A TRANSLATOR'S GUIDE TO
THE GOSPEL OF LUKE

Helps for Translators Series

Technical Helps:

Handbooks:

Guides:

HELPS FOR TRANSLATORS

A TRANSLATOR'S GUIDE
to
THE GOSPEL OF LUKE

by

ROBERT G. BRATCHER

UNITED BIBLE SOCIETIES

London, New York,
Stuttgart

Books in the series of **Helps for Translators** may be ordered from a national Bible Society, or from either of the following centers:

United Bible Societies
European Production Fund
D-7000 Stuttgart 80
Postfach 81 03 40
West Germany

United Bible Societies
1865 Broadway
New York, New York 10023
U.S.A.

L.C. Catalog Card Number: 82-213977

ISBN 0-8267-0181-7

ABS-1988-700-2,200-CM-2-08712

Contents

Preface

A *Translator's Guide to the Gospel of Luke* is another volume in the new series of Guides prepared as part of the general series, *Helps for Translators*. The Handbooks were formerly the only exegetical materials on various books of the Bible published by the United Bible Societies for the use of translators.

The Handbooks have proven to be valuable for a good number of translators. They are full-range commentaries that deal with problems of the original text, interpretation, vocabulary analysis, and discourse structure. They also include analyses of translation problems that may occur, and they provide suggestions for dealing with such problems. Some translators, however, prefer material in a more condensed form and from which they can easily retrieve information. Therefore the Translator's Guides do not, for example, attempt to explain the reasons for the exegesis of a passage nor for a suggested solution to a translation problem. A Guide does not take away from the translator the responsibility to make his own decisions, but it does attempt to give him practical information and to alert him to pitfalls he may otherwise overlook. On the basis of such information the translator should be able to prepare a manuscript that is faithful to the meaning of the original and faithful to the style of his own language that is most appropriate for conveying the message to the reader.

Other Guides are in preparation, covering material from both the Old Testament and the New Testament. Meanwhile, preparation of the Handbooks continues, so that the needs of all translators may be met. The United Bible Societies Subcommittee on Translations will welcome any suggestions for making both the Handbooks and the Guides more effective and useful for translators.

Abbreviations Used in This Volume

Books of the Bible:

1,2 Chr	1,2 Chr
Col	Colossians
Dan	Daniel
Deut	Deuteronomy
Exo	Exodus
Gal	Galatians
Gen	Genesis
Isa	Isaiah
Jer	Jeremiah
1,2 Kgs	1,2 Kgs
Lev	Leviticus
Mal	Malachi
Matt	Matthew
Num	Numbers
Psa	Psalms

Other Abbreviations:

A.D.	anno Domini (in the year of our Lord)
B.C.	before Christ
KJV	King James Version
RSV	Revised Standard Version
TEV	Today's English Version

Translating the Gospel of Luke

The purpose of this Guide is to help translators recognize and solve some of the problems they will encounter in translating the Gospel of Luke. This Guide is not intended to replace standard commentaries or the Handbook, which is also published by the United Bible Societies. Rather, it seeks to show, in a simple and consistent way, what the translator must do in order to provide in his or her own language a text that is faithful to the meaning of the original and that is clear and simple for the reader. The translator is encouraged to seek additional help from available commentaries and Bible dictionaries, and to consult other translations.

The Gospel is divided into sections, each with a heading that indicates the content or the main idea of the section. The translator should carefully read the whole section before starting to translate the first verse of the section.

The Guide uses the Today's English Version (TEV) section headings, and prints the text of both TEV and the Revised Standard Version (RSV). The translator will notice that in many places the two are considerably different in form, although in the vast majority of instances the meaning is the same. The differences are due to the fact that RSV is a translation that tries to reflect, as far as possible, the form of the original Greek in terms of vocabulary, word classes, word order, and grammatical constructions. TEV attempts to express the meaning of the Greek text as simply and naturally as possible, using a vocabulary and grammatical constructions that will be easily understood by most people who read English.

The translator is encouraged to imitate TEV in this respect, and to express the meaning of the text in a form that will be easy for the reader to understand.

After each TEV section heading other suggestions are made for different ways to translate the heading. However, this Guide does not provide the parallel references that accompany such section headings in TEV. A translator who wishes to include those references may find them in a copy of the Good News Bible.

After each verse, printed in full in both the TEV (left-hand column) and the RSV (right-hand column) texts, key passages are selected for explanation; these are underlined, as are all quotations from the TEV text, and the suggestions are provided to enable the translator to understand better what is being proposed.

The Guide takes notice of places where there are important differences among the Greek manuscripts of the Gospel. In some places RSV and TEV differ in their decision on the Greek text (see 8.43); the Guide states the matter concisely and recommends what a translator should do.

Translating Luke

The most important thing is that a translator be thoroughly acquainted with a whole passage (a section or a chapter) before starting to translate, so as to reflect the author's style, the unity of the passage, and the development of the text.

Title

THE GOSPEL ACCORDING TO LUKE

Gospel: usually there is a word already in use to represent "Gospel."
The Greek word means "good news." If a more explicit statement is needed,
"The Good News about Jesus Christ."

according to Luke: this was not written by the author of the Gospel,
but represents the opinion of the early church at a time when the book
was being widely read by Christians. The book itself does not say who
wrote it. The words "according to" do not necessarily mean that Luke
actually wrote this account. It means that in some way this Gospel is
related to a man named Luke, who is assumed to be the friend and companion of Paul (Philemon 24; Col 4.14). Many languages say simply "of Luke,"
which is satisfactory as long as it does not imply that the Gospel is
about a man named Luke, or that the gospel message is proclaimed by Luke.

Chapter 1

SECTION HEADING

Introduction: "Preface," "The Author to Theophilus."

Verses 1-4 are one sentence in Greek. In most languages it is better to have at least two sentences. The author briefly states the reason
why he has written this book, the method he has used, and the purpose of
his account of what Jesus did and taught.

1.1-2 TEV	RSV
Dear Theophilus: Many people have done their best to write a report of the things that have taken place among us. 2 They wrote what we have been told by those who saw these things from the beginning and who pro-claimed the message.	Inasmuch as many have under-taken to compile a narrative of the things which have been accomplished among us, 2 just as they were de-livered to us by those who from the beginning were eyewitnesses and ministers of the word,

RSV follows the word order of the Greek; TEV has begun the book
with the words Dear Theophilus, which is more in keeping with modern
style. Nothing is said about Theophilus other than what appears in
verses 3-4; his name appears also in the beginning of Acts (1.1).

Many people: the expression is as vague in Greek as it is in English. There is no way of knowing precisely how many the writer had in mind.

have done their best: "have tried," "have attempted," "have made an effort." There is the implication that the work that the Many people did was not adequate, and that is why the author has written his account.

write a report: "prepare an account," "write a comprehensive account."

the things that have taken place: "the events that have occurred," "the things that have happened." The author is referring to the beginning and spread of the Christian movement.

us: this is probably exclusive, that is, "among us believers," referring to the people who belong to the Christian community. But in a broader sense it could refer to the people who belonged to that generation.

In verse 2 the author excludes himself and his contemporaries from the original eyewitnesses of the events to be described. Here we includes the author and his fellow Christians at that time. Among them are included the people who had drawn up the previous accounts to which he made reference.

the beginning: in a general sense, the beginning of the Christian movement.

those who...proclaimed the message: this translates the Greek phrase "servants of the word," which is a way of speaking about those whose task it was to proclaim the Christian message.

1.3	TEV		RSV

1.3   TEV

And so, Your Excellency, because I have carefully studied all these matters from their beginning, I thought it would be good to write an orderly account for you.

RSV

it seemed good to me also, having followed all things closely[a] for some time past, to write an orderly account for you, most excellent Theophilus,

[a]Or accurately

Your Excellency: this expression shows that Theophilus was a man of high rank, perhaps an official in the Roman government. It is the same term that the Roman army commander Claudius Lysias uses in the letter he writes to the Roman governor Felix (Acts 23.26). Most languages have standard greeting terms or expressions used in addressing people of high rank, such as officials or nobility.

carefully studied: "carefully investigated." Here studied is not used in the sense of reading written texts, but of personal investigation: "I have made a thorough investigation (of these matters)."

from their beginning: this seems preferable to RSV "for some time past."

an orderly account: this means not only chronological order, but a clear statement of what Jesus did and taught.

1.4 TEV	RSV
I do this so that you will know the full truth about everything which you have been taught.	that you may know the truth concerning the things of which you have been informed.

I do this: or "I write this account for you."

you have been taught: RSV has "you have been informed," which differs in meaning from TEV. There is no way of knowing for sure whether the Greek term used here means that Theophilus was a Christian who had been taught the Christian faith, or that as a government official he had heard reports about what Christians did and taught.

SECTION HEADING

The Birth of John the Baptist Is Announced: "The Angel Gabriel Promises Zechariah that He Will Have a Son."

The story of the gospel starts here, with the promise of the birth of John the Baptist.

1.5 TEV	RSV
During the time when Herod was king of Judea,^{a} there was a priest named Zechariah, who belonged to the priestly order of Abijah. His wife's name was Elizabeth; she also belonged to a priestly family.	In the days of Herod, king of Judea, there was a priest named Zechariah,^{b} of the division of Abijah; and he had a wife of the daughters of Aaron, and her name was Elizabeth.
^{a}JUDEA: *The term here refers to the whole land of Palestine.*	^{b}Greek *Zacharias*

Herod was king of Judea: this is Herod the Great, king of all the land of Israel from 37 B.C. to 4 B.C. As TEV footnote makes clear, Judea here refers to the whole country, not only to the southern province.

the priestly order of Abijah: the eighth of the twenty-four orders into which the priests were divided (see 1 Chr 24.10).

she also belonged to a priestly family: this translates the Greek expression "of the daughters of Aaron" (RSV). The meaning could be expressed, "she also was a descendant of (the High Priest) Aaron."

1.6 TEV	RSV
They both lived good lives in God's sight and obeyed fully all the Lord's laws and commands.	And they were both righteous before God, walking in all the commandments and ordinances of the Lord blameless.

lived good lives in God's sight: "lived in such a way as to please God," "lived lives pleasing to God."

obeyed fully: "obeyed completely," "followed without fail."

[5]

the Lord's: this refers to God, and it may be better to use the possessive pronoun "his."

1.7   TEV   RSV

They had no children because Eliza-   But they had no child, because Elizabeth could not have any, and she   beth was barren, and both were ad-
and Zechariah were both very old.   vanced in years.

Elizabeth could not have any: "Elizabeth was barren" (RSV). This is the main reason why Zechariah and Elizabeth had no children; but the writer adds that at this time both of them were quite old, beyond the normal age for having children.

1.8   TEV   RSV

One day Zechariah was doing   Now while he was serving as
his work as a priest in the Temple,   priest before God when his division
taking his turn in the daily serv-   was on duty,
ice.

After the background information in verses 5-7, the writer now shifts to the specific time, place, and circumstances of the events he is going to narrate. So TEV begins in normal storytelling style, One day.

doing his work as a priest: "performing his priestly functions (or, duties)."

in the Temple: this represents the Greek "before God" (RSV); this could be expressed by "at the altar" or "in the divine service," "in the Temple worship."

taking his turn in the daily service: or "while his division (Abijah) was on duty." Each division would serve in the Temple in Jerusalem for one week at a time, twice a year (see 1 Chr 24.19; 2 Chr 23.8).

1.9-10   TEV   RSV

According to the custom followed   according to the custom of the
by the priests, he was chosen by   priesthood, it fell to him by lot
lot to burn incense on the altar.   to enter the temple of the Lord and
So he went into the Temple of the   burn incense. 10 And the whole mul-
Lord, 10 while the crowd of people   titude of the people were praying
outside prayed during the hour when   outside at the hour of incense.
the incense was burned.

According to the custom: this clause, in Greek, may go with what precedes or with what follows; most translations, like TEV, take it with what follows.

he was chosen by lot: this refers to the way in which such decisions were made. The Greek verb could have the general sense of "he was chosen" or "it was his turn." But the more restricted sense seems preferable: "It was the custom of the priests to draw lots to decide which one would

burn incense on the altar. This time the lot fell on Zechariah, and so
he went into the Temple."

The altar on which incense was burned was located inside the Holy
Place, the large sanctuary of the Temple (compare Exo 30.6-8).

the hour: or "the time." This was at 9:00 a.m.

1.11	TEV	RSV
An angel of the Lord appeared to him, standing at the right side of the altar where the incense was burned.		And there appeared to him an angel of the Lord standing on the right side of the altar of incense.

an angel of the Lord: "an angel sent by God," "an angel who served
God." The Greek word for angel means "messenger," and here a heavenly
messenger is meant. Angels were God's messengers, sent for specific purposes.

appeared: this does not mean the angel was not real; it means he
became visible.

standing at the right side of the altar: Zechariah was facing the
altar, so the angel was standing to the left of Zechariah. Since the
altar has already been identified, it is not absolutely necessary to add
where the incense was burned.

1.12-13	TEV	RSV
When Zechariah saw him, he was alarmed and felt afraid. 13 But the angel said to him, "Don't be afraid, Zechariah! God has heard your prayer, and your wife Eliza- beth will bear you a son. You are to name him John.		And Zechariah was troubled when he saw him, and fear fell upon him. 13 But the angel said to him, "Do not be afraid, Zechariah, for your prayer is heard, and your wife Elizabeth will bear you a son, and you shall call his name John.

he was alarmed and felt afraid: or "Zechariah was upset (or, alarmed)
when he saw the angel, and he was afraid" or "Fright and alarm overcame
Zechariah when he saw the angel."

Don't be afraid: or "Stop being afraid."

God has heard your prayer: as the context indicates, this was Zechariah's prayer that he and his wife might have children.

will bear you a son: this is the normal English way of saying this
and represents the identical idea in the Greek. A wife gives birth to a
child to (or, for) her husband. If such an expression is unnatural in
some languages, the simple "will bear (or, give birth to) a son" is sufficient.

1.14	TEV	RSV
How glad and happy you will be, and how happy many others will be when he is born!		And you will have joy and gladness, and many will rejoice at his birth;

1.14

Some translations may wish to imitate RSV and render verses 14-17 in poetic form.

Not only Zechariah himself but many others will also be happy when the boy is born.

1.15 TEV	RSV
He will be a great man in the Lord's sight. He must not drink any wine or strong drink. From his very birth he will be filled with the Holy Spirit,	for he will be great before the Lord, and he shall drink no wine nor strong drink, and he will be filled with the Holy Spirit, even from his mother's womb.

a great man in the Lord's sight: RSV translates "for he will be great." This may be taken as the reason why Zechariah and many others will rejoice when John is born. The expression in the Lord's sight means that God will consider John an important person (compare the similar "in God's sight" in verse 6).

not drink any wine or strong drink: this requirement is similar to the Old Testament requirements for Nazirites, people who dedicated themselves either for a limited time or permanently to the service of God (see Num 6.3; Judges 13.4).

strong drink: or "beer." This would not be drink made by distillation but by fermentation. So the translation could be "neither wine nor any other fermented (or, alcoholic) drink."

From his very birth: as RSV shows, the biblical idiom is "from his mother's womb." It is not absolutely necessary to translate this idiom literally, as though it were important to maintain that John was filled with the Holy Spirit before his birth. But the translation could be "Even before he is born" (see Gal 1.15).

filled with the Holy Spirit: this kind of expression may not make sense in some languages, and it may be necessary to say "as soon as he is born the Holy Spirit will be with him," or "the power of the Holy Spirit will be upon him," or "he will be led (or, controlled) by the Spirit of God."

1.16 TEV	RSV
and he will bring back many of the people of Israel to the Lord their God.	And he will turn many of the sons of Israel to the Lord their God,

bring back: or "lead back," or "cause many Israelites to turn back to the Lord their God." This action is that of worshiping God or of obeying his laws.

1.17 TEV	RSV
He will go ahead of the Lord, strong and mighty like the prophet	and he will go before him in the spirit and power of Elijah,

[8]

Elijah. He will bring fathers and
children together again; he will
turn disobedient people back to the
way of thinking of the righteous;
he will get the Lord's people ready
for him."

to turn the hearts of the fa-
    thers to the children,
and the disobedient to the wis-
    dom of the just,
to make ready for the Lord a
    people prepared."

He will go ahead of the Lord: the literal translation of this biblical phrase may not carry much sense. The meaning may be that the Lord
God is coming to his people, and John will be his forerunner, to prepare
the way for him (reflecting the language of Mal 3.1; and see 1.76 below).
Or else the Greek may simply mean that John will go as the Lord's messenger. The former is most likely the meaning intended by the writer.

strong and mighty like the prophet Elijah: this translates "in the
spirit and power of Elijah." Here "in the spirit...of Elijah" means to
be like Elijah, not in appearance, but in mission and in attitude—a
fearless and outspoken prophet.

he will turn disobedient people...way of thinking of the righteous:
John's future mission is described as that of reconciling fathers and
their children (see Mal 4.5-6) and of causing disobedient people to return to the principles (the way of thinking) of righteous people. Here
disobedient people are those who do not obey God, while the righteous
are those who obey God's laws and commandments.

get the Lord's people ready for him: this foretells the coming of
the Lord God, for which his people must be ready. The phrase the Lord's
people could be translated "the people who belong especially to God" or
"the people God has chosen to be his own."

1.18   TEV
    Zechariah said to the angel,
"How shall I know if this is so?
I am an old man, and my wife is
old also."

          RSV
And Zechariah said to the angel,
"How shall I know this? For I am
an old man, and my wife is advanced
in years."

How shall I know: "How can I be sure (or, certain)...?" See Abraham's response in Genesis 15.8.

this: that is, the birth of a son. Since he and his wife are old,
Zechariah cannot believe that they will have a son.

1.19-20   TEV
    "I am Gabriel," the angel an-
swered. "I stand in the presence
of God, who sent me to speak to
you and tell you this good news.
20 But you have not believed my
message, which will come true at
the right time. Because you have
not believed, you will be unable

          RSV
And the angel answered him, "I am
Gabriel, who stand in the presence
of God; and I was sent to speak to
you, and to bring you this good
news. 20 And behold, you will be
silent and unable to speak until
the day that these things come to
pass, because you did not believe

to speak; you will remain silent
until the day my promise to you
comes true."

my words, which will be fulfilled
in their time."

The angel identifies himself as Gabriel, one of the chief angels
(see Dan 8.16). In verse 20 Gabriel tells Zechariah that he will be punished for his lack of faith.

RSV "behold" represents a Greek word used frequently as an attention
getter; it may be represented by "Listen" or "Look." But it is used so
often that it loses much of its effect, which is why it is not always
formally represented in TEV.

you will be unable to speak: "you will remain silent." It is not
necessary to repeat the angel's statement, as TEV does. Perhaps "Because
you have not believed my message (or, promise), you will not be able to
speak until..." or "...you will be struck dumb until...."

The various elements in verse 20 may be rearranged as follows: "My
promise to you will come true at the proper time. But since you have not
believed me, you will be unable to speak until your son is born."

1.21-22	TEV	RSV
	In the meantime the people were waiting for Zechariah and wondering why he was spending such a long time in the Temple. 22 When he came out, he could not speak to them, and so they knew that he had seen a vision in the Temple. Unable to say a word, he made signs to them with his hands.	And the people were waiting for Zechariah, and they wondered at his delay in the temple. 22 And when he came out, he could not speak to them, and they perceived that he had seen a vision in the temple; and he made signs to them and remained dumb.

In the meantime: "While this was going on."
and wondering why: "and were worried because."
seen a vision: this may be difficult to express, since the word
"vision" implies that what Zechariah saw was not real. What is meant,
however, is that Zechariah had had a supernatural experience, had received a revelation from God. The word vision here corresponds to appeared in verse 11. Zechariah's inability to speak led the crowd to con-
clude that God, or an angel, had appeared to him in the Temple.

1.23	TEV	RSV
	When his period of service in the Temple was over, Zechariah went back home.	And when his time of service was ended, he went to his home.

period of service: one week (see verse 8).
went back home: only in verses 39-40 are we told where Zechariah
lived.

[10]

1.24-25 TEV	RSV
Some time later his wife Eliza-beth became pregnant and did not leave the house for five months. 25 "Now at last the Lord has helped me," she said. "He has taken away my public disgrace!"	After these days his wife Elizabeth conceived, and for five months she hid herself, saying, 25 "Thus the Lord has done to me in the days when he looked on me, to take away my reproach among men."

Some time later: an indefinite period of time; "Soon after this," "After this."

did not leave the house: "remained secluded," "lived in seclusion."

Elizabeth's statement to herself (verse 25) reflects the thinking of that time. A wife who did not bear a child was despised, and her condition was seen as God's punishment on her.

helped me: this translates the literal "looked on me" (RSV), which may be understood as representing compassion, pity, or awareness. One could translate "The Lord has finally taken notice of me" or "...had compassion on me."

He has taken away my public disgrace may be represented by "He has made it so that people will no longer despise me." See Genesis 30.23 for Rachel's statement.

SECTION HEADING

The Birth of Jesus Is Announced: "The Angel Gabriel Promises Mary that She Will Have a Son."

This section parallels the previous section; in the first section John the Baptist's birth is announced, and now Jesus' birth is announced.

1.26-27 TEV	RSV
In the sixth month of Eliza-beth's pregnancy God sent the angel Gabriel to a town in Galilee named Nazareth. 27 He had a message for a girl promised in marriage to a man named Joseph, who was a descendant of King David. The girl's name was Mary.	In the sixth month the angel Gabriel was sent from God to a city of Galilee named Nazareth, 27 to a virgin betrothed to a man whose name was Joseph, of the house of David; and the virgin's name was Mary.

In these two verses the writer sets the stage for the coming narrative, giving the time and place of the event and the names of the people involved.

In the sixth month of Elizabeth's pregnancy: it may not be enough to say simply "In the sixth month," as RSV does.

Gabriel: already known from verse 19.

Galilee: the province in the north of the country; Zechariah and Elizabeth lived in Judea, the province in the south (verses 39-40).

[11]

Nazareth was a small town some 26 kilometers west of the southern tip of Lake Galilee.

He: this refers to the angel. The material might be reconstructed as follows: "God sent the angel Gabriel to Nazareth, a town in Galilee, with a message for...."

a girl: this translates the Greek word usually rendered "virgin" (RSV). The word means an unmarried female of marriageable age, and in this context is not used in the more restricted sense of lack of sexual experience; this emphasis is made in verse 34. According to the custom of the time Mary would have been a teenager. At age 12 a Jewish girl was considered old enough to be married.

promised in marriage: this was a formal relationship which could be broken only by an act of divorce. If the man were to die the woman would consider herself a widow, even though they had not married. The expression "engaged to" or "the fiancée of" may not be quite adequate, since this kind of a relationship is not usually regarded as being so permanent and serious. In some translations a footnote may be required (see comments at 2.5).

a descendant of King David: this translates the literal "of the house of David" (RSV).

The girl's name was Mary: the last item of information is the girl's name. It may be preferable to restructure verse 27 as follows: "Gabriel was sent to a girl named Mary, who was promised in marriage to Joseph, a descendant of King David."

1.28 TEV	RSV
The angel came to her and said, "Peace be with you! The Lord is with you and has greatly blessed you!"	And he came to her and said, "Hail, O favored one, the Lord is with you!"*c*
	*c*Other ancient authorities add *"Blessed are you among women!"*

came: or "went." The Greek "went in to her" seems to mean "went into her room" or "went in where she was."

Peace be with you: this translates the Greek word "Greetings" (RSV "Hail"). The Jewish greeting was "Peace be with you." "I greet you," or the standard form of greeting employed in a language may be used. It should be somewhat formal, not casual or informal such as "Hi!" or "Hello" in English.

The Lord is with you: in Greek there is no verb, and so the words could be understood not as a statement but as a wish, "The Lord be with you." But the declarative form seems preferable.

has greatly blessed you: this translates the passive participle of the verb "to be kind to," "to bless." A possible meaning is "the one whom God has chosen." The traditional "full of grace" has been taken to mean that Mary possessed divine grace to a degree beyond that of anyone else; but it seems clear that the Greek term means that Mary was the object of God's goodness, or favor.

Textual Note: many Greek manuscripts and ancient versions add at the end of the verse "you are the most blessed of all women," as in verse 42. But these words do not belong here.

1.29-30

TEV	RSV
Mary was deeply troubled by the angel's message, and she wondered what his words meant. 30 The angel said to her, "Don't be afraid, Mary; God has been gracious to you.	But she was greatly troubled at the saying, and considered in her mind what sort of greeting this might be. 30 And the angel said to her, "Do not be afraid, Mary, for you have found favor with God.

deeply troubled: "disturbed," "upset," "perplexed."
his words: "his greeting."
Don't be afraid: as in verse 13.
God has been gracious to you: or "God is pleased with you." The biblical expression "to find grace (or, favor)" with someone means to win someone's approval, gain that person's pleasure.

1.31

TEV	RSV
You will become pregnant and give birth to a son, and you will name him Jesus.	And behold, you will conceive in your womb and bear a son, and you shall call his name Jesus.

You will become pregnant: there is nothing in this statement to indicate anything unusual; it is simply a way of saying to Mary that in time she will give birth to a son.
Jesus: this represents the Greek form of a fairly common Hebrew proper name, Joshua. The name means "The Lord is Savior" or "He saves."

1.32-33

TEV	RSV
He will be great and will be called the Son of the Most High God. The Lord God will make him a king, as his ancestor David was, 33 and he will be the king of the descendants of Jacob forever; his kingdom will never end!"	He will be great, and will be called the Son of the Most High; and the Lord God will give to him the throne of his father David, 33 and he will reign over the house of Jacob for ever; and of his kingdom there will be no end."

The angel tells Mary that her son will be the king of Israel.
he...will be called: the passive form often has God as the subject of the action, so here the translation could be "God will call him his Son."
the Most High God: this translates "the highest (one)," a title for God in the Old Testament.

RSV preserves the literal form of the Greek, "the Lord God will give to him the throne of David." This means that God will make Mary's son inherit David's kingdom, that is, be a successor of David as king of Israel.

his ancestor David: in verse 27 we are told that Joseph was a descendant of King David.

the descendants of Jacob: literally "the house of Jacob" (RSV). This is a way of speaking of the people of Israel: "he will reign over the people of Israel forever," "he will be king forever of the people of Israel."

his kingdom will never end: here in the sense of royal power, sovereign rule. It is a way of saying "he will reign forever," "he will always be king."

	1.34 TEV	RSV
	Mary said to the angel, "I am a virgin. How, then, can this be?"	And Mary said to the angel, "How shall this be, since I have no husband?"

I am a virgin: this translates the words "I do not know (any) man," which is a Semitic way of saying she had never had sexual relations. She was already promised in marriage to Joseph, and in the normal course of events she would marry and have children by Joseph. But the angel's words seem to imply that she would bear a son before the time she normally would have one by Joseph.

	1.35 TEV	RSV
	The angel answered, "The Holy Spirit will come on you, and God's power will rest upon you. For this reason the holy child will be called the Son of God.	And the angel said to her, "The Holy Spirit will come upon you, and the power of the Most High will overshadow you; therefore the child to be born^d will be called holy, the Son of God.

^{d}Other ancient authorities add *of you*

The Holy Spirit...God's power: these are two parallel expressions, and the expressions mean the same. The second one in Greek is "the power of the Most High" (see verse 32).

will rest upon you: this translates the Greek "will overshadow you" (RSV). The expression is used in the Old Testament for God's glory coming down on a place. In 9.34 the same verb is used for the cloud, the symbol of God's presence, appearing at the transfiguration of Jesus.

the holy child will be called: as RSV and TEV show, the Greek text may be understood in two different ways. Child translates the passive participle "that which is born"; RSV translates "the child to be born."

The adjective holy may be taken as the object of the verb shall be called: "shall be called holy" (so RSV). Or it may modify the phrase "the one to be born"; so "the holy one to be born" (so TEV). The quality holy, when attached to a person or thing, means principally "dedicated to God's service," "used for God's purpose," or "used for the worship of God."

the Son of God: this is similar to the promise in verse 32.

Textual Note: as RSV footnote shows, some Greek manuscripts and early versions have "to be born of you," not "to be born." The text without the added "of you" is to be preferred. But some translations may need to say "the child which you will have" or something similar.

1.36-37 TEV	RSV
Remember your relative Elizabeth. It is said that she cannot have children, but she herself is now six months pregnant, even though she is very old. 37 For there is nothing that God cannot do."	And behold, your kinswoman Elizabeth in her old age has also conceived a son; and this is the sixth month with her who was called barren. 37 For with God nothing will be impossible."

relative: the term is quite general, and there is no way of knowing how close a relative Elizabeth was.

It is said: "People say" or "She is called barren." It is impossible to decide whether the angel is telling Mary something she had not known before, or simply reminding Mary of Elizabeth's pregnancy. The context makes it appear that Gabriel is informing Mary of Elizabeth's pregnancy: "You should know that your relative Elizabeth, as old as she is, is now pregnant. She was (called) barren, but she is now six months pregnant."

The angel's words in verse 37 recall the Lord's statement to Abraham (Gen 18.14), when he told him that Sarah would give birth to a son.

Instead of the double negative form, the positive might be preferable: "For God can do anything," "Everything is possible for God."

1.38 TEV	RSV
"I am the Lord's servant," said Mary; "may it happen to me as you have said." And the angel left her.	And Mary said, "Behold, I am the handmaid of the Lord; let it be to me according to your word." And the angel departed from her.

I am the Lord's servant: "I am at the Lord's service," "I am ready to serve the Lord."

may it happen: "may your prediction happen to me" or "may the Lord do to me as you have said."

SECTION HEADING

Mary Visits Elizabeth.

In this section the story is told of Mary's visit to Elizabeth. The purpose of this story is to emphasize again the extraordinary nature of the child that Mary will bear.

1.39-40 TEV	RSV
Soon afterward Mary got ready and hurried off to a town in the hill country of Judea. 40 She went into Zechariah's house and greeted Elizabeth.	In those days Mary arose and went with haste into the hill country, to a city of Judah, 40 and she entered the house of Zechariah and greeted Elizabeth.

Soon afterward: this translates another vague reference to time; "at that time" or something similar expresses the meaning.

got ready and hurried off: or "went in a hurry."

the hill country of Judea: or "the hilly (or mountainous) region of the province of Judea." Judea was the province in the southern part of the country; from Nazareth to Jerusalem it was a distance of some 88 kilometers.

1.41-42 TEV	RSV
When Elizabeth heard Mary's greeting, the baby moved within her. Elizabeth was filled with the Holy Spirit 42 and said in a loud voice, "You are the most blessed of all women, and blessed is the child you will bear!	And when Elizabeth heard the greeting of Mary, the babe leaped in her womb; and Elizabeth was filled with the Holy Spirit 42 and she exclaimed with a loud cry, "Blessed are you among women, and blessed is the fruit of your womb!

the baby moved within her: or "the baby stirred in her womb." The literal translation "leaped" (RSV) does not correspond to normal English usage in this context. A six-month-old fetus may stir or move or turn in the womb, but it does not jump.

filled with the Holy Spirit: "the Holy Spirit came upon Elizabeth" (see 1.15).

the most blessed of all women: this represents the passive form of the Greek verb; it may be translated, "God has blessed you more than he has any other woman." It should be noticed that the Greek verb here is not the same as the one used in verse 28, which TEV translates has greatly blessed.

the child you will bear: literally "the fruit of your womb" (RSV). Elizabeth's words may be translated, "God has blessed you more than any other woman, and he has also blessed the child you will bear" (or, "... the child you are carrying").

1.43-44 TEV	RSV
Why should this great thing happen to me, that my Lord's mother comes to visit me? 44 For as soon as I	And why is this granted me, that the mother of my Lord should come to me? 44 For behold, when the

heard your greeting, the baby within me jumped with gladness.	voice of your greeting came to my ears, the babe in my womb leaped for joy.

Why should this great thing happen to me...?: this rhetorical question is a way of saying "I don't deserve to have such a wonderful thing as this happen to me!"

my Lord's mother: here "Lord" refers to Jesus.

In verse 44 Elizabeth explains why she knows of the wonderful thing that has happened to Mary. She describes the baby's movement in her womb as an expression of joy: the baby...jumped with gladness.

1.45 TEV	RSV
How happy you are to believe that the Lord's message to you will come true!"	And blessed is she who believed that there would be^e a fulfilment of what was spoken to her from the Lord."

^{e}Or *believed, for there will be*

As RSV shows, the form of the Greek is impersonal: "And blessed is she who believed...." The reference is to Mary, and so TEV has made this explicit: How happy you are to believe.

The text may be understood in two different ways: (1) "Happy are you to believe that the Lord's promise to you will come true"; or (2) "Happy are you to have believed, for the Lord's promise to you will come true" (see RSV footnote). The first one seems the more probable.

SECTION HEADING

Mary's Song of Praise: "Mary Praises God."

Mary's song of praise is known as the "Magnificat," which is the first word of the song ("magnifies") in the Latin translation, the Vulgate. If possible, a translation should try to preserve the poetic style of the song.

1.46-47 TEV	RSV
Mary said, "My heart praises the Lord; 47 my soul is glad because of God my Savior,	And Mary said, "My soul magnifies the Lord, 47 and my spirit rejoices in God my Savior,

My heart...my soul: RSV prefers "My soul...my spirit." It should be remembered that these are not regarded as separate elements of the person, but are ways of speaking of an individual in terms of that person's thinking and willing; or, in more general terms, they are what could be called the emotional and the spiritual dimensions of the individual. So two terms which represent this can be used: "With all my heart I praise the Lord; I am filled with joy because...."

1.48-49

TEV	RSV
for he has remembered me, his lowly servant!	for he has regarded the low estate of his handmaiden.
from now on all people will call me happy,	For behold, henceforth all generations will call me blessed;
49 because of the great things the Mighty God has done for me.	49 for he who is mighty has done great things for me,
His name is holy;	and holy is his name.

he has remembered me, his lowly servant: this translates "he has looked upon the condition of his (female) servant." Mary is talking about herself; and the Greek verb for "look upon" is identical in meaning with the similar verb for "look upon" in verse 25. Here the translation could be "He has looked with concern (or, tenderness)."

all people: literally "all generations." "For all time to come people will call me happy."

happy: "fortunate" or even "very lucky."

the Mighty God: this translates "the Powerful One," a title for God.

His name is holy: the "name" of God stands for God himself, and so the statement "God's name is holy" is a way of saying "God is holy." When used of God (see 1.35), holy refers to the nature of God as one who is separate and apart from humanity, one in whom there is no flaw or evil, who is to be approached and worshiped as being pure and perfect.

1.50

TEV	RSV
from one generation to another	And his mercy is on those who fear him
he shows mercy to those who honor him.	from generation to generation.

This verse speaks of God's mercy, or goodness.

from one generation to another: or "in all generations," or "to people of all times."

those who honor him: the verb that RSV translates "fear" is used in the Bible of the proper attitude of respect, reverence, awe, which people should have toward God. If a word like "fear" is used, it should not imply terror, but reverence and respect.

1.51-52

TEV	RSV
He has stretched out his mighty arm	He has shown strength with his arm,

[18]

and scattered the proud with all their plans.	he has scattered the proud in the imagination of their hearts,
52 He has brought down mighty kings from their thrones, and lifted up the lowly.	52 he has put down the mighty from their thrones, and exalted those of low degree;

his mighty arm: these two verses use familiar language in describing God's action in history. God's "arm" is a figure of his power and strength, used against the arrogant. If such metaphors are not acceptable, the translation can speak of God's power: "With his mighty power he has scattered...."

the proud with all their plans: or "men of proud hearts," or "those who were proud in heart and mind."

brought down...lifted up: "humbled...exalted."

1.53	TEV	RSV
	He has filled the hungry with good things, and sent the rich away with empty hands.	he has filled the hungry with good things, and the rich he has sent empty away.

with empty hands: or "without anything"—in contrast with the poor, whom God fills with good things. The language is figurative but the meaning is clear. God reverses the situation of the rich and the poor, giving the poor many good things and sending the rich away without giving them anything.

1.54-55	TEV	RSV
	He has kept the promise he made to our ancestors, and has come to the help of his servant Israel.	He has helped his servant Israel, in remembrance of his mercy,
	55 He has remembered to show mercy to Abraham and to all his descendants forever!"	55 as he spoke to our fathers, to Abraham and to his posterity for ever."

RSV shows the Hebrew order of the lines of poetry, which must be revised for most other languages. TEV has changed the order of the four lines of these two verses as follows: 3-1-2-4. Line 2 goes with line 4, and not with line 3 as in RSV. Another possibility would be 1-2-4-3:

[1] He has come to the help of Israel, his servant;
[2]   he has remembered to be merciful
[4]   to Abraham and his descendants forever,
[3] as he promised our ancestors.

[19]

One could also use the order 1-3-2-4.

<u>our ancestors</u>: the <u>our</u> is inclusive: Mary, Elizabeth, and any others there (who would all be Jews).

<u>his servant Israel</u>: here <u>Israel</u> stands for the people of Israel, spoken of as a person: "his servants, the people of Israel," or "the people of Israel, who serve him."

<u>to show mercy</u>: "to be merciful," "to be kind."

1.56	TEV	RSV
	Mary stayed about three months with Elizabeth and then went back home.	And Mary remained with her about three months, and returned to her home.

<u>about three months</u>: it would seem that Mary returned home before the birth of John.

SECTION HEADING

<u>The Birth of John the Baptist</u>: "John the Baptist Is Born."

In this section the writer tells the story of John's birth and the name given him when he was circumcised. The section is related to the one that follows, but it seems better to keep the two separate.

1.57	TEV	RSV
	The time came for Elizabeth to have her baby, and she gave birth to a son.	Now the time came for Elizabeth to be delivered, and she gave birth to a son.

<u>The time came</u>: or "When it was time for Elizabeth to bear her child, she gave birth to a son" (or, "...to a baby boy").

1.58	TEV	RSV
	Her neighbors and relatives heard how wonderfully good the Lord had been to her, and they all rejoiced with her.	And her neighbors and kinsfolk heard that the Lord had shown great mercy to her, and they rejoiced with her.

<u>heard how wonderfully good the Lord had been to her</u>: "heard that the Lord had blessed her greatly" or "...had been very good (or, kind) to her." This refers to her bearing a son, especially when she was so old.

<u>they all rejoiced with her</u>: this could imply that they went to see her. The translation could make this explicit, "they went to congratulate her," or else, "they were all very happy over what had happened to her."

1.59-60   TEV   RSV

When the baby was a week old,   And on the eighth day they came to
they came to circumcise him, and   circumcise the child; and they
they were going to name him Zecha-   would have named him Zechariah after
riah, after his father. 60 But his   his father, 60 but his mother said,
mother said, "No! His name is to   "Not so; he shall be called John."
be John."

a week old: this translates "on the eighth day" (RSV); it could be
rendered "a week after the baby was born." The Law required that a boy
be circumcised on the eighth day (see Lev 12.3).

they came: the subject is not explicit, but the circumcision was a
public ceremony, and friends and relatives would be there for the joyous
occasion; "people came." Or else the Greek may mean "They (that is,
Zechariah and Elizabeth) took the child to be circumcised." But the TEV
and RSV rendering seems preferable, since the subject of the next verb
(they were going to name him) can hardly be Zechariah and Elizabeth.

circumcise: the ritual of cutting off the foreskin from the penis
of a Jewish baby boy as a sign of God's covenant with the people of Israel (see Gen 17.9-14).

name him: the translation should be quite clear: "they tried to
name him" or "they wanted to name him."

name him Zechariah, after his father: "give him the same name his
father had, Zechariah."

His name is to be John: "He must be named John," "John will be his
name."

1.61   TEV   RSV

They said to her, "But you   And they said to her, "None of your
don't have any relative with that   kindred is called by this name."
name!"

you: here you is singular, referring only to Elizabeth. "You don't
have any relative called (or, named) John." It was to be expected that
the boy would be named after some relative.

1.62   TEV   RSV

Then they made signs to his father,   And they made signs to his father,
asking him what name he would like   inquiring what he would have him
the boy to have.   called.

they made signs to his father: this clearly implies that Zechariah
could not hear, and not just that he was unable to speak.

1.63   TEV   RSV

Zechariah asked for a writing   And he asked for a writing tablet,
pad and wrote, "His name is John."   and wrote, "His name is John." And
How surprised they all were!   they all marveled.

a writing pad: this would be a small wooden board covered with wax; in English "a writing tablet" (RSV) is perhaps the best; TEV writing pad suggests paper.

surprised: this implies that Zechariah had not told his friends and relatives about the angel's command (verse 13).

1.64

TEV	RSV
At that moment Zechariah was able to speak again, and he started praising God.	And immediately his mouth was opened and his tongue loosed, and he spoke, blessing God.

able to speak again: the biblical phrase "his mouth was opened and his tongue" (see RSV) indicates a miracle. "God gave back to him the power of speech," "God enabled him to talk again." A literal translation may be difficult to understand; in most languages it will be quite strange.

praising: "thanking," "giving thanks to."

1.65

TEV	RSV
The neighbors were all filled with fear, and the news about these things spread through all the hill country of Judea.	And fear came on all their neighbors. And all these things were talked about through all the hill country of Judea;

filled with fear: as is common in the Bible, the word fear in a context like this means rather "awe" or even "wonder."

the news about these things spread: "everybody was talking about these things," "people were telling one another what had happened."

hill country of Judea: see verse 39.

1.66

TEV	RSV
Everyone who heard of it thought about it and asked, "What is this child going to be?" For it was plain that the Lord's power was upon him.	and all who heard them laid them up in their hearts, saying, "What then will this child be?" For the hand of the Lord was with him.

thought about it: literally "stored (it up) in their hearts" (see RSV). The idea is not so much to remember as to ponder, that is, to reflect about the meaning of the events.

What is this child going to be?: that is, when he grows up. The unusual circumstances of his birth indicated that he would be an unusual person.

the Lord's power: this translates "the Lord's hand" (see RSV), which is God's power to help, to lead, to direct. The second part of the verse is taken by most commentators and translators to be the author's comment, and not part of what the people were saying. But some include this as part of their statement, which is possible but does not seem very probable.

was upon him: "was with him" (RSV). It may be better to speak of the Lord, and not of his power; for example, "For it was plain that the Lord was guiding (or, blessing) the child."

SECTION HEADING

Zechariah's Prophecy: "Zechariah Praises God," "The Song of Zechariah."

In this section we have Zechariah's song of praise, traditionally known as the "Benedictus," which is the first word of verse 68 in the Latin translation, the Vulgate; the word means "blessed be." The song divides naturally into two parts: (1) verses 68-75 (one sentence in Greek) are a song of praise, and (2) verses 76-79 (another sentence in Greek) speak of what John will do.
If the poetic style of the original can be effectively imitated, it should be done in translation.

1.67	TEV	RSV
	John's father Zechariah was filled with the Holy Spirit, and he spoke God's message:	And his father Zechariah was filled with the Holy Spirit, and prophesied, saying,

John's father Zechariah: it is important to note that Zechariah is identified in terms of his relation to John, who plays the major role in the narrative.
was filled with the Holy Spirit: "the Holy Spirit came upon Zechariah," "the Holy Spirit took possession of Zechariah" (see 1.15).
spoke God's message: this represents the Greek verb usually translated "prophesied" (RSV). In what follows, Zechariah praises God and then he predicts what John will be (verse 76). One possibility here would be to say "spoke what God wanted him to speak," or "spoke in the name of God," or "spoke like a prophet."

1.68	TEV	RSV
	"Let us praise the Lord, the God of Israel! He has come to the help of his people and has set them free.	"Blessed be the Lord God of Israel, for he has visited and redeemed his people,

Let us praise: this is usually translated "Blessed be" (RSV)—a biblical phrase which declares that God should be thanked, or praised. Since "to bless" in English is usually used of God's activity toward people (that is, of the superior toward the inferior), it is not natural to speak of people "blessing" God, in the normal sense of causing good things to happen to someone.
He has come to the help of: this translates the verb "he visited" (see RSV), which in Hebrew is often used in the Old Testament for God's

[23]

action on behalf of someone. It describes God's help as his personal
activity on their behalf.

has set them free: RSV "redeemed"; or else "saved," "rescued." This
language reflects the experience of the people of Israel in being set
free from slavery in Egypt. However, there is no idea of paying money to
set a slave free.

1.69	TEV	RSV
	He has provided for us a mighty Savior, a descendant of his servant David.	and has raised up a horn of sal- vation for us in the house of his servant Da- vid,

provided: the verb "to raise" (see RSV), with God as subject, means
to cause to appear, to send forth, to bring.

us: this includes all the people there, or all the people of Israel.

a mighty Savior: this translates the Old Testament phrase "a horn
of salvation" (RSV; see Psa 18.2). In the Old Testament, "horn" is a
symbol of strength.

a descendant of his servant David: this kind of language is used of
the Messiah. Zechariah is not speaking of John; David was of the tribe
of Judah, and Zechariah, as a priest, was of the tribe of Levi (see 1.5).
The angel had told Zechariah that his son would be the forerunner of
God's saving activity (1.17).

1.70	TEV	RSV
	He promised through his holy prophets long ago	as he spoke by the mouth of his holy prophets from of old,

In Greek this verse begins with "as he spoke" (RSV), referring to
the previous verse; it is not advisable, however, to imitate RSV and
have verses 68-75 as one sentence. If a break is made here, the verse may
begin: "He did this as he had promised,...."

holy prophets: a prophet was one who spoke for God, who proclaimed
God's message to the people. Holy here is a title of respect applied to
the great prophets in Israel's history.

1.71	TEV	RSV
	that he would save us from our enemies, from the power of all those who hate us.	that we should be saved from our enemies, and from the hand of all who hate us;

The two lines of this verse are parallel: our enemies and all those
who hate us mean the same thing. The phrases refer to the enemies of
Israel, God's people, especially those who in Israel's long history had
conquered and enslaved them: Assyrians, Babylonians, Persians, Greeks,
Syrians, Romans.

1.72

TEV	RSV
He said he would show mercy to our ancestors and remember his sacred covenant.	to perform the mercy promised to our fathers, and to remember his holy covenant,

He said he would: TEV starts a new sentence here, and so adds this verbal phrase. RSV "to perform" seems to connect this back with verses 68b-69, which is possible.

show mercy to: "be merciful to," "save," "help." RSV translates "to perform the mercy promised to our fathers," interpreting the verse to mean that salvation had been promised to the "fathers," and the promise is now being fulfilled. This is a possible interpretation. TEV takes the words to mean that the ancestors are involved in the salvation God achieves, since they were the objects of God's sacred covenant. The form of the Greek favors the TEV interpretation.

remember: not simply to recollect or to remind himself of it, but to carry it out, to fulfill it. So something like "keep" or "fulfill" would be better.

covenant: "agreement," "alliance," "pact." God made this agreement with Abraham, Isaac, and Jacob—the "ancestors" of the Israelites—and then with the people of Israel themselves.

1.73-74

TEV	RSV
With a solemn oath to our ancestor Abraham he promised to rescue us from our enemies and allow us to serve him without fear,	the oath which he swore to our father Abraham, 74 to grant us that we, being delivered from the hand of our enemies, might serve him without fear,

A comparison of TEV and RSV shows that there has been some restructuring of the material by TEV in order to keep the various matters in more of a chronological order. The passage refers to God's promise to Abraham in Genesis 22.16-17; Zechariah says us, meaning the people of Israel of his own time. God will soon rescue his people from the power of their enemies.

With a solemn oath...he promised: this attempts to preserve the compound phrase in Greek; "he promised earnestly," "he swore," "he made a (solemn) vow."

without fear: that is, without being afraid that enemies may persecute them for worshiping Yahweh, the God of Israel.

1.75

TEV	RSV
so that we might be holy and righteous before him all the days of our life.	in holiness and righteousness before him all the days of our life.

1.75

so that we might be: instead of this result clause, a closer equivalent of the Greek would be "and be holy and righteous...."

holy: dedicated to God, separated for his service, devoted to him.

righteous: obeying God's will, doing what is right.

before him: in his presence, that is, with an active consciousness that God always sees what one is doing.

The verse may be restructured as follows:

> and to live in his presence all our lives,
> dedicated to him and doing his will.

1.76

TEV	RSV
"You, my child, will be called a prophet of the Most High God. You will go ahead of the Lord to prepare his road for him.	And you, child, will be called the prophet of the Most High; for you will go before the Lord to prepare his ways,

Here Zechariah changes subject, addresses the child directly, and speaks of what he will be and do (verses 76-79).

will be called: this passive probably represents divine activity (see 1.32), "God will call you." Or, in a more general way, it could be taken to mean "You will be known as," "You will have the title of," "You will be."

prophet: see 1.70.

the Most High God: see 1.32.

You will go ahead...road for him: this reflects the language of Isaiah 40.3 and Malachi 3.1.

go ahead of the Lord: that is, to go as a messenger announcing to God's people that God is coming to save them. In this context of Zechariah's song, the Lord refers to God.

prepare his road for him: "get a road ready for him," "cut a path on which he can come." This is a figurative expression, meaning to take the necessary measures that will make it possible for God to come to his people. If possible, the figurative language should be kept in translation.

1.77

TEV	RSV
to tell his people that they will be saved by having their sins forgiven.	to give knowledge of salvation to his people in the forgiveness of their sins,

TEV expresses in verbs what are nouns in Greek: to tell...that they will be saved for "to give knowledge of salvation" (RSV), and having their sins forgiven for "the forgiveness of their sins" (RSV). In both

[26]

cases the actor is God: God saves and God forgives the people's sins. This can be expressed as follows:

> to tell his people
> that God will forgive their sins
> and in this way (he will) save them.

1.78

	TEV	RSV
	Our God is merciful and tender.	through the tender mercy of our God,
	He will cause the bright dawn of salvation to rise on us	when the day shall dawn upon^f us from on high

^{f} Or *whereby the dayspring will visit.* Other ancient authorities read *since the dayspring has visited*

merciful and tender: "merciful and kind." This expresses the reason why God will forgive his people's sins and save them. So this can be joined more closely to what precedes, by beginning: "For our God is."

The second part of the verse uses the sun as a figure of salvation, the sun which rises and with its bright rays dispels the shadows and the darkness. In order to show that this is a figure, TEV has of salvation, which is not in the Greek. The abstract noun may not be adequate in some languages, so a verbal phrase, "He will save us," or a noun phrase, "He will send a Savior," may be better. What follows will then be in the form of a comparison: "That (or, He) will be like the rising sun...."

Textual Note: as RSV footnote shows, some Greek manuscripts have the verb in the past tense, "has risen," instead of the future tense, "will rise." The future tense seems to be the correct text.

1.79

	TEV	RSV
	and to shine from heaven on all those who live in the dark shadow of death,	to give light to those who sit in darkness and in the shadow of death,
	to guide our steps into the path of peace."	to guide our feet into the way of peace."

This verse continues with the figure of sunlight and darkness representing life and death.

to guide: the subject is God; it might be better to say "in order to guide," which links it more closely with He in verse 78b.

path of peace: "path that leads to peace."

peace: in the Bible this is usually not just absence of conflict, but spiritual prosperity, wholeness, salvation. This peace is the salvation that God's Messiah will bring.

TEV	RSV
The child grew and developed in body and spirit. He lived in the desert until the day when he appeared publicly to the people of Israel.	And the child grew and became strong in spirit, and he was in the wilderness till the day of his manifestation to Israel.

grew and developed in body and spirit: "grew physically and developed spiritually." Both his bodily growth and his spiritual growth are stated.

the desert: probably the desolate region on the west side of the Jordan River, not far from where it empties into the Dead Sea. The meaning can be expressed by "a place where no people live," "a wilderness," "wild country."

he appeared publicly: "he began his public ministry."

Chapter 2

The Birth of Jesus.

The story of the birth of Jesus in Bethlehem, given in verses 1-7, is followed by the account of the shepherds' visit to the place of Jesus' birth (verses 8-20). Most translations, like TEV, divide this material into two sections.

2.1 TEV	RSV
At that time Emperor Augustus ordered a census to be taken throughout the Roman Empire.	In those days a decree went out from Caesar Augustus that all the world should be enrolled.

At that time: this vague expression of time does not mean the time when (or after) John began his public ministry (1.80), but around the time of his birth and early childhood. So a translation could say "Soon after John was born."

Emperor: this translates the Roman title "Caesar" (RSV). Augustus was also a title. The emperor's name was Gaius Octavius, and he ruled from 27 B.C. to A.D. 14.

the Roman Empire: this is the meaning here of the Greek phrase "all the (inhabited) world" (see RSV). The Emperor's order that a census be taken was for purposes of taxation.

2.2 TEV	RSV
When this first census took place, Quirinius was the governor of Syria.	This was the first enrollment, when Quirinius was governor of Syria.

The Greek text may be understood differently from the way RSV and TEV interpret it. The meaning may be "This was the first census taken while Quirinius was the governor of Syria." But most translations agree with RSV and TEV.

Syria: at that time this was a Roman province, and some translations may need to state this, either in the text or in a footnote.

2.3 TEV	RSV
Everyone, then, went to register himself, each to his own hometown.	And all went to be enrolled, each to his own city.

2.3

All citizens of the Roman Empire were required to register, by heads of family, in their birthplaces.

town: this translates a Greek word which may mean either "city" or "town," according to the modern point of view. Few places in the empire at that time would qualify as a city today.

2.4   TEV   RSV

Joseph went from the town of   And Joseph also went up from Gali-
Nazareth in Galilee to the town of   lee, from the city of Nazareth, to
Bethlehem in Judea, the birthplace   Judea, to the city of David, which
of King David. Joseph went there   is called Bethlehem, because he was
because he was a descendant of   of the house and lineage of David,
David.

The fact that Joseph was a descendant of King David has already been stated in 1.27.

Nazareth and Galilee: see 1.26.

Bethlehem: a small town about 8 kilometers south of Jerusalem.

Judea: the southern province of the country.

the birthplace of King David: this translates "the city (or, town) of David" (see RSV). A literal translation may be misunderstood as meaning that Bethlehem was the "city" where David lived when he was king, or else that Bethlehem belonged to David.

a descendant of David: this translates the Greek "of the house and family of David" (see RSV), a way of saying that David was Joseph's ancestor. There is no need to have two different words in a translation to express this relationship; a verbal phrase may be used, "he was descended from King David." The descent would be counted through the fathers.

2.5-6   TEV   RSV

He went to register with Mary, who   to be enrolled with Mary, his be-
was promised in marriage to him.   trothed, who was with child. 6 And
She was pregnant, 6 and while they   while they were there, the time
were in Bethlehem, the time came   came for her to be delivered.
for her to have her baby.

who was promised in marriage to him: this translates the same verb used in 1.27. The relationship is that of "betrothal" (see RSV and other English translations), by which is meant "promised in marriage." Later Greek manuscripts added the word "wife" (or, "woman"), which is the text represented in KJV as "his espoused wife." As suggested in 1.27, perhaps a footnote would be helpful, as follows: "According to Jewish custom at that time, a couple who planned to marry would first enter into a binding agreement to marry; this agreement could be broken only by a formal act of divorce."

The time between the agreement and the wedding was usually one year.

the time came for her to have her baby: see the similar expression used of Elizabeth in 1.57.

2.7 TEV	RSV
She gave birth to her first son, wrapped him in cloths and laid him in a manger—there was no room for them to stay in the inn.	And she gave birth to her first-born son and wrapped him in swaddling cloths, and laid him in a manger, because there was no place for them in the inn.

her first son: or "her first-born son" (RSV). The word seems to imply that Mary had other children besides Jesus.

wrapped him in cloths: "swaddled him." Cloth strips were wrapped tightly around the body of a newborn child.

a manger: this was a feeding trough for cattle. At that time the stable was often built onto the house itself; it was not a separate building.

the inn: or "the house." It is not certain that this was a public lodging place. It may have been a private home where Joseph and Mary hoped to find lodging, but there was "no room (or, place) for them (to spend the night)."

SECTION HEADING

The Shepherds and the Angels: "The Shepherds Go and See the Baby Jesus."

The shepherds are told by an angel, God's messenger, about the birth of Jesus, and they go and see him that very night.

2.8 TEV	RSV
There were some shepherds in that part of the country who were spending the night in the fields, taking care of their flocks.	And in that region there were shepherds out in the field, keeping watch over their flock by night.

shepherds: it may be necessary to describe them by a phrase, "men who took care of (or, looked after) sheep." Or else one could simply translate "men," as follows: "Some men were taking care of (or, watching over) their sheep that night in a field." If possible, an expression should be used to show that this was their usual work and not just something they were doing that night.

in that part of the country: "not far from Bethlehem," "in that same region."

taking care of: "looking after," "watching over."

their flocks: "their sheep," "their flock" (RSV).

2.9 TEV	RSV
An angel of the Lord appeared to them, and the glory of the Lord shone over them. They were terribly afraid,	And an angel of the Lord appeared to them, and the glory of the Lord shone around them, and they were filled with fear.

An angel of the Lord: see 1.11.
appeared to them: literally "stood before them." It is often assumed that the angel was in the air, but the text itself does not say exactly where he was. In verse 15 went...back into heaven seems to imply that the angels were standing on the ground.
glory: "bright light," "brightness." In the Old Testament "the glory of Yahweh" was the way in which he appeared to his people, as a bright light or a shining cloud.
shone over them: or "shone around them" (RSV).

2.10

TEV	RSV
but the angel said to them, "Don't be afraid! I am here with good news for you, which will bring great joy to all the people.	And the angel said to them, "Be not afraid; for behold, I bring you good news of a great joy which will come to all the people;

RSV "behold" represents a Greek word used frequently as an attention getter; it may be represented by "Pay attention," "Listen," "Look." But it is used so frequently as to lose much of its effect as an attention getter, which is the reason why it is not always formally represented in TEV.
I am here with good news for you: this translates "I am bringing good news to you" or "I am telling you good news." The Greek verb is related to the noun translated "gospel," literally "good news."
all the people: that is, all the people of Israel.

2.11

TEV	RSV
This very day in David's town your Savior was born—Christ the Lord!	for to you is born this day in the city of David a Savior, who is Christ the Lord.

RSV begins verse 11 with "for"; the Greek particle could be read as "that," meaning "that is," giving the content of the good news announced in verse 10.
David's town: Bethlehem (see verse 4).
your Savior: "the one who will save you," "the one who will set you free." The same title is applied to God in 1.47.
Christ the Lord: or "the Messiah, the Lord," as two titles. Christ is the Greek form of the Hebrew "Messiah," which means "the anointed one," that is, the one who has been chosen and commissioned by God to save his people Israel. Lord is the Greek form of the Hebrew title which in the Old Testament is applied to God.

2.12

TEV	RSV
And this is what will prove it to you: you will find a baby wrapped in cloths and lying in a manger."	And this will be a sign for you: you will find a babe wrapped in swaddling cloths and lying in a manger."

will prove it to you: that is, will prove that what the angel is saying is true. This translates the Greek noun "sign" (RSV). A possible translation would be "this is how you will be able to know (or, recognize) that my message is true."

wrapped in cloths: as in verse 7.

lying in a manger: as in verse 7.

2.13

TEV	RSV
Suddenly a great army of heaven's angels appeared with the angel, singing praises to God:	And suddenly there was with the angel a multitude of the heavenly host praising God and saying,

a great army: the word army (RSV "host") is used to represent the Greek word which refers to the angels as a military group, a company of soldiers. This reflects the Old Testament concept of angels as heavenly warriors.

singing praises to God: "praising God" (RSV), "giving praise (or, thanks) to God."

2.14

TEV	RSV
"Glory to God in the highest heaven, and peace on earth to those with whom he is pleased!"	"Glory to God in the highest, and on earth peace among men with whom he is pleased!"*g* *g*Other ancient authorities read *peace, good will among men*

Glory to God: here the sense is "Thanks be to God," "God is to be praised," "Praise God." It is to be noted that, in keeping with the form of the Greek, neither RSV nor TEV has a verb in either of the two lines; Glory to God...peace...to those. It may be better to have verbal phrases as follows:

'May God, who lives in the highest heaven, be praised,
and may there be peace on earth...."

the highest heaven: this translates the plural "highest places," a way of speaking about heaven, God's abode, as located in the distant heights above the earth. The whole phrase, "Glory in the highest," may be a way of saying "May those who live in the highest heaven (that is, the angels) praise God." Most translations, however, connect "the highest" with God, as the place where he lives.

peace: see 1.79.

to those: or "among those."

those with whom he is pleased: "people who please him," "people he likes (or, chooses)." In line with TEV, a translation should avoid the exclusive language "men" (RSV), as though women were not included.

Textual Note: as RSV footnote shows, some Greek manuscripts read "and on earth (may there be) peace among people, and good will." There is no doubt that the Greek text translated by RSV and TEV is correct.

2.15	TEV	RSV

<table>
<tr>
<td>When the angels went away from them back into heaven, the shepherds said to one another, "Let's go to Bethlehem and see this thing that has happened, which the Lord has told us."</td>
<td>When the angels went away from them into heaven, the shepherds said to one another, "Let us go over to Bethlehem and see this thing that has happened, which the Lord has made known to us."</td>
</tr>
</table>

When the angels went away from them back into heaven: "After the angels left them and returned to heaven"; or, as a complete sentence, "Then the angels left the shepherds and returned to heaven."

Let's go to Bethlehem: the implication is that they are not far from the town.

this thing that has happened: a reference to the baby born that day (verse 11).

the Lord: God.

2.16	TEV	RSV

<table>
<tr>
<td>So they hurried off and found Mary and Joseph and saw the baby lying in the manger.</td>
<td>And they went with haste, and found Mary and Joseph, and the babe lying in a manger.</td>
</tr>
</table>

found: this implies a purposeful search. To avoid the idea of an accidental find, the translation could say, if necessary, "After looking for them, the shepherds found Mary and Joseph."

and saw the baby: this is said in order to avoid the possibility (see RSV) of making it sound as if all three—Mary, Joseph, the baby— were in the manger.

2.17	TEV	RSV

<table>
<tr>
<td>When the shepherds saw him, they told them what the angel had said about the child.</td>
<td>And when they saw it they made known the saying which had been told them concerning this child;</td>
</tr>
</table>

saw him: the Greek text has no direct object, so the meaning could be "saw them," that is, Mary, Joseph, and the baby. But since the focus of attention is on the baby, probably "the child" or "the baby" is the object of the verb.

they told them: again the Greek has no direct object; so it may be preferable to translate "they reported" or "they told everybody (there)."

what the angel had said: this translates "the saying which had been told them" (RSV), a reference to what the angel had told them (verses 11-12). It is better to make the reference to the angel explicit, as TEV has done.

2.18-19	TEV	RSV

<table>
<tr>
<td>All who heard it were amazed at what the shepherds said. 19 Mary</td>
<td>and all tho heard it wondered at what the shepherds told them. 19 But</td>
</tr>
</table>

remembered all these things and thought deeply about them.	Mary kept all these things, pondering them in her heart.

were amazed: "were astounded," "were surprised."

remembered: this translates a verb meaning "keep, preserve, store up"—an obvious reference to storing up in her mind.

thought deeply about them: the Greek verb (RSV "pondering") means "to throw together," "to compare"; in some instances it means "to talk with." The meaning here is a process of meditation and reflection.

2.20	TEV	RSV
	The shepherds went back, singing praises to God for all they had heard and seen; it had been just as the angel had told them.	And the shepherds returned, glorifying and praising God for all they had heard and seen, as it had been told them.

singing praises to God: "praising God with songs" or "glorifying and praising God" (RSV). RSV "glorifying" represents the Greek verb which is related to the noun Glory used in verse 14.

as the angel had told them: again TEV has represented the passive verb in Greek (so RSV "as it had been told them") by a verb in the active voice, with the subject (the angel) made explicit.

SECTION HEADING

Jesus Is Named: "The Circumcision of Jesus."

In TEV this verse is a separate paragraph, since in the next section (verses 22-38) the scene shifts to Jerusalem. Some translations join this verse to the preceding section; others, to the following section. The emphasis is on the name of the child, not on his circumcision.

2.21	TEV	RSV
	A week later, when the time came for the baby to be circumcised, he was named Jesus, the name which the angel had given him before he had been conceived.	And at the end of eight days, when he was circumcised, he was called Jesus, the name given by the angel before he was conceived in the womb.

A week later: as in the case of John the Baptist (see 1.59).

circumcised: see 1.59.

Jesus: see 1.31.

before he had been conceived: or "before Mary got pregnant." Or the material may be restructured: "...he was named Jesus, as the angel had commanded Mary before she got pregnant."

[35]

SECTION HEADING

Jesus Is Presented in the Temple: "Mary and Joseph Take Jesus to the Temple."

This section includes three distinct events: (1) Joseph and Mary present the baby boy Jesus to God, in the Temple in Jerusalem (verses 22-24); (2) the meeting with Simeon (verses 25-35); and (3) the meeting with Anna (verses 36-38). Some translators may want to divide the material into three sections, with the following section headings: (1) Mary and Joseph Take Jesus to the Temple; (2) Simeon and the Baby Jesus; (3) Anna and the Baby Jesus.

2.22 TEV	RSV
The time came for Joseph and Mary to perform the ceremony of purification, as the Law of Moses commanded. So they took the child to Jerusalem to present him to the Lord,	And when the time came for their purification according to the law of Moses, they brought him up to Jerusalem to present him to the Lord

The Greek text says "When the days of their purification were fulfilled, according to the Law of Moses." The plural "their" is hard to understand, since the rite of purification (Lev 12.1-4,6-7) applied only to the woman; according to the Law, only she became impure when she gave birth to a child. It is not certain whom the author means by "their"— probably Mary and her husband, but it could be Mary and her son.
After the birth of a son a woman was ritually unclean for forty days.
perform the ceremony of purification: this is an attempt to make clear what is meant by purification. The following translation might be better: "The day came when Mary and Joseph had to purify themselves by means of the ritual prescribed in (or, required by) the Law of Moses." Either in a footnote, or in a Word List at the end of the translation, some explanation should be given about the concept of ritual impurity in Jewish society of the first century A.D.
present him to the Lord: the Law of Moses required that every first-born male, human and animal, be offered to God, in recognition of the fact that God claimed that male child or animal for his own.

2.23 TEV	RSV
as it is written in the Law of the Lord: "Every first-born male is to be dedicated to the Lord."	(as it is written in the law of the Lord, "Every male that opens the womb shall be called holy to the Lord")

as it is written: this is a standard formula for quoting the Old Testament. Other expressions may be used: "as the Scriptures say (or, state)," "according to what the Law of God requires." The passage cited is from Exodus 13.2,12.

first-born male: it is not necessary to translate the Hebrew idiom literally, as does RSV. Since here the word male refers both to human beings and to animals, care must be taken to choose a word that can apply to both; or else, "every first-born baby boy and every first-born male of your domestic animals."

is to be dedicated: "shall be offered to the Lord," "shall be consecrated to the Lord's service," "shall be set apart for God's service." For the concept of "holy" see 1.35.

2.24

TEV	RSV
They also went to offer a sacrifice of a pair of doves or two young pigeons, as required by the Law of the Lord.	and to offer a sacrifice according to what is said in the law of the Lord, "a pair of turtledoves, or two young pigeons."

This verse is connected directly to verse 22 (see RSV), but it is simpler to begin a new sentence, as does TEV.

Leviticus 12.8 states that if a woman cannot afford to offer a lamb as a sacrifice in the rite of her purification, she may offer two doves or two pigeons. The implication is that Joseph and Mary could not afford a lamb.

a pair of doves or two young pigeons: the words a pair of do not mean a male and a female, but simply two. If two different kinds of such birds are unknown in a given language, the translation may say something like "two pigeons or two small birds of another kind."

as required by the Law of the Lord: "as the Law of the Lord says (or, commands)."

2.25

TEV	RSV
At that time there was a man named Simeon living in Jerusalem. He was a good, God-fearing man and was waiting for Israel to be saved. The Holy Spirit was with him	Now there was a man in Jerusalem, whose name was Simeon, and this man was righteous and devout, looking for the consolation of Israel, and the Holy Spirit was upon him.

Four things are said about Simeon: (1) he was good, or "righteous" (RSV). In the context of the Jewish religion, this meant that he obeyed the Law of Moses, fulfilling all duties and obligations of a faithful Jew. (2) He was God-fearing, or "devout" (RSV), "pious," "religious." (3) He was waiting for Israel to be saved, or "waiting for God to save the people of Israel." This refers to the hope that God would soon keep the promise he had made through the prophets to rescue his people from their enemies, either doing it himself, or by sending the Messiah. (4) The Holy Spirit was with him, or "the Spirit of God was upon him," or whatever may be the normal way of speaking of the Spirit's presence with a person.

2.26	TEV	RSV

and had assured him that he would not die before he had seen the Lord's promised Messiah.	And it had been revealed to him by the Holy Spirit that he should not see death before he had seen the Lord's Christ.

(The Holy Spirit) had assured him: "had promised him," "had told him."

he would not die: literally "he would not see death" (see RSV). Another biblical expression is "to taste death" (see 9.27).

the Lord's promised Messiah: or "the Savior that God had promised to send," or "the Savior chosen by God."

The verse may also be translated as follows: "The Holy Spirit had promised him that he would live to see the Savior whom God would send."

2.27-28	TEV	RSV

Led by the Spirit, Simeon went into the Temple. When the parents brought the child Jesus into the Temple to do for him what the Law required, 28 Simeon took the child in his arms and gave thanks to God:	And inspired by the Spirit[h] he came into the temple; and when the parents brought in the child Jesus, to do for him according to the custom of the law, 28 he took him up in his arms and blessed God and said,

[h]Or *in the Spirit*

Led by the Spirit: the Greek expression "in the Spirit" means that God's Spirit is in control; Simeon went to the Temple because the Spirit made him go. However, no word should be used which would imply that Simeon went reluctantly or unwillingly.

into the Temple: or "to the Temple." The Temple as a whole included several courts and buildings, and here no specific indication is given of where Simeon went.

the parents: or "Jesus' father and mother."

to do for him: that is, to perform the necessary ritual, as required by the Law of Moses.

what the Law required: RSV "the custom of the law" is obscure English. What is meant is the ritual that the Law commanded people to do.

took...in his arms: "held in his arms," "held close to his chest."

gave thanks to God: see "blessed" in 1.68.

2.29	TEV	RSV

"Now, Lord, you have kept your promise, and you may let your servant go in peace.	"Lord, now lettest thou thy servant depart in peace, according to thy word;

Simeon's prayer of praise is traditionally called the "Nunc Dimittis" (which means "Now you dismiss"), the first two words of the translation in the Latin version, the Vulgate.

TEV restructures the two lines of this verse; in Greek the second line is "according to your word" (see RSV), which TEV represents by you have kept your promise. Simeon immediately recognizes the baby Jesus as God's promised Messiah, and so he confesses that God has kept his promise to Simeon. The main statement is to be understood either as a petition, "let your servant go in peace," or as a permission, you may let, as TEV has it.

Lord here translates a rarely used title for God: "Master," "Owner." It fits the way Simeon speaks of himself, your servant (or "your slave"). To make it clear that Simeon is speaking about himself, it may be better to say "you may let me, your servant, die in peace." Now that the Master has kept his promise, his servant's task is finished, and so the Master can send him away.

go: Simeon is talking about his death; so instead of go it may be better to translate "you may let your servant die in peace." The verb and tense used for the verb "to die" should not imply that death would be at that very moment.

in peace: here in the sense of "serene," "tranquil," "calm."

2.30-31	TEV	RSV
	With my own eyes I have seen your salvation,	for mine eyes have seen thy salvation
31	which you have prepared in the presence of all peoples:	31 which thou hast prepared in the presence of all peoples,

your salvation: this impersonal, abstract concept refers to the baby boy he is holding in his arms. "I have seen the one who will save your people." With the following line (verse 31), the translation could be:

> For I have (personally) seen the Savior
> (whom) you have provided in the sight of all peoples.

in the presence of all peoples: it may be that the meaning of the Greek is "for all people to see" (see Isa 52.10).

2.32	TEV	RSV
	A light to reveal your will to the Gentiles and bring glory to your people Israel."	a light for revelation to the Gentiles, and for glory to thy people Israel."

This verse explains the nature of the salvation which God has prepared: it is a light "for revelation to the Gentiles" (RSV). Here this noun "revelation" may mean, as TEV has it, to reveal your will; or else, in a more general sense, "a light to shine on the Gentiles," or else "a light to make your truth known to the Gentiles." In the Old Testament, light is used as a figure of life, salvation, as opposed to death and destruction.

The second line of verse 32 is "and glory for your people Israel."
Here "glory" may mean honor, fame, renown. But as a parallel with light,
it seems better to relate glory to God and not to Israel as such. God's
glory was his visible presence with his people (see verse 9). God's salvation is light for the Gentiles, and God's glory is for the Israelites.
So, to translate this verse in accordance with the suggestion made for
verses 30-31, one could say:

> He will bring your saving light to the Gentiles,
>   and your saving presence to your people Israel.

2.33   TEV   RSV
   The child's father and mother   And his father and his mother
were amazed at the things Simeon   marveled at what was said about him;
said about him.

   The child's father and mother: the same language as in verse 27 (the
parents) and in verse 41 (the parents); and see in verse 48 Your father
and I.

2.34   TEV   RSV
Simeon blessed them and said to   and Simeon blessed them and said to
Mary, his mother, "This child is   Mary his mother,
chosen by God for the destruction   "Behold, this child is set for
and the salvation of many in Israel.   the fall and rising of many
He will be a sign from God which   in Israel,
many people will speak against   and for a sign that is spoken
                                          against

   blessed them: or "asked God to bless them." If it is necessary to
make it explicit, them probably refers to the parents of Jesus. For
bless see 1.68.
   is chosen by God: this translates a verb in Greek which means "to
be placed" (RSV "is set"), referring here to God's decision about the
child. Another translation could be "This child is destined (by God)
to...."
   the destruction and the salvation: this translates the Greek "for
the falling and the rising" (RSV). What is meant is not that the same
group (many in Israel) will fall and then will rise, but that many will
fall and many will rise. People's reaction to the child will determine
whether they will be saved or be destroyed.
   a sign from God: here in the sense of a warning sign. This sign
does not refer to any miracle, but to the person and message of Jesus,
who will confront the people of Israel with God's demands.
   will speak against: "will oppose," "will refuse," "will not accept."

2.35 TEV	RSV
and so reveal their secret thoughts. And sorrow, like a sharp sword, will break your own heart."	(and a sword will pierce through own soul also), that thoughts out of many hearts may be revealed."

As a comparison of TEV and RSV shows, the material in verse 35 has been restructured by TEV so as to keep together the saying about the child, followed by Simeon's direct statement to Mary. RSV preserves the order of the Greek and places within parentheses the first line of verse 35. This may not be effective in other languages.

and so: this seems to be related directly to will speak against in the preceding verse; the subject will be the same, many people. It may be difficult to represent reveal as a transitive verb, so another form may be used, "and so their secret thoughts will become known (to others)," or "and so others will know their (secret) thoughts." But the subject may be Jesus himself. If so, Simeon is saying "and so he will bring to light their secret thoughts."

sharp sword: in the saying to Mary, "a sword" (RSV) is a figure of pain, suffering, or punishment. Here sorrow, like a sharp sword seems to express the idea well; or else "pain will pierce your heart like a sword."

2.36-37 TEV	RSV
There was a very old prophetess, a widow named Anna, daughter of Phanuel of the tribe of Asher. She had been married for only seven years and was now eighty-four years old.*b* She never left the Temple; day and night she worshiped God, fasting and praying.	And there was a prophetess, Anna, the daughter of Phanuel, of the tribe of Asher; she was of a great age, having lived with her husband seven years from her virginity, 37 and as a widow till she was eighty-four. She did not depart from the temple, worshiping with fasting and prayer night and day.

*b*was now eighty-four years old; *or* had been a widow eighty-four years.

TEV has the two verse numbers together because the word widow is in the first part of the verse. In Greek the fact that she was a widow is stated in verse 37.

tribe: in some languages a tribe is made up of people who are looked down on by other people, and some explanation of the term as used in the Bible may be necessary.

She had been married for only seven years: she could have married as early as the age of twelve (see note on 1.27) and so have become a widow at nineteen or twenty years of age.

The next statement can be understood in two different ways, as TEV text and footnote show. Most translations prefer the meaning found in TEV text (and in RSV). If this interpretation is preferred, it would be more natural to translate verses 36-37 as follows: "There was a very old prophetess (or, a very old woman who spoke in God's name) named Anna, the

[41]

daughter of Phanuel (or, whose father was Phanuel), of the tribe of Asher. She was an eighty-four year old widow who had been married (only) seven years."

If the meaning in TEV footnote is preferred, a translation could read: "There was a very old prophetess (or, woman who spoke in God's name) named Anna, the daughter of Phanuel, of the tribe of Asher. Her husband had died after they had been married seven years, and she had been a widow for eighty-four years."

She never left the Temple: this is an emphatic way of saying "She went often to the Temple"; she would not have lived in the Temple.

The same kind of exaggeration is seen in day and night she worshiped God. This describes her activity in the Temple.

fasting and praying: this is the way in which Anna worshiped God. Where fasting is unknown, one may say "going without food for a religious motive."

2.38	TEV	RSV
	That very same hour she arrived and gave thanks to God and spoke about the child to all who were waiting for God to set Jerusalem free.	And coming up at that very hour she gave thanks to God, and spoke of him to all who were looking for the redemption of Jerusalem.

That very same hour: that is, at the time Simeon was there.

waiting for God to set Jerusalem free: this refers to the same great act of salvation spoken of in verse 25, waiting for Israel to be saved. As the location of the Temple, God's dwelling place on earth, Jerusalem was the most sacred of all places in Israel.

SECTION HEADING

The Return to Nazareth: "Joseph and Mary Return with Jesus to Nazareth."

2.39	TEV	RSV
	When Joseph and Mary had finished doing all that was required by the Law of the Lord, they returned to their hometown of Nazareth in Galilee.	And when they had performed everything according to the law of the Lord, they returned into Galilee, to their own city, Nazareth.

all that was required by the Law of the Lord: see the similar expressions in verses 22,27.

Nazareth in Galilee: see 1.26.

2.40	TEV	RSV
	The child grew and became strong; he was full of wisdom, and God's blessings were upon him.	And the child grew and became strong, filled with wisdom; and the favor of God was upon him.

The statement about Jesus in verse 40 is similar to the one made about John the Baptist in 1.80.

he was full of wisdom: "he was very wise (or, intelligent)." "The child grew, becoming ever stronger and wiser."

God's blessings were upon him: "God kept on blessing him"; or "God was pleased with him."

SECTION HEADING

The Boy Jesus in the Temple: "The Boy Jesus and the Teachers in the Temple."

This is the only story in the Gospels about Jesus as a boy. Nothing else is said about him between the time of his birth and the beginning of his public ministry as an adult.

2.41-42   TEV

Every year the parents of Jesus went to Jerusalem for the Passover Festival. 42 When Jesus was twelve years old, they went to the festival as usual.

2.41-42   RSV

Now his parents went to Jerusalem every year at the feast of the Passover. 42 And when he was twelve years old, they went up according to custom;

Passover Festival: this was held every year on the fourteenth day of the month Nisan (around April 1) to commemorate the liberation of the ancient Hebrews from their slavery in Egypt (see Exo 12.24-27; Deut 16.1-8). The Passover was one of the three Jewish festivals during which every male Jew twenty years and older was supposed to go to Jerusalem. The festival lasted eight days.

twelve years old: at this age a Jewish boy became "a son of the Law" and had certain religious duties to fulfill.

they went: this includes all three, Jesus and his parents.

2.43   TEV

When the festival was over, they started back home, but the boy Jesus stayed in Jerusalem. His parents did not know this;

2.43   RSV

and when the feast was ended, as they were returning, the boy Jesus stayed behind in Jerusalem. His parents did not know it,

they started back home: "Joseph and Mary started back to Nazareth."

Verse 43 can be translated as one sentence: "When the festival was over, Joseph and Mary started back home (to Nazareth), not knowing that (the boy) Jesus had stayed (behind) in Jerusalem."

2.44   TEV

they thought that he was with the group, so they traveled a whole day

2.44   RSV

but supposing him to be in the company they went a day's journey, and

[43]

2.44

and then started looking for him   they sought him among their kinsfolk
among their relatives and friends.   and acquaintances;

 with the group: that is, with relatives and friends from Nazareth,
who had gone to Jerusalem for the festival.
 and then started looking: this gives the impression that Joseph and
Mary started looking for Jesus only after the first day's journey, that
is, on the second day. However, the Greek may mean that the search for
the boy began that first day: "so they traveled a whole day, all the
while looking for him...." A day's trip would be between 25 and 30 kilometers.

2.45-46   TEV   RSV
They did not find him, so they went   and when they did not find him, they
back to Jerusalem looking for him.   returned to Jerusalem, seeking him.
46 On the third day they found him   46 After three days they found him
in the Temple, sitting with the   in the temple, sitting among the
Jewish teachers, listening to them   teachers, listening to them and ask-
and asking questions.   ing them questions;

 they went back to Jerusalem: the return trip would take a whole day.
 the third day: probably the day after their arrival back in Jerusalem; the time is calculated from the day they left the city, not from the
day they arrived back there. So the translation could be: verse 45, "They
did not find him, so the following day they went back..."; verse 46, "The
next day they found him...." The Greek text may mean that they spent
three days looking for him in Jerusalem, but this is not very probable.
 with the Jewish teachers: or "with the teachers of the Law," "with
some teachers of the Law."

2.47   TEV   RSV
All who heard him were amazed at   and all who heard him were amazed
his intelligent answers.   at his understanding and his an-
                                         swers.

 were amazed: this translates a different Greek verb from the one
used in 2.18,33; here the translation could be "astounded," "astonished."
 his intelligent answers: as RSV shows, the Greek text has two nouns,
"his understanding and (his) answers," which may be understood to mean
two different things: his understanding (or, insight), and the answers
he gave. In either case, the picture is that of Jesus asking and answering questions, showing intelligence in both the questions and the answers.

2.48   TEV   RSV
His parents were astonished when   And when they saw him they were
they saw him, and his mother said   astonished; and his mother said to
to him, "Son, why have you done   him, "Son, why have you treated us

[44]

this to us? Your father and I have   so? Behold, your father and I have
been terribly worried trying to   been looking for you anxiously."
find you."

His parents: the Greek says only "they" (RSV), but it is better to
be explicit.
were astonished: this translates still another Greek verb, which
expresses strong surprise: "were astounded," "marveled."
Son: or "Child," whichever is more appropriate on the lips of a
woman talking to her twelve-year-old son.
this: that is, caused Joseph and Mary much trouble and worry when
he did not start back to Nazareth at the same time when they left.
have been terribly worried trying to find you: "have been looking
for you, and we have been very upset."

2.49-50   TEV   RSV
He answered them, "Why did you   And he said to them, "How is it that
have to look for me? Didn't you   you sought me? Did you not know that
know that I had to be in my Fa-   I must be in my Father's house?"
ther's house?" 50 But they did not 50 And they did not understand the
understand his answer.   saying which he spoke to them.

Why did you have to look for me?: as Jesus' next statement shows,
this question implies that Joseph and Mary should have realized where
Jesus was, and they did not have to worry about him. They should have
gone back straight to the Temple, knowing they would find him there. The
question may be phrased as a statement, a slight rebuke: "You didn't have
to waste any time (and trouble) looking for me," "You didn't have to be
worried about where to find me."
I had to be: "I was bound to be"; this kind of compulsion is inner,
arising out of the heart. It was his duty to be in the Temple, the house
of his Father.
in my Father's house: some older translations have "(busy) at my
Father's business." But similar constructions in other Greek sources
demonstrate that the idiom means "in house" and not "at business." The
Temple was God's house.

2.51   TEV   RSV
So Jesus went back with them   And he went down with them and came
to Nazareth, where he was obedient to Nazareth, and was obedient to
to them. His mother treasured all   them; and his mother kept all these
these things in her heart.   things in her heart.

went back with them to Nazareth: the Greek "went down...and arrived"
is a way of talking about traveling away from Jerusalem. One always "went
up" to Jerusalem and "went down" away from it. It is not necessary to
represent this idiom, unless it is a natural way of speaking of departing
from the most important city in the country.
treasured...in her heart: "kept in mind," "remembered"; see similar
language in 2.19.

[45]

2.52	TEV	RSV

Jesus grew both in body and in wisdom, gaining favor with God and men.

And Jesus increased in wisdom and in stature,[i] and in favor with God and man.

[i] Or *years*

grew both in body and in wisdom: this reverses the order of the Greek phrase, which has wisdom first. The word translated body means either physical height (RSV "stature") or age, that is, "he grew older." If this is the sense intended, the translation can be "As Jesus grew older (or, grew up) he became wiser and...."

gaining favor with God and men: see a similar statement in verse 40. Here the translation could be "he gained approval from God and from people" or "...divine and human approval." Or else "he pleased God and everyone who knew him."

Chapter 3

The Preaching of John the Baptist: "The Message Proclaimed by John the Baptist," "John the Baptist Proclaims His Message to the People."

In this section the time, place, content, and effect of John the Baptist's preaching are given. He appears like one of the Old Testament prophets, calling on the people of Israel to repent and turn to God. He also proclaims the coming of the Messiah, which will be soon.

3.1–2 TEV	RSV
It was the fifteenth year of the rule of Emperor Tiberius; Pontius Pilate was governor of Judea, Herod was ruler of Galilee, and his brother Philip was ruler of the territory of Iturea and Trachonitis; Lysanias was ruler of Abilene, 2 and Annas and Caiaphas were high priests. At that time the word of God came to John son of Zechariah in the desert.	In the fifteenth year of the reign of Tiberius Caesar, Pontius Pilate being governor of Judea, and Herod being tetrarch of Galilee, and his brother Philip tetrarch of the region of Ituraea and Trachonitis, and Lysanias tetrarch of Abilene, 2 in the high-priesthood of Annas and Caiaphas, the word of God came to John the son of Zechariah in the wilderness;

Tiberius was Roman Emperor A.D. 14-37; the fifteenth year of his rule would have been A.D. 28 or 29. For Emperor see 2.1.

Pontius Pilate: Roman governor of the provinces of Judea, Samaria, and Idumea, A.D. 26 to 36.

Herod: Herod Antipas, ruler of the province of Galilee and Perea, 4 B.C. to A.D. 39; he was son of Herod the Great (see 1.5).

Philip ruled Iturea and Trachonitis, regions in the northeast part of the country, 4 B.C. to A.D. 34; he was an older half brother of Herod Antipas, also son of Herod the Great, but by a different wife.

Lysanias: nothing is known about him.

Abilene: a region west of Iturea.

Annas had been High Priest from about A.D. 6 to 15; his son-in-law Caiaphas was High Priest A.D. 18 to 36.

high priest: the priest who occupied the highest office in the Jewish priestly system, and who was president of the Supreme Council of the Jews.

the word of God came: "the message from God came," or "God sent his message."

desert: see 1.80.

[47]

3.3 TEV	RSV
So John went throughout the whole territory of the Jordan River, preaching, "Turn away from your sins and be baptized, and God will forgive your sins."	and he went into all the region about the Jordan, preaching a baptism of repentance for the forgiveness of sins.

the whole territory of the Jordan River: it is commonly assumed that this means specifically the west side of the river near the north end of the Dead Sea; it does not mean all the region between Lake Galilee and the Dead Sea.

preaching: "proclaiming his message," "announcing," "telling people." The word used should not imply a church setting with pulpit and congregation.

Turn away from your sins: "Repent of your sins," "Repent of the wrong things you have done." The Greek verb does not mean simply "be sorry," "feel bad," "regret"; it means "to change one's mind," but the command is not only to change one's opinion or attitude, but also one's conduct. In the Old Testament the verb often used means "change," "turn around."

and be baptized: or "and I will baptize you" (see verses 7,16). For "baptize" there is usually a word already current in the Christian community to refer to the Christian rite, and this should generally be used. The Greek verb itself means "to dip," "to immerse," but in some languages the word generally used for baptism does not necessarily imply this.

It is to be noticed that TEV uses direct speech to represent John's message. The Greek uses indirect speech, "preaching a baptism of repentance for the forgiveness of sins" (RSV). In many languages direct speech is more effective and clearer.

forgive: the biblical meaning of the verb is that of God's action whereby sin, as a debt, is canceled or, as a transgression of the Law, is pardoned. There are many ways in which different languages express this action: "to forget about," "erase," "wipe out," "pay back," "lose," "throw away," "be set free from," "turn one's back on," "cover over," "take away," "do away with." A translator should consider carefully the implications of the verb or phrase used, to make sure that it does not introduce an element unworthy of God.

3.4 TEV	RSV
As it is written in the book of the prophet Isaiah: "Someone is shouting in the desert: 'Get the road ready for the Lord; make a straight path for him to travel!	As it is written in the book of the words of Isaiah the prophet, "The voice of one crying in the wilderness: Prepare the way of the Lord, make his paths straight.

As it is written: see 2.23. The passage is from Isaiah 40.3-5 and is quoted according to the ancient Greek version of the Old Testament,

the Septuagint, and not according to the Hebrew text. In the last line
of verse 4, for him replaces "for our God" in Isaiah 40.3.
   prophet: see 1.70.
   shouting: the RSV "crying" should not be understood as "weeping."
   the desert: the same word as in verse 2; in translation the same
word should be used, to make the connection clear.
   Get the road ready: "Prepare a road," "Cut a path." This command is
said in a figurative sense; it means to provide the necessary conditions
that would make it possible for the Lord to come to his people. By turning away from their sins the people would provide those necessary conditions. If possible, the figurative language should be maintained in the
translation.
   the Lord: for the Christian reader this meant Jesus; in the Old
Testament passage it meant God.
   make a straight path: this command means the same as the first one.
   to travel: "to come to his people," "to come to us."

	TEV	RSV
3.5	Every valley must be filled up, every hill and mountain leveled off. The winding roads must be made straight, and the rough paths made smooth.	Every valley shall be filled, and every mountain and hill shall be brought low, and the crooked shall be made straight, and the rough ways shall be made smooth;

This verse uses the same figurative language of verse 4. Both verses
state what has to be done in order to make it possible for the Lord to
come to save his people.
   The verbs in Greek are in the future tense, which may have the force
of an imperative—so TEV must. But most translations use the future tense,
as in verse 6, making these actions refer to what will happen in the future. Some hold that the passive voice of the verbs in this verse denotes
divine activity: God will do all these things to prepare for his coming.
   valley...hill and mountain: if there are no specific words for such
features of the terrain, a translation may use general terms such as "low
places" and "high places." If there are not two words for hill and mountain, one word is enough: "all hills," "every mountain."

	TEV	RSV
3.6	All mankind will see God's salvation!'"	and all flesh shall see the sal- vation of God."

This verse expresses the same idea found in 2.29-30.
   All mankind: "Everyone," "All people everywhere." The Greek word
"flesh" (RSV) means "humanity," "the human race."
   will see God's salvation: "will see how God will save them" or "will
see the Savior that God will send" (see note on 2.30-31).

[49]

3.7 TEV	RSV
Crowds of people came out to John to be baptized by him. "You snakes!" he said to them. "Who told you that you could escape from the punishment God is about to send?	He said therefore to the multitudes that came out to be baptized by him, "You brood of vipers! Who warned you to flee from the wrath to come?

Crowds of people: "Many people."
came out: or "went out."
You snakes: an insulting way of calling them clever hypocrites; they evidently thought that all they had to do was to be baptized by John. The vivid metaphor may be represented by a simile, "You are as wicked (or, as clever) as snakes."
the punishment God is about to send: God's coming would include his judgment on mankind, his punishment of unrepentant sinners. Unless people repented, God would punish them. The whole warning could be translated, "How clever you think you are! You think that just by being baptized you will escape the punishment that God is soon going to send on the wicked!"

3.8 TEV	RSV
Do those things that will show that you have turned from your sins. And don't start saying among yourselves that Abraham is your ancestor. I tell you that God can take these rocks and make descendants for Abraham!	Bear fruits that befit repentance, and do not begin to say to yourselves, 'We have Abraham as our father'; for I tell you, God is able from these stones to raise up children to Abraham.

Do those things: "Perform the actions," "Live in such a way"—literally "Produce fruits" (see RSV). It was not enough to claim to have repented; they had to prove their claim by right actions, by a change from their sinful ways.
turned from your sins: see verse 3.
saying among yourselves that Abraham is your ancestor: or "saying to yourselves, 'Abraham is our ancestor.'" John warns them not to think that they are exempt from God's punishment of sinners because they are Jews, that is, descendants of Abraham.
these rocks: no doubt with a gesture John pointed to the many rocks in the region where he was baptizing.
make descendants for Abraham: a vivid way of saying that God could provide all the descendants Abraham needed. The fact that these people were Jews did not mean a thing.

3.9 TEV	RSV
The ax is ready to cut down the trees at the roots; every tree that does not bear good fruit will be cut down and thrown in the fire."	Even now the axe is laid to the root of the trees; every tree therefore that does not bear good fruit is cut down and thrown into the fire."

The ax: a symbol of God's judgment, which would soon destroy the wicked, that is, those people who did not do what God required (every tree that does not bear good fruit). If the figure ax is difficult or impossible to represent in translation, one may say "God is ready to cut down (or, knock down)."

be cut down and thrown: the passive form of the verbs refers to God's action: "God will cut down and throw."

the fire: a symbol of hell, the place of punishment; but it is not advisable to translate "hell."

3.10-11	TEV	RSV
	The people asked him, "What are we to do, then?"	And the multitudes asked him, "What then shall we do?" 11 And he
	11 He answered, "Whoever has two shirts must give one to the man who has none, and whoever has food must share it."	answered them, "He who has two coats, let him share with him who has none; and he who has food, let him do likewise."

What are we to do, then?: implicit in the question is the assumption that by doing something they will escape being punished by God. So the translation could be "What can we do in order not to be punished by God?"

shirt: this was a short-sleeved, knee-length garment worn next to the body.

share it: or "share it with someone who doesn't have any."

3.12-13	TEV	RSV
	Some tax collectors came to be baptized, and they asked him, "Teacher, what are we to do?"	Tax collectors also came to be baptized, and said to him, "Teacher, what shall we do?" 13 And he said
	13 "Don't collect more than is legal," he told them.	to them, "Collect no more than is appointed you."

tax collectors: these were Jews who collected taxes for the Roman government on goods or produce taken in or out of the town.

Teacher: a respectful form of address; John was not a teacher as such, but a prophet, a recognized religious authority.

collect: "tell (or, force) people to pay."

more than is legal: "more than what you have been ordered to collect." Usually the tax collectors were instructed on the amount they should charge.

3.14	TEV	RSV
	Some soldiers also asked him, "What about us? What are we to do?"	Soldiers also asked him, "And we, what shall we do?" And he said to
	He said to them, "Don't take money from anyone by force or accuse anyone falsely. Be content with your pay."	them, "Rob no one by violence or by false accusation, and be content with your wages."

soldiers: Roman occupation troops.

What about us?: the emphatic form of the question shows that they, non-Jews, believe that John's warnings apply to them as well.

In RSV John's answer has to do only with one specific thing which he orders them not to do: "Rob no one." TEV, however, interprets the Greek to refer to two things. But the text may also mean: "Don't use force on anyone, don't blackmail anyone." (To blackmail is to extort money by threatening to make charges of misconduct against a person.) Most translations follow the interpretation found in RSV: "Don't rob anyone by (threat of) violence or by blackmail."

Be content with your pay: "Be satisfied with the wages you earn."

3.15	TEV	RSV
	People's hopes began to rise, and they began to wonder whether John perhaps might be the Messiah.	As the people were in expectation, and all men questioned in their hearts concerning John, whether perhaps he were the Christ,

People's hopes began to rise: "All the people there were expecting something marvelous (or, unusual) to happen."

and they began to wonder whether...: it might be easier to use the direct form, as follows: "and they began to wonder (or, think), 'Could he be the Messiah?'" or "...'Maybe he is the Messiah!'"

Messiah: see 2.11.

3.16	TEV	RSV
	So John said to all of them, "I baptize you with water, but someone is coming who is much greater than I am. I am not good enough even to untie his sandals. He will baptize you with the Holy Spirit and fire.	John answered them all, "I baptize you with water; but he who is mightier than I is coming, the thong of whose sandals I am not worthy to untie; he will baptize you with the Holy Spirit and with fire.

I baptize you with water: "I use water to baptize you."

is much greater than I am: "has more authority than I do," "is more important than I," "has more power than I have."

I am not good enough: "I am not important enough," "I don't deserve," "I do not qualify."

untie his sandals: this was the work of a slave. John is saying that he doesn't deserve to be the servant of the one who is coming.

He will baptize you with the Holy Spirit and fire: this balances I baptize you with water at the beginning of the verse. One could translate "He will use the Holy Spirit and fire to baptize you."

the Holy Spirit and fire: in the Bible God's Spirit is his power at work, creating, renewing, transforming; fire is a destroying and purifying force. Obviously fire is used figuratively here. The meaning of John's statement is that the baptism administered by Jesus will destroy those who are sinful and will give power and life to those who believe his message.

3.17 TEV	RSV
He has his winnowing shovel with him, to thresh out all the grain and gather the wheat into his barn; but he will burn the chaff in a fire that never goes out."	His winnowing fork is in his hand, to clear his threshing floor, and to gather the wheat into his granary, but the chaff he will burn with unquenchable fire."

winnowing shovel: a tool like a shovel or large fork with which the worker threw the threshed grain into the air; the wind carried away the chaff, and the grain fell to the ground. This is a figure of God's judgment, separating the good from the worthless.

If possible, the metaphors should be kept; if not, they can be changed into similes: "He will judge all people, separating the good from the bad, as a farmer separates the grain from the chaff. The good (people) he will keep safe in heaven, as grain is kept in the barn, and the bad (people) he will cause to be destroyed in hell, as chaff is burned in the fire."

3.18 TEV	RSV
In many different ways John preached the Good News to the people and urged them to change their ways.	So, with many other exhortations, he preached good news to the people.

preached the Good News: see 2.10. If the simple Good News does not communicate much meaning, one can say "the Good News of salvation."

What RSV has represented by "exhortations" TEV has represented by urged them to change their ways. John's preaching emphasized the need for people to change their conduct, which is the reason for TEV's expression. But a translation need not follow TEV; it may have something like "John made many other exhortations (or, appeals) to the people as he preached the Good News to them."

3.19 TEV	RSV
But John reprimanded Governor Herod, because he had married Herodias, his brother's wife, and had done many other evil things.	But Herod the tetrarch, who had been reproved by him for Herodias, his brother's wife, and for all the evil things that Herod had done,

Governor Herod: Herod Antipas, governor of Galilee (see 3.1).

his brother: this was his half brother Philip (see Mark 6.17), who lived in Rome (not to be confused with the Philip mentioned in 3.1).

3.20 TEV	RSV
Then Herod did an even worse thing by putting John in prison.	added this to them all, that he shut up John in prison.

did an even worse thing: to all the other crimes Herod had committed he added another one, even worse.

[53]

by putting John in prison: since Herod did not do this personally, it may be necessary to say "by having John arrested and put in prison" or "by ordering his officials to put John in prison."

SECTION HEADING

The Baptism of Jesus: "Jesus Is Baptized," "John Baptizes Jesus."

In this brief account of the baptism of Jesus the emphasis is on the heavenly voice and its message. The baptism of other people, the baptism of Jesus, and his praying are all described in dependent clauses which set the stage for the action that follows, namely, heaven opens, the Spirit descends, and a voice speaks from heaven to Jesus.

3.21 TEV	RSV
After all the people had been baptized, Jesus also was baptized. While he was praying, heaven was opened,	Now when all the people were baptized, and when Jesus also had been baptized and was praying, the heaven was opened,

By using two passive participles, the Gospel writer avoids mentioning the name of John the Baptist. In some languages such passives may not be normal style and may be difficult to understand; in such a case the translation can be "After John had baptized all the people, and Jesus also" or "John baptized all the people, and then he baptized Jesus. And while Jesus was praying...."

all the people: the text says that all those people who were there were baptized by John.

baptized: see 3.3.

praying: the normal posture was to stand and look at the sky.

heaven was opened: the action described represents an opening in the sky which took place at that moment. The text does not specify exactly how this "opening" took place; the impression is that of a door or gate being opened.

3.22 TEV	RSV
and the Holy Spirit came down upon him in bodily form like a dove. And a voice came from heaven, "You are my own dear Son. I am pleased with you."	and the Holy Spirit descended upon him in bodily form, as a dove, and a voice came from heaven, "Thou art my beloved Son,^{j} with thee I am well pleased."^{k}
	^{j}Or my Son, my (or the) Beloved
	^{k}Other ancient authorities read today I have begotten thee

the Holy Spirit came down: the picture seems to be that of the Holy Spirit, in the form of a dove, coming down from heaven through the opening.

in bodily form like a dove: the meaning seems to be that a bird came down, a dove, which was the bodily form taken by the Spirit. Or else, the meaning could be that the Spirit assumed a bodily form which is not specified, and in that form came down upon Jesus in the same way that a dove comes down. The first interpretation seems better.

dove: see 2.24.

a voice came from heaven: "a voice in heaven spoke," "a voice from heaven was heard." The voice is obviously God's, but this should not be explicitly stated in translation unless the language requires it.

You are: the voice speaks to Jesus alone. Whether others heard it (or saw heaven opening) is neither implied nor denied by the text. The message given by the voice reflects such Old Testament passages as Psalm 2.7; Genesis 22.2; Isaiah 42.1.

my own dear Son: or "my only Son"; or "my Son, the Beloved" (see RSV footnote)—in which case "the Beloved" is a title for the Messiah.

I am pleased with you: or "you please me (very much)."

Textual Note: one Greek manuscript and some ancient versions have "You are my Son; today I have become your Father." This comes from Psalm 2.7. Most commentaries and translations prefer the text translated by RSV and TEV.

SECTION HEADING

The Ancestors of Jesus: "The Genealogy of Jesus," "The Family Line of Jesus."

The family line of Jesus is traced back through Joseph to Adam and to God. In Greek, verses 23-38 are one sentence.

3.23-38 TEV	RSV
When Jesus began his work, he was about thirty years old. He was the son, so people thought, of Joseph, who was the son of Heli, 24 the son of Matthat, the son of Levi, the son of Melchi, the son of Jannai, the son of Joseph, 25 the son of Mattathias, the son of Amos, the son of Nahum, the son of Esli, the son of Naggai, 26 the son of Maath, the son of Mattathias, the son of Semein, the son of Josech, the son of Joda, 27 the son of Joanan, the son of Rhesa, the son of Zerubbabel, the son of Shealtiel, the son of Neri, 28 the	Jesus, when he began his ministry, was about thirty years of age, being the son (as was supposed) of Joseph, the son of Heli, 24 the son of Matthat, the son of Levi, the son of Melchi, the son of Jannai, the son of Joseph, 25 the son of Mattathias, the son of Amos, the son of Nahum, the son of Esli, the son of Naggai, 26 the son of Maath, the son of Mattathias, the son of Semein, the son of Josech, the son of Joda, 27 the son of Joanan, the son of Rhesa, the son of Zerubbabel, the son of Shealtiel,^{l} the son of Neri, 28 the son of Melchi, the son

son of Melchi, the son of Addi, the son of Cosam, the son of Elmadam, the son of Er, 29 the son of Joshua, the son of Eliezer, the son of Jorim, the son of Matthat, the son of Levi, 30 the son of Simeon, the son of Judah, the son of Joseph, the son of Jonam, the son of Eliakim, 31 the son of Melea, the son of Menna, the son of Mattatha, the son of Nathan, the son of David, 32 the son of Jesse, the son of Obed, the son of Boaz, the son of Salmon, the son of Nahshon, 33 the son of Amminadab, the son of Admin, the son of Arni, the son of Hezron, the son of Perez, the son of Judah, 34 the son of Jacob, the son of Isaac, the son of Abraham, the son of Terah, the son of Nahor, 35 the son of Serug, the son of Reu, the son of Peleg, the son of Eber, the son of Shelah, 36 the son of Cainan, the son of Arphaxad, the son of Shem, the son of Noah, the son of Lamech, 37 the son of Methuselah, the son of Enoch, the son of Jared, the son of Mahalaleel, the son of Kenan, 38 the son of Enosh, the son of Seth, the son of Adam, the son of God.

of Addi, the son of Cosam, the son of Elmadam, the son of Er, 29 the son of Joshua, the son of Eliezer, the son of Jorim, the son of Matthat, the son of Levi, 30 the son of Simeon, the son of Judah, the son of Joseph, the son of Jonam, the son of Eliakim, 31 the son of Melea, the son of Menna, the son of Mattatha, the son of Nathan, the son of David, 32 the son of Jesse, the son of Obed, the son of Boaz, the son of Sala, the son of Nahshon, 33 the son of Amminadab, the son of Admin, the son of Arni, the son of Perez, the son of Judah, 34 the son of Jacob, the son of Isaac, the son of Abraham, the son of Terah, the son of Nahor, 35 the son of Serug, the son of Reu, the son of Peleg, the son of Eber, the son of Shelah, 36 the son of Cainan, the son of Arphaxad, the son of Shem, the son of Noah, the son of Lamech, 37 the son of Methuselah, the son of Enoch, the son of Jared, the son of Mahalaleel, the son of Cainan, 38 the son of Enos, the son of Seth, the son of Adam, the son of God.

[l]Greek *Salathiel*

began his work: "began his public ministry," "began his activities." so people thought: "as was supposed" (RSV). The author adds this to make clear to the readers that Joseph was not Jesus' father.

The best way to translate this list of names is to say the son of (or, "whose father was") in each instance, including the last one (verse 38), Adam, the son of God. Some translations have "When Jesus began his public work he was about thirty years old. He was the son, so people thought, of Joseph. This is the list of his ancestors: Joseph, Heli... Seth, Adam, who was created by God." This may be better, but it does change the flow of the original, which speaks of Adam as the son of God.

It should be noticed that TEV follows the Hebrew form of the names: in verse 27 Shealtiel (Greek *Salathiel*); verse 32 Salmon (Greek *Sala*); verse 37 Kenan (Greek *Cainan*) and verse 38 Enosh (Greek *Enos*). For the last two names see 1 Chronicles 1.1. In translating names which are found both in the Old Testament and the New Testament, it is recommended that the same form be used in both Testaments.

Chapter 4

The Temptation of Jesus: "Jesus Is Tempted by the Devil," "The Devil Tries to Make Jesus Do Wrong."

The events described in this section take place immediately after Jesus is baptized by John. For forty days in the desert Jesus fasts and is tempted by the Devil; after this (in the next section) Jesus begins his public ministry.

4.1	TEV	RSV
	Jesus returned from the Jordan full of the Holy Spirit and was led by the Spirit into the desert,	And Jesus, full of the Holy Spirit, returned from the Jordan, and was led by the Spirit

returned from the Jordan: where he had been baptized by John the Baptist (see 3.3).

full of the Holy Spirit: see 1.15,41,67.

was led by the Spirit: "was guided (or, taken) by the Spirit"; or else, using the active form of the verb, "the Spirit took (or, led) Jesus." The word used should not imply that Jesus went unwillingly.

the desert: the place is unspecified (see 3.2); "a place where no people live," "a wilderness."

4.2	TEV	RSV
	where he was tempted by the Devil for forty days. In all that time he ate nothing, so that he was hungry when it was over.	for forty days in the wilderness, tempted by the devil. And he ate nothing in those days; and when they were ended, he was hungry.

he was tempted: "he was put to the test." The active form could be used, "the Devil tempted him," "the Devil tried to make him do wrong." The Greek verb is used in two senses: "to test" by means of misfortunes and sufferings, in order to find out how morally or spiritually strong a person is; and "to tempt," that is, to try to make someone do wrong. Here it is used in the latter sense.

the Devil: this is a translation of a Greek noun which means "accuser, opponent." He is represented as the leader of all forces of evil, and is also called "Satan" (see 10.18), which represents the Hebrew word for "accuser, opponent."

he ate nothing: this is fasting as a religious duty, a voluntary action (see Deut 9.18 concerning Moses' forty-day fast).

he was hungry: of course he would have started to get hungry before the fortieth day; the text simply summarizes the result of going without food for forty days.

when it was over: "at the end of that time," "after those days had passed."

4.3

TEV	RSV
The Devil said to him, "If you are God's Son, order this stone to turn into bread."	The devil said to him, "If you are the Son of God, command this stone to become bread."

The reader may assume that the three temptations described in this section take place after the forty days; but they could have happened any time during that period. The latter explanation seems correct, because verse 2 says he was being tempted throughout the forty days, and here in verse 3 there is no statement such as "the Devil approached him."

If you are God's Son: in Greek the form used is known as "a fulfilled condition." This means that at least for the purpose of this occasion the Devil assumes that Jesus is in fact God's Son: "Since you are God's Son"; "Of course you are God's Son; so...."

this stone: presumably the Devil picks out a particular stone.

to turn into bread: "to become (a loaf of) bread." At that time a loaf of bread looked somewhat like a stone, small and round.

The purpose of the temptation was to get Jesus to use his power as God's Son (see 3.22) to relieve his hunger.

4.4

TEV	RSV
But Jesus answered, "The scripture says, 'Man cannot live on bread alone.'"	And Jesus answered him, "It is written, 'Man shall not live by bread alone.'"

The scripture: this expression nearly always refers to a specific passage in the Old Testament. The Greek says "It is written" (RSV), which reflects the attitude that the words quoted have the force of divine law. The passage quoted is from Deuteronomy 8.3; a reading of Deuteronomy 8.2-3 will give the translator a good idea of the background of this saying. In translating The scripture, care should be taken to avoid a word which means "Bible," that is, the Old Testament and the New Testament. Perhaps "The Hebrew Scriptures" or "The holy book (of the Jews)."

Man cannot: "No one can," "Nobody is able to." Women are not excluded.

bread: here this stands for "food." The statement expresses the conviction that life is more than physical existence. A translation could say "In order to have (real) life a person needs more than just food."

4.5	TEV	RSV

Then the Devil took him up and showed him in a second all the kingdoms of the world.

And the devil took him up, and showed him all the kingdoms of the world in a moment of time,

took him up: the text does not say where Jesus was taken (unlike Matt 4.8, which speaks of a very high mountain). It could be either some high place or high up in midair.

in a second: "in a flash," "in one glance."

all the kingdoms of the world: the style is exaggerated, but it must be respected by the translator. Kingdoms here is used in the sense of "countries," "nations"; it does not mean only countries ruled by kings. The word for world is the same one translated Roman Empire in 2.1.

4.6	TEV	RSV

"I will give you all this power and all this wealth," the Devil told him. "It has all been handed over to me, and I can give it to anyone I choose.

and said to him, "To you I will give all this authority and their glory; for it has been delivered to me, and I give it to whom I will.

all this power and all this wealth: "the power and wealth in all the world," "all the power and wealth that everybody has." What is meant is that Jesus will be given the authority over the whole world and everything in it.

this wealth: this represents the Greek "their glory" (RSV), that is, the "glory" of the kingdoms, in terms of fame or wealth.

It has all been handed over to me: nothing is said as to when, how, or where this was done. The passive probably is used for God as the actor: "God handed (or, gave) it over to me."

to anyone I choose: "to whomever I wish."

4.7	TEV	RSV

All this will be yours, then, if you worship me."

If you, then, will worship me, it shall all be yours."

All this will be yours: "I will give you all this." It may be more natural in some languages to follow the order of the Greek, with the condition first and the consequence last: "if you worship me, all this will be yours" (see RSV).

worship: "confess that I am your god" or "...your master."

4.8	TEV	RSV

Jesus answered, "The scripture says, 'Worship the Lord your God and serve only him!'"

And Jesus answered him, "It is written,

'You shall worship the Lord your God,
and him only shall you serve.'"

   The scripture: this is from Deuteronomy 6.13, where these words are addressed to Israel. If the command, Worship, makes it appear that the words are directed to Satan, the translation could be "The scripture says that a person should worship the Lord his God and serve only him."
   serve: in a religious sense, parallel in meaning with Worship.

4.9	TEV	RSV
	Then the Devil took him to Jerusalem and set him on the highest point of the Temple, and said to him, "If you are God's Son, throw yourself down from here.	And he took him to Jerusalem, and set him on the pinnacle of the temple, and said to him, "If you are the Son of God, throw yourself down from here;

   took: Jesus goes willingly; he is not forced to go.
   set him: "made him stand," "had him stand." The translation should not make it appear that the Devil was carrying Jesus.
   highest point: it is not certain what specific place on the Temple is indicated by the Greek word. Some translate it as "pinnacle" (RSV), the top of a tower; others as "parapet," the top of a roof. It is enough to indicate a very high place on the Temple.
   If you are God's Son: see verse 3.

4.10-11	TEV	RSV
For the scripture says, 'God will order his angels to take good care of you.' 11 It also says, 'They will hold you up with their hands so that not even your feet will be hurt on the stones.'"		for it is written, 'He will give his angels charge of you, to guard you,' 11 and 'On their hands they will bear you up, lest you strike your foot against a stone.'"

   the scripture: Psalm 91.11-12. In this context, the passage cited means that at God's order his angels would come and hold Jesus on his fall from the top of the Temple to the ground so that he would not hurt himself on the stones below.
   take good care of you: "protect (you) and keep you safe." You and your are singular and are here taken to refer to Jesus.
   not even your feet will be hurt: the Greek says "so that you will not hit your foot against a stone." What is meant is not that just the feet will be safe, but that the whole body will not be hurt. In such a fall at least the feet would be hurt, on the assumption that he would fall feet first; so TEV says not even your feet. The translation could say "so that you won't be hurt in the least," "you won't suffer any injury."

4.12	TEV	RSV
	But Jesus answered, "The scripture says, 'Do not put the Lord your God to the test.'"	And Jesus answered him, "It is said, 'You shall not tempt the Lord your God.'"

The scripture says: this translates "It is said" (RSV). The quotation is from Deuteronomy 6.16.

put...to the test: the Greek verb is a stronger form of the verb used in 4.2. The meaning here is "to make God prove that he cares for (or, will take care of) you." The passage, Deuteronomy 6.16, refers back to 'Massah' in Exodus 17.1-7, where the Israelites tested God's patience with them. What they did was the same as if they were saying to God, "If you don't give us water right now, this means that you don't love us." The application to Jesus in this passage is obvious: to throw himself down from the Temple and then to expect that God would send his angels to keep him from hurting himself would be the same as if he were saying to God, "If you don't send your angels to keep me safe, this means that you don't love me."

your God: in Deuteronomy 6.16 "your" refers to Israel; here it does not refer to the Devil. Jesus is applying the scripture to his own situation; he must not put the Lord, the God of Israel, to the test. The command may be stated in the third person, "No one must put the Lord his God to the test."

4.13 TEV	RSV
When the Devil finished tempting Jesus in every way, he left him for a while.	And when the devil had ended every temptation, he departed from him until an opportune time.

tempting Jesus: "trying to make Jesus sin," "trying to make Jesus do (something) wrong."

in every way: "in different ways," "in all the ways he could."

for a while: RSV "until an opportune time" is another possible interpretation of the Greek text. Most translations give the sense that TEV gives. In any case these were not the only temptations of Jesus (see 22.28).

SECTION HEADING

Jesus Begins His Work in Galilee: "Jesus Goes to Galilee and Begins Proclaiming His Message."

This short two-verse section can be joined to the next section; but it seems better to keep it separate, since this section speaks of how Jesus was successful at first in all of Galilee, while the next one speaks of his rejection in Nazareth.

4.14 TEV	RSV
Then Jesus returned to Galilee, and the power of the Holy Spirit was with him. The news about him spread throughout all that territory.	And Jesus returned in the power of the Spirit into Galilee, and a report concerning him went out through all the surrounding country.

4.14

Galilee: see 1.26.
the power of the Holy Spirit: see Verse 1. The Spirit of God con-
trols Jesus.
The news about him spread: "His fame spread," or "Everywhere in
that region people were talking about him" or "...people were hearing
about him."

4.15 TEV	RSV
He taught in the synagogues and was praised by everyone.	And he taught in their synagogues, being glorified by all.

taught: not in the sense of a school teacher, but of instructing
people about their religious duties and about the meaning of the Hebrew
Scriptures.
synagogues: "houses of prayer," "houses of worship," where Jews
gathered every Sabbath. A word should be used that would preserve the
difference between the many synagogues and the one Temple in Jerusalem.
The Greek "their synagogues" (RSV) means the synagogues in the various towns that Jesus visited.

SECTION HEADING

Jesus Is Rejected at Nazareth: "The People of Nazareth Reject Jesus"
or "...Do Not Accept Jesus."

This is a detailed account of how the people in Nazareth reacted to
Jesus and his message. The story suggests that this was the first time
that Jesus was in Nazareth after his baptism.

4.16 TEV	RSV
Then Jesus went to Nazareth, where he had been brought up, and on the Sabbath he went as usual to the synagogue. He stood up to read the Scriptures	And he came to Nazareth, where he had been brought up; and he went to the synagogue, as his custom was, on the sabbath day. And he stood up to read;

Jesus: TEV gives the name (Greek says only "he went") because this
is the beginning of a new section.
went: or "came" (RSV). The translation will depend on the point of
view taken; if it is the point of departure, went will be used; if it is
the point of arrival, "came" is appropriate.
where he had been brought up: "where he had grown up."
Sabbath: the day of rest, the seventh day of the Jewish week. A day
was counted from sundown to sundown, so the Sabbath began at sundown on
our Friday and ended at sundown on our Saturday. Possible translations
of the name can be "the rest day (of the Jews)," "the holy day of the
Jews," "the day when no work was done," or simply "Saturday," but never
"Sunday."

as usual: "as he always did," "as was his custom."

synagogue: see verse 15.

stood up: in front, facing the people, who were seated. The presiding officer could invite any adult male Jew to read the Scriptures in the worship service.

to read: that is, aloud.

the Scriptures: TEV adds this for clarity. A word or expression should be used that means only the Hebrew Scriptures, the Old Testament, and not the complete Bible with both Old and New Testaments.

4.17 TEV	RSV
and was handed the book of the prophet Isaiah. He unrolled the scroll and found the place where it is written,	and there was given to him the book of the prophet Isaiah. He opened the book and found the place where it was written,

was handed: by the attendant (see verse 20).

the book: a long, rolled-up scroll made of parchment. So TEV has He unrolled the scroll, which is better than "He opened the book" (RSV), which implies a codex, that is, separate pages bound together on one edge.

of the prophet Isaiah: this could be taken to mean that the book belonged to a prophet named Isaiah. So it would be better to translate "the book with the words (or, messages) of the prophet Isaiah" or "the book that the prophet Isaiah had written."

it is written: in Isaiah 61.1-2. The text here follows the ancient Greek version, the Septuagint, and not the Hebrew text.

4.18 TEV	RSV
18 "The Spirit of the Lord is upon me, because he has chosen me to bring good news to the poor. He has sent me to proclaim liberty to the captives and recovery of sight to the blind, to set free the oppressed	18 "The Spirit of the Lord is upon me, because he has anointed me to preach good news to the poor. He has sent me to proclaim release to the captives and recovering of sight to the blind, to set at liberty those who are oppressed,

The Spirit of the Lord: "The Spirit of God" or "The Spirit sent by God."

is upon me: "is with me"; see full of the Holy Spirit in verse 1.

because: thus translated, the text seems to say that God has chosen him, and because of this God's Spirit is upon him. But the meaning is more likely to be that because the Lord's Spirit is with him, God has chosen him for the task. Some translations handle this by making the two statements parallel:

The Spirit of the Lord is upon me.
He (the Lord) has chosen me....

4.18

Others translate:

> The Spirit of the Lord is upon me,
>   and because of this he (the Lord) has chosen me....

chosen: this translates the Greek verb "to anoint" (see Christ in 2.11). To anoint someone in Israel was to pour olive oil on that person's head as a sign that he had been chosen by God to be a priest or a king. In this passage the meaning is not literal; the descent of the Spirit on Jesus at his baptism (3.21) was his anointing.

bring good news: or "take the Good News" (see 2.10; 3.18).

the poor: in the context this is meant literally, "people who don't have much," "people who have very little" (see 7.22). The same is true of the others to whom he is sent: the captives are "the prisoners," "those who are not free"; the blind are "people who cannot see"; the oppressed are "people who are mistreated (or, exploited)," "people who are robbed of their rights."

to proclaim liberty: instead of the noun liberty, a verb phrase might be better, "to tell the captives (or, prisoners) that they are free" or "to tell the prisoners, 'You are free!'"

recovery of sight: here again a verbal phrase might be better, "and to tell blind people that they can see" or "to tell blind people, 'You can see!'" In both instances this proclamation brings about what is being proclaimed: captives are set free and the blind recover their sight.

to set free the oppressed: this last clause is from Isaiah 58.6.

4.19	TEV	RSV
	and announce that the time has come when the Lord will save his people."	to proclaim the acceptable year of the Lord."

It will be noticed that the Greek noun phrase "the acceptable year of the Lord" (RSV) is represented in TEV by the time has come when the Lord will save his people. This is because the adjective "acceptable" here means "favorable" in the sense "the year that the Lord will show (or, manifest) his favor." TEV has represented this "favor" by will save his people. Others translate "the year when the Lord's favor (or, goodness) will be manifested"; "the year when the Lord will forgive his people"; "the year when the Lord wants to save his people."

4.20	TEV	RSV
	Jesus rolled up the scroll, gave it back to the attendant, and sat down. All the people in the synagogue had their eyes fixed on him,	And he closed the book, and gave it back to the attendant, and sat down; and the eyes of all in the synagogue were fixed on him.

rolled up the scroll: see unrolled the scroll in verse 17.
the attendant: the men responsible for taking care of such matters
as storing the scrolls in the wooden chest, or ark.
sat down: facing the people. This was the position of a teacher.
had their eyes fixed on him: "looked at him intently," "kept looking
(straight) at him." In one language the idiom is "to nail one's eyes on a
person."

4.21   TEV   RSV

TEV	RSV
as he said to them, "This passage of scripture has come true today, as you heard it being read."	And he began to say to them, "Today this scripture has been fulfilled in your hearing."

has come true today: this means that what the prophet Isaiah had
said many years before was now happening. The one upon whom the Lord's
Spirit would come was now present to carry out his mission.

4.22   TEV   RSV

TEV	RSV
They were all well impressed with him and marveled at the eloquent words that he spoke, They said, "Isn't he the son of Joseph?"	And all spoke well of him, and wondered at the gracious words which proceeded out of his mouth; and they said, "Is not this Joseph's son?"

were all well impressed with him: or "thought that he was a good
person"; or, in direct form, "thought, 'What a fine person he is!'"
marveled: see 2.18.
eloquent words: literally "words of grace," that is, "persuasive
words," "fine talking," "elegant speaking." They were surprised that he
spoke so well.
Isn't he the son of Joseph?: this is not a request for information;
it is a rhetorical question expressing surprise that such a person could
speak so well, or else indignation that he would make such high claims
for himself. "He is only the son of Joseph!" or "This fellow is Joseph's
son—that's all he is!"

4.23   TEV   RSV

TEV	RSV
He said to them, "I am sure that you will quote this proverb to me, 'Doctor, heal yourself.' You will also tell me to do here in my hometown the same things you heard were done in Capernaum.	And he said to them, "Doubtless you will quote to me this proverb, 'Physician, heal yourself; what we have heard you did at Capernaum, do here also in your own country.'"

proverb: "saying," "wise word."
Doctor, heal yourself: the point of the proverb is that a man who
claims to be able to heal others should be able to prove his claim by
healing himself. Jesus should prove his claim to be the one of whom Isaiah spoke by doing in Nazareth (his hometown) the same kinds of miracles
he had done in Capernaum.

In order to make clear that what follows is not part of the proverb that Jesus quotes, TEV has put that into indirect form (You will also tell me to do...), which in Greek is direct address.

hometown: where he had been raised (4.16).

were done in Capernaum: nothing has yet been said in this Gospel about Jesus' miracles in Capernaum, a town on the northwest shore of Lake Galilee, some 35 kilometers from Nazareth.

4.24 TEV	RSV
I tell you this," Jesus added, "a prophet is never welcomed in his hometown.	And he said, "Truly, I say to you, no prophet is acceptable in his own country.

I tell you this: this translates "Amen I say to you" (RSV "Truly, I say to you"), an emphatic way to begin a statement.

a prophet: "a man who speaks God's message" (see 1.70).

is never welcomed: "is not accepted," "is not liked." The passive can be transformed into an active: "People never welcome (or, like) a prophet who is a native of their own town."

hometown: see verse 23.

4.25-26 TEV	RSV
Listen to me: it is true that there were many widows in Israel during the time of Elijah, when there was no rain for three and a half years and a severe famine spread throughout the whole land. 26 Yet Elijah was not sent to anyone in Israel, but only to a widow living in Zarephath in the territory of Sidon.	But in truth, I tell you, there were many widows in Israel in the days of Elijah, when the heaven was shut up three years and six months, when there came a great famine over all the land; 26 and Elijah was sent to none of them but only to Zarephath, in the land of Sidon, to a woman who was a widow.

Listen to me: it is true: this translates what RSV renders as "But in truth, I tell you." The RSV translation is an even more emphatic way of beginning a statement.

Elijah: for the story about Elijah see 1 Kings 17.1-16.

The two verses contain many items of information, and it may be better to use more complete sentences than TEV has done. One way might be: "When the prophet Elijah was alive, there was a period of three and a half years when it did not rain in Israel. This caused a severe famine in all the land. And although there were many widows in Israel (at that time), 26 God didn't send Elijah to (help) any of them. Instead, God sent him to (help) a widow who lived in Zarephath, in the territory of Sidon."

when there was no rain: "when no rain fell," "when it didn't rain." This translates the biblical idiom "the sky was locked up" (see RSV).

three and a half years: see the same figure in James 5.17. The Old Testament account is not that precise (see 1 Kgs 17.1; 18.1,45).

the whole land: "all the land of Israel."

Elijah was not sent: the active form may be clearer, "God did not send Elijah" or "God did not order Elijah to go."

<u>to anyone in Israel</u>: it is better to say "to any of them in Israel" or "to any widow in Israel" (see "to none of them" in RSV).

<u>Sidon</u>: an important Phoenician city on the Mediterranean coast, north of the land of Israel. The point is that God did not send Elijah to help an Israelite widow but a foreign (that is, Gentile) widow.

4.27 TEV	RSV
And there were many people suffering from a dreaded skin disease who lived in Israel during the time of the prophet Elisha; yet not one of them was healed, but only Naaman the Syrian."	And there were many lepers in Israel in the time of the prophet Elisha; and none of them was cleansed, but only Naaman the Syrian."

The second example, that of <u>the prophet Elisha</u>, is taken from 2 Kings 5.1-16.

<u>a dreaded skin disease</u>: this translates the word ordinarily translated "leprosy" (see RSV). But there is convincing evidence that the Hebrew word used in the Old Testament was applied to a number of skin diseases, so that it is impossible to be certain that the specific disease leprosy is meant. Some translations keep the traditional word "leper" (or "leprosy") in the text, but either in a footnote or in a Word List they provide an explanation of the biblical terms. In most languages it is best to avoid the word for "leper."

<u>was healed</u>: the Greek says "was made clean" (see RSV). The skin disease rendered a person ceremonially impure, that is, unfit to take part in religious services and other activities. When the sick person was cured, then he or she was declared clean in this religious sense. See Leviticus 13—14. If a translation uses "was made clean" in the text, an explanation should be provided either in a footnote or in a Word List (see 5.12-14).

It may be necessary to use the active form of the verb: "yet Elijah did not heal any of them; the only leper he healed was Naaman the Syrian."

The point of these two biblical incidents is that in both cases there was no special consideration given to the prophet's own people, the Israelites; the people they helped were not Israelites but foreigners. In the same way the people of Nazareth, citizens of Jesus' hometown, would not receive any special treatment from Jesus.

4.28 TEV	RSV
When the people in the synagogue heard this, they were filled with anger.	When they heard this, all in the synagogue were filled with wrath.

<u>were filled with anger</u>: "were very angry," "were furious."

4.29 TEV	RSV
They rose up, dragged Jesus out of town, and took him to the top of	And they rose up and put him out of the city, and led him to the brow of

the hill on which their town was   the hill on which their city was
built. They meant to throw him over built, that they might throw him
the cliff,   down headlong.

    They rose up: here the Greek verb is probably used in the literal
sense of standing up (after being seated). But the verb could be used in
a general sense of beginning an action, as it often is used in the Bible.
    dragged Jesus out of town: care must be taken not to use a word that
might suggest what dragged may suggest, that is, pulling Jesus by the
arms along the path. The Greek verb is "to expel" (see RSV "put...out"),
which suggests that they held him securely by the arms and walked along
with him to the hill.
    on which their town was built: or "on which their town stood."
    over the cliff: this might prove difficult because of the mention
of the hill; so it might be better to translate "over the side" or "down
the hill."

4.30   TEV   RSV
but he walked through the middle of But passing through the midst of
the crowd and went his way.   them he went away.

    walked through: the narrative does not imply anything miraculous or
supernatural; it simply states that Jesus walked, not ran, through the
midst of the people, with no attempt being made to stop him.

SECTION HEADING

    A Man with an Evil Spirit: "Jesus Expels an Evil Spirit from a Man."

    This section gives the first of Jesus' miracles reported in this
Gospel. The expulsion of the demon, which takes place in the synagogue
in Capernaum, shows the power and authority of Jesus.

4.31   TEV   RSV
    Then Jesus went to Capernaum,   And he went down to Capernaum,
a town in Galilee, where he taught   a city of Galilee. And he was teach-
the people on the Sabbath.   ing them on the sabbath;

    went: the Greek has "went down" (RSV). Capernaum was on the north-
west shore of Lake Galilee, some 275 meters lower in altitude than Nazareth.
    taught: see verse 15. The setting is the synagogue (verse 33), and
some translations may want to make this explicit here: "where on the
Sabbath he taught the people in the synagogue" or "where on the Sabbath
he went to the synagogue and taught the people." For synagogue see verse
15.
    Sabbath: see verse 16.

[68]

4.32   TEV

They were all amazed at the way he taught, because he spoke with authority.

       RSV

and they were astonished at his teaching, for his word was with authority.

amazed: the same verb used in 2.48.

the way he taught: this translates the noun "teaching" (RSV), which may refer to the content of his message or to the way in which he delivered it. Here "teaching" probably refers to the content of Jesus' message: "They were amazed at what he taught." But the following explanation, "for his word was with authority" (RSV), seems to emphasize the manner of Jesus' teaching, the way he taught.

he spoke with authority: "he spoke as though he had the right to command (them what to do)," "he taught them as though he knew that what he said was completely true." This is authority in its absolute sense, that is, authority that does not depend on any outward circumstance (such as status, learning, position of power) but springs solely from the evident truth of what is being said. The order of the sentence may be reversed: "He spoke with such (an air of) authority that they were all astonished."

4.33   TEV

In the synagogue was a man who had the spirit of an evil demon in him; he screamed out in a loud voice,

       RSV

And in the synagogue there was a man who had the spirit of an unclean demon; and he cried out with a loud voice,

a man who had the spirit of an evil demon in him: instead of who had...in him it might be better to say "who was possessed by" or "who was under the control of."

the spirit of an evil demon: this translates "the spirit of an unclean demon" (RSV), which is an elaborate way of referring to what is elsewhere called simply "a demon" (see verse 35), or "an unclean spirit" (see verse 36), or "an evil spirit" (see 7.21), or simply "a spirit" (see 9.39). The terms are different, but what they refer to is always the same. The spirit is called "unclean" because when it took possession of a person it caused certain bodily disorders or actions which made that person ritually defiled; the person was therefore unable to take part in public worship and other activities until the defilement was removed. If a translation uses the expression "unclean spirit," it must say something more than simply "a dirty spirit"; it must say something like "a spirit which made a person ritually unclean," or else there should be a footnote or a Word List where the matter is explained.

The full phrase "the spirit of an unclean demon" may lead some readers to think that the man was possessed by the spirit (or ghost) of an unclean demon who had died; so it would be better to translate "an unclean spirit," or "a demon," or "a demon, that is, an unclean (or, evil) spirit."

he screamed: the Greek does not specify who is the subject of the verb; it could be the spirit or the man speaking. But in the case of a

[69]

demon-possessed man, what he says is the spirit in him speaking; he has lost his own personality and has become, in effect, an embodied evil spirit.

4.34	TEV	RSV

TEV: "Ah! What do you want with us, Jesus of Nazareth? Are you here to destroy us? I know who you are: you are God's holy messenger!"

RSV: "Ah!^{m} What have you to do with us, Jesus of Nazareth? Have you come to destroy us? I know who you are, the Holy One of God."

^{m}Or *Let us alone*

Ah!: as RSV footnote shows, the Greek may mean "Leave (us) alone"; but it seems more probable that it is meant as an interjection, a cry expressing hostility.

What do you want with us...?: this translates a biblical expression which is literally "What to us and to you?" It means "Why are you meddling with us?" "Why are you interfering in our affairs?" It is not so much a question as it is a rebuke: "Don't meddle with us!" "Don't get involved in our affairs!"

us: this probably refers to all evil spirits as a group. In this particular case only one evil spirit is in possession of the man.

Jesus of Nazareth: frequently a person was identified by the place he was from, such as Elijah of Tishbe (1 Kgs 17.1), Joseph of Arimathea (Mark 15.43).

Are you here to destroy us?: the Greek may be punctuated as a statement, "You have come to destroy us." But a question seems more likely; it is a question, however, that reveals the demon's fear that Jesus had come to destroy the evil spirits. The demon regards Jesus as an enemy.

I know: it is still the demon who speaks.

God's holy messenger: this translates "the Holy One of God" (see RSV), which is to be understood as a title of the Messiah. The possessive "of God" is probably to be understood as "the messenger (or, Holy One) who is sent by God."

4.35	TEV	RSV

TEV: Jesus ordered the spirit, "Be quiet and come out of the man!" The demon threw the man down in front of them and went out of him without doing him any harm.

RSV: But Jesus rebuked him, saying, "Be silent, and come out of him!" And when the demon had thrown him down in the midst, he came out of him, having done him no harm.

ordered the spirit: the Greek verb (RSV "rebuked") has the meaning of stopping an action in progress or of preventing an action from starting. In view of its use elsewhere (see verse 36) it is better to translate "He commanded," "He gave an order."

threw the man down: the man's fall to the ground is attributed to the spirit's violent departure. The fall, however, did not hurt the man.

in front of them: or "in the midst of them." The scene portrayed is that of Jesus and the demon-possessed man facing each other, with the people standing around them, watching.

It may be better to divide the material into two complete sentences: "The spirit threw the man down in front of them and went out of him. But the spirit did not hurt him."

4.36   TEV   RSV
    The people were all amazed and   And they were all amazed and said
said to one another, "What kind of   to one another, "What is this word?
words are these? With authority and   For with authority and power he
power this man gives orders to the   commands the unclean spirits, and
evil spirits, and they come out!"   they come out."

    were all amazed: this translates the phrase "amazement came upon all"; the Greek noun appears only here and in 5.9 in this Gospel.

    What kind of words are these?: the people are amazed that simply by means of an oral command Jesus is able to send the spirit away. So an exclamation may be used: "What powerful words he speaks!" or "The order he gives is very strong!" A translation should not give the impression that the people did not understand the meaning of the words Jesus spoke to the demon.

    authority and power: the two words mean much the same, but each has its own particular area of meaning: authority is the right to command, and power is the capacity to have one's command obeyed.

    gives orders: RSV "he commands." It is to be noticed that the Greek verb here is the same one that in verse 35 RSV translates "rebuked" (TEV ordered). The people's statement may be rephrased, "This man has authority and power! He orders the evil spirits to come out, and they do!"

    evil spirits: the Greek is "unclean spirits" (see verse 33).

4.37   TEV   RSV
And the report about Jesus spread   And reports of him went out into
everywhere in that region.   every place in the surrounding re-
                                        gion.

    the report about Jesus spread: this statement is similar to The news about him spread in verse 14. "People all over that region talked about what Jesus was doing."

    that region: undefined; "all around the town of Capernaum" or "all over (northern) Galilee."

SECTION HEADING

Jesus Heals Many People.

The cures done by Jesus in this section all take place that same day, which was the Sabbath before the sun set, but was considered the

4.38

first day of the week after the sun set. Some translations have two small
sections: the first one (verses 38-39), "Jesus Heals Simon's Mother-in-
Law; and the second one (verses 40-41), "Jesus Heals Many People."

4.38 TEV	RSV
Jesus left the synagogue and went to Simon's home. Simon's mother-in-law was sick with a high fever, and they spoke to Jesus about her.	And he arose and left the syna-gogue, and entered Simon's house. Now Simon's mother-in-law was ill with a high fever, and they besought him for her.

Again, since it is the beginning of a new section, TEV has Jesus and
not simply "He" as in the Greek text.
    left the synagogue: RSV "arose and left the synagogue" shows that
the Greek text has the verb used also in verse 29; but it seems probable
that here the verb "arose" is used to reinforce the verb "left," and does
not mean literally "he arose (from his seat)."
    Simon's home: Simon is introduced as though known by the readers;
this is the first time he appears in this Gospel. His call to be a disciple is given in chapter 5. His home is in Capernaum.
    they spoke: the text does not say who spoke; presumably the friends
there who were helping to take care of Simon's mother-in-law. The text
could be translated "they asked Jesus to help (or, heal) her."

4.39 TEV	RSV
He went and stood at her bedside and ordered the fever to leave her. The fever left her, and she got up at once and began to wait on them.	And he stood over her and rebuked the fever, and it left her; and immediately she rose and served them.

    stood at her bedside: this translates the Greek "stood over her"
(RSV); the translation could be "leaned over her" (she was lying down).
    ordered...to leave: this is the same verb used in verse 35 of Jesus'
command to the demon.
    and began to wait on them: her action seems to imply that she was
the mistress of the house. It is possible that Simon was a widower and
that his mother-in-law, a widow, lived with him. It is not clear in this
verse who them is; presumably they are Jesus and his disciples. But nothing has been said of Jesus' disciples, and the only other person named
in this story is Simon himself. So them must be taken generally of Jesus
and the others there at the house. Here began to wait on is to be understood in terms of the food and drink she would offer her guests.

4.40 TEV	RSV
After sunset all who had friends who were sick with various diseases brought them to Jesus; he placed his hands on every one of them and healed them all.	Now when the sun was setting, all those who had any that were sick with various diseases brought them to him; and he laid his hands on every one of them and healed them.

[72]

After sunset: this is important because sunset marked the beginning of the first day of the week, when people could carry their sick relatives and friends to Jesus—work they could not do on the Sabbath.

friends who were sick with various diseases: not that any one person had several diseases, but that the various people had different diseases: "all kinds of sick people."

The language is exaggerated. All means all the people living in Capernaum who had sick friends and relatives.

brought: or "took." Many of them would be carried on mats; others would be helped as they walked to Simon's house.

he placed his hands: this is the way Jesus healed them, not with a command but with a touch. The relation between the action and the cure should be more clearly stated than in TEV; for example, "he healed them all by placing his hands on each (or, every) one." Perhaps he placed his hands on the afflicted part of the body.

4.41	TEV	RSV
	Demons also went out from many people, screaming, "You are the Son of God!"	And demons also came out of many, crying, "You are the Son of God!" But he rebuked them, and would not allow them to speak, because they knew that he was the Christ.
	Jesus gave the demons an order and would not let them speak, because they knew he was the Messiah.	

Demons also went out: that is, besides the other cures, Jesus also expelled demons, presumably by an oral command as in verse 35. But it would not be proper here to say "At his command, demons went out of...."

You are the Son of God!: the same kind of knowledge shown by the first demon Jesus expelled (verse 34).

gave...an order: the same verb used in verses 35,39. Instead of gave...an order and would not let them speak, as though two different actions are involved, it would be better to say "and with an order (or, a command) Jesus kept the demons from saying anything." Or "Jesus ordered the demons not to say anything."

the Messiah: see 2.11. Jesus does not allow the demons to say who he is.

SECTION HEADING

Jesus Preaches in the Synagogues: "Jesus Proclaims His Message Everywhere."

In this section, emphasis is placed on Jesus' compulsion to proclaim his message about the Kingdom of God all over Israel.

4.42	TEV	RSV
	At daybreak Jesus left the town and went off to a lonely	And when it was day he departed and went into a lonely place. And

place. The people started looking for him, and when they found him, they tried to keep him from leaving.	the people sought him and came to him, and would have kept him from leaving them;

At daybreak: "Next morning"; this would be our Sunday morning, the first day of the week.

left the town: "went out of Capernaum."

a lonely place: "a place where there were no people," "an isolated spot."

tried to: the Greek implies that they were unable to keep Jesus from leaving them. These people are from Capernaum, and they want him to stay in their town.

4.43 TEV	RSV
But he said to them, "I must preach the Good News about the Kingdom of God in other towns also, because that is what God sent me to do."	but he said to them, "I must preach the good news of the kingdom of God to the other cities also; for I was sent for this purpose."

preach the Good News: see 2.10; 3.18; for preach see 3.3.

about the Kingdom of God: in the Gospels the Kingdom of God refers to the time or circumstances when God will rule completely over the world and mankind. Sometimes it is spoken of as a present reality, at other times as a future event; in some instances it is equivalent to eternal life with God. A verbal phrase may be used here: "I must proclaim in other towns also the Good News that God will (soon) establish his rule (or, dominion) over the world."

God sent me to do: as RSV shows ("I was sent"), the Greek has a passive verb, which indicates God's activity. See the passive form of this same verb in 1.19.

4.44 TEV	RSV
So he preached in the synagogues throughout the country.	And he was preaching in the synagogues of Judea.[n]

[n] Other ancient authorities read *Galilee*

he preached: "he went and proclaimed."

throughout the country: as RSV shows, the Greek text says "Judea." In some instances (see 1.5) this Gospel uses "Judea" as the name for the whole land of Israel, and this is how TEV understands the word here.

Textual Note: as RSV footnote shows, many Greek manuscripts and ancient versions have "Galilee" instead of "Judea." The change was made because Jesus is in the northern part of the country, Galilee, and not in the southern part. (But as said above, "Judea" here may mean the whole country.)

Chapter 5

Jesus Calls the First Disciples: "Jesus Tells Three Fishermen to Follow Him," "The First Disciples of Jesus."

This description of the call of the first disciples differs somewhat from the accounts in Mark (1.16-20) and Matthew (4.18-22). Simon's brother Andrew is not mentioned, and the unusual catch of fish is not included in the other accounts.

5.1	TEV	RSV
	One day Jesus was standing on the shore of Lake Gennesaret while the people pushed their way up to him to listen to the word of God.	While the people pressed upon him to hear the word of God, he was standing by the lake of Gennesaret.

One day: this is simply an introductory marker in English; the Greek text does not indicate the relation in time between this incident and the previous one. The introduction in Greek is quite vague: "It happened that while...."

Lake Gennesaret: this is another name for Lake Galilee, a body of fresh water in the province of Galilee, some 21 kilometers long and 13 kilometers wide at its greatest width.

pushed their way up: as Jesus stood on the shore, the people were crowded around him. TEV pushed their way up may be misleading, since it could be understood to mean to go from a lower level to a higher one; here "to push up" is used in the sense of trying to get to the front row, near Jesus.

to listen to the word of God: this should not be translated in such a way as to imply that the author is calling Jesus God. It might be better to translate "to listen to the message from God" or "to listen to Jesus' message about God."

5.2	TEV	RSV
	He saw two boats pulled up on the beach; the fishermen had left them and were washing the nets.	And he saw two boats by the lake; but the fishermen had gone out of them and were washing their nets.

pulled up on the beach: since there was no dock, the boats would be pulled up out of the water (or part way out), so as not to drift out on the lake.

the nets: or "their nets" (RSV) might be more natural. These nets were large dragnets (see verses 4-5), not the smaller casting nets. In order to introduce the information that there was nobody in the boats, a translation could say "They were empty, because the fishermen had left and were washing their nets."

5.3   TEV   RSV

TEV	RSV
Jesus got into one of the boats— it belonged to Simon—and asked him to push off a little from the shore. Jesus sat in the boat and taught the crowd.	Getting into one of the boats, which was Simon's, he asked him to put out a little from the land. And he sat down and taught the people from the boat.

The order of elements in this verse may be changed: "One of the boats belonged to Simon. Jesus got into that boat and asked Simon to...." The text does not say whether Jesus knew who was the owner of the boat before he got in.

push off a little from the shore: "push the boat out in the water a short distance" or "...a few feet from shore." The boat is close enough to shore that from it Jesus can easily teach the people who are standing on shore, at the water's edge.

sat...and taught: see 4.20.

5.4   TEV   RSV

TEV	RSV
When he finished speaking, he said to Simon, "Push the boat out further to the deep water, and you and your partners let down your nets for a catch."	And when he had ceased speaking, he said to Simon, "Put out into the deep and let down your nets for a catch."

Push the boat out: this might give the idea of pushing the boat out with a pole. Or it could have been by rowing, or else by hoisting the sails and sailing. In the absence of a specific word for moving the boat on water, a general expression may be sufficient: "Get the boat farther out in the lake, where the water is deep," "Make the boat go out...." The command is addressed to Simon.

the deep water: this does not mean there was only one such spot; "to a place where the water is (real) deep."

you and your partners let down: TEV has you and your partners because the verb let down is plural; Jesus is now talking to Simon and his partners (see verse 7). A large dragnet was placed in the water and hauled in by men working in two boats, with the net between the boats. Here, however, the description shows that the men in the one boat were handling the nets.

for a catch: "to catch (or, net) fish."

5.5   TEV   **RSV**
"Master," Simon answered, "we   And Simon answered, "Master, we
worked hard all night long and   toiled all night and took nothing!
caught nothing. But if you say so,   But at your word I will let down
I will let down the nets."   the nets."

Master: this translates a word that in this Gospel is always used by
the disciples, except in 17.13. It should not be translated "Owner" or
"Boss"; perhaps in some languages the equivalent of "Chief" would be acceptable. Or else something equivalent to the English "Sir"; or, if nothing else seems appropriate, "Teacher" might be used. (But it is interest-
ing to notice that in this Gospel the Greek word for "Teacher" is used of
Jesus always by people who are not disciples, with the single exception
of 21.7.)
     we worked hard: "we kept fishing," "we didn't stop fishing."
     all night long: a good time for fishing.
     and caught nothing: "but we didn't catch a thing," "but we netted no
fish."
     if you say so: or "since you say so," "because you tell me to do it,"
"at your command."

5.6   TEV   RSV
They let them down and caught such   And when they had done this, they
a large number of fish that the   enclosed a great shoal of fish; and
nets were about to break.   as their nets were breaking,

     They: "Simon Peter and his partners."
     let them down: it might be necessary to say explicitly, "They went
out to where the water was deep and let down the nets."
     were about to break: or whatever verb best suits nets; "tear,"
"split," "come apart." It would seem that the Greek text means that the
nets were at the bursting point, not that they actually "were breaking"
(RSV). As the men pulled the nets toward shore, if there were too many
fish in them the nets could split; once they began to come apart the fish
would swim free.

5.7   TEV   RSV
So they motioned to their partners   they beckoned to their partners in
in the other boat to come and help   the other boat to come and help
them. They came and filled both   them. And they came and filled both
boats so full of fish that the   the boats, so that they began to
boats were about to sink.   sink.

     motioned: the use of such a verb, instead of a verb "to call," indi-
cates a purely visual means of communication; "gestured," "made signs,"
"waved their arms."
     partners: verse 10 says that James and John were Simon's partners;
nothing is said about Simon's brother Andrew. It may be that Andrew was
in the same boat with Simon, while James and John were in the other boat.

filled both boats: the men pulled the nets full of fish up into the boats.

were about to sink: "were in danger of sinking." It does not appear that the boats were actually sinking (RSV).

5.8

TEV	RSV
When Simon Peter saw what had happened, he fell on his knees before Jesus and said, "Go away from me, Lord! I am a sinful man!"	But when Simon Peter saw it, he fell down at Jesus' knees, saying, "Depart from me, for I am a sinful man, O Lord."

When Simon Peter saw what had happened: this might seem strange, since Simon was there all the time and could not but see what had happened. But this is the writer's way of introducing what follows, and a translator should not try to improve the author's style.

he fell on his knees before Jesus: the writer may have meant to indicate that two boats were now at shore, and the people were back on land. This is possible, since the business of hauling in the nets and getting the overloaded boats safely to shore would take up the time and energy of the fishermen. But verse 11 seems to indicate that the incident here in verse 8 took place while the boat was still out on the lake. The Greek text says "he fell (or, threw himself down) at the knees of Jesus" (see RSV). This seems to suggest that Peter knelt and bowed his head on a level with Jesus' knees. The more natural expression in English is "he threw himself down in front of Jesus."

Go away from me: "Leave me," "Don't have anything to do with me." This expresses Simon's sense of unworthiness to continue in Jesus' company.

Lord: the writer probably intends the word to have its full Christian meaning here. It is the distinctive word that believers apply to Jesus.

a sinful man: "a sinner." It is not easy to decide the precise meaning of the phrase here. It may reflect Peter's lack of faith that seems implied in verse 5. Whatever the meaning may be, the incident gave Peter an insight into Jesus' extraordinary nature, so that Peter felt himself unworthy to be Jesus' friend or follower.

5.9

TEV	RSV
He and the others with him were all amazed at the large number of fish they had caught.	For he was astonished, and all that were with him, at the catch of fish which they had taken;

the others with him: in the next verse James and John are named, in addition to the others mentioned in this verse; therefore someone else besides Andrew is there (assuming that Andrew is present).

were all amazed: see 4.36.

5.10	TEV	RSV

The same was true of Simon's partners, James and John, the sons of
Zebedee. Jesus said to Simon,
"Don't be afraid; from now on you
will be catching men."

and so also were James and John,
sons of Zebedee, who were partners
with Simon. And Jesus said to Simon,
"Do not be afraid; henceforth you
will be catching men."

the sons of Zebedee: it is not said whether Zebedee had other sons
besides James and John. It is assumed that James, the brother named first,
is the older one.

you will be catching men: this is not simply a statement of what
will happen; it has the force of an imperative: "from now on you are to
catch men." The figurative language means that Simon will quit his work
of catching fish and start "catching" people. The figure may be difficult
to express, since it might make it appear that Simon is to catch people
physically, that is, to arrest them. So it may be necessary to say "I
will teach (or, train) you to bring people to me (or, cause people to
become my disciples), as you now catch fish in a net." Or, "Just as you
have worked to bring in fish, from now on you will work to bring people
to me." Most translations keep the figurative language. The use of the
word men should not imply that women would not be included; so "people"
would be better.

5.11	TEV	RSV

They pulled the boats up on
the beach, left everything, and
followed Jesus.

and when they had brought their
boats to land, they left everything
and followed him.

the boats: the two boats of verse 2.
pulled the boats up on the beach: "beached the boats," "brought the
boats to land."
followed: "went with," "accompanied (as disciples)."

SECTION HEADING

Jesus Heals a Man: "Jesus Makes a Man Well."

The place where this cure takes place is not identified. The man is
suffering from a skin disease which, according to Jewish Law and current
practice, keeps him from leading a normal life. So the cure not only
heals the man physically but also restores him to his family and community.

5.12	TEV	RSV

Once Jesus was in a town
where there was a man who was suffering from a dreaded skin disease.

While he was in one of the
cities, there came a man full of
leprosy; and when he saw Jesus, he

5.12

When he saw Jesus, he threw himself down and begged him, "Sir, if
you want to, you can make me
clean!"*c*

fell on his face and besought him,
"Lord, if you will, you can make me
clean."

*c*MAKE ME CLEAN: *This disease was
considered to make a person ritually unclean.*

Once Jesus was: this is a way of beginning a new incident; the Greek
text has "And it happened that he was."

a dreaded skin disease: this translates the Greek phrase "full of
leprosy" (RSV), showing that he had a severe case (see 4.12).

threw himself down: the action is described by the phrase "fell on
his face" (RSV), by which is meant that he lay face down at Jesus' feet.

Sir: this translates a Greek title which may mean Lord, lord, master,
or owner; here it is the appropriate polite form of address; it is not
used in the Christian sense (see verse 8). But RSV "Lord" takes it in
this sense.

if you want to: "if you wish," "if you are willing." The man doesn't
directly ask Jesus to heal him; he believes Jesus can, and his only question is: will Jesus be willing?

make me clean: as the TEV footnote indicates, this disease made a
person ritually unclean; that is, it prevented that person from taking
part in normal social and religious activities such as public worship
until he or she had been cleansed. In some languages make me clean means
only physical cleanliness, and some translations may say simply, "You can
heal me"—but this does omit an important element of the original cultural context.

5.13   TEV   RSV
    Jesus reached out and touched   And he stretched out his hand, and
him. "I do want to," he answered.   touched him, saying, "I will; be
"Be clean!" At once the disease   clean." And immediately the leprosy
left the man.   left him.

Jesus reached out and touched him: all physical contact with a person suffering from such a disease was carefully avoided, to keep from
being infected with the sufferer's "impurity"; so Jesus' gesture is highly significant.

I do want to: "I am willing." Jesus answers the implied question in
verse 12: "Are you willing?"

Be clean!: it may be difficult to use the passive imperative. It may
therefore be necessary to translate "I heal you" or "God heals you"—but
such a statement misses the force of the command. Again, if clean is a
problem, the translation can be "Be healed!"

the disease left the man: this translates the Greek idiom literally;
it may be better in some languages to say "his disease disappeared" or
"he was cured of his disease."

5.14 TEV	RSV
Jesus ordered him, "Don't tell anyone, but go straight to the priest and let him examine you; then to prove to everyone that you are cured, offer the sacrifice as Moses ordered."	And he charged him to tell no one; but "go and show yourself to the priest, and make an offering for your cleansing, as Moses commanded, for a proof to the people."^O

^OGreek *to them*

Don't tell anyone: "Don't say anything about this to anybody." The man was told to lose no time in obeying Jesus' instructions.

go straight to the priest and let him examine you: it is not certain whether the man was to go to a local priest, or to a priest on duty in the Temple in Jerusalem. Probably it was the latter, since the Temple was the place where the cured man would offer the sacrifice, as required by the Law of Moses. After the priest had examined the man and pronounced him clean, the man would offer the sacrifice. Leviticus 14.1-32 has the instructions, which a translator should read if the language has to specify what kind of sacrifice or offering was required.

as Moses ordered: "as required by the Law of Moses." In a general sense this refers to the Torah, the first five books of the Hebrew Scriptures.

5.15 TEV	RSV
But the news about Jesus spread all the more widely, and crowds of people came to hear him and be healed from their diseases.	But so much the more the report went abroad concerning him; and great multitudes gathered to hear and to be healed of their infirmities.

spread all the more widely: "kept on spreading more and more"; see similar statements in 4.14,37. The statement is made this way since it goes against Jesus' wish not to arouse publicity (verse 14).

be healed from their diseases: if this passive form proves difficult, it is possible to use an active form of the verb in a complete sentence: "They also came to ask (or, get) Jesus to heal them" or "...so that Jesus would heal them."

5.16 TEV	RSV
But he would go away to lonely places, where he prayed.	But he withdrew to the wilderness and prayed.

would go away: this expression is meant to indicate that Jesus did this often, or regularly. "But he used to go away and pray in places where there were no people" or "...in places where there was no one else."

lonely places: away from towns (see 4.42).

5.17

SECTION HEADING

Jesus Heals a Paralyzed Man: the translation of <u>Paralyzed Man</u> will follow the translation of the term in verse 18.

The cure of this man shows not only Jesus' power to restore him to physical health, but even more importantly his authority to forgive sins. And in this incident there appears the first sign of opposition from the religious leaders to Jesus and his claims.

5.17 TEV	RSV
One day when Jesus was teaching, some Pharisees and teachers of the Law were sitting there who had come from every town in Galilee and Judea and from Jerusalem. The power of the Lord was present for Jesus to heal the sick.	On one of those days, as he was teaching, there were Pharisees and teachers of the law sitting by, who had come from every village of Galilee and Judea and from Jerusalem; and the power of the Lord was with him to heal.[p]

[p]Other ancient authorities read *was present to heal them*

One day: this is a vague expression of time used to begin the story; the time and place of this incident are not given.
teaching: "teaching people," "telling people about God (or, the Kingdom of God)." Jesus was in a house (verse 18), or perhaps a synagogue.
Pharisees: these were Jews who were strict in obeying the Law of Moses as well as other regulations which had been added to it through the centuries. Most of these regulations had to do with personal conduct and with specific rules intended to keep a person from becoming ceremonially impure. The Pharisees were highly respected by the people for their devotion to the Law of Moses.
teachers of the Law: men who were qualified to interpret the Hebrew Scriptures, particularly the first five books.
every town in Galilee and Judea: the statement is not intended literally, but is an emphatic way of describing Jesus' popularity.
The power of the Lord was present: here the Lord is God, and the abstract phrase The power of the Lord indicates that Jesus was able to heal people because God gave him the power to do so. If this abstract concept is difficult to translate, it may be represented by "God gave Jesus the power (or, capacity) to heal sick people." No word should be used, however, that might imply natural medical skill.

5.18 TEV	RSV
Some men came carrying a paralyzed man on a bed, and they tried to carry him into the house and put him in front of Jesus.	And behold, men were bringing on a bed a man who was paralyzed, and they sought to bring him in and lay him before Jesus;[q]

[q]Greek *him*

[82]

carrying...on a bed: this was not a bed in the usual sense of the word (wood or metal frame, springs, mattress), but a more simple thing, easily carried, such as a sleeping mat.

a paralyzed man: "a man who couldn't walk" or "a man who couldn't move."

they tried: the next verse shows why they were unable to get the paralyzed man to Jesus.

the house: the Greek says only "carry him in," but the story shows that Jesus was inside a house, so it is necessary to say this here.

put him in front of Jesus: obviously they wanted Jesus to heal their friend; and since Jesus generally healed by touching people (4.40), they had to get him close to Jesus.

5.19 TEV	RSV
Because of the crowd, however, they could find no way to take him in. So they carried him up on the roof, made an opening in the tiles, and let him down on his bed into the middle of the group in front of Jesus.	but finding no way to bring him in, because of the crowd, they went up on the roof and let him down with his bed through the tiles into the midst before Jesus.

Because of the crowd: the large crowd inside the house made it impossible for the men to carry their sick friend in to Jesus.

carried him up on the roof: the roof was flat and was reached by outside steps. Here the writer speaks of tiles, which were common in houses in places where Greek culture was prevalent. These tiles were probably made of clay.

made an opening in the tiles: it would be better to say "made an opening in the roof by removing some of the tiles" or "they removed some of the tiles and lowered the man, on his mat, through the opening...."

the group in front of Jesus: "the people who were sitting in front of (or, facing) Jesus."

5.20 TEV	RSV
When Jesus saw how much faith they had, he said to the man, "Your sins are forgiven, my friend."	And when he saw their faith he said, "Man, your sins are forgiven you."

saw: "perceived," "recognized," "sensed."

how much faith they had: here faith is their belief that Jesus can heal their friend: "how strongly they believed that he could heal the sick man."

they: this refers to the men carrying the sick man; it may include the sick man also.

Your sins are forgiven: the passive are forgiven is a way of speaking of God's activity: "God forgives you," "God forgives your sins." If possible, the passive voice should be kept in translation, in light of the reaction of the teachers of the Law and the Pharisees (verse 21). Or else, "You are free from your sins."

forgiven: some languages use set phrases such as "God forgets our wrong" or "God takes back what we have done wrong"; or else, "God throws away our sins," "God no longer thinks about our sins." The basic idea in the Bible is the restoration of the relationship between God and the person—a relationship which has been broken by sin.

my friend: this translates the Greek 'Man' (RSV). There is no idea of rebuke in the word; it is a friendly term, applied to someone who is not known personally or intimately.

5.21

TEV	RSV
The teachers of the Law and the Pharisees began to say to themselves, "Who is this man who speaks such blasphemy! God is the only one who can forgive sins!"	And the scribes and the Pharisees began to question, saying, "Who is this that speaks blasphemies? Who can forgive sins but God only?"

began to say to themselves: or "began to argue (or, dispute) among themselves."

Who is this man: that is, "Who does this man think he is?" They presumably knew who Jesus was; their question was not a request for information but a rebuke of Jesus for speaking as he did.

blasphemy: "words which are insulting to God." "This man is insulting (or, dishonoring) God."

God is the only one: as RSV shows, the Greek is in the form of a question, but it is a way of making an affirmation. The reaction of the religious leaders is caused by the fact that they see Jesus doing something that only God can do.

5.22

TEV	RSV
Jesus knew their thoughts and said to them, "Why do you think such things?	When Jesus perceived their questionings, he answered them, "Why do you question in your hearts?

knew: "perceived" (RSV), "sensed," "caught on to what they were thinking."

their thoughts: this is rather strange, since verse 21 states they were talking among themselves. But this noun ("questions," "doubts," "opinions"; RSV "questionings") and Jesus' question make it appear that the Pharisees and the teachers of the Law were thinking these matters, not saying them out loud. It could be, therefore, that the participle "saying" in verse 21 (see RSV) does not actually mean to talk out loud, but is the Greek equivalent to modern quotation marks.

think such things: the Greek adds "in your hearts" (RSV); but in English it is unnatural to add this phrase to the verb "to think."

5.23

TEV	RSV
Is it easier to say, 'Your sins are forgiven you,' or to say, 'Get up and walk'?	Which is easier, to say, 'Your sins are forgiven you,' or to say, 'Rise and walk'?

Is it easier: in this extended question, the point is that it is in fact easier to say "Your sins are forgiven," because there is no way to prove that the statement is false; to say "Get up and walk" is much harder, because it requires a most unusual result to prove it to be true. The whole matter, as Jesus says in the next verse, is a question of whether or not he has authority; and the command to the paralyzed man to get up and walk will show whether or not Jesus has authority to forgive sins.

If the rhetorical question proves misleading, the translation can use a declarative form: "It is, of course, easier to say, 'Your sins are forgiven' than to say, 'Get up and walk.'" Or the two quoted statements may be expressed in indirect form: "It is easier to say to this man that his sins are forgiven than to tell (or, command) him to get up and walk."

5.24	TEV	RSV
	I will prove to you, then, that the Son of Man has authority on earth to forgive sins." So he said to the paralyzed man, "I tell you, get up, pick up your bed, and go home!"	But that you may know that the Son of man has authority on earth to forgive sins"—he said to the man who was paralyzed—"I say to you, rise, take up your bed and go home."

I will prove to you: this translates the Greek "In order that you may know."

the Son of Man: this is a title of uncertain meaning in the Gospels. It is the main title which Jesus applied to himself. In the Old Testament the phrase "the son of man" means "person" or "human being," emphasizing that human beings are weak and mortal. In Daniel 7.13-14 it is the title of one who is more than an ordinary human being. As used by Jesus, it does not emphasize his humanity; it is a title of honor and power.

Here Jesus speaks of himself as the Son of Man, so it may be necessary to translate "I, the Son of Man," "I who am the Son of Man."

authority on earth: the words on earth are important; they show that the Son of Man has been given authority by God to forgive sins on earth.

Jesus' command to the paralyzed man proves that he, the Son of Man, has authority from God to forgive people's sins. RSV follows the form of the Greek text, in which verse 24 is one complex sentence; TEV has restructured the material to make it easier to understand.

5.25	TEV	RSV
	At once the man got up in front of them all, took the bed he had been lying on, and went home, praising God.	And immediately he rose before them, and took up that on which he lay, and went home, glorifying God.

in front of them all: "in the presence of all," "while they all watched."

took the bed he had been lying on: "picked up the mat he had been lying on."

praising God: "giving thanks to God," "saying, 'Thank you, God'"; "saying to God, 'I thank you.'"

[85]

5.26 TEV	RSV
They were all completely amazed! Full of fear, they praised God, saying, "What marvelous things we have seen today!"	And amazement seized them all, and they glorified God and were filled with awe, saying, "We have seen strange things today."

<u>completely amazed</u>: the Greek noun "amazement" (RSV) is related to the verb used in 2.47.

<u>fear</u>: "awe" (RSV).

<u>marvelous things</u>: "wonderful things," "surprising things," "unusual things"; or "things that are hard to believe," "things we don't understand."

SECTION HEADING

<u>Jesus Calls Levi</u>: "Jesus Tells Levi to Follow Him," "...to Become His Disciple."

There is no certain indication of time and place in this incident; in verse 27 <u>Jesus went out</u> may mean he left the house he had been in, or else that he left the town. The former is probably intended; but the latter could be meant, since the tax collector's place of business would be on the main road on which people entered and left town.

5.27-28 TEV	RSV
After this, Jesus went out and saw a tax collector named Levi, sitting in his office. Jesus said to him, "Follow me." 28 Levi got up, left everything, and followed him.	After this he went out, and saw a tax collector, named Levi, sitting at the tax office; and he said to him, "Follow me." 28 And he left everything, and rose and followed him.

<u>went out</u>: of the house or of the town.

<u>a tax collector</u>: the office of collecting taxes from the people was held by Jews who on behalf of the Roman authorities collected duties on produce taken in and out of the towns.

<u>Levi</u>: as in Mark 2.14; in Matthew 9.9 he is called Matthew. If helpful, a footnote could indicate that this man is the same one known as Matthew, with a reference to Matthew 9.9; it is recommended that the name <u>Levi</u> be kept in the text here.

<u>office</u>: not an elaborate structure; "toll booth," "customs shed."

<u>Follow me</u>: "Come with me as my follower," "Be my disciple."

<u>left everything, and followed him</u>: as in verse 11.

5.29 TEV	RSV
Then Levi had a big feast in his house for Jesus, and among the	And Levi made him a great feast in his house; and there was a large

| guests was a large number of tax collectors and other people. | company of tax collectors and others sitting at table[r] with them. |

[r]Greek *reclining*

a big feast: "an elaborate reception," "a splendid banquet."
for Jesus: "in Jesus' honor," "to honor Jesus."
among the guests: this translates the Greek "were reclining" (see RSV text and footnote). This denotes the way in which meals were eaten. People lay stretched out on their left sides on rugs or cushions on the floor, and the food was placed on low tables in front of them.

5.30 TEV	RSV
Some Pharisees and some teachers of the Law who belonged to their group complained to Jesus' disciples. "Why do you eat and drink with tax collectors and other outcasts?" they asked.	And the Pharisees and their scribes murmured against his disciples, saying, "Why do you eat and drink with tax collectors and sinners?"

who belonged to their group: "who were also Pharisees."
The sentence could be restructured: "There were present some Pharisees, including teachers of the Law, and they complained...."
complained: "grumbled," "criticized."
disciples: in the Gospels this word usually applies to the close followers of Jesus, the men who learned from him and helped him in his work. Care should be taken not to use a word that means only "students" or "learners," as though they were pupils in school. "Followers," or "helpers," or even "apprentices," would be better.
eat and drink: to join such people at a meal indicated a degree of close friendship which, in the opinion of the Pharisees, Jesus and his followers should not show.
other outcasts: this translates the Greek "sinners" (RSV). The word is used here in a specialized sense for Jews who, like the tax collectors, were despised by the religious leaders because of their refusal to obey every one of the religious rules, especially those which prohibited eating certain foods and associating with Gentiles. TEV says other because the tax collectors themselves were also considered "sinners." If the use of the usual word for "sinners" would be misleading, and if something like "outcasts" is difficult, the translation could say "people who had a bad reputation," "people who did not obey all the rules," "people who were despised by others."

5.31 TEV	RSV
Jesus answered them, "People who are well do not need a doctor, but only those who are sick.	And Jesus answered them, "Those who are well have no need of a physician, but those who are sick;

It may be that Jesus is quoting a popular proverb: "It is sick people who need a doctor, not healthy people." Jesus' words imply that a religious teacher such as he should associate with those who needed his teachings, and not with people like the religious leaders, who did not need them. Jesus' reply does not seem particularly hostile.

5.32

TEV	RSV
I have not come to call respectable people to repent, but outcasts."	I have not come to call the righteous, but sinners to repentance."

come: here it is hard to decide whether "I have (not) come teaching and preaching" is meant, or "I have (not) come into the world." Perhaps the best translation is "My mission (or, task) is not to call...but to call...."

call: here in the sense of inviting or exhorting people to repent.

respectable people: "good people," "people who obey the Law of Moses"; this reflects the opinion the religious leaders had of themselves, as compared with the "sinners."

Instead of the negative form of the statement, the positive form may be better: "I have come to call (or, exhort) the outcasts to repent, not the respectable people."

repent: see 3.3.

SECTION HEADING

The Question about Fasting: "Jesus Teaches about Fasting" or "... about Not Eating as a Religious Duty."

In this section the question about fasting as a religious duty gives Jesus the opportunity to teach why he and his followers do not conform to the practices of the Pharisees and of John the Baptist and his followers. Different situations require different practices; those which suit the Pharisees and John the Baptist's group are not fit for Jesus' group.

5.33

TEV	RSV
Some people said to Jesus, "The disciples of John fast frequently and offer prayers, and the disciples of the Pharisees do the same; but your disciples eat and drink."	And they said to him, "The disciples of John fast often and offer prayers, and so do the disciples of the Pharisees, but yours eat and drink."

Some people said: this translates the Greek "And they said" (RSV), which makes it appear that the people speaking are the Pharisees and teachers of the Law (of verse 30). It seems more likely, however, that this is a separate incident, and that Jesus is no longer in the house of Levi.

disciples of John: the same word, disciples, is used to refer to the followers of John the Baptist, of the Pharisees, and of Jesus (see verse 30).

fast: at that time pious Jews went without food on the second and fifth days of the week as an expression of their devotion to God. Fasting as a religious duty may not be known in certain parts of the world, so it is important not to use an expression that means only "not to eat" or "to go on a diet." It may be possible to say "were not eating as a way of worshiping God," "were going without food as a religious duty."

offer prayers: "pray." Perhaps at stated times; or else prayers that went with fasting.

eat and drink: this implies self-indulgence.

5.34   TEV

Jesus answered, "Do you think you can make the guests at a wedding party go without food as long as the bridegroom is with them? Of course not!

RSV

And Jesus said to them, "Can you make wedding guests fast while the bridegroom is with them?

Do you think: this kind of question implies that the answer is Of course not! (as TEV has). This is another example of what is called a rhetorical question, which means that it is not a request for information but a way of making a strong statement. So the translation could be "You can't make the guests at a wedding party go without food...."

guests at a wedding party: or "a bridegroom's attendants" or "the friends of the bridegroom."

as long as the bridegroom is with them: this means while the wedding festivities are going on (they would last a week).

5.35   TEV

But the day will come when the bridegroom will be taken away from them, and then they will fast."

RSV

The days will come, when the bridegroom is taken away from them, and then they will fast in those days."

the day will come: "the time will come." Nothing in the text says whether that time is near or far away.

will be taken away: the Greek verb means a violent removal by force, and it is probable that the language is a way of saying "will be killed," and that Jesus is referring to himself. His answer is that his own disciples do not fast as long as he is with them; but after he is gone they will fast. Jesus regards fasting not as a required religious duty but as an expression of grief.

A translation should not identify the bridegroom as Jesus, nor be taken away as the crucifixion, but should maintain the figurative language of the text.

5.36   TEV

Jesus also told them this parable: "No one tears a piece off a new coat to patch up an old coat.

RSV

He told them a parable also: "No one tears a piece from a new garment and puts it upon an old garment; if he

If he does, he will have torn the new coat, and the piece of new cloth will not match the old.	does, he will tear the new, and the piece from the new will not match the old.

parable: essentially a story which uses real, everyday situations in order to teach spiritual truths. Various terms are used: "comparison, figure, illustration, analogy"; or else more descriptive phrases such as "comparison word, picture with words, message in the manner of comparison, a story told for teaching." One language says "story from which understanding comes." The word is used quite often in the Gospels, so if there is no short and simple translation (such as "tale" or "story"), a note may be needed in a Word List at the end of the translation.

new coat: here coat translates the word for the long outer garment worn at that time; it is not necessary to designate a particular piece of clothing, so a general word such as "garment" or "clothes" will do.

patch: here the idea is that the patch will not look or feel like the garment onto which it is being sown; "will clash with," "will be different from," "will not form one whole with."

5.37-38   TEV   RSV

Nor does anyone pour new wine into used wineskins, because the new wine will burst the skins, the wine will pour out, and the skins will be ruined. 38 Instead, new wine must be poured into fresh wineskins!	And no one puts new wine into old wineskins; if he does, the new wine will burst the skins and it will be spilled, and the skins will be destroyed. 38 But new wine must be put into fresh wineskins.

new wine: wine that is still fermenting; "wine beginning to ferment," "wine that has not stopped fermenting." As wine ferments, gas is released; if it cannot escape, the pressure within the wineskin increases.

wineskins: made generally of goatskins; a used wineskin would be old and brittle, and would not expand as the wine inside fermented, but would burst as a result of the increasing pressure.

will be ruined: "will become useless," "will no longer be useful."

fresh wineskins: not yet used, and so able to expand as the wine inside ferments.

5.39   TEV   RSV

And no one wants new wine after drinking old wine. 'The old is better,' he says."	And no one after drinking old wine desires new; for he says, 'The old is good.'"[8]

[8]Other ancient authorities read better

new wine: wine that is still fermenting, and so not quite "ripe" or ready for drinking (see verses 37-38).

old wine: wine that has had a chance to settle and ripen.

better: the Greek text has "good" (RSV); but since a comparison is implicit, TEV translates better. Something like "tastier," "has a better bouquet," may be used, or whatever other way is used to praise a good wine. TEV is not translating the Greek adjective "better" found in many Greek manuscripts and ancient versions (see RSV footnote).

Chapter 6

SECTION HEADING

The Question about the Sabbath: "The Controversy about the Sabbath," "Jesus and the Pharisees Argue about the Sabbath."

This is the story of another conflict between Jesus and the Pharisees, who were very strict about what could and couldn't be done on the Sabbath, the holy day of rest and worship.

6.1 TEV	RSV
Jesus was walking through some wheat fields on a Sabbath. His disciples began to pick the heads of wheat, rub them in their hands, and eat the grain.	On a sabbath,^{t} while he was going through the grainfields, his disciples plucked and ate some heads of grain, rubbing them in their hands.

^{t}Other ancient authorities read *On the second first sabbath* (on the second sabbath after the first)

It may be better to begin the verse with an indication of time: "One Sabbath," "On a certain Sabbath Jesus was walking...."

walking through: public footpaths often went across grain fields; it is not implied that Jesus and his disciples were trespassing on someone's property.

some wheat fields: "a wheat field," "a field in which wheat was growing." Or, if wheat is unknown, a more general expression may be used, "a grain field."

Sabbath: see 4.16.

rub them in their hands: to get the grains loose from the husks.

Textual Note: as the RSV footnote shows, many Greek manuscripts and early versions have "second first sabbath"; this may mean "the second Sabbath after the first one" or "the second Sabbath of the first month."

6.2 TEV	RSV
Some Pharisees asked, "Why are you doing what our Law says you cannot do on the Sabbath?"	But some of the Pharisees said, "Why are you doing what is not lawful to do on the sabbath?"

Pharisees: see 5.17.

Why are you doing...?: this is a rhetorical question, intended as a rebuke; "You shouldn't be doing...!"

you is plural; the Pharisees are talking to the disciples.

our Law: the our here is inclusive; it is the Law that all Jews obeyed, and not just the one which the Pharisees obeyed. This is the Law of Moses, otherwise known as the Torah, the first five books of the Hebrew Scriptures. It may be better to use a plural form, "our laws," or else "our holy writings."

you cannot do: "you shouldn't do," "you are not allowed to do." They are talking against picking the heads of wheat, which was classified as reaping, and rubbing the heads in the hands, which would be classified as threshing; both of these activities were forbidden on the Sabbath. The disciples were not being accused of stealing; on the other six days of the week, it was all right to pick and eat heads of grain as they walked on paths that led through a wheat field.

6.3

TEV	RSV
Jesus answered them, "Haven't you read what David did when he and his men were hungry?	And Jesus answered, "Have you not read what David did when he was hungry, he and those who were with him:

It is to be noticed that RSV follows the form of the Greek text and has verses 3-4 as one long question. TEV has broken the material into several sentences, to make the text easier to understand.

Haven't you read...?: this is another rhetorical question. The Pharisees would have known what is reported in 1 Samuel 21.1-6. One could translate "You know very well what David did..." or "You know that scripture passage that tells about what David did...."

his men: "his companions," "his followers," or even "his soldiers."

6.4

TEV	RSV
He went into the house of God, took the bread offered to God, ate it, and gave it also to his men. Yet it is against our Law for anyone except the priests to eat that bread."	how he entered the house of God, and took and ate the bread of the Presence, which it is not lawful for any but the priests to eat, and also gave it to those with him?"

the house of God: not the Temple in Jerusalem (it had not yet been built), but the Tent of the Lord's Presence in Nob.

the bread offered to God: see Leviticus 24.5-9. Every week the priests baked twelve fresh loaves of bread and placed them on a special table as an offering to God; the priests alone were authorized to eat the old loaves which had been replaced by the fresh ones.

our Law: the same as in verse 2.

In some languages it may be necessary to restructure the last part of the verse as follows: "Yet our Law says that only priests are allowed to eat that bread; no one else may eat it."

6.5	TEV	RSV

And Jesus concluded, "The Son of Man is Lord of the Sabbath." | And he said to them, "The Son of man is lord of the sabbath."

And Jesus concluded: "And (or, Then) he said to them."
The Son of Man: see 5.24.
is Lord of the Sabbath: "has the authority to make rules about the Sabbath," "rules over the Sabbath," "has the right to do as he wishes on the Sabbath." For Lord see 5.12.

SECTION HEADING

The Man with a Paralyzed Hand: "Jesus Heals a Man Who Had a Paralyzed Hand."

This is another story about conflict with the religious leaders, centering again on the Sabbath. The incident takes place in a synagogue, but the town is not identified.

6.6	TEV	RSV

On another Sabbath Jesus went into a synagogue and taught. A man was there whose right hand was paralyzed. | On another sabbath, when he entered the synagogue and taught, a man was there whose right hand was withered.

Sabbath: see 4.16.
synagogue: see 4.15.
paralyzed: stiff, and so the man was unable to use it. RSV "withered" gives the wrong idea that the hand had shrunk in size because it had not been used.

6.7	TEV	RSV

Some teachers of the Law and some Pharisees wanted a reason to accuse Jesus of doing wrong, so they watched him closely to see if he would heal on the Sabbath. | And the scribes and the Pharisees watched him, to see whether he would heal on the sabbath, so that they might find an accusation against him.

teachers of the Law...Pharisees: see 5.17.
wanted a reason to accuse: from Jesus' past actions they were sure that Jesus would heal the man if he were asked to do so.
doing wrong: specifically "breaking (or, disobeying) the Law of Moses." They believed that the Law of Moses prohibited curing someone on the Sabbath.

6.8	TEV	RSV

But Jesus knew their thoughts and said to the man, "Stand up and come | But he knew their thoughts, and he said to the man who had the withered

here to the front." The man got up
and stood there.

hand, "Come and stand here." And he
rose and stood there.

knew their thoughts: "knew their intentions" (see 5.22). Here
thoughts translates the same Greek word used in 5.22.

come here to the front: "come here in front of everyone." TEV assumes that Jesus was seated up front, where the one who did the teaching
would sit, and that the man was sitting farther back. Or else the translation could be "Come here," "Come and stand here by me."

6.9   TEV   RSV

Then Jesus said to them, "I ask
you: What does our Law allow us to
do on the Sabbath? To help or to
harm? To save a man's life or destroy it?"

And Jesus said to them, "I ask you,
is it lawful on the sabbath to do
good or to do harm, to save life or
to destroy it?"

our Law: as in verse 2.
To help or to harm?: "To do good or to do evil?" Jesus' questions
refute the assumption of his opponents that a cure violated the Sabbath
law; they knew that the Law allowed measures on the Sabbath that would
save a person's life. The question may be restructured as follows: "What
does our Law (or, our laws) say: that we should do good things on the
Sabbath, or do bad things?"

6.10   TEV   RSV

He looked around at them all; then
he said^d to the man, "Stretch out
your hand." He did so, and his hand
became well again.

And he looked around on them all,
and said to him, "Stretch out your
hand." And he did so, and his hand
was restored.

^dsaid; *some manuscripts have* said
angrily.

Stretch out: "Extend," "Reach out." The command indicates the man's
fingers were drawn up into the palm of the hand.

became well again: the Greek verb implies that the hand at one time
had been strong and healthy.

Textual Note: as the TEV footnote shows, a few Greek manuscripts add
"angrily" (see Mark 3.5).

6.11   TEV   RSV

They were filled with rage and
began to discuss among themselves
what they could do to Jesus.

But they were filled with fury and
discussed with one another what
they might do to Jesus.

rage: only here in the Gospels is this strong word used; it is violent anger, unreasoning fury. The translation could say "They became very
angry."

[95]

6.11

what they could do to Jesus: this could be stated in direct form, "...discuss among themselves: 'What can (or, shall) we do to Jesus?'"

SECTION HEADING

Jesus Chooses the Twelve Apostles: "The Twelve Men Jesus Chose to Be Apostles."

The indication of time (verse 12) is vague, and the location of the hill that Jesus climbed is not given. The choosing of the apostles is followed immediately by a long discourse to them and to a very large crowd.

6.12-13   TEV   RSV
At that time Jesus went up a   In these days he went out to
hill to pray and spent the whole   the mountain to pray; and all night
night there praying to God. 13 When   he continued in prayer to God. 13 And
day came, he called his disciples   when it was day, he called his dis-
to him and chose twelve of them,   ciples, and chose from them twelve,
whom he named apostles: whom he named apostles;

a hill: there is no way of knowing what hill this was. In terms of size, probably hill is better than "mountain" (RSV) in this context.
When day came: "Next morning," "Early the next day."
disciples: see 5.12. From a larger number of disciples, Jesus chose twelve men.
whom he named apostles: most translations will prefer to have a complete sentence: "Jesus named (or, called) them apostles."
apostles: men who are sent out. They are more than messengers; they speak and act with the authority of the one who sent them; so the translation could be "men who would be sent out with Jesus' authority."

6.14-16   TEV   RSV
Simon (whom he named Peter) and his   Simon, whom he named Peter, and
brother Andrew; James and John,   Andrew his brother, and James and
Philip and Bartholomew, 15 Matthew   John, and Philip, and Bartholomew,
and Thomas, James son of Alphaeus,   15 and Matthew, and Thomas, and
and Simon (who was called the Pa-   James the son of Alphaeus, and Si-
triot), 16 Judas son of James, and   mon who was called the Zealot,
Judas Iscariot, who became the   16 and Judas the son of James, and
traitor.   Judas Iscariot, who became a traitor.

Peter: this name is not intended to replace the name Simon, but is an additional name; it has already been used by the writer in 5.8.
Andrew: his name appears here for the first time in the Gospel.
James and John: see 5.10.
the Patriot: the Greek word means "Zealot" (RSV), "Revolutionary," "Nationalist." The title indicates that this Simon was, or had been, a

[96]

member of a nationalist party that advocated the removal of the Roman authority, by force if necessary.

who became the traitor: "who (later) betrayed Jesus."

SECTION HEADING

Jesus Teaches and Heals: "Jesus Heals Many People."

This short section sets the stage for what follows. Nothing is said in these three verses about Jesus' teaching. His teaching begins in verse 20. The people present include the apostles, a larger number of disciples, and a huge crowd of people.

6.17-18 TEV	RSV
When Jesus had come down from the hill with the apostles, he stood on a level place with a large number of his disciples. A large crowd of people was there from all over Judea and from Jerusalem and from the coast cities of Tyre and Sidon; 18 they had come to hear him and to be healed of their diseases. Those who were troubled by evil spirits also came and were healed.	And he came down with them and stood on a level place, with a great crowd of his disciples and a great multitude of people from all Judea and Jerusalem and the seacoast of Tyre and Sidon, who came to hear him and to be healed of their diseases; 18 and those who were troubled with unclean spirits were cured.

a level place: probably level ground at the foot of the hill.

with a large number of his disciples: these people are present there with Jesus. The text does not say that they had been on the hill with Jesus the night before.

Judea: this could refer to the whole country (see 1.5).

Tyre and Sidon: Gentile (Phoenician) cities on the Mediterranean coast, north of Galilee.

to hear him and to be healed of their diseases: see 5.15.

troubled by: that is, possessed by (see 4.33).

evil spirits: this translates the Greek "unclean spirits" (RSV); see 4.33.

A comparison of RSV with TEV shows that they disagree as to where verse 18 begins; TEV follows the United Bible Societies' Greek New Testament.

6.19 TEV	RSV
All the people tried to touch him, for power was going out from him and healing them all.	And all the crowd sought to touch him, for power came forth from him and healed them all.

power...healing: see 5.17. This is the same divine power present with Jesus.

was going out: the tense of the Greek verb implies a continuous flow of healing power.

SECTION HEADING

Happiness and Sorrow: "Promises and Warnings," "Blessings and Woes."

This long discourse of Jesus goes from 6.20 to 6.49. Much of the material here is found also in Matthew 5—7, where it is traditionally called "The Sermon on the Mount." Here, however, Jesus is on a level spot (verse 17), presumably at the foot of a hill.

The material may be conveniently divided (as TEV does) into five sections.

6.20	TEV	RSV
	Jesus looked at his disciples and said, "Happy are you poor; the Kingdom of God is yours!	And he lifted up his eyes on his disciples, and said: "Blessed are you poor, for yours is the kingdom of God.

looked at his disciples: or "turned to his disciples."

Happy: the Greek word here is not the one that means "Blessed" (RSV) as such (as in 1.42), but another word, with the same idea as the Hebrew word translated "Happy" in Psalm 1.1 and elsewhere. It means "fortunate," "to be in a truly good state," "to be well off."

you poor: "you people who have little."

Kingdom of God: see 4.43.

is yours: not that they own it, but that they belong to it and enjoy the blessings of those who are ruled by God. The present tense of the verb is should be noticed.

6.21	TEV	RSV
	"Happy are you who are hun- gry now; you will be filled! "Happy are you who weep now; you will laugh!	"Blessed are you that hunger now, for you shall be satisfied. "Blessed are you that weep now, for you shall laugh.

are hungry: "don't have enough to eat."

you will be filled: "you will get (or, have) all you need." The passive voice of the verb indicates God as the actor: "God will fill you," "God will give you all you need."

weep: "cry," "mourn." No specific reason is given for this crying; the saying emphasizes the reversal of feelings. People who are now sad, Jesus says, will be happy.

6.22 TEV	RSV
"Happy are you when people hate you, reject you, insult you, and say that you are evil, all because of the Son of Man!	"Blessed are you when men hate you, and when they exclude you and revile you, and cast out your name as evil, on account of the Son of Man!

hate you, reject you, insult you: Jesus is still talking to his disciples (verse 20), and this saying foresees difficult times ahead for them.

say that you are evil: this translates "throw out your name as evil" (see RSV), a way of saying "condemn you as being evil."

because of the Son of Man: "because you are followers of the Son of Man." It is their allegiance to the Son of Man—Jesus—that causes them to be hated and persecuted. Jesus here speaks of himself in the third person; it may be necessary to translate "because you follow me, the Son of Man." For Son of Man see 5.24.

6.23 TEV	RSV
Be glad when that happens and dance for joy, because a great reward is kept for you in heaven. For their ancestors did the very same things to the prophets.	Rejoice in that day, and leap for joy, for behold, your reward is great in heaven; for so their fathers did to the prophets.

when that happens: that is, when you are hated and persecuted.

because: what follows is the reason why they are to be very happy when they are persecuted. The reason for their happiness is their assurance that God will reward them.

a great reward is kept...in heaven: this is a way of saying that God will reward them: "because God keeps a great reward for you in heaven." The words in heaven indicate that God is the giver and that the reward will be safe.

For their ancestors: this statement provides an additional explanation of why Jesus' followers will be hated and persecuted. In the past the prophets of Israel were persecuted for speaking the message of God. The people who will hate and persecute the followers of Jesus, the Son of Man, are descendants (not necessarily in a physical sense but in a moral sense) of the people who persecuted the prophets, and they will act as their ancestors did. So persecution is evidence that the followers of Jesus are being faithful. The connection indicated by For may not be very clear, and it may be better to begin this last statement as follows: "Remember that the ancestors of the people who will persecute you hated and persecuted the prophets (of long ago)."

prophets: see 1.70.

6.24	TEV	RSV

"But how terrible for you who are rich now; you have had your easy life!	"But woe to you that are rich, for you have received your consolation.

In verses 24-26 there are four sayings which are the exact opposites
of the four sayings in verses 20-23. A translator should take care to see
that each saying matches its opposite.

how terrible: this expression (RSV "woe") is a mixture of condemnation and regret. It is the very opposite of the word translated Happy in
verses 20-22. Translations use a variety of words to indicate the condition of those who are being condemned: "pain, trouble, misfortune, disaster, distress."

you: obviously these are not disciples of Jesus; they are people
present there in the crowd listening to Jesus.

who are rich now: the opposite of you poor in verse 20. The Greek
text does not have the word now, and it is not necessary here.

you have had your easy life: this translates the Greek "you have
received your consolation" (RSV). Here the word "consolation" represents
the thing or condition that brings satisfaction, happiness, fulfillment.
"You have had your time of happiness" or "your true happiness (or, comfort) is over," "that is all the happiness (or, prosperity) you will
have."

6.25	TEV	RSV

"How terrible for you who are full now; you will go hungry! "How terrible for you who laugh now; you will mourn and weep!	"Woe to you that are full now, for you shall hunger. "Woe to you that laugh now, for you shall mourn and weep.

full now...hungry: the opposite of hungry now...filled of verse 21a.
laugh now...mourn and weep: the opposite of weep now...laugh of
verse 21b.

6.26	TEV	RSV

"How terrible when all people speak well of you; their ancestors said the very same things about the false prophets.	"Woe to you, when all men speak well of you, for so their fathers did to the false prophets.

As the opposite of verses 22-23, this saying indicates that praise
from all is not to be a source of happiness but of sorrow, because such
universal praise comes only to people who are like the false prophets of
the past who were also praised by their contemporaries.

false prophets: "people who claim to be God's messengers but are
not" or "people whose messages about God are untrue."

SECTION HEADING

Love for Enemies: "Jesus Teaches that People Should Love Their Enemies" or "...Love Those Who Hate Them."

In this section Jesus teaches the attitude his followers should have
toward people who hate and mistreat them. Their attitude is to be the
same as God's, who loves all and is good to all, even to the ungrateful
and the wicked.

6.27-28 TEV	RSV
"But I tell you who hear me: Love your enemies, do good to those who hate you, 28 bless those who curse you, and pray for those who mistreat you.	"But I say to you that hear, Love your enemies, do good to those who hate you, 28 bless those who curse you, pray for those who abuse you.

you who hear me: in the context, this refers to all the people gathered to hear Jesus (verses 17-18). But the contrast between those who are
exhorted to behave as Jesus wants them to and those whom he calls "sinners" (verses 32-34) shows that Jesus is addressing his followers in particular.

The people who hate and mistreat Jesus' followers are described in
four ways: your enemies...those who hate you...those who curse you...
those who mistreat you. These are not four different groups, but are the
different ways in which enemies of the followers of Jesus act toward
them.

bless: "ask God to bless" or "speak well of"; probably the former,
as a close parallel to the following pray for.

curse you: "speak evil of you," "say bad things about you." Quite
specifically, to curse someone is to express a desire that evil and suffering will come upon that person.

mistreat: the Greek verb (RSV "abuse") could mean verbal abuse, that
is, insults and curses, or else physical ill-treatment. Most translations
take it in the latter sense.

6.29 TEV	RSV
If anyone hits you on one cheek, let him hit the other one too; if someone takes your coat, let him have your shirt as well.	To him who strikes you on the cheek, offer the other also; and from him who takes away your coat do not withhold even your shirt.

hits you on one cheek: here you is singular; not that Jesus is talking to a particular person, but that he addresses his words to every person as an individual. A blow on the cheek seems to represent a deliberate
insult; Jesus' follower is not to strike back but is to let the person
hit him on the other cheek.

coat: the flowing outer garment, which reached to the feet; the
shirt is the inner short-sleeved garment which reached to the knees

(see 3,11). A robber would naturally grab the outer garment and try to run away with it. If in a given language there are no exact equivalents for the two garments, the outer one and the inner one, the translation may say "If someone takes part of your clothes, let him have the rest of them, too."

6.30   TEV   RSV

Give to everyone who asks you for something, and when someone takes what is yours, do not ask for it back.	Give to every one who begs from you; and of him who takes away your goods do not ask them again.

asks you for something: the verb "to ask" means "to make a request," "to ask for something."
do not ask for it back: "do not try to get it back." In some instances it may be more natural to use the direct form of address: "do not say to that person, 'Give that back to me.'"

6.31   TEV   RSV

Do for others just what you want them to do for you.	And as you wish that men would do to you, do so to them.

Here the plural form of the verb is used again; you means the people Jesus is talking to. TEV reverses the order of the saying in Greek (see RSV); but in some languages it may be more natural to follow the order of the Greek: "As you would like for others to treat you, that is how you should treat them."

6.32   TEV   RSV

"If you love only the people who love you, why should you receive a blessing? Even sinners love those who love them!	"If you love those who love you, what credit is that to you? For even sinners love those who love them.

In verses 32-34 Jesus contrasts the motivation of the conduct of his followers with that of people he calls "sinners." These contrasts are all presented as questions ending with why should you receive a blessing? This is simply a way of saying "You shouldn't expect to receive a blessing." It may be better to translate as a statement, not as a question.
why should you receive a blessing?: the Greek text may be understood in different ways: (1) "What credit is that to you?" (RSV); that is, "you have not done anything for which you deserve credit (or, should be praised)." (2) "What (unusual) kindness (or, favor) have you shown?" That is, "you haven't shown any unusual kindness (or, goodness)." (3) What divine reward awaits you?" That is, "you shouldn't expect God to reward you."
sinners: here the word is used in the particular sense of people who are not religious, who are not consciously trying to obey God's rules, people who are behaving in a normal human way, without reference to the

demands of religion. So a translation could be "Even people who do not pay any attention to God's laws love those who love them!"

6.33-34   TEV   RSV

TEV	RSV
And if you do good only to those who do good to you, why should you receive a blessing? Even sinners do that! 34 And if you lend only to those from whom you hope to get it back, why should you receive a blessing? Even sinners lend to sinners, to get back the same amount!	And if you do good to those who do good to you, what credit is that to you? For even sinners do the same. 34 And if you lend to those from whom you hope to receive, what credit is that to you? Even sinners lend to sinners, to receive as much again.

Verse 33 follows the exact same pattern as verse 32; do good: "do good things for someone," "be kind to."

Verse 34 is more specific; get it back: "be repaid," "be paid back." "And if you lend only to people you hope (or, expect) will pay you back."

lend: many languages require a direct object: "lend something" or "lend money."

get back the same amount: that is, to be completely repaid, to be repaid the full amount. "Even sinners lend to sinners, on the assumption that they will be repaid in full."

6.35   TEV   RSV

TEV	RSV
No! Love your enemies and do good to them; lend and expect nothing back. You will then have a great reward, and you will be sons of the Most High God. For he is good to the ungrateful and the wicked.	But love your enemies, and do good, and lend, expecting nothing in return;[v] and your reward will be great, and you will be sons of the Most High; for he is kind to the ungrateful and the selfish.

[v]Other ancient authorities read *despairing of no man*

No!: TEV thus tries to represent the strong adversative: "On the contrary"—that is, unlike what sinners do.

and expect nothing back: "without expecting to be repaid," "and don't expect to be paid back."

you will be sons: "you will become sons." In this kind of saying the word sons means to have the same nature as, the same attitude as, to behave like, the one who is called "father"—in this case, the Most High God (see 1.32).

good: "kind."

the ungrateful: "people who are not grateful," "people who do not say 'Thank you.'"

the wicked: "people who are evil (or, bad)." The word means more than just "selfish" (RSV).

Textual Note: as the RSV footnote shows, some Greek manuscripts and early versions, instead of and expect nothing back, have "and don't lose

6.35

confidence in anyone." Most modern translations follow the text translated by TEV.

6.36   TEV   RSV
Be merciful just as your Father is   Be merciful, even as your Father is
merciful.   merciful.

Be merciful: "Be compassionate," "Be kind." Since God shows the same mercy toward all people, this idea could be made explicit in translation: "Be merciful to everyone, just as God, your Father, is merciful to everyone."

your Father: in some languages the use of your would implicitly exclude Jesus; in effect it would mean that the one who is called the Father of the disciples is not the Father of Jesus. In such cases, "our Father" should be used: "...just as God, (who is) our Father, is merciful."

SECTION HEADING

Judging Others: "Jesus Teaches about Judging Other People," "... about Condemning Other People."

This section includes warnings against judging and condemning others (verses 37-38), the point being that we should use the same standards for judging others that we expect God will use for judging us. The two short illustrations (verses 39-40) do not fit too well in the context of judging, but in verses 41-42 the subject is dealt with again in terms of a person's willingness to judge himself before judging his brothers.

6.37   TEV   RSV
"Do not judge others, and God   "Judge not, and you will not
will not judge you; do not condemn   be judged; condemn not, and you will
others, and God will not condemn   not be condemned; forgive, and you
you; forgive others, and God will   will be forgiven;
forgive you.

Do not judge others: "Do not pass judgment on others." This is followed immediately by do not condemn others, so that it is clear that Jesus is talking against harsh or hasty judgment of others. Jesus does not forbid forming an opinion; he forbids a readiness to judge and condemn, as though one knew all the facts on which to base a fair and even judgment.

All the second person verbs and pronouns in verses 37-38 are plural.

God will not judge you: the Greek passive form (see RSV "you will not be judged") shows that God is the actor. The future will not judge refers most likely to God's final judgment of all people. The same is true of the other two similar statements: God will not condemn you...God will forgive you.

forgive: see 5.20.

6.38 TEV	RSV
Give to others, and God will give to you. Indeed, you will receive a full measure, a generous helping, poured into your hands—all that you can hold. The measure you use for others is the one that God will use for you."	give, and it will be given to you; good measure, pressed down, shaken together, running over, will be put into your lap. For the measure you give will be the measure you get back."

Give...God will give: this follows the same pattern of the three sayings in verse 37.

a full measure, a generous helping: RSV gives the literal meaning of the Greek text, which uses several phrases to describe a very large and generous gift. The language seems to imply grain, which is "pressed down, shaken together" in the bowl that holds it; the grain fills the bowl to the brim so that it runs over. All of this "will be put into your lap." The Greek word translated "lap" refers to the fold in the outer garment that was used as a pocket. In translation, "Pocket(s)" would be better than "lap." Or else this particular feature need not be presented, and it is enough simply to say "you will be given" or "you will receive" (instead of TEV into your hands).

The measure you use for others: here the figurative sense is obvious and refers to the degree of generosity we show to others. God will be as generous to us as we are generous to others.

6.39 TEV	RSV
And Jesus told them this parable: "One blind man cannot lead another one; if he does, both will fall into a ditch.	He also told them a parable: "Can a blind man lead a blind man? Will they not both fall into a pit?

parable: see 5.36.

As RSV shows, this verse has two rhetorical questions, the first of which expects the answer "No" and the second one the answer "Yes." TEV represents both with statements.

lead: "guide," "go with to show the way."

ditch: "hole," "gully," "pit."

6.40 TEV	RSV
No pupil is greater than his teacher; but every pupil, when he has completed his training, will be like his teacher.	A disciple is not above his teacher, but every one when he is fully taught will be like his teacher.

No pupil is greater than his teacher: or "No pupil is as great as his teacher," "A teacher is always greater than his pupil"; here greater means "more important," "has more prestige," or "is wiser."

when he has completed his training: "when he has learned everything he should know," "when he has been taught everything he needs to learn."

will be like: "will be as wise as," "will be as important as."

6.41 TEV	RSV
"Why do you look at the speck in your brother's eye, but pay no attention to the log in your own eye?	Why do you see the speck that is in your brother's eye, but do not notice the log that is in your own eye?

Why do you...?: this may be represented as a statement: "You should not...."

you: singular, as are the other verbs and pronouns through verse 42.

look at: "notice," "pay (or, call) attention to," or even "be concerned about."

speck...log: this is another instance of an exaggerated way of speaking, used for vividness; it is impossible that a log could get stuck, unnoticed, in someone's eye. The vivid language should be retained, if at all possible: "a little speck...a big stick (or, a plank)."

brother: a member of the same religious group; here, a fellow Christian.

6.42 TEV	RSV
How can you say to your brother, 'Please, brother, let me take that speck out of your eye,' yet cannot even see the log in your own eye? You hypocrite! First take the log out of your own eye, and then you will be able to see clearly to take the speck out of your brother's eye.	Or how can you say to your brother, 'Brother, let me take out the speck that is in your eye,' when you yourself do not see the log that is in your own eye? You hypocrite, first take the log out of your own eye, and then you will see clearly to take out the speck that is in your brother's eye.

How can you say: "Do you think it is right to say...?" Or the question may be transformed into a statement: "You should not say...."

Please, brother, let me...: this can be put into indirect form, "You shouldn't ask your brother to let you remove the speck from his eye."

even see: "even notice," "even be aware of."

hypocrite: "a person who pretends," "a person who appears to be one thing but is really another thing."

you will be able to see clearly to take: "you will see clearly, and so be able to take."

SECTION HEADING

A Tree and Its Fruit: "The Kind of Fruit a Tree Bears," "Good Fruit and Bad Fruit."

This short section uses figurative language to show the relation between character and deeds, character and speaking.

6.43   TEV   RSV
   "A healthy tree does not bear   "For no good tree bears bad
bad fruit, nor does a poor tree   fruit, nor again does a bad tree
bear good fruit.   bear good fruit;

   A healthy tree: "A tree that is growing well," "A tree that is not
dying."
   bad fruit: "fruit that tastes bad," "fruit that no one wants to eat."
   a poor tree: "a tree that isn't healthy," "a tree that isn't growing
well."
   good fruit: "tasty fruit," "fruit that people like to eat."

6.44   TEV   RSV
Every tree is known by the fruit it   for each tree is known by its own
bears; you do not pick figs from   fruit. For figs are not gathered
thorn bushes or gather grapes from   from thorns, nor are grapes picked
bramble bushes.   from a bramble bush.

   is known by: that is, can be identified by the fruit it bears. The
fruit reveals what kind of tree it is. "The fruit that a tree bears shows
what kind of tree it is."
   figs from thorn bushes...grapes from bramble bushes: or, to reverse
it, "thorn bushes do not bear figs, nor do bramble bushes bear grapes";
or "figs don't grow on thorn bushes, nor do grapes grow on bramble
bushes." A bramble bush is a prickly plant, like the blackberry plant. In
each case edible and valuable fruit (figs and grapes) are mentioned together with worthless weeds. If necessary, appropriate cultural equivalents may be substituted.

6.45   TEV   RSV
A good person brings good out of   The good man out of the good treas-
the treasure of good things in his   ure of his heart produces good, and
heart; a bad person brings bad out   the evil man out of his evil treas-
of his treasure of bad things. For   ure produces evil; for out of the
the mouth speaks what the heart is   abundance of the heart his mouth
full of.   speaks.

   The same thought is represented by two parallel statements comparing
good and bad: the treasure of good things and treasure of bad things. It
is not natural to speak of a treasure of bad things since "treasure" implies something valuable, something worth saving. So instead of treasure
a translation may say "collection, store, accumulation, deposit." Or in
a simpler way, "the good things he has...the bad things he has." But if
the figure proves too difficult to represent, the meaning may be expressed
as follows: "A good person has good thoughts (or, feelings) in his mind
(or, heart) and so says good things; a bad person has bad thoughts and so
says bad things."
   what the heart is full of: this pictures the heart, or mind, as the
source of thoughts or feelings which are put into words by the mouth.

6.45

"Your words come from (or, express) the thoughts (or, feelings) that fill your heart (or, mind)."

SECTION HEADING

The Two House Builders: "Two Different Kinds of Foundations," "The House that Stood and the House that Fell."

The discourse ends with a vivid picture which stresses the importance of putting into practice the teachings of Jesus, of obeying his commands. Obedience leads to success, disobedience ends in failure.

6.46 TEV	RSV
"Why do you call me, 'Lord, Lord,' and yet don't do what I tell you?	"Why do you call me 'Lord, Lord,' and not do what I tell you?

A rebuke is intended. The order may be reversed: "You don't do what I tell you; so why do you call me 'Lord. Lord'?" Or else as a statement: "It does you no good to call me 'Lord, Lord' and not do what I tell you" or "You should not call me 'Lord, Lord' unless you do what I tell you."

Lord, Lord: in some languages the repetition Lord, Lord may be inappropriate; so just "Lord" or "My Lord" may be preferable. For Lord see 5.12.

6.47 TEV	RSV
Anyone who comes to me and listens to my words and obeys them—I will show you what he is like.	Every one who comes to me and hears my words and does them, I will show you what he is like:

comes to me: "to listen to me" or "to be my follower."
my words: "my teachings."

6.48 TEV	RSV
He is like a man who, in building his house, dug deep and laid the foundation on rock. The river flooded over and hit that house but could not shake it, because it was well built.	he is like a man building a house, who dug deep, and laid the foundation upon rock; and when a flood arose, the stream broke against that house, and could not shake it, because it had been well built.[w]

[w]Other ancient authorities read
founded upon the rock

in building his house: or "when he built his house." Obviously the foundation comes first, so it may be preferable to say "He is like a man who decided to build a house. He dug deep in the ground and laid (or, built) the foundation on rock."

[108]

rock: underlying rock, what is called "bedrock," and not simply stones or stony ground.

flooded over: "overflowed its banks" (as the result of heavy rains).

Textual Note: as RSV footnote shows, many Greek manuscripts and early versions, instead of "because it was well built," have "because its foundation had been laid on rock." The TEV text should be preferred.

6.49	TEV	RSV
	But anyone who hears my words and does not obey them is like a man who built his house without laying a foundation; when the flood hit that house it fell at once—and what a terrible crash that was!"	But he who hears and does not do them is like a man who built a house on the ground without a foundation; against which the stream broke, and immediately it fell, and the ruin of that house was great."

without laying a foundation: that is, he did not dig down into the soil, but simply constructed his house on the ground, with no foundation.

the flood: "the river in flood."

crash: or "it was destroyed completely," "it was a total loss."

Chapter 7

SECTION HEADING

Jesus Heals a Roman Officer's Servant: the wording of this heading will be determined by the translation of Roman officer and servant in verse 2.

The healing of the Roman officer's servant is one of the very few times that Jesus was involved with Gentiles. The Roman demonstrates strong faith in Jesus' power to cure and receives high praise from Jesus.

7.1	TEV	RSV
	When Jesus had finished saying all these things to the people, he went to Capernaum.	After he had ended all his sayings in the hearing of the people he entered Capernaum.

When Jesus had finished saying: "After Jesus said," or "Jesus finished saying all these things to the people, and then he went to Capernaum."

he went to: this is the natural way in English of saying this; RSV "he entered" is a literal translation of the Greek.

Capernaum: see 4.31.

7.2	TEV	RSV
	A Roman officer there had a servant who was very dear to him; the man was sick and about to die.	Now a centurion had a slave who was dear^x to him, who was sick and at the point of death.

^{x}Or *valuable*

Roman officer: usually the Greek word is translated by the technical term "centurion" (RSV), an officer normally in charge of 100 soldiers. The modern equivalent in rank would be something like "captain," and a translation should use a modern term. Roman troops were stationed in cities throughout Palestine, which at that time was under Roman domination.

servant: or "slave" (RSV). In verse 7 a different word is used, which RSV and TEV translate "servant." It is not necessary to use two different words in translation. It is not certain whether the man is a military aide or a slave. The best translation would be a word which designates a person who is forced to work without pay.

who was very dear to him: "whom he liked very much."

[110]

7.3

TEV

When the officer heard about Jesus, he sent some Jewish elders to ask him to come and heal his servant.

RSV

When he heard of Jesus, he sent to him elders of the Jews, asking him to come and heal his slave.

heard about Jesus: or "heard that Jesus was in Capernaum."

elders: respected religious leaders, some of whom were members of the Supreme Council in Jerusalem; a translation may use the phrase "older men" (with the implied idea of prestige), "important men."

to ask him to come: in some instances direct address may be better: "to ask him, 'Please come and heal the Roman officer's servant!'"

7.4

TEV

They came to Jesus and begged him earnestly, "This man really deserves your help.

RSV

And when they came to Jesus, they besought him earnestly, saying, "He is worthy to have you do this for him,

came: or "went"; or else, "approached." Languages differ in the matter of the point of view of movement from one place to the other. In some languages the point of departure is preferred ("went"); in others, the point of arrival ("came").

begged him earnestly: "asked him strongly (or, insistently)."

deserves your help: this expresses the elders' opinion of the officer as a good man and worthy of Jesus' help.

7.5

TEV

He loves our people and he himself built a synagogue for us."

RSV

for he loves our nation, and he built us our synagogue."

our people: that is, the Jews. Here our is inclusive, since Jesus was also a Jew. RSV "nation" is meant to refer to the people as such, not the country.

he himself built: it is to be inferred that the Roman officer paid the expenses of building the synagogue; it is not meant that he alone built the synagogue.

synagogue: see 4.15.

for us: here us is probably exclusive, since it means "us citizens of Capernaum." Jesus' hometown was Nazareth (see 4.16).

7.6

TEV

So Jesus went with them. He was not far from the house when the officer sent friends to tell him, "Sir, don't trouble yourself. I do not deserve to have you come into my house,

RSV

And Jesus went with them. When he was not far from the house, the centurion sent friends to him, saying to him, "Lord, do not trouble yourself, for I am not worthy to have you come under my roof;

the house: "the Roman officer's home."
friends: there is no way of knowing whether these people were Jews
or Romans. Most likely, however, they were Jews.
Sir: see 5.12. This is a title of respect; in translation a word
should be used which would be appropriate on the lips of an army officer.
don't trouble yourself: that is, don't take the time and effort to
come all the way to my house. As the rest of the message shows, the officer believes that Jesus can cure his servant without being present.
I do not deserve: "I am not worthy" (RSV), "I'm not important enough,"
"I don't merit." The officer regards Jesus as too important a person to
enter his house.

7.7	TEV	RSV
	neither do I consider myself worthy to come to you in person. Just give the order, and my servant will get well.	therefore I did not presume to come to you. But say the word, and let my servant be healed.

come to you in person: or "speak to you personally." The officer is
saying that there is such a great difference between himself and Jesus
that he does not have the right to address Jesus personally or have him
in his own home.
give the order: "command," "say a word." All that Jesus had to do
was give a command then and there; there was no need for him to go to the
house in person.

7.8	TEV	RSV
	I, too, am a man placed under the authority of superior officers, and I have soldiers under me. I order this one, 'Go!' and he goes; I or-der that one, 'Come!' and he comes; and I order my slave, 'Do this!' and he does it."	For I am a man set under authority, with soldiers under me: and I say to one, 'Go,' and he goes; and to another, 'Come,' and he comes; and to my slave, 'Do this,' and he does it."

I, too: the Roman officer justifies his request that Jesus give a
command by comparing Jesus to himself; he, the officer, was part of a
chain of command; he himself was under the authority of superior officers
and had authority over soldiers lower in rank than he. With this comparison he is saying that Jesus also was under authority (of God) and so
could issue orders that would be obeyed.
soldiers under me: "soldiers who have to obey my orders," "soldiers
of inferior rank."
It is not necessary to preserve the direct order of the commands in
the second part of the verse. It may be better to translate "I tell one
soldier to go, and he goes; I tell another soldier to come, and he comes;
I order my slave to do something, and he does it."

7.9 TEV	RSV
Jesus was surprised when he heard this; he turned around and said to the crowd following him, "I tell you, I have never found faith like this, not even in Israel!"	When Jesus heard this he marveled at him, and turned and said to the multitude that followed him, "I tell you, not even in Israel have I found such faith."

was surprised: "was astonished" (see 1.21). Jesus' reaction is caused by the Roman officer's belief that Jesus could effect the cure with just an oral command, without actually seeing and touching the sick man.

never found faith like this: "never found anyone who had such faith (as this man has)," "...anyone who believes as he does."

in Israel: that is, among the Jews, God's people. The translation should not make it appear that Jesus was outside the country of Israel. Jesus was saying that this Gentile—the Roman officer—was showing faith greater than that of any Jew that Jesus had met.

7.10 TEV	RSV
The messengers went back to the officer's house and found his servant well.	And when those who had been sent returned to the house, they found the slave well.

The messengers: this translates "those who had been sent" (RSV). Since The messengers were the friends mentioned in verse 6, it may be better to say here, "The officer's friends went back to his home...."

found: it must not be made to appear that the messengers were looking for him, as though he had been lost. It may be better to say "And when the messengers returned to the officer's house, they found out (or, were told) that the servant was well."

well: "healed," "in good health," "completely restored."

SECTION HEADING

Jesus Raises a Widow's Son: "Jesus Brings Back to Life a Widow's Son."

This incident, not reported by any other Gospel, shows Jesus' power over death. The extraordinary quality of the miracle is emphasized by the public nature of the act, with eyewitnesses present besides the family of the dead man.

7.11 TEV	RSV
Soon afterward[e] Jesus went to a town named Nain, accompanied by his disciples and a large crowd.	Soon afterward[y] he went to a city called Nain, and his disciples and a great crowd went with him.

[e]Soon afterward; *some manuscripts have* The next day.

[y]Other ancient authorities read *Next day*

7.11

Nain: a town some 36 kilometers southwest of Capernaum.
Textual Note: many Greek manuscripts and some early versions have "many of his disciples" and not his disciples. Modern translations prefer the text represented by RSV and TEV.

7.12

TEV	RSV
Just as he arrived at the gate of the town, a funeral procession was coming out. The dead man was the only son of a woman who was a widow, and a large crowd from the town was with her.	As he drew near to the gate of the city, behold, a man who had died was being carried out, the only son of his mother, and she was a widow; and a large crowd from the city was with her.

the gate of the town: evidently Nain was a walled city, and the gate opened up onto the main road leading out of the city. A more generic word such as "entrance" or "exit" may be used; or "the gate in the wall of (or, around) the town."
a funeral procession was coming out: this translates "a dead man was being carried out." The phrase funeral procession may not be satisfactory in some languages, and the more literal form may be preferable. If it is necessary to say how the corpse was being carried, the information in verse 14 should be included here.
There are several items of information in this verse: the dead man (in verse 14 Young man) was the only son, and his mother was a widow—which means that she was left helpless and would be dependent on relatives and friends. The phrase a large crowd shows that the woman had many friends, who were trying to console her in this time of grief.
Another way in which the verse can be translated would be as follows: "As he got near to the entrance of the town, a large crowd was coming out. A man had died and they were accompanying the body to the place of burial. The man was his mother's only son, and she was a widow."

7.13

TEV	RSV
When the Lord saw her, his heart was filled with pity for her, and he said to her, "Don't cry."	And when the Lord saw her, he had compassion on her and said to her, "Do not weep."

the Lord: see 5.12.
his heart was filled with pity for her: "he felt very sorry for her," "he was overcome with compassion for her."
Don't cry: or "Stop crying."

7.14

TEV	RSV
Then he walked over and touched the coffin, and the men carrying it stopped. Jesus said, "Young man! Get up, I tell you!"	And he came and touched the bier, and the bearers stood still. And he said, "Young man, I say to you, arise."

the coffin: RSV "the bier." This would not be an elaborate construction such as a modern casket, but a simple wooden stretcher on which the corpse would be laid and carried out for burial. (In English a bier is the stand on which a coffin is placed.)

Young man: the Greek word indicates a man probably in his late teens or early twenties.

It may be more forceful to follow the order of the Greek: "Young man, I tell you: 'Arise (or, Get up)!'"

7.15	TEV	RSV
	The dead man sat up and began to talk, and Jesus gave him back to his mother.	And the dead man sat up, and began to speak. And he gave him to his mother.

The dead man sat up: if this should appear ridiculous in some languages (a dead person doesn't sit up), it may be better to say "The young man sat up" or "The young man, now alive, sat up."

gave him back: that is, walked with him over to the man's mother. It should not appear that Jesus carried him to his mother.

7.16	TEV	RSV
	They all were filled with fear and praised God. "A great prophet has appeared among us!" they said; "God has come to save his people!"	Fear seized them all; and they glorified God, saying, "A great prophet has arisen among us!" and "God has visited his people!"

filled with fear: the same reaction as in 5.26.

praised God: "gave thanks to God" (see 5.26).

A great prophet: "An unusual (or, powerful) prophet"; for prophet see 1.70.

appeared: this translates the passive of the verb "to raise"; "has been raised" means "has been sent by God." See the use of the verb in 1.69.

has come to save: this translates the verb "has visited" (RSV), which in the Old Testament is used of God as he "visits" his people, either to save or to punish.

his people: that is, the Jews. Since these are Jews talking, it may be better to say "to save us, his people."

7.17	TEV	RSV
	This news about Jesus went out through all the country and the surrounding territory.	And this report concerning him spread through the whole of Judea and all the surrounding country.

This news about Jesus: see similar statements in 4.37; 5.15.

all the country: this translates "all of Judea, (see RSV); since Nain was in Galilee, it does not seem likely that the writer meant the province of Judea in the south (see 1.5).

surrounding territory: "the neighboring regions," that is, places outside the borders of Israel.

SECTION HEADING

The Messengers from John the Baptist: "John the Baptist Sends Messengers to Jesus," "John the Baptist Sends Two of His Disciples to Jesus."

In this long section John the Baptist appears for the first time since the beginning of Jesus' ministry, when he was baptized by John. John had been put in prison (3.20), and it is assumed that he is now in prison as he sends his message to Jesus. John the Baptist's death is not described, but Herod Antipas, governor of Galilee, refers to it (9.7-8).

7.18-19 TEV	RSV
When John's disciples told him about all these things, he called two of them 19 and sent them to the Lord to ask him, "Are you the one John said was going to come, or should we expect someone else?"	The disciples of John told him of all these things. 19 And John, calling to him two of his disciples, sent them to the Lord, saying, "Are you he who is to come, or shall we look for another?"

It may be better to have John's complete name: "The disciples of John the Baptist told him about all these things."
disciples: see 5.30.
all these things: the resurrection of the widow's only son, and the healing of the Roman officer's slave.
to the Lord: "to the Lord Jesus." In many languages it will be necessary to say explicitly "the Lord Jesus," so as to distinguish him from God, who is also spoken of as "the Lord."
to ask him: as RSV "saying" shows, in Greek this participle agrees in number and gender with John: in effect, the Greek says "John asked." But his disciples carry his message to Jesus, and he himself does not speak to him.
the one John said was going to come: see 3.16-17; "the man John was talking about when he said, 'He will come.'" The question seems prompted by the fact that Jesus' ministry did not conform to the severe picture John had drawn of "the Coming One" who would judge and punish the wicked.
John said: TEV needs this to make clear that the question refers back to what John had said in 3.16-17.
we: that is, people in general, not just John's two disciples.
Textual Note: it should be noticed that TEV and RSV differ on where verse 19 begins; TEV follows the United Bible Societies' Greek New Testament.

7.20 TEV	RSV
When they came to Jesus, they said, "John the Baptist sent us to ask if you are the one he said was	And when the men had come to him, they said, "John the Baptist has sent us to you, saying, 'Are you

going to come, or should we expect   he who is to come, or shall we look
someone else?"   for another?'"

Here, if it is more appropriate, two levels of direct discourse may
be used (as in RSV): "John the Baptist sent us to ask you: 'Are you the
one he said was going to come, or should we expect someone else?'"

7.21	TEV	RSV
	At that very time Jesus healed many people from their sicknesses, diseases, and evil spirits, and gave sight to many blind people.	In that hour he cured many of diseases and plagues and evil spirits, and on many that were blind he bestowed sight.

At that very time: the Greek "hour" (RSV) here does not mean a
sixty-minute period.

sicknesses, diseases: these two words mean the same. It is not necessary to use two different words in translation; in some languages it
will be better to use only one word.

evil spirits: literally "unclean spirits"—see 4.33. In the Greek
evil spirits is governed by the verb healed; but in some languages it
may be more appropriate to say "he expelled," or "he exorcised," or "he
drove out."

gave sight to: or "restored the sight of blind people," "made it so
that blind people could see." This describes a complete and permanent
cure.

7.22	TEV	RSV
	He answered John's messengers, "Go back and tell John what you have seen and heard: the blind can see, the lame can walk, those who suffer from dreaded skin diseases are made clean,^{f} the deaf can hear, the dead are raised to life, and the Good News is preached to the poor.	And he answered them, "Go and tell John what you have seen and heard: the blind receive their sight, the lame walk, lepers are cleansed, and the deaf hear, the dead are raised up, the poor have good news preached to them.

^{f}MADE CLEAN: *See 5.12.*

what you have seen and heard: "what you yourselves have seen and
what others have told you." This refers to the cures that are listed next.

Five of the miracles performed by Jesus are listed: the healing of
the blind, of the lame, of those suffering from skin diseases, of the
deaf, and the raising of the dead.

are made clean: for the meaning of this see 5.12.

the Good News is preached to the poor: or "the poor are hearing the
Good News"; or "people are proclaiming the Good News to the poor."

the poor: this is meant literally of destitute people; it does not
mean "spiritually poor."

7.23   TEV   RSV
How happy are those who have no   And blessed is he who takes no of-
doubts about me!"   fense at me."

    happy: see 6.20.
    have no doubts about me: "are not offended by what I do," or "who
don't lose their faith in me," "whose faith in me is not destroyed (or,
weakened) by what I do." There is here an implicit rebuke of John, who
doubted that Jesus was the Messiah. He doubted because of the activities
of Jesus.
    Some translations might wish to start a new section with verse 24
(through verse 35), which can be entitled: "Jesus Talks about John the
Baptist."

7.24   TEV   RSV
    After John's messengers had   When the messengers of John had
left, Jesus began to speak about   gone, he began to speak to the
him to the crowds: "When you went   crowds concerning John: "What did
out to John in the desert, what did   you go out into the winderness to
you expect to see? A blade of grass   behold? A reed shaken by the wind?
bending in the wind?

    the crowds: that is, "the very large crowd"; this does not mean dif-
ferent groups of people, but one large group.
    went out to John: "went out to hear John," "...to listen to John's
message." Or the whole question can be phrased, "What did you expect to
see when you went out to listen to John?"
    the desert: see 3.2.
    A blade of grass: here this is a figure of a weak, uncertain, vacil-
lating man, one who did not have strong convictions and would easily be
swayed by public opinion.
    The question in this verse expects a negative answer: "No, you didn't
go out for that purpose."

7.25   TEV   RSV
What did you go out to see? A man   What then did you go out to see? A
dressed up in fancy clothes? Peo-   man clothed in soft clothing? Behold,
ple who dress like that and live in   those who are gorgeously appareled
luxury are found in palaces!   and live in luxury are in kings'
                                        courts.

    dressed up in fancy clothes: a figure of a rich man who cares only
for material things, for physical comforts; one who indulges himself.
    live in luxury: a style of living characterized by spending money on
unnecessary, expensive things. The question in this verse also expects a
negative answer: "No, you didn't go out expecting to find a rich man living out in the desert."

7.26   TEV
Tell me, what did you go out to
see? A prophet? Yes indeed, but you
saw much more than a prophet.

                         RSV
What then did you go out to see? A
prophet? Yes, I tell you, and more
than a prophet.

prophet: see 1.70.
much more than a prophet: "one who is much greater than a prophet"
or "a very extraordinary prophet." Jesus was not denying that John was a
prophet; he was saying that John's mission was more important than that
of the average prophet.

7.27   TEV
For John is the one of whom the
scripture says: 'God said, I will
send my messenger ahead of you to
open the way for you.'

                         RSV
This is he of whom it is written,
  'Behold, I send my messenger be-
    fore thy face,
  who shall prepare thy way before
    thee.'

of whom the scripture says: "referred to (or, spoken of) in the (passage of) scripture that says."
the scripture: see 2.23.
God said: these words are necessary in order to identify the speaker
in I will send; otherwise it might appear that Jesus is speaking of himself. The passage quoted is Malachi 3.1, where the messenger is sent to
prepare the way for God himself; here, however, you refers to Jesus and
my messenger is John the Baptist. If possible, it is better not to be
specific about who you is; but if it must be made specific, it can be "I
will send my messenger ahead of the Messiah," "...ahead of the Christ."
open the way: "prepare the road," "make the road ready for your coming."

7.28   TEV
I tell you," Jesus added, "John is
greater than any man who has ever
lived. But he who is least in the
Kingdom of God is greater than
John."

                         RSV
I tell you, among those born of wom-
en none is greater than John; yet he
who is least in the kingdom of God
is greater than he."

greater: "more important."
any man: "any person," "anyone."
any man who has ever lived: literally "those born of women" (RSV).
he who is least: "the one who is least important," "the most insignificant."
Kingdom of God: see 4.43. In this comparison, by implication John
the Baptist is not part of the Kingdom of God; John belongs to the old
order; he was the point of transition between the old and the new. He was
the culmination of the old, but not part of the new. And the new order is
superior to the old order.

TEV	RSV
All the people heard him; they and especially the tax collectors were the ones who had obeyed God's righteous demands and had been baptized by John.	(When they heard this all the people and the tax collectors justified God, having been baptized with the baptism of John;

As RSV parentheses show, this is an explanatory note by the Gospel writer, not the words of Jesus. Some, however, take them as part of Jesus' words to the crowd—for which (as shown below) certain changes will have to be made in translation.

All the people heard him: TEV takes him to be Jesus; but it could refer to John (see below). Since in this verse All the people and the tax collectors are contrasted with the Pharisees and the teachers of the Law in the next verse, it seems likely that people here means "common people, "average folk," "the mass of people."

and especially the tax collectors: something like this is necessary, since tax collectors are people also; perhaps it would be better to say "including also the tax collectors." For tax collectors see 3.12.

had obeyed God's righteous demands: this translates the phrase "justified God" (RSV). The verb means to acknowledge or declare someone is right or just. Here, in connection with John the Baptist's message and his demand that people be baptized, the verb indicates that by means of their baptism these people recognized, or confessed, God's "justice." Or else, in the sense of "putting (someone) in the right," the verb may be understood to mean that these people, by being baptized, admitted that John the Baptist's message was from God and should be obeyed. TEV has attempted to include these two shades of meaning by translating obeyed God's righteous demands.

But some take the words to mean "praised God," "gave God due praise, "praised God for his goodness." This supposes that the verbal phrase refers to what these people did at that very time when Jesus spoke to them about John, whereas TEV takes it to refer to their action when they heard John's message. It is difficult to be dogmatic about which interpretation is to be preferred, but it seems clear enough that the two verses, 29 and 30, must be interpreted in the same way. Verse 30 hardly reads as a statement of what the Pharisees and teachers of the Law did when they heard Jesus praise John; it describes how they had reacted to John's message. On this basis it would appear that TEV is correct in regarding verses 29-30 as a statement of how the people had reacted to John's message of repentance and baptism.

and had been baptized by John: or "because they had been baptized by John."

It seems preferable—following the interpretation given by TEV—to translate verse 29 as follows: "All the common people, including the tax collectors, who had heard John, had obeyed God's righteous demands and had been baptized by John."

But if the translation follows the RSV interpretation, that this verse describes how Jesus' hearers reacted to his high praise of John, a translation could say "When they heard him say this, all the people there including the tax collectors, praised God, because they had been baptized by John the Baptist."

7.30 TEV	RSV
But the Pharisees and the teachers of the Law rejected God's purpose for themselves and refused to be baptized by John.	but the Pharisees and the lawyers rejected the purpose of God for themselves, not having been baptized by him.)

the Pharisees and the teachers of the Law: see 5.17.

rejected God's purpose for themselves: "did not do what God wanted them to do," "refused to obey God's will for them."

Since this refers (as TEV interprets it) to what had happened during John's ministry, it would be better to translate "But the Pharisees and the teachers of the Law had rejected God's purpose for them, and had refused to be baptized by John."

If the translation takes verses 29-30 to be Jesus' words, that is, part of his speech to the crowd, the translation could be something like this:

> 29 "And all the common people, including the tax collectors, let John baptize them, and in this way they obeyed God's demands. 30 But the Pharisees and the teachers of the Law did not let John baptize them, and in this way they refused to do what God wanted them to do.

7.31 TEV	RSV
Jesus continued, "Now to what can I compare the people of this day? What are they like?	"To what then shall I compare the men of this generation, and what are they like?

Jesus continued: this follows the TEV interpretation that verses 29-30 are the writer's comment; if verses 29-30 are translated as the words of Jesus, then verse 31 will begin without these introductory words.

to what can I compare: "what shall I say (the people of this day) are like?" Or as a statement: "I will tell you what the people of this day are like." The text has two separate questions (as TEV and RSV show), but they mean the same, and it may be more natural to use only one question in translation.

the people of this day: "this generation" (RSV), "the people living now."

7.32 TEV	RSV

They are like children sitting in the marketplace. One group shouts to the other, 'We played wedding music for you, but you wouldn't dance! We sang funeral songs, but you wouldn't cry!'	They are like children sitting in the market place and calling to one another,
	  'We piped to you, and you did
	    not dance;
	  we wailed, and you did not weep.'

7.32

the marketplace: or "the streets," or "the parks"—wherever children get together to play.

We played: the Greek word indicates "play on a flute," which RSV "We piped" means to represent.

wedding music...funeral songs: the first group of children tries to get the other group to play with them, either in a make-believe wedding or a make-believe funeral, but the second group isn't willing, in either instance. Jesus compares his contemporaries to this second group of children.

7.33   TEV   RSV

TEV	RSV
John the Baptist came, and he fasted and drank no wine, and you said, 'He has a demon in him!'	For John the Baptist has come eating no bread and drinking no wine; and you say, 'He has a demon.'

John the Baptist came: "John the Baptist came proclaiming his message."

fasted: see 5.33. The literal "eating no bread" (RSV) means "not eating any food."

drank no wine: "abstained from drinking wine." John is pictured as an ascetic, a man who would not indulge in any luxuries.

He has a demon in him!: John's behavior was so strange that some people thought he was possessed by a demon.

7.34   TEV   RSV

TEV	RSV
The Son of Man came, and he ate and drank, and you said, 'Look at this man! He is a glutton and wine-drinker, a friend of tax collectors and other outcasts!'	The Son of man has come eating and drinking; and you say, 'Behold, a glutton and a drunkard, a friend of tax collectors and sinners!'

Son of Man: see 5.24.

he ate and drank: "he enjoyed eating and drinking (wine)." Jesus was a person who enjoyed eating with others and who enjoyed the simple pleasures of life.

He is a glutton and wine-drinker: "He eats too much and drinks too much," "He's always eating and drinking."

tax collectors: see 5.27.

other outcasts: see 5.30.

7.35   TEV   RSV

TEV	RSV
God's wisdom, however, is shown to be true by all who accept it."	Yet wisdom is justified by all her children."

God's wisdom: the Greek says only "wisdom" (RSV), but in the context it seems clear that Jesus is not speaking of human wisdom but of divine wisdom. In the context, this saying means that the results of any course of action will determine whether it was dictated by divine wisdom or by human folly. The contemporaries of Jesus were not following God's instructions, and the results of their actions would prove it.

[122]

shown to be true: this translates the same Greek verb, "justify," used in verse 29.

all who accept it: literally "her children" (RSV).

SECTION HEADING

Jesus at the Home of Simon the Pharisee: "Jesus and the Sinful Woman."

This incident serves to illustrate the different ways in which people reacted to Jesus. On the one hand, a sinful woman, conscious of her needs, accepts him; a Law-obeying Pharisee, proud of his righteousness, rejects him. They are reacting to him as people had to John the Baptist. Nothing is said about the time or place of this incident.

7.36 TEV	RSV
A Pharisee invited Jesus to have dinner with him, and Jesus went to his house and sat down to eat.	One of the Pharisees asked him to eat with him, and he went into the Pharisee's house, and took his place at table.

have dinner: "have a meal." The main meal of the day was served around 3:00 p.m.

sat down: "reclined" (see 5.29).

7.37 TEV	RSV
In that town was a woman who lived a sinful life. She heard that Jesus was eating in the Pharisee's house, so she brought an alabaster jar full of perfume	And behold, a woman of the city, who was a sinner, when she learned that he was at table in the Pharisee's house, brought an alabaster flask of ointment,

lived a sinful life: "was immoral," "was a prostitute."

brought: "took with her," "carried," "took."

alabaster: a soft stone of light, creamy color, from which vases and jars were made. A more generic term may be used: "a stone jar," "an expensive jar." Or else the jar can be described explicitly: "a jar made of stone called alabaster."

perfume: or "ointment" (RSV); "fragrant anointing oil," meant to be used on the head.

7.38 TEV	RSV
and stood behind Jesus, by his feet, crying and wetting his feet with her tears. Then she dried his feet with her hair, kissed them, and poured the perfume on them.	and standing behind him at his feet, weeping, she began to wet his feet with her tears, and wiped them with the hair of her head, and kissed his feet, and anointed them with the ointment.

behind Jesus, by his feet: this can be understood only if it is clear that Jesus is reclining, full-length, on cushions or rugs, and not sitting on a bench or chair.

wetting his feet with her tears: it should not appear that the woman did this on purpose. "She was crying, and her tears fell on Jesus' feet."

Verses 37-38 may be restructured as follows: "A prostitute in that town heard that Jesus was having a meal in the Pharisee's house. So she went there, taking an alabaster jar full of perfume. As she stood behind Jesus, at his feet, she began to cry, and her tears fell on Jesus' feet. Then she dried his feet with her hair, kissed them, and poured the perfume on them."

7.39	TEV	RSV
	When the Pharisee saw this, he said to himself, "If this man really were a prophet, he would know who this woman is who is touching him; he would know what kind of sinful life she lives!"	Now when the Pharisee who had invited him saw it, he said to himself, "If this man were a prophet, he would have known who and what sort of woman this is who is touching him, for she is a sinner."

said to himself: or "thought."

TEV omits as redundant "who had invited him" (RSV). If a translator wants to include this, the translation could say "When his host, the Pharisee, saw this...."

a prophet: here in the sense of "a man of God," one who should be able to judge people's character. The Pharisee is saying that Jesus is not a prophet. So the translation could be "This man is not a prophet, for he doesn't know what kind of person this woman is who is touching him."

As RSV shows, the Greek says "who and what kind of woman this is." It is not necessary to represent these two expressions, for they mean the same thing.

he would know what kind of sinful life she lives: "he would know she is a prostitute."

7.40	TEV	RSV
	Jesus spoke up and said to him, "Simon, I have something to tell you." "Yes, Teacher," he said, "tell me."	And Jesus answering said to him, "Simon, I have something to say to you." And he answered, "What is it, Teacher?"

spoke up: RSV "answering" is not quite appropriate. Jesus senses the Pharisee's attitude, and so he speaks.

Simon: for the first time the Pharisee's name is given.

Teacher: a title of respect; in Hebrew, "Rabbi."

7.41   TEV

"There were two men who owed
money to a moneylender," Jesus began. "One owed him five hundred
silver coins, and the other owed
him fifty.

RSV

"A certain creditor had two debtors;
one owed five hundred denarii, and
the other fifty.

The two amounts owed the moneylender are 500 denarii and 50 denarii.
A denarius was the daily wage of a rural worker at that time. The important thing in translation is not to find an equivalent amount in terms of
purchasing power, but to maintain the ratio of ten to one between the
amounts owed. It may be enough to say "One owed ten times as much as the
other." Some translations may prefer to use the name of the coin, "denarius," and explain it in a footnote or in a Word List.

Jesus began: in some languages it may be better to say "Jesus said."
It may be better to reverse the order of components: "Two men went
to a man whose business was lending money, and borrowed some money. One
borrowed five hundred (silver) coins and the other borrowed fifty (silver)
coins."

7.42   TEV

Neither of them could pay him back,
so he canceled the debts of both.
Which one, then, will love him
more?"

RSV

When they could not pay, he forgave
them both. Now which of them will
love him more?"

canceled the debts of both: or "said to both of them, 'You don't
have to pay back what you owe me.'" Some languages are able to use the
equivalent of RSV, "he forgave them both."

will love him more: "will be more grateful," "will like him better."
But the Greek verb is "to love," and it is probably better to represent
it in translation.

7.43   TEV

"I suppose," answered Simon,
"that it would be the one who was
forgiven more."
"You are right," said Jesus.

RSV

Simon answered, "The one, I suppose,
to whom he forgave more." And he
said to him, "You have judged rightly."

I suppose: "In my opinion," "I should think," "It seems to me."
the one who was forgiven more: "the one whose debt was greater,"
"the one who owed the larger amount."
You are right: "You have answered correctly," "Your answer is correct."

7.44   TEV

Then he turned to the woman and
said to Simon, "Do you see this woman? I came into your home, and you

RSV

Then turning toward the woman he
said to Simon, "Do you see this woman? I entered your house, you gave

gave me no water for my feet, but
she has washed my feet with her
tears and dried them with her hair.

me no water for my feet, but she
has wet my feet with her tears and
wiped them with her hair.

In verses 44-46 Jesus describes the woman's actions in contrast
with those of his host.

Do you see this woman?: with this question Jesus is calling Simon's
attention to what the woman has been doing. "You see this woman, don't
you?" or "You see what this woman has been doing, don't you?"

no water for my feet: "no water for me to wash my feet"—this was a
common courtesy as guests came in off the dusty roads and streets.

7.45-46   TEV

You did not welcome me with a kiss,
but she has not stopped kissing my
feet since I came. 46 You provided
no olive oil for my head, but she
has covered my feet with perfume.

RSV

You gave me no kiss, but from the
time I came in she has not ceased
to kiss my feet. 46 You did not
anoint my head with oil, but she
has anointed my feet with ointment.

welcome...with a kiss: a normal way of welcoming a guest, with a
kiss on the cheeks.

no olive oil for my head: a host would provide olive oil for his
guest to rub on his hair and face, as a tonic and restorative, after coming in from the hot sun.

7.47   TEV

I tell you, then, the great love
she has shown proves that her many
sins have been forgiven. But whoever has been forgiven little shows
only a little love."

RSV

Therefore I tell you, her sins,
which are many, are forgiven, for
she loved much; but he who is forgiven little, loves little."

A comparison of RSV with TEV shows that the two differ on the meaning of the first part of this verse. RSV interprets the Greek to mean
"Her great love is the reason why her many sins are forgiven." TEV takes
the Greek to mean "Her great love is evidence of the fact that her many
sins are forgiven."

The TEV interpretation fits better with what follows: "he who is
forgiven little, loves little" (so RSV). That is, little love is evidence
of being forgiven little. And the TEV interpretation makes more sense in
relation to the parable, whose point is not that the debtors were forgiven because they loved; rather, their different levels of love were
evidence of having been forgiven different amounts, one more, one less.
It is recommended that the TEV interpretation be preferred.

7.48   TEV

Then Jesus said to the woman,
"Your sins are forgiven."

RSV

And he said to her, "Your sins are
forgiven."

Your sins are forgiven: see 5.20.

7.49   TEV   RSV
     The others sitting at the   Then those who were at table with
table began to say to themselves,   him began to say among themselves,
"Who is this, who even forgives   "Who is this, who even forgives
sins?"   sins?"

     The reaction of the other guests is the same as that recorded in
5.21.
     The others sitting at the table: "The other guests," "The other peo-
ple who were eating."
     The question Who is this...? may be a genuine question; but it seems
more likely that it implies condemnation (as in 5.21): "Who does he think
he is...?" It may be better to say "Who is this man...?"

7.50   TEV   RSV
     But Jesus said to the woman,   And he said to the woman, "Your faith
"Your faith has saved you; go in   has saved you; go in peace."
peace."

     Your faith has saved you: "You are saved because of your faith" or
"...because you believe." If an object is needed, it could be either
"faith in God" or "faith in me."
     in peace: without any doubts or worries, full of assurance and con-
fidence.

Chapter 8

SECTION HEADING

Women Who Accompanied Jesus: "Some Women Who Traveled with (or, Who Helped) Jesus and His Disciples."

This bit of information is in keeping with the nature of this Gospel, which gives prominence to women, their faith, and their activities.

8.1 TEV	RSV
Some time later Jesus traveled through towns and villages, preaching the Good News about the Kingdom of God. The twelve disciples went with him,	Soon afterward he went on through cities and villages, preaching and bringing the good news of the kingdom of God. And the twelve were with him,

Some time later: a vague expression of time, similar to the one in 7.11.
 preaching: see 3.3.
 the Kingdom of God: see 4.43.
 The twelve disciples: as RSV shows, the Greek text says only "the twelve"; most languages will have to say The twelve disciples.

8.2 TEV	RSV
and so did some women who had been healed of evil spirits and diseases: Mary (who was called Magdalene), from whom seven demons had been driven out;	and also some women who had been healed of evil spirits and infirmities: Mary, called Magdalene, from whom seven demons had gone out,

who had been healed: it may not be clear that they had been healed by Jesus, so it may be better to say "some women whom Jesus had healed and from whom he had driven out evil spirits."
 healed of evil spirits and diseases: see the similar statement in 7.21.
 Magdalene: this means "from Magdala," a town on the west bank of Lake Galilee.
 seven demons: here the Greek word for "demons" is used, meaning the same as "evil spirits"; see 4.33.
 had been driven out: that is, by Jesus.

[128]

8.3 TEV	RSV
Joanna, whose husband Chuza was an officer in Herod's court; and Susanna, and many other women who used their own resources to help Jesus and his disciples.	and Joanna, the wife of Chuza, Herod's steward, and Susanna, and many others, who provided for them[z] out of their means.

[z]Other ancient authorities read *him*

an officer: the Greek word means "administrator," "manager," "steward" (RSV). His specific duties are not clear, but they were probably in the area of finances.

Herod: Herod Antipas, governor of Galilee (see 3.1).

their own resources: that is, their money, their possessions. They paid the costs of food and lodging for Jesus and his disciples.

Jesus and his disciples: this translates the Greek "them" (RSV); as RSV footnote shows, some Greek manuscripts and many early versions have "him," that is, Jesus. The plural "them" is to be preferred.

SECTION HEADING

The Parable of the Sower: "The Story of the Man Who Sowed Grain," "The Parable of the Soils."

In this Gospel the section on the parables about the Kingdom is shorter than in Matthew 13 and Mark 4. After telling the first parable (verses 4-8), Jesus speaks of the purpose of the parables (verses 9-10) and then explains this parable (verses 11-15). After this he tells another parable, together with related parabolic sayings (verses 16-18).

8.4 TEV	RSV
People kept coming to Jesus from one town after another; and when a great crowd gathered, Jesus told this parable:	And when a great crowd came together and people from town after town came to him, he said in a parable:

A comparison of TEV with RSV shows that TEV attempts a more natural style by speaking first of people as they came to Jesus from different towns, and then of the crowd that was formed. RSV follows the order of the Greek text. The text does not say where Jesus was when he told these parables.

parable: see 5.36.

8.5 TEV	RSV
"Once there was a man who went out to sow grain. As he scattered the seed in the field, some of it fell along the path, where it was stepped on, and the birds ate it up.	"A sower went out to sow his seed; and as he sowed, some fell along the path, and was trodden under foot, and the birds of the air devoured it.

Once: this is a conventional way in English of beginning a story which is not specifically located in time.

a man: RSV translates literally "A sower," but it should not appear that the only thing this man did was to sow grain, and nothing else.

went out: "went out to his field."

to sow grain: at that time grain seed (wheat or barley) was scattered by hand on the soil as the farmer walked through his field. In some translations it will be helpful if a footnote is added which explains how sowing was done in Palestine at that time.

As he scattered the seed in the field: "As he sowed the grain."

along the path: the soil on the narrow footpath through the field would be hard, and the seeds would lie exposed on the ground, making it easy for birds to eat them.

where it was stepped on: "where people stepped on it," as they walked on the path.

birds: wild birds, not domesticated fowl.

8.6	TEV	RSV
	Some of it fell on rocky ground, and when the plants sprouted, they dried up because the soil had no moisture.	And some fell on the rock; and as it grew up, it withered away, because it had no moisture.

rocky ground: that part of the field where there was a thin layer of soil over the underlying bedrock. This explains why the soil had no moisture; the moisture would quickly evaporate under the hot sun.

8.7	TEV	RSV
	Some of the seed fell among thorn bushes, which grew up with the plants and choked them.	And some fell among thorns; and the thorns grew with it and choked it.

thorn bushes: "briers," "thistles," "brambles." It is enough to refer to any common weed or plant (preferably one that has thorns) that grows naturally and quickly. What the parable describes is that these bushes had been cleared off but had not been taken out by the roots, so that they grew up quickly at the same time the grain sprouted and grew.

choked them: "made it impossible for them to bear grain" or "stopped them from growing." In some languages this is expressed by "they threw a shadow over them."

8.8	TEV	RSV
	And some seeds fell in good soil; the plants grew and bore grain, one hundred grains each."	And some fell into good soil and grew, and yielded a hundredfold."
	And Jesus concluded, "Listen, then, if you have ears!"	As he said this, he called out, "He who has ears to hear, let him hear."

good soil: "rich soil," "fertile ground."

bore grain: "produced a good harvest," "there was a good crop."

one hundred grains each: it may be preferable to have a separate sentence for this information: "And each plant (or, stalk) produced one hundred grains."

Listen, then, if you have ears: the meaning of this command may be expressed "If you can hear, pay close attention!" It is not to be thought that the saying puts in doubt whether the listeners have ears, that is, whether they can hear; it is a vivid way of telling them to pay attention. "You have ears, don't you? Well, then, listen to what I'm saying!"

SECTION HEADING

The Purpose of the Parables: "Why Jesus Told Parables."

8.9-10   TEV

His disciples asked Jesus what this parable meant, 10 and he answered, "The knowledge of the secrets of the Kingdom of God has been given to you, but to the rest it comes by means of parables, so that they may look but not see, and listen but not understand.

RSV

And when his disciples asked him what this parable meant, 10 he said, "To you it has been given to know the secrets of the kingdom of God; but for others they are in parables, so that seeing they may not see, and hearing they may not understand.

the secrets: "the secret truths," "the truths people cannot discover," "the truths that others don't know."

the Kingdom of God: see 4.43.

has been given to you: "God has given to you," "God has made you able to know (or, understand)." Here you means the twelve disciples. The whole saying may be translated, "God has made it possible for you to know the secret (or, unknown) truths about the Kingdom of God."

to the rest: to other people.

it comes by means of parables: the Greek says only "but to the others in parables"; TEV takes The knowledge of the secrets of the Kingdom of God to be implied; RSV takes "secrets" to be implied. Better than either one would be something like "but to other people the secret truths are told (or, taught) by means of parables."

so that they may look but not see, and listen but not understand: this language is taken from Isaiah 6.9-10. Another way of expressing it would be "so that even if they look hard they will not see, and even if they listen closely they will not hear (or, understand)." Since God has not given these people the knowledge of the secret truths about the Kingdom of God, they do not understand.

SECTION HEADING

Jesus Explains the Parable of the Sower: "Jesus Tells His Disciples What the Parable of the Sower Means" or "...What the Parable of the Soils Means."

[131]

8.11

TEV	RSV
"This is what the parable means: the seed is the word of God.	Now the parable is this: The seed is the word of God.

the word of God: "the message from God"; this is Jesus' own message (see 5.1).

8.12 TEV	RSV
The seeds that fell along the path stand for those who hear; but the Devil comes and takes the message away from their hearts in order to keep them from believing and being saved.	The ones along the path are those who have heard; then the devil comes and takes away the word from their hearts, that they may not believe and be saved.

along the path: see verse 5.
stand for: "represent," "are a figure of," "symbolize."
the Devil: see 4.2.
the message: literally, "the word"—referring to the word of God in verse 11.
takes...away from their hearts: this language may cause some difficulty. The Devil's action is compared to that of the birds that ate up the seeds on the path. It may be better to say something like "causes them to forget" or "makes their hearts (or, minds) as though they had never heard."
believing: that is, the message.

8.13 TEV	RSV
The seeds that fell on rocky ground stand for those who hear the message and receive it gladly. But it does not sink deep into them; they believe only for a while but when the time of testing comes, they fall away.	And the ones on the rock are those who, when they hear the word, receive it with joy; but these have no root, they believe for a while and in time of temptation fall away.

See verse 6.
does not sink deep into them: literally "these have no root," that is, no depth of understanding or commitment. This is a figure of superficial hearing, without any lasting effects.
the time of testing comes: "when things happen that test their faith." A way of speaking about troubles, difficulties, persecutions.
they fall away: the Greek verb is related to the noun that means "apostasy"; it means to abandon, to defect, to forsake. Here it is to lose faith in the Christian message, to quit believing.

8.14 TEV	RSV
The seeds that fell among thorn bushes stand for those who hear;	And as for what fell among the thorns, they are those who hear, but

but the worries and riches and pleasures of this life crowd in and choke them, and their fruit never ripens.	as they go on their way they are choked by the cares and riches and pleasures of life, and their fruit does not mature.

See verse 7.

hear: "listen to," or even (in this context) "believe." There is a progression in the condition of the hearers in verses 12,13,14.

As RSV shows, there is in Greek a participle translated "as they go on their way." This may mean "eventually," "in the course of time," "as time goes by," which is not made explicit in TEV. The idea can be made explicit as follows: "...those who hear; but as time goes by the worries and riches..." or "...but little by little the worries...."

worries: "troubles," "anxieties."

riches and pleasures: although apparently desirable, they serve to distract the mind from spiritual matters, and so are harmful.

crowd in and choke them: these two verbs translate one Greek verb which is in the passive voice, "they are choked by" (RSV).

their fruit never ripens: the spiritual lesson is clear enough; their faith never reaches fulfillment in deeds and actions.

8.15 TEV	RSV
The seeds that fell in good soil stand for those who hear the message and retain it in a good and obedient heart, and they persist until they bear fruit.	And as for that in the good soil, they are those who, hearing the word, hold it fast in an honest and good heart, and bring forth fruit with patience.

See verse 8.

good and obedient heart: "loyal and good," or "very good."

they persist: "they hold fast," "they endure" (the opposite of those who give up in verse 13).

SECTION HEADING

A Lamp under a Bowl: "A Lamp Is for Giving Light."

8.16 TEV	RSV
"No one lights a lamp and covers it with a bowl or puts it under a bed. Instead, he puts it on the lampstand, so that people will see the light as they come in.	"No one after lighting a lamp covers it with a vessel, or puts it under a bed, but puts it on a stand, that those who enter may see the light.

a lamp: an oil-burning wick lamp, the wick lying in a shallow clay bowl filled with olive oil.

a bowl: for holding grain. It is not absolutely necessary to specify the object with which the lamp is covered; it is enough to say "...and then covers it up...."

[133]

8.16

> a bed: if "bed" is a mat spread flat on the floor, something like "bench" or "sleeping platform" will have to be used.
> the lampstand: in the poorer homes this would be a niche in the wall, high enough so that the light would shine all over the room.

8.17

TEV	RSV
"Whatever is hidden away will be brought out into the open, and whatever is covered up will be found and brought to light.	For nothing is hid that shall not be made manifest, nor anything secret that shall not be known and come to light.

There is no obvious relation between this saying and the one that comes before, other than the idea of light shining and revealing. This verse says that eventually all secret truths about the Kingdom of God will be revealed. The same thing is said in two statements. The time when the revelation will take place is the final Day of Judgment; and the passive verbs denote divine activity: "God will reveal...God will uncover and show."

8.18

TEV	RSV
"Be careful, then, how you listen; because whoever has something will be given more, but whoever has nothing will have taken away from him even the little he thinks he has."	Take heed then how you hear; for to him who has will more be given, and from him who has not, even what he thinks that he has will be taken away."

> then: this means that this saying is an inference from the preceding saying, but the precise connection is not clear.
> will be given more: God is the giver; "God will give more to that person." In the same way will have taken away from him represents divine activity: "God will take away from him."
> has nothing...the little he thinks he has: logically this seems to be a contradiction, since someone who has nothing can hardly think he has a little. But this is a way of expressing having a small amount; the meaning is that whoever does not wish to listen and learn, even the little that he understands about the Kingdom of God will be taken away from him.

SECTION HEADING

> Jesus' Mother and Brothers: "Jesus' Family," "Jesus' Real Family."

In this brief account, the family of Jesus appears for the first time since the account of the birth of Jesus and of the visit to Jerusalem when he was twelve years old (chapters 1 and 2).

8.19 TEV	RSV
Jesus' mother and brothers came to him, but were unable to join him because of the crowd.	Then his mother and his brothers came to him, but they could not reach him for the crowd.

brothers: some interpreters, especially Roman Catholics, take the Greek word for "brother" in the general sense of "relative" and not in the restricted sense of "(blood) brother," because of the teaching that Mary had no children besides Jesus. Some translations, therefore, such as Bible de Jérusalem, in some passages add a footnote saying that the word does not mean brothers but cousins or relatives. But it is to be noticed that some Roman Catholic translations (such as New American Bible) translate "brothers" in the text and do not have any note; and the interconfessional Traduction oecuménique de la Bible and La Biblia interconfessional: Nuevo Testamento do the same. The translation should read brothers; whether a footnote indicating this other point of view should be added will depend on the local situation.

because of the crowd: as in 5.19.

8.20-21 TEV	RSV
Someone said to Jesus, "Your mother and brothers are standing outside and want to see you." 21 Jesus said to them all, "My mother and brothers are those who hear the word of God and obey it."	And he was told, "Your mother and your brothers are standing outside, desiring to see you." 21 But he said to them, "My mother and my brothers are those who hear the word of God and do it."

outside: that is, outside the house Jesus was in.

them all: TEV shows clearly that Jesus is talking to all the people there, not to his mother and brothers.

the word of God: as in verse 11.

obey it: "do what it commands," "put it into practice."

SECTION HEADING

Jesus Calms a Storm: "Jesus Commands a Storm to Stop."

This incident shows the power of Jesus over the forces of nature, which were seen not simply as impersonal powers, but as evil forces which threatened to undo the order imposed on creation by God. In the same way that Jesus ordered evil spirits out of people (4.35,41) and ordered the fever to leave Simon Peter's mother-in-law (4.39), so he orders the winds and the waves to stop.

8.22 TEV	RSV
One day Jesus got into a boat with his disciples and said to them,	One day he got into a boat with his disciples, and he said to them,

"Let us go across to the other side   "Let us go across to the other side
of the lake." So they started out.   of the lake." So they set out,

     One day: a vague expression of time (see 5.17).
     a boat: a sailboat (see verse 23, sailing).
     his disciples: it is not said how many of them were with him, pre-
sumably all twelve. It may be better to say "Jesus and his disciples got
into a boat."
     the other side: the east side.
     the lake: Lake Galilee, which in this Gospel is called Lake Gennes-
aret (see 5.1). A translation may wish to make the name explicit.

8.23   TEV   RSV
As they were sailing, Jesus fell   And as they sailed he fell asleep.
asleep. Suddenly a strong wind blew   And a storm of wind came down on
down on the lake, and the boat be-   the lake, and they were filling with
gan to fill with water, so that   water, and were in danger.
they were all in great danger.

     the boat began to fill with water: this translates the verb "they
were filling"; a literal translation (see RSV) may give the impression
that Jesus and the disciples were filling with water, instead of the
boat. The huge waves created by the strong wind filled the boat with
water and threatened to sink it.

8.24   TEV   RSV
The disciples went to Jesus and   And they went and woke him, saying,
woke him up, saying, "Master, Mas-   "Master, Master, we are perishing!"
ter! We are about to die!"   And he awoke and rebuked the wind
     Jesus got up and gave an order   and the raging waves; and they
to the wind and to the stormy   ceased, and there was a calm.
water; they quieted down, and there
was a great calm.

     Master: see 5.5.
     We are about to die: "We are in danger of dying," "We're drowning."
The We here is inclusive: it means the disciples and Jesus, and not just
the disciples. They were concerned not only for their own safety but for
Jesus' safety also.
     gave an order: "commanded," "rebuked" (RSV); the same verb which in
4.35,41 is used with evil spirits, and in 4.39 is used with the fever.

8.25   TEV   RSV
Then he said to the disciples,   He said to them, "Where is your
"Where is your faith?"   faith?" And they were afraid, and
     But they were amazed and   they marveled, saying to one another,
afraid, and said to one another,   "Who then is this, that he commands
"Who is this man? He gives orders   even wind and water, and they obey
to the winds and waves, and they   him?"
obey him!"

Where is your faith?: this is a rebuke. "Why don't you have faith?" "Why don't you believe in me?"

amazed: see 2.18.

afraid: this is fear mixed with awe (see 5.26).

Who is this man?: this is an expression of amazement and wonder. They really do not know how Jesus is able to do what he did.

He gives orders to the winds and waves: "He commands even the winds and waves."

SECTION HEADING

Jesus Heals a Man with Demons: "Jesus Heals a Man Possessed by Demons," "Jesus Drives Out Demons from a Man."

This incident takes place on the east side of Lake Galilee, in Gentile territory. There is considerable confusion over the name of the place, but it seems to have been one of the ten semi-independent Greek towns known as the Decapolis (TEV the Ten Towns).

8.26 TEV	RSV
Jesus and his disciples sailed on over to the territory of Gerasa,*g* which is across the lake from Galilee.	Then they arrived at the country of the Gerasenes,*a* which is opposite Galilee.
*g*GERASA; *some manuscripts have* Gadara *(see Mt 8.28); others have* Gergesa.	*a*Other ancient authorities read *Gadarenes*, others *Gergesenes*

Jesus and his disciples: TEV makes this explicit (RSV "they"), since this is the beginning of a new section.

Gerasa: as the footnotes in RSV and TEV show, there is disagreement among the Greek manuscripts and early versions as to the name of the place. Gerasa was one of the Ten Towns, about 60 kilometers southeast of Lake Galilee; Gadara (Matt 8.28) was another of the Ten Towns, some 8 kilometers south of the lake; and Gergesa seems to have been right on the shore of the lake. Most modern translations follow the text represented in RSV and TEV.

8.27 TEV	RSV
As Jesus stepped ashore, he was met by a man from the town who had demons in him. For a long time this man had gone without clothes and would not stay at home, but spent his time in the burial caves.	And as he stepped out on land, there met him a man from the city who had demons; for a long time he had worn no clothes, and he lived not in a house but among the tombs.

    <u>he was met</u>: some languages distinguish between accidental and intentional meetings; in such languages the expression used here should denote an intentional meeting.

    <u>who had demons in him</u>: "who was possessed (or, controlled) by demons"; see 4.33.

    <u>had gone without clothes</u>: "wore no clothes," "went around naked."

    <u>burial caves</u>: at that time people were buried in cavelike openings dug into the rock. The openings were big enough for a person to enter on foot, and usually high enough inside to allow a person to stand upright. Such a place would provide shelter for a man who had no other place to live.

8.28 TEV	RSV
When he saw Jesus, he gave a loud cry, threw himself down at his feet, and shouted, "Jesus, Son of the Most High God! What do you want with me? I beg you, don't punish me!"	When he saw Jesus, he cried out and fell down before him, and said with a loud voice, "What have you to do with me, Jesus, Son of the Most High God? I beseech you, do not torment me."

    <u>threw himself down at his feet</u>: or "bowed before him," "fell on his knees in front of Jesus."

    <u>Son of the Most High God</u>: the title "the Most High" is appropriate on the lips of a Gentile speaking of the God of the Jews (see <u>Most High God</u> in 1.32). The full title used by the demon-possessed man is a Christian title, expressing the belief that Jesus was, in a unique sense, the Son of God.

    <u>What do you want with me?</u>: the same kind of expression appears in an identical context in 4.34.

    <u>don't punish me</u>: "don't torment me," "don't make me suffer." The man sees Jesus not as a friend but as an enemy. What kind of punishment is implied is difficult to determine. In the mind of the writer of the Gospel, however, the word probably means that the demon, who speaks by means of the man, is afraid that Jesus is about to send him to the place of punishment, that is, hell.

8.29 TEV	RSV
He said this because Jesus had ordered the evil spirit to go out of him. Many times it had seized him, and even though he was kept a prisoner, his hands and feet tied with chains, he would break the chains and be driven by the demon out into the desert.	For he had commanded the unclean spirit to come out of the man. (For many a time it had seized him; he was kept under guard, and bound with chains and fetters, but he broke the bonds and was driven by the demon into the desert.)

    <u>had ordered</u>: this gives the reason why the man was afraid of Jesus. If preferable, direct speech may be used: "...because Jesus had said to the evil spirit, 'Come out of the man!'"

the evil spirit: literally "the unclean spirit" (see 4.33). Notice that different names are used in this narrative for this evil power: demons, unclean spirit, and demon.

The man's abnormal strength is described; not even chains on his hands and feet could keep him a prisoner.

be driven by the demon: "the demon would make him go."

into the desert: or "to uninhabited places" (see 4.1).

RSV places within parentheses the information about the man's great strength, since it has to do with what had happened before. There are several items of information in this one sentence, and it may be better to divide the material into two or more sentences: "Many times the demon would take possession of the man. People would try to keep him tied up with chains on his hands and on his feet, but he would break the chains, and the demon would make him run off to places where there were no people." All of this refers back to things that had happened before the man met Jesus. A translation may want to rearrange the various items of information in order to reflect a chronological order of events. RSV does it by placing this material within parentheses.

8.30	TEV	RSV
	Jesus asked him, "What is your name?" "My name is 'Mob,'" he answered—because many demons had gone into him.	Jesus then asked him, "What is your name?" And he said, "Legion"; for many demons had entered him.

My name is 'Mob': this translates the Greek "Legion" (RSV). The legion was a unit in the Roman army composed of from four thousand to six thousand men. By use of the word the demon-possessed man is saying that he is possessed by many evil spirits. A word such as "Crowd" or "Mob" may be easier than the technical word for "Legion." If such a technical word is used, a footnote should explain the meaning of the term.

8.31	TEV	RSV
	The demons begged Jesus not to send them into the abyss.[h]	And they begged him not to command them to depart into the abyss.

[h]ABYSS: *It was thought that the demons were to be imprisoned in the depths of the earth until their final punishment.*

begged: "kept begging." The request may be put into direct speech. "The demons kept begging Jesus: 'Don't order us to go into the abyss!'"

the abyss: as the TEV footnote shows, the abyss was thought of as a place where evil spirits were kept prisoner until their final punishment. It may be necessary in some languages to use the word for "hell" or "place of (final) punishment," and not just a word meaning a very deep hole.

8.32 TEV	RSV
There was a large herd of pigs near by, feeding on a hillside. So the demons begged Jesus to let them go into the pigs, and he let them.	Now a large herd of swine was feeding there on the hillside; and they begged him to let them enter these. So he gave them leave.

The presence of the pigs shows that this is Gentile territory, not Jewish; Jews considered pigs unclean animals.

near by: or "there" (RSV).

The evil spirits ask Jesus to send them off into the pigs. The request is prompted by their conviction that Jesus is going to expel them from the man, and so they ask his permission to enter the animals.

begged Jesus to let them: or, in direct form, "begged Jesus, 'Let us go into the pigs.'"

8.33 TEV	RSV
They went out of the man and into the pigs. The whole herd rushed down the side of the cliff into the lake and was drowned.	Then the demons came out of the man and entered the swine, and the herd rushed down the steep bank into the lake and were drowned.

the side of the cliff: or "down the hillside."

the lake: Lake Galilee.

The drowning of the pigs was proof that the demons had been destroyed.

8.34 TEV	RSV
The men who had been taking care of the pigs saw what happened, so they ran off and spread the news in the town and among the farms.	When the herdsmen saw what had happened, they fled, and told it in the city and in the country.

The men who had been taking care of the pigs: in some languages a proper term such as "pig herders" or "swine keepers" is available. Or else "The owners of the pigs"; this is not certain, however, since these men could have been hired men, paid by the owner of the pigs to take care of them.

the town: presumably Gerasa (verse 26).

among the farms: or "in the rural areas."

8.35-36 TEV	RSV
People went out to see what had happened, and when they came to Jesus, they found the man from whom the demons had gone out sitting at the feet of Jesus, clothed and in his right mind; and they were all afraid. 36 Those who had	Then people went out to see what had happened, and they came to Jesus, and found the man from whom the demons had gone, sitting at the feet of Jesus, clothed and in his right mind; and they were afraid. 36 And those who had seen it told

seen it told the people how the
man had been cured.

them how he who had been possessed
with demons was healed.

The three things said of the man—sitting at the feet of Jesus, clothed, and in his right mind—show that he was completely free of the demons.

Those who had seen it: presumably the pig herders; perhaps others also. Here it refers to the whole incident.

8.37   TEV

Then all the people from that territory asked Jesus to go away, because they were terribly afraid.
So Jesus got into the boat and
left.

                RSV

Then all the people of the surrounding country of the Gerasenes[a] asked
him to depart from them; for they
were seized with great fear; so he
got into the boat and returned.

[a]Other ancient authorities read
Gadarenes, others Gergesenes

all the people: the exaggerated language is not to be taken literally.

that territory: that is, the territory around the town of Gerasa.
TEV has chosen not to use the name "Gerasa" here, but a translation can
do so as follows: "Then all the people in the territory around Gerasa...."

asked Jesus to go away: or "said to Jesus, 'Go away!'"

because they were terribly afraid: his power, which caused the loss
of the pigs, frightened them.

Jesus got into the boat: it is assumed that the disciples are with
him, but they are not explicitly named.

As happens often in this Gospel, the writer finishes the account of
an incident, and then reports other happenings which took place before
the formal ending, not after. Here, what is described in verses 38-39a
obviously took place before Jesus left in the boat.

8.38-39   TEV

The man from whom the demons had
gone out begged Jesus, "Let me go
with you."

But Jesus sent him away, saying, 39 "Go back home and tell what
God has done for you."

The man went through the town,
telling what Jesus had done for him.

                RSV

The man from whom the demons had
gone begged that he might be with
him; but he sent him away, saying,
39 "Return to your home and declare
how much God has done for you." And
he went away, proclaiming throughout the whole city how much Jesus
had done for him.

Let me go with you: TEV puts this in direct address; it can be expressed in indirect form, as in Greek: "The man...begged Jesus to let
him go with him." The Greek says "be" (so RSV), but in the context go is
more natural, since Jesus is leaving.

the town: Gerasa.

[141]

8.40

Jairus' Daughter and the Woman Who Touched Jesus' Cloak: the two
incidents are narrated together, and so the heading has to include them
both. A shorter form may be used: "Jairus' Daughter and a Sick Woman."
Or else it is possible to divide this section into three sections as
follows: "A Father's Request (verses 40-42a); "Jesus Heals a Sick Woman"
(verses 42b-48); "Jesus Restores Jairus' Daughter to Life" (verses 49-56).

The two cures are effected the same day. The place is not identified, except that it is a town on the west shore of Lake Galilee. In both
instances the length of time, twelve years, is mentioned: the age of
Jairus' daughter (verse 42) and the time the woman had suffered from
severe bleeding (verse 43). The whole account is quite similar to the
account in Mark 5.21-43, but is less detailed.

8.40   TEV   RSV
    When Jesus returned to the   Now when Jesus returned, the
other side of the lake, the people   crowd welcomed him, for they were
welcomed him, because they had all   all waiting for him.
been waiting for him.

    Jesus: only he is mentioned, but presumably the disciples are with
him.
    the other side: the west side of Lake Galilee.
    the people: the Greek says "the crowd" (RSV), as though this partic-
ular group had been referred to before.

8.41   TEV   RSV
Then a man named Jairus arrived; he   And there came a man named Jairus,
was an official in the local syna-   who was a ruler of the synagogue;
gogue. He threw himself down at Je-   and falling at Jesus' feet he be-
sus' feet and begged him to go to   sought him to come to his house,
his home,

    an official in the local synagogue: not a professional (like a
priest) but one whom we would call a layman, who helped conduct Sabbath
services in the synagogue. This title is mentioned again in verse 49.
The text does not say what town Jairus lived in.
    synagogue: see 4.15.
    threw himself down: or "bowed low," "prostrated himself."
    and begged him to go: or "and begged him, 'Please come home with
me!' 42 He did this because....'"

8.42   TEV   RSV
because his only daughter, who was   for he had an only daughter, about
twelve years old, was dying.   twelve years of age, and she was
    As Jesus went along, the peo-   dying.
ple were crowding him from every   As he went, the people pressed
side.   round him.

[142]

his only daughter: that is, in Greek, his only child.

twelve years old: more precisely "about twelve years old." At age twelve a Jewish girl was considered old enough to be married.

As Jesus went along: both RSV and TEV begin a new paragraph here because it introduces the separate incident involving the woman who touched him.

8.43	TEV	RSV
Among them was a woman who had suffered from severe bleeding for twelve years; she had spent all she had on doctors,^{i} but no one had been able to cure her.	And a woman who had had a flow of blood for twelve years^b and could not be healed by any one,	
^{i}*Some manuscripts do not have* she had spent all she had on doctors.	^{b}Other ancient authorities add *and had spent all her living upon physicians*	

severe bleeding: due to menstrual disorder. It is not to be thought that she had bled without stopping for twelve years; rather, she had had menstrual disorder all that time. In that kind of physical condition she was considered ceremonially impure by the Law of Moses (see Lev 15.25) and could not take part in the synagogue services and other religious activities.

she had spent all she had on doctors: "she had spent all her money paying doctors to cure her." As TEV footnote shows, a few old Greek manuscripts and several early versions omit this clause, and RSV is probably correct in not including it in the text. In some translations, a footnote like the one in TEV could be used; in others, the clause may be included within round brackets (parentheses).

8.44	TEV	RSV
She came up in the crowd behind Jesus and touched the edge of his cloak, and her bleeding stopped at once.	came up behind him, and touched the fringe of his garment; and immediately her flow of blood ceased.	

the edge: at that time pious Jews had tassels on the edge of their outer garment as a sign of their devotion to God (see Num 15.37-41; Matt 23.5).

cloak: the outer garment (see 6.29, coat).

8.45	TEV	RSV
Jesus asked, "Who touched me?" Everyone denied it, and Peter said, "Master, the people are all around you and crowding in on you."	And Jesus said, "Who was it that touched me?" When all denied it, Peter^c said, "Master, the multitudes surround you and press upon you!"	
	^{c}Other ancient authorities add *and those who were with him*	

8.45

Who touched me?: the reason Jesus knew someone had touched him is given in verse 46.

Master: see 5.5.

As RSV footnote shows, many Greek manuscripts and early versions have "Peter and those with him," that is, his fellow disciples (see Mark 5.31).

It should be noticed (see KJV) that many Greek manuscripts and early versions add (as in Mark 5.31) at the end of the verse: "...and yet you ask who touched you?" But quite certainly this is not part of the original text of Luke and should not be included in a translation.

8.46 TEV	RSV
But Jesus said, "Someone touched me, for I knew it when power went out of me."	But Jesus said, "Some one touched me; for I perceive that power has gone forth from me."

knew: "sensed," "felt," "was aware of."

power went out of me: the cure was effected by Jesus' power, without any conscious participation on his part; it was the divine power at work in the person of Jesus (see 5.17; 6.19). The translation should not give the impression that all of Jesus' power left him.

8.47 TEV	RSV
The woman saw that she had been found out, so she came trembling and threw herself at Jesus' feet. There in front of everybody, she told him why she had touched him and how she had been healed at once.	And when the woman saw that she was not hidden, she came trembling, and falling down before him declared in the presence of all the people why she had touched him, and how she had been immediately healed.

saw that she had been found out: "realized that she could not conceal what had happened to her" or "...could not keep her cure a secret."

threw herself at Jesus' feet: or "knelt down in front of Jesus"—similar to what Jairus did (verse 41).

8.48 TEV	RSV
Jesus said to her, "My daughter, your faith has made you well. Go in peace."	And he said to her, "Daughter, your faith has made you well; go in peace."

My daughter: a term of affection; it does not imply that she was younger than Jesus.

your faith has made you well: "because you believed I could heal you." The words in Greek are exactly the same as in 7.50, the words that Jesus said to the prostitute. Here the Greek verb "to save" means "to heal, to make well."

Go in peace: see 7.50.

8.49	TEV		RSV

<table>
<tr><td>8.49</td><td>TEV
While Jesus was saying this, a messenger came from the official's house. "Your daughter has died," he told Jairus; "don't bother the Teacher any longer."</td><td>RSV
While he was still speaking, a man from the ruler's house came and said, "Your daughter is dead; do not trouble the Teacher any more."</td></tr>
</table>

a messenger came: the Greek says only "someone (male) came."

he told Jairus: TEV makes explicit the fact that the messenger is speaking to Jairus. Most translations will have to supply this information, either as TEV has done it (in the narrative) or else by having the messenger say "Mr. Jairus, your daughter has died."

bother: that is, by insisting that he go on home with you.

the Teacher: a title of respect. If, as is the case in some languages, the title has to be possessed, the rendering would be "our Teacher."

<table>
<tr><td>8.50</td><td>TEV
But Jesus heard it and said to Jairus, "Don't be afraid; only believe, and she will be well."</td><td>RSV
But Jesus on hearing this answered him, "Do not fear; only believe, and she shall be well."</td></tr>
</table>

heard it: heard what the messenger said.

said to Jairus: a literal translation (see RSV) might make it appear that Jesus was talking to the messenger.

be afraid: that is, doubtful, uncertain.

believe: or "keep on believing." There is no object given, and so it may be faith either in God or in Jesus himself. Perhaps the latter is better: "Believe that I can restore your daughter to life." But if the verb "to believe" or the phrase "to have faith" can be used without an object, it is better not to give one in translation.

she will be well: this translates the same verb as in verse 48; here the implication is that she will be restored to life and health.

<table>
<tr><td>8.51</td><td>TEV
When he arrived at the house, he would not let anyone go in with him except Peter, John, and James, and the child's father and mother.</td><td>RSV
And when he came to the house, he permitted no one to enter with him, except Peter and John and James, and the father and mother of the child.</td></tr>
</table>

anyone: that is, anyone else besides the five people mentioned.

go in with him: since the girl's mother is mentioned here for the first time, it is probable that the Greek means to say, "When Jesus entered the house he did not let anyone go in with him to the room where the girl was except...."

8.52-53 TEV	RSV
Everyone there was crying and mourning for the child. Jesus said, "Don't cry; the child is not dead—she is only sleeping!" 53 They all made fun of him, because they knew that she was dead.	And all were weeping and bewailing her; but he said, "Do not weep; for she is not dead but sleeping." 53 And they laughed at him, knowing that she was dead.

mourning: the verb in Greek (RSV "bewailing") means literally "to beat (upon one's breast)," an expression of grief that often accompanied weeping.

made fun of him: "jeered at him," "laughed at him."

8.54 TEV	RSV
But Jesus took her by the hand and called out, "Get up, child!"	But taking her by the hand he called, saying, "Child, arise."

Get up: the same Greek verb is used here that was used in the command to the widow's dead son (7.14).

child: a term should be used that would be appropriate for a girl twelve years old.

8.55 TEV	RSV
Her life returned, and she got up at once, and Jesus ordered them to give her something to eat.	And her spirit returned, and she got up at once; and he directed that something should be given her to eat.

Her life returned: RSV "her spirit returned." Or the translation could be "She began to breathe again" or "She became alive again." Care should be taken not to use an expression used of a person who only regains consciousness.

got up: from her bed.

ordered them: no one in particular is named. The direct form may be used: "and Jesus ordered, 'Give her something to eat.'"

8.56 TEV	RSV
Her parents were astounded, But Jesus commanded them not to tell anyone what had happened.	And her parents were amazed; but he charged them to tell no one what had happened.

were astounded: as in 2.47.

not to tell anyone: as in 5.14.

Chapter 9

<u>Jesus Sends Out the Twelve Disciples</u>: "Jesus Sends Out the Disciples to Preach and to Heal."

Jesus gives his disciples the power to heal and to drive out demons, and commands them to proclaim the message about the Kingdom of God. As they traveled about, they were to depend on friendly people for their food and lodging, and were to waste no time trying to persuade unfriendly people to give them a hearing. Their purpose was to proclaim as widely as possible that the Kingdom of God was near.

9.1	TEV	RSV
	Jesus called the twelve disciples together and gave them power and authority to drive out all demons and to cure diseases.	And he called the twelve together and gave them power and authority over all demons and to cure diseases,

<u>Jesus</u>: TEV gives the name, since this is the beginning of a new section.

<u>the twelve disciples</u>: this translates "the twelve" (RSV); the translation could be "the twelve apostles" (see 6.13).

<u>power and authority</u>: there is no sharp distinction between the two in this context (see their use in 4.36).

<u>demons</u>: see 4.33.

9.2	TEV	RSV
	Then he sent them out to preach the Kingdom of God and to heal the sick,	and he sent them out to preach the kingdom of God and to heal.

<u>Then</u>: this translates the Greek "and" (see RSV).

<u>sent...out</u>: this translates the Greek verb which is related to the noun "apostles" (see 6.13). It is to be noticed that when they return they are referred to as apostles (verse 10).

<u>preach the Kingdom of God</u>: "proclaim the message about the Kingdom of God."

<u>preach</u>: see 3.3.

<u>the Kingdom of God</u>: see 4.43.

[147]

9.3   TEV   RSV
after saying to them, "Take noth-   And he said to them, "Take nothing
ing with you for the trip: no   for your journey, no staff, nor bag,
walking stick, no beggar's bag, no   nor bread, nor money; and do not
food, no money, not even an extra   have two tunics.
shirt.

    after saying to them: TEV thus translates the literal "and he said
to them" (RSV) because the instructions would be given before the twelve
left. Or else, a translation can end verse 2 with a complete stop and begin verse 3, "Before they left, Jesus told them...."
    walking stick: to help as they traveled.
    beggar's bag: or "traveler's bag," "knapsack," or anything else in
which provisions may be carried. But nothing so modern as "suitcase" or
"trunk" should be used. The twelve were to travel without carrying any
provisions with them.
    an extra shirt: this translates the Greek "two tunics" (RSV). For
shirt see 3.11. The instruction is that no one take along a tunic in
addition to the one he would be wearing. A translation might wish to make
clear that the order applies to each one: "do not have (or, take) two
shirts apiece."

9.4   TEV   RSV
Wherever you are welcomed, stay in   And whatever house you enter, stay
the same house until you leave that there, and from there depart.
town;

    This verse instructs the twelve not to move about from house to
house when they are in a town. It does not mean that they are to stay inside the house all the time they are in town; it means they are to remain
as guests of that family and not seek lodging in some other home. The
translation may be "When you arrive in a town and the people there welcome you, stay (as a guest) in the same house (or, with the same family)
until you leave that town." The text in this Gospel pictures the twelve
traveling as a group. In some languages it may be necessary to make clear
that each apostle is to stay in the same house where he has been made
welcome. In small Palestinian villages very few homes would be able or
willing to accommodate twelve men as guests at one time.

9.5   TEV   RSV
wherever people don't welcome you,   And wherever they do not receive
leave that town and shake the dust   you, when you leave that town shake
off your feet as a warning to   off the dust from your feet as a
them."   testimony against them."

    shake the dust off your feet: this is an action indicating that the
town is ceremonially unclean and will be punished by God; all contact
with it must be carefully avoided. So it is an action expressing both
disapproval and condemnation. If the action is unintelligible or carries
the wrong meaning, the translation may have to say "leave that town after

telling the people there that they have sinned by refusing to listen to
you" or "...that they will be punished because they would not listen to
you."

as a warning to them: or "That will show them that they will be
punished (by God)."

9.6   TEV   RSV
    The disciples left and trav-   And they departed and went through
eled through all the villages,   the villages, preaching the gospel
preaching the Good News and heal-   and healing everywhere.
ing people everywhere.

    traveled through all the villages: or "went from village to village,"
"went from one village to another."
    preaching the Good News: see 2.10; 3.18.

SECTION HEADING

    Herod's Confusion: "Herod Worries about Jesus," "Herod Wonders Who
Jesus Is."

    Unlike the other Synoptic Gospels, Luke does not describe John the
Baptist's death but refers to it only as a remark made by Herod. In this
Gospel this section serves as background information for the confession
of Jesus as Messiah (verses 18-20), and is placed between the disciples'
departure (verse 6) and their return (verse 10).

9.7   TEV   RSV
    When Herod, the ruler of Gal-   Now Herod the tetrarch heard
ilee, heard about all the things   of all that was done, and he was
that were happening, he was very   perplexed, because it was said by
confused, because some people were   some that John had been raised from
saying that John the Baptist had   the dead,
come back to life.

    Herod: Herod Antipas (see 3.1).
    all the things that were happening: the cures and miracles performed
by Jesus and the twelve disciples.
    very confused: "upset," "did not know what to think."
    had come back to life: it was believed that a person could come back
to life, that is, that God could bring a dead person back to life. Some
people were saying that the miracles and cures were being performed by a
resurrected John the Baptist.

9.8   TEV   RSV
Others were saying that Elijah had   by some that Elijah had appeared,
appeared, and still others that one   and by others that one of the old

9.8

of the prophets of long ago had   prophets had risen.
come back to life.

    Elijah: a Hebrew prophet who was expected to return and prepare the
way for the coming of the Messiah (see Mal 4.5-6).
    appeared: that is, returned. Of Elijah it is not said "raised to
life," because he had been taken up to heaven alive (see 2 Kgs 2.11-12).
    prophets: see 1.70.
    had come back to life: "had been raised to life (by God)."

9.9   TEV   RSV

Herod said, "I had John's head cut   Herod said, "John I beheaded; but
off; but who is this man I hear   who is this about whom I hear such
these things about?" And he kept   things?" And he sought to see him.
trying to see Jesus.

    I had John's head cut off: "I had John executed." The language ("I
cut off John's head") should not be understood to mean that Herod had
done it personally; he had ordered it done.
    but who is this man...?: or "who, then, is this man...?" Perhaps
two sentences will be better: "I hear strange (or, unusual) things about
this man. Who is he?"
    kept trying to see Jesus: in the sense of having Jesus brought to
him so that he could talk with him. (Herod's wish is finally realized:
see 23.6-12.)

SECTION HEADING

    Jesus Feeds Five Thousand Men: "Jesus Feeds a Large Crowd." (To say
only "Five Thousand Men" gives the impression there were no women or
children present. It is to be noticed that the text says "about five
thousand men" [verse 14] but says nothing about women or children.)

    In this section the emphasis is more on Jesus and the twelve dis-
ciples than on Jesus and the crowd. The twelve return to Jesus, they report on their travels, and Jesus goes off with them for what is intended
to be a time of rest. But the people follow him and the feeding miracle
takes place.

9.10   TEV   RSV

    The apostles came back and   On their return the apostles
told Jesus everything they had   told him what they had done. And he
done. He took them with him, and   took them and withdrew apart to a
they went off by themselves to a   city call Bethsaida.
town named Bethsaida.

    apostles: see 6.13.
    came back: from the trip on which Jesus had sent them (verses 1-6).

to a town: the narrative (verse 12) makes it clear that they did not enter the town, so a translation should use an expression meaning "to" or "in the direction of" Bethsaida.

Bethsaida: a town on the northeast shore of Lake Galilee.

9.11 TEV	RSV
When the crowds heard about it, they followed him. He welcomed them, spoke to them about the Kingdom of God, and healed those who needed it.	When the crowds learned it, they followed him; and he welcomed them and spoke to them of the kingdom of God, and cured those who had need of healing.

the crowds: the literal translation makes it appear that there were separate groups of people, but what is meant is only "many people." The translation could be "Many people heard that Jesus was going to Bethsaida, and so they followed him."

welcomed them: or "said to them, 'Welcome!'" The normal way of extending a friendly greeting should be expressed.

healed those who needed it: "healed the sick (people)."

9.12 TEV	RSV
When the sun was beginning to set, the twelve disciples came to him and said, "Send the people away so that they can go to the villages and farms around here and find food and lodging, because this is a lonely place."	Now the day began to wear away; and the twelve came and said to him, "Send the crowd away, to go into the villages and country round about, to lodge and get provisions; for we are here in a lonely place."

the sun was beginning to set: "the sun was about to set," "the day was almost over." The Greek expression may not mean exactly what TEV has; perhaps, it means in a more general manner, "It was getting late in the day," that is, late afternoon.

farms: see 8.34.

food and lodging: "something to eat and a place to spend the night." There was not enough time for the people to return home that day.

a lonely place: "an isolated place" (see 4.42). The Greek text says "we are here in a lonely place" (RSV). If a translation uses this form, the "we" should be inclusive. It may be better to reverse the order of the Greek and translate "This is an isolated place. So send the people away, to go to the villages and farms around here where they can find food and lodging (for the night)."

9.13 TEV	RSV
But Jesus said to them, "You yourselves give them something to eat."	But he said to them, "You give them something to eat." They said, "We have no more than five loaves and

[151]

They answered, "All we have are five loaves and two fish. Do you want us to go and buy food for this whole crowd?" two fish—unless we are to go and buy food for all these people."

You yourselves give them something to eat: the Greek is emphatic; Jesus is telling his disciples to take the necessary measures to feed the large crowd.

we...us: in both cases this first person plural pronoun refers to the twelve.

loaves: "loaves of bread." They were round, fairly small.

two fish: cooked fish, not fresh.

Do you want us to go and buy...?: TEV has expressed this as a question (see RSV for the form of the Greek). The Greek implies this is an impossible thing, so a better way of translating would be "You don't expect us to go and buy food for this whole crowd, do you?" or "We can't go and buy food for this whole crowd!"

9.14   TEV   RSV
(There were **ab**out five thousand men there.)   For there were about five thousand men. And he said to his disciples,
       Jesus said to his disciples, "Make the people sit down in groups of about fifty each."   "Make them sit down in companies, about fifty each."

The information about the number of men present is placed by TEV within parentheses, since it interrupts the dialogue.

Jesus said: his order may be placed in indirect form: "Jesus told his disciples to order the men to sit down in groups of about fifty men in each group."

Make: that is, to order or command. Physical force is not implied.

9.15-16   TEV   RSV
       After the disciples had done so, 16 Jesus took the five loaves and two fish, looked up to heaven, thanked God for them, broke them, and gave them to the disciples to distribute to the people.   And they did so, and made them all sit down. 16 And taking the five loaves and the two fish he looked up to heaven, and blessed and broke them, and gave them to the disciples to set before the crowd.

looked up to heaven: "looked up to the sky" or "looked up." This was the attitude of prayer.

thanked God for them: "said a prayer of thanks." RSV translates "and blessed...them." This would be equivalent to "and asked God to bless them."

broke them: "broke the loaves and the fish into small pieces." It should not be said that he broke them into tiny crumbs.

9.17   TEV   RSV
They all ate and had enough, and   And all ate and were satisfied. And
the disciples took up twelve bas-   they took up what was left over,
kets of what was left over.   twelve baskets of broken pieces.

    and had enough: "and each one there had as much as he wanted," "and
everyone was satisfied."
    the disciples took up: the Greek uses the passive form, "twelve
baskets...were taken up," which could mean "people took up twelve baskets." But it seems reasonable to suppose that the disciples are meant.
    what was left over: not crumbs and bits on the ground, but pieces
of bread and of fish that had not been eaten.

SECTION HEADING

    Peter's Declaration about Jesus: "Peter Confesses that Jesus Is the
Messiah."

    This incident is not related to what precedes. It begins with an
indefinite statement of time and does not say where Jesus and the twelve
disciples were. This section goes with the one telling of Herod's Confusion (verses 7-9), which describes the rumors going around about who Jesus was.

9.18   TEV   RSV
    One day when Jesus was praying   Now it happened that as he was
alone, the disciples came to him.   praying alone the disciples were
"Who do the crowds say I am?" he   with him; and he asked them, "Who
asked them.   do the people say that I am?"

    One day: a way in English of beginning a story where no particular
time or place is specified (see 1.8).
    the disciples came to him: or, as RSV has it, "the disciples were
with him." The Greek verb means "to be together with"; in the context,
where Jesus is praying alone, it seems probable that the Greek means to
say that the disciples joined Jesus.
    the crowds: better "the people" (RSV).

9.19   TEV   RSV
    "Some say that you are John   And they answered, "John the Baptist;
the Baptist," they answered. "Oth- but others say, Elijah; and others,
ers say that you are Elijah, while that one of the old prophets has
others say that one of the prophets risen."
of long ago has come back to life."

    Some say: "Some people are saying."
    John the Baptist...Elijah...one of the prophets: as in verses 7-8.

9.20 TEV	RSV
"What about you," he asked them. "Who do you say I am?" Peter answered, "You are God's Messiah."	And he said to them, "But who do you say that I am?" And Peter answered, "The Christ of God."

you: TEV makes this emphatic, trying to represent the emphatic form of the Greek.

God's Messiah: "the Messiah sent by God," "the Savior whom God promised to send." For Messiah see 2.11,26.

It is to be noticed that RSV joins verses 21-22 to what precedes, whereas TEV joins them to what follows. What RSV has done may be preferable, since the words in verses 21-22 follow immediately after Peter's confession, and Jesus is talking directly to the twelve. Verse 23 begins And he said to them all, clearly implying that Jesus is speaking to more people than just the twelve disciples. So a translation may wish to include verses 21-22 in the preceding section, and begin a new section at verse 23.

SECTION HEADING

Jesus Speaks about His Suffering and Death: "Jesus Speaks about His Death and Resurrection," "Jesus Tells His Disciples that He Will Be Put to Death and Then Come Back to Life."

After ordering his disciples not to tell people that he is the Messiah, Jesus speaks about the coming suffering, death, and resurrection of the Son of Man. This leads into his declaration to his listeners about the nature of discipleship.

9.21 TEV	RSV
Then Jesus gave them strict orders not to tell this to anyone.	But he charged and commanded them to tell this to no one,

not to tell this to anyone: "not to tell anyone that he was the Messiah." If preferable, a direct form can be used, "Then Jesus gave them a strict order: 'Don't tell anyone that I am the Messiah.'"

9.22 TEV	RSV
He also told them, "The Son of Man must suffer much and be rejected by the elders, the chief priests, and the teachers of the Law. He will be put to death, but three days later he will be raised to life."	saying, "The Son of man must suffer many things, and be rejected by the elders and chief priests and scribes, and be killed, and on the third day be raised."

Son of Man: see 5.24. Jesus is referring to himself, so it may be necessary to say "I, who am the Son of Man."

must suffer much: "must be made to suffer many things," "will have to undergo great suffering," "will be badly mistreated."

must: "will have to." The language is clear, and this must indicates that the sufferings of the Son of Man are the result of God's will.

be rejected: "not be accepted," "be condemned."

elders: see 7.3.

chief priests: the heads of the twenty-four orders into which the Jewish priests were divided, as well as the priestly members of the family of the High Priest. They may be called "the important priests," "the priests who have more authority."

teachers of the Law: see 5.17.

He will be put to death: or "I, the Son of Man, will be put to death." The text does not say who will kill him, and a translation should not imply that the elders, the chief priests, and the teachers of the Law will kill Jesus. Nor should it appear that the sufferings that he will endure will result in his death; his death is a separate event. The language means that the Son of Man will be killed, will die as the result of violent action against him. "The Son of Man will be made to die" or "People will kill the Son of Man."

three days later: or "two days later." The numbering of the days included the day on which the numbering started. Most translations use a standard phrase, "on the third day (after that)" or "after three days."

he will be raised to life: "he will live again," "God will raise him to life."

In Greek the whole sentence is so constructed that the expression must governs all the verbs and verbal phrases that follow: "must suffer much...must be rejected...must be put to death...must be raised to life." All the things that will happen to the Son of Man will happen because God has willed it.

9.23   TEV   RSV
    And he said to them all, "If   And he said to all, "If any
anyone wants to come with me, he   man would come after me, let him
must forget himself, take up his   deny himself and take up his cross
cross every day, and follow me.   daily and follow me.

The way this verse begins shows that it is a separate incident, and RSV does well to begin a new paragraph here, as does TEV.

them all: the disciples and others who were there.

to come with me: or "to go with me," "to follow me," "to be my disciple."

forget himself: "deny himself (RSV),""renounce himself," "give up his own plans and wishes," "say no to his own plans and wishes."

take up his cross every day: the language is figurative but the meaning is quite plain. To carry a cross meant to be on the way to execution; a condemned man carried the horizontal crossbar to the place of execution. Here Jesus is saying that anyone who wants to be his disciple must be prepared to share his fate, to be persecuted and to die, as he was about to experience it (verse 22). The addition, every day, means that this is a daily resolution, a constantly renewed vow.

9.24	TEV	RSV
	For whoever wants to save his own life will lose it, but whoever loses his life for my sake will save it.	For whoever would save his life will lose it; and whoever loses his life for my sake, he will save it.

save his own life will lose it...loses his life...will save it: here the word "life" is used with two meanings: in the first instance life is physical existence, and in the other instance (it) it is future life, or true life, or eternal life. It may be necessary to expand somewhat if a literal translation results in what appears to be a flat contradiction. Something like the following might serve: "For if someone is determined to save his life, then he will not gain (or, have) true life (or, eternal life); but if someone loses his life for my sake, that person will have true life."

lose: the word does not mean to misplace, or to leave somewhere by mistake, but to renounce, to give up on purpose.

for my sake: "in order to be my disciple," "because he is willing to follow me."

9.25	TEV	RSV
	Will a person gain anything if he wins the whole world but is himself lost or defeated? Of course not!	For what does it profit a man if he gains the whole world and loses or forfeits himself?

TEV has retained the form of the rhetorical question (Will a person gain...?) but has made the answer clear, Of course not! A translation may prefer to use the form of a statement: "A person does not gain anything if..."; if a rhetorical question is used, it should be clear that the answer is negative.

the whole world: "everything there is," "everything he wants." Jesus is saying that true life is more than all the material possessions a person can get.

lost or defeated: these are not two possible ways of losing true life, but two ways of expressing that loss. It is not necessary in translation to use two different words. The Greek word translated defeated (RSV "forfeits himself") may mean "be destroyed," that is, in the punishment after death.

9.26	TEV	RSV
	If a person is ashamed of me and of my teaching, then the Son of Man will be ashamed of him when he comes in his glory and in the glory of the Father and of the holy angels.	For whoever is ashamed of me and of my words, of him will the Son of man be ashamed when he comes in his glory and the glory of the Father and of the holy angels.

is ashamed of me: "does not follow me," "rejects me," "denies he is my disciple."

is ashamed...of my teaching: "does not believe what I teach," "does not obey my teaching," "does not proclaim what I teach."

the Son of Man: or "I, the Son of Man."

will be ashamed of him: "will deny that he (or, that person) is his disciple."

when he comes in his glory: referring to the future coming of the Son of Man as judge of all people. Here the word glory is used of the Son of Man, of the Father, and of the angels. In the Old Testament "the glory of Yahweh" was his visible manifestation to his people, seen as a bright light or a shining cloud. This glory will be shining from the Son of Man, the same kind of glory that God and the angels have. So it represents the greatness, the power, the majesty of God.

the Father: it may be necessary to say "his (that is, the Son of Man's) Father" or else "our Father."

the holy angels: "God's angels," "God's heavenly servants" (see 1.81).

9.27	TEV	RSV
	I assure you that there are some here who will not die until they have seen the Kingdom of God."	But I tell you truly, there are some standing here who will not taste death before they see the kingdom of God."

I assure you: "I am telling you the truth," "Believe me," "You may be sure."

there are some here: the Greek is more precise: "there are some people standing here." The language is quite specific, and Jesus was referring to those who were listening to him, that is, the twelve disciples and others (verse 23).

will not die: the Greek "will not taste death" (RSV) is a way of saying "will not experience death." It does not mean to come close to death without actually dying.

It may be better to use a positive statement: "I assure you that some of you here will live to see the Kingdom of God."

seen the Kingdom of God: here the meaning is quite specifically the final day, when all people everywhere will acknowledge God as ruler and judge. So it might be well to expand somewhat: "...will live to see the final day when God will establish his Kingdom (or, God will manifest his complete power as King)."

SECTION HEADING

The Transfiguration: "Jesus Is Transfigured," "The Appearance of Jesus Changes." This idea may be difficult to express in a short section heading (see verse 29, below). It may be better, therefore, to have something like "Jesus, Moses, and Elijah" as a section heading.

This incident prepares the way for the beginning of Jesus' journey to Jerusalem (verse 51). The key elements here are the subject of the

9.28

conversation between Jesus, Moses, and Elijah; the glory which surrounds Jesus; and the heavenly voice announcing God's approval of Jesus.

9.28 TEV	RSV
About a week after he had said these things, Jesus took Peter, John, and James with him and went up a hill to pray.	Now about eight days after these sayings he took with him Peter and John and James, and went up on the mountain to pray.

About a week: this translates "about eight days" (RSV).

these things: those reported in verses 21-27.

went up a hill: there is no way of knowing what hill this was (see 6.12).

to pray: it would seem that the text means that Jesus went in order to pray, and that he took the three disciples to be with him while he prayed.

9.29 TEV	RSV
While he was praying, his face changed its appearance, and his clothes became dazzling white.	And as he was praying, the appearance of his countenance was altered, and his raiment became dazzling white.

his face changed its appearance: "his face became different." The text does not say how it was different. Most languages will have ways of expressing a change in appearance without specifying the exact nature of the change. (In one language the phrase "his face was changed" is an idiomatic way of saying "he died," so quite clearly the phrase should not be used.)

dazzling white: the meaning is that the clothes shone brightly. The Greek expression "shining white" uses a verb which means to flash like lightning, indicating intense brilliance.

9.30 TEV	RSV
Suddenly two men were there talking with him. They were Moses and Elijah,	And behold, two men talked with him, Moses and Elijah,

Suddenly: this represents the Greek word which RSV translates "behold" (see 1.20).

two men were there: "two men appeared," "two men were seen there."

9.31 TEV	RSV
who appeared in heavenly glory and talked with Jesus about the way in which he would soon fulfill God's purpose by dying in Jerusalem.	who appeared in glory and spoke of his departure, which he was to accomplish at Jerusalem.

[158]

appeared in heavenly glory: this translates "were seen (or, appeared) in glory." For glory see 2.6. Here glory indicates brightness, light, shining, and the expression means that the two men shone with a bright splendor, which indicated their heavenly origin.

For the subject of their conversation with Jesus, the Greek says "his departure which he was about to fulfill in Jerusalem" (see RSV). Here "departure" is a clear reference to Jesus' death. TEV has taken the Greek verb "fulfill" to be a way of saying fulfill God's purpose (or, accomplish God's will). Another way of expressing this would be "They talked with Jesus about his coming death in Jerusalem, which was what God wanted him to undergo."

Others, however, take the Greek to mean simply "They talked with Jesus about the death he was going to suffer (or, experience) in Jerusalem."

9.32   TEV

Peter and his companions were sound asleep, but they woke up and saw Jesus' glory and the two men who were standing with him.

RSV

Now Peter and those who were with him were heavy with sleep, and when they wakened they saw his glory and the two men who stood with him.

Peter and his companions: "Peter and the two other disciples."
were sound asleep: "were sleeping soundly." As verse 37 seems to indicate, this took place at night.
they woke up: either the brilliant light or the conversation between Jesus and the heavenly visitors woke up the three disciples.
Jesus' glory: Jesus himself was radiating that same heavenly light that was shining from Moses and Elijah.

9.33   TEV

As the men were leaving Jesus, Peter said to him, "Master, how good it is that we are here! We will make three tents, one for you, one for Moses, and one for Elijah." (He did not really know what he was saying.)

RSV

And as the men were parting from him, Peter said to Jesus, "Master, it is well that we are here; let us make three booths, one for you and one for Moses and one for Elijah"— not knowing what he said.

were leaving: presumably back to heaven.
Master: see 5.5.
we: this could be: (1) the three disciples; (2) the three disciples and Jesus; or (3) the three disciples, Jesus, Moses, and Elijah. It would seem that the meaning is (1), Peter and his two fellow disciples. The statement how good it is that we are here is explained by what follows, that is, the three disciples will put up three shelters for Jesus and the two heavenly visitors.
tents: "booths" (RSV), "shelters," "lean-tos"; these are temporary constructions, not solid and fixed. Peter's offer is made on the

understanding that the heavenly visitors will remain there for a while with Jesus.

The information given by the writer of the Gospel at the end of the verse interrupts the narrative and so is placed within parentheses by TEV. The meaning is that Peter's proposal to build three shelters was quite meaningless in this situation.

9.34	TEV	RSV
	While he was still speaking, a cloud appeared and covered them with its shadow; and the disciples were afraid as the cloud came over them.	As he said this, a cloud came and overshadowed them; and they were afraid as they entered the cloud.

a cloud: this indicates the presence of God.

covered them with its shadow: "threw its shadow over them." Here them would probably include all those present on the mountain, but the three disciples are in focus. The next statement "they were afraid" (RSV) means the disciples were afraid.

as the cloud came over them: this translates the Greek "as they entered the cloud" (RSV). Of course it was the cloud that was moving, not the three disciples.

9.35	TEV	RSV
	A voice said from the cloud, "This is my Son, whom I have chosen— listen to him!"	And a voice came out of the cloud, saying, "This is my Son, my Chosen;[d] listen to him!"

[d]Other ancient authorities read *my Beloved*

A voice said from the cloud: "A voice speaking from (or, in) the cloud said." The sound of the voice came out of the cloud. God is the speaker, and if necessary the translation may say "God spoke from (inside) the cloud."

This is my Son, whom I have chosen: see the similar language in 3.22. The heavenly voice seems to be speaking to the three disciples, since the command listen to him seems to be addressed to them.

whom I have chosen: this reflects Old Testament language about the one Yahweh chooses to accomplish his purposes (see Isa 42.1; see also Luke 23.35). "The Chosen One" is equivalent to "the Messiah."

Textual Note: as RSV footnote shows, instead of my Son, whom I have chosen, many Greek manuscripts and early versions have "my Beloved" (as in 3.22). The text followed by TEV and RSV should be preferred.

listen to him: "pay attention to what he says" or "obey him."

9.36	TEV	RSV
	When the voice stopped, there was Jesus all alone. The disciples	And when the voice had spoken, Jesus was found alone. And they kept

kept quiet about all this and told   silence and told no one in those
no one at that time anything they   days anything of what they had seen.
had seen.

the voice stopped: "the voice stopped speaking"; or "After the voice
had spoken."
there was Jesus all alone: this translates the Greek "Jesus was
found alone" (RSV), an idiomatic way of describing the situation. The
passive of the verb "to find" does not mean that someone had been looking for Jesus and had found him. The two heavenly visitors were gone, and
the disciples saw only Jesus there.
The disciples kept quiet about all this: "The disciples said nothing
about this." The Greek text uses two different expressions to say the
same thing, that is, that the disciples told no one at that time what
they had seen on the hill. It is not clear how long a period at that time
covers; perhaps the rest of the time that Jesus was with them.

SECTION HEADING

Jesus Heals a Boy with an Evil Spirit: "Jesus Expels an Evil Spirit
from a Boy."

This event follows immediately after the transfiguration of Jesus.
The cure of the demon-possessed boy not only demonstrates again Jesus'
power over the forces of evil, but also the disciples' inability to expel the demon. Jesus' angry rebuke (verse 41) seems to include the disciples.

9.37   TEV   RSV
The next day Jesus and the   On the next day, when they had
three disciples went down from the   come down from the mountain, a great
hill, and a large crowd met Jesus.   crowd met him.

It is to be noticed that TEV has made explicit Jesus and the three
disciples (Greek "they") and Jesus (Greek "him"). The setting is that of
a large crowd waiting at the foot of the hill, together with the nine
disciples who had not gone up the hill the day before with Jesus.

9.38   TEV   RSV
A man shouted from the crowd,   And behold, a man from the crowd
"Teacher! I beg you, look at my   cried, "Teacher, I beg you to look
son—my only son!   upon my son, for he is my only child;

Teacher: see 3.12 and 5.5.
my son: the use of the word boy in verse 42 shows that the son is an
adolescent.
my only son: an additional bit of information, to emphasize the father's distress.

9.39   TEV   RSV
A spirit attacks him with a sudden   and behold, a spirit seizes him,
shout and throws him into a fit,   and he suddenly cries out; it con-
so that he foams at the mouth; it   vulses him till he foams, and
keeps on hurting him and will   shatters him, and will hardly leave
hardly let him go!   him.

A spirit: here meaning, of course, "evil spirit"; in verse 42a it
is called "the demon" and in verse 42b "the unclean spirit" (RSV; see
4.33).
The description of the boy's condition is quite detailed, and there
are various ways of interpreting the Greek text and different ways of
reconstructing it in translation.
attacks him with a sudden shout: or "seizes him, and he suddenly
cries out" (RSV). This seems to say, either (1) the spirit cries out as
it suddenly seizes the boy, or (2) after the demon has seized him, the
boy cries out suddenly. Probably the latter is meant; the initial seizure
by the demon is accompanied by a scream from the boy; it is the demon (in
the text) who is said to shout suddenly, but the writer probably meant
that the scream was produced by the seizure. So it would be better to
translate "From time to time an evil spirit seizes (or, possesses) my son
and makes him scream (or, shout) all of a sudden," or else "...seizes my
son and gives a sudden scream."
throws him into a fit: "makes him go into convulsions."
he foams at the mouth: that is, globules of saliva appear on his
mouth. The mention of foam and convulsions fits the description of an
epileptic seizure.
keeps on hurting him: the Greek verb means "to inflict suffering
on," "to torment," "to break." It is a vivid description of the terrible
effects of the seizure on the boy.
The material may be reconstructed as follows: "From time to time an
evil spirit comes upon (or, takes possession of) my son, and it makes
him scream all of a sudden. The spirit makes him go into convulsions and
to foam at the mouth. It keeps on hurting him and will hardly leave him."

9.40   TEV   RSV
I begged your disciples to drive it   And I begged your disciples to cast
out, but they couldn't."   it out, but they could not."

I begged: the same verb used in verse 38.
your disciples: the ones who did not go up the hill with Jesus.
they couldn't: evidently they tried to expel the demon, but were unable.

9.41   TEV   RSV
Jesus answered, "How unbeliev-   Jesus answered, "O faithless and
ing and wrong you people are! How   perverse generation, how long am I
long must I stay with you? How long   to be with you and bear with you?
do I have to put up with you?" Then   Bring your son here."

he said to the man, "Bring your son
here."

unbelieving: "no faith," "without faith."

wrong: "confused," "misguided," "perverted." The Greek verb "turned
around" has here a moral meaning. The whole sentence may be translated
"You people are unbelieving and sinful" or "You people do not believe
(or, do not have faith) and are sinful."

How long...?: as RSV shows, the Greek text has here one rhetorical
question with two verbs, which TEV represents by two rhetorical questions.

How long must I stay with you?: as a wish, "I hope I will not be
with you much longer."

How long do I have to put up with you?: this means the same as the
first rhetorical question. "I can't stand you people much longer" or "I
hope I don't have to endure you much longer."

Then he said to the man: TEV adds this to make clear that the command that follows is directed to the father.

Bring: not in the sense of carrying but of taking him by the hand
to Jesus.

9.42	TEV	RSV
	As the boy was coming, the de-mon knocked him to the ground and threw him into a fit. Jesus gave a command to the evil spirit, healed the boy, and gave him back to his father.	While he was coming, the demon tore him and convulsed him. But Jesus rebuked the unclean spirit, and healed the boy, and gave him back to his father.

knocked him to the ground: RSV takes the Greek verb to be one meaning "to tear, to rip apart"; but this does not fit the context. TEV
takes the Greek verb to be one which means "throw to the ground."

threw him into a fit: this verb in Greek is related to the one used
in verse 39.

gave a command: see this same Greek verb in 4.35. The command, of
course, was for the spirit to leave the boy. This may have to be explicitly stated in some languages.

the evil spirit: the Greek is "the unclean spirit" (see 4.33).

healed the boy: this should not be seen as a second act in addition
to the expulsion of the demon, but a result of the expulsion. So a translation may say "Jesus healed the boy by ordering the evil (or, unclean)
spirit to go out of him. Then he returned the boy to his father."

gave him back: not in the sense of handing the boy over bodily, but
of turning him back to his father's care.

9.43a	TEV	RSV
	All the people were amazed at the mighty power of God.	And all were astonished at the maj-esty of God.

9.43a

amazed: see 2.48.
<u>the mighty power</u>: "the greatness," "this demonstration of God's great power."

SECTION HEADING

<u>Jesus Speaks Again about His Death</u>: see the section heading at 9.21.

It is to be noticed that in this second statement to the disciples about his forthcoming suffering, Jesus says nothing about his resurrection, and speaks in a very vague way about being arrested.
TEV and RSV both make the break in the middle of verse 43. The structure in Greek demands that 43b go with what follows, not with what precedes.

9.43b	TEV	RSV
	The people were still marveling at everything Jesus was doing, when he said to his disciples,	But while they were all marveling at everything he did, he said to his disciples,

<u>marveling</u>: see 2.18.
<u>everything Jesus was doing</u>: in the context this refers specifically to the expulsion of the demon from the boy.

9.44	TEV	RSV
	"Don't forget what I am about to tell you! The Son of Man is going to be handed over to the power of men."	"Let these words sink into your ears; for the Son of man is to be delivered into the hands of men."

<u>Don't forget what I am about to tell you</u>: see RSV for the idiomatic language of the Greek. Other translations could be "Pay close attention to what I am about to say," "Listen to this and don't forget it."
<u>The Son of Man</u>: see 5.24. Jesus is talking about himself, and so it may be necessary to say "I, the Son of Man."
<u>to be handed over</u>: "to be arrested," "to be handed over to the authorities." The Greek verb may mean "to betray," but here it seems more likely that "hand over" is meant. No subject is given, that is, it is not said who will turn Jesus over to the authorities; if a passive cannot be used, it will be necessary to say "Some people will hand over the Son of Man to men."
<u>to the power of men</u>: here a reference to the authorities or to hostile opponents; it might be better to say "to the authorities," "to the people who are powerful."

9.45	TEV	RSV
	But the disciples did not know what this meant. It had been hidden from	But they did not understand this saying, and it was concealed from

[164]

them so that they could not under- stand it, and they were afraid to ask him about the matter.	them, that they should not per- ceive it; and they were afraid to ask him about this saying.

The inability of the disciples to grasp the meaning of Jesus' words is described in two different ways: (1) the disciples did not know, they didn't understand what he said; and (2) God had hidden the meaning (literally "covered it over") so they could not perceive it. The passive had been hidden denotes divine activity.

they were afraid to ask him about the matter: the depth of their perplexity is further indicated by this statement. They really did not want the plain truth.

SECTION HEADING

Who Is the Greatest?: "Jesus Says How to Become Important."

This small section combines two different sayings, both of which make use of the status of a child. The answer to the disciples' argument comes at the end of verse 48; the saying about welcoming a child in the name of Jesus in the beginning of the verse does not logically relate to the disciples' argument.

9.46 TEV	RSV
An argument broke out among the disciples as to which one of them was the greatest.	And an argument arose among them as to which of them was the greatest.

The English idiom An argument broke out may not be suitable for a literal translation, so something else may be said: "The disciples began to argue."

among the disciples: this is said to make clear the meaning of "among them" (RSV).

was the greatest: "was the most important," "had the highest standing in the group."

9.47 TEV	RSV
Jesus knew what they were thinking, so he took a child, stood him by his side,	But when Jesus perceived the thought of their hearts, he took a child and put him by his side,

Jesus knew what they were thinking: this seems strange, if the argument was oral (see similar situation in 5.21,22). Here it could be that the disciples were not with Jesus when they argued, or at least they were far enough away from him so that he couldn't hear what they were arguing about.

a child: in this context, a young boy or girl.

9.47

stood him by his side: "made the child stand near him." In Greek the pronoun referring to the child is neuter; the child could have been either a girl or a boy.

9.48 TEV	RSV
and said to them, "Whoever welcomes this child in my name, welcomes me; and whoever welcomes me, also welcomes the one who sent me. For he who is least among you all is the greatest."	and said to them, "Whoever receives this child in my name receives me, and whoever receives me receives him who sent me; for he who is least among you all is the one who is great."

welcomes: "receives" (RSV), "says, 'Welcome!'"

this child: of course the child serves as an example; the saying does not refer to the child as an individual but as a representative of unimportant people in general.

in my name: "as my follower," "because he is my disciple," "as my representative."

the one who sent me: that is, God. To welcome a child means to welcome Jesus, which means to welcome God.

he who is the least: "the one who is least important," "the one who considers himself least important."

the greatest: "the most important." The Greek has the positive form "great" (RSV), but in this context it has the superlative force greatest (as the comparative "smaller" in Greek has the superlative force of "smallest").

SECTION HEADING

Whoever Is Not against You Is for You: "One Who Is Not Your Enemy Is Your Friend."

These two verses could well be joined to the preceding section; but since the question they deal with is different, it may be better to keep them as a separate section.

9.49 TEV	RSV
John spoke up, "Master, we saw a man driving out demons in your name, and we told him to stop, because he doesn't belong to our group."	John answered, "Master, we saw a man casting out demons in your name, and we forbade him, because he does not follow with us."

John: the disciple, son of Zebedee (see 5.10; 6.14).

spoke up: the literal translation "answered" (RSV) makes it appear that John's remark is in response to what Jesus had said. It is better to use an expression like the one in TEV.

Master: see 5.5.

[166]

driving out demons: "expelling demons from people," "ordering demons to go out of people."

in your name: "using your authority (or, your power)," "claiming to be your follower (or, representative)." It is to be noticed that the person who is doing this is not a disciple of Jesus.

we told him to stop: or "we tried to stop him," "we tried to make him quit."

he doesn't belong to our group: "he is not one of us," "he is not one of your disciples." Here our is inclusive.

9.50

TEV	RSV
"Do not try to stop him," Jesus said to him and to the other disciples, "because whoever is not against you is for you."	But Jesus said to him, "Do not forbid him; for he that is not against you is for you."

Do not try to stop him: "Don't tell him to quit."
The Greek text has "Jesus said to him (that is, John), 'You (plural) are not to stop him, because whoever is not against you (plural) is for you (plural).'" That is why TEV has Jesus said to him and to the other disciples. Or else, "Jesus said to his disciples."

against you...for you: "your enemy...your friend." The plural you refers to the disciples as a group, and somehow seems to exclude Jesus. So some translations have "against us...for us" (as the Greek text says in Mark 9.40). But if there is no great problem involved, it is better to have "you (plural)" and not "us."

SECTION HEADING

A Samaritan Village Refuses to Receive Jesus: "Jesus Starts on His Way to Jerusalem," "The Unfriendly Samaritans."

Here begins a section in Luke that goes through 19.27, where Jesus finally reaches Jerusalem. Throughout this long middle section of the Gospel, Jesus is on his way to Jerusalem with his disciples, knowing that betrayal and death await him there. The refusal of the people in a village in Samaria to welcome Jesus reflects ancient racial and religious hostility.

9.51

TEV	RSV
As the time drew near when Jesus would be taken up to heaven, he made up his mind and set out on his way to Jerusalem.	When the days drew near for him to be received up, he set his face to go to Jerusalem.

taken up to heaven: this translates the Greek noun "ascension," which is related to the verb "to ascend" used in Acts 1.2,11,22. There are various ways translations have expressed this: "go up to heaven," "be received in heaven (by God)," "be taken away from this world." It is not recommended that "be taken back to heaven" be used.

he made up his mind and set out on his way: "he decided firmly that he would go to Jerusalem." Most languages have vivid and clear expressions to indicate a firm decision and unshakable resolution.

9.52 TEV	RSV
He sent messengers ahead of him, who went into a village in Samaria to get everything ready for him.	And he sent messengers ahead of him, who went and entered a village of the Samaritans, to make ready for him;

messengers: most likely some of the twelve disciples, but this is not said explicitly.

Samaria: the province between Galilee and Judea. There was much hostility between Jews and Samaritans because of differences in race, customs, politics, and religion.

to get everything ready for him: "to arrange a place for him to stay (or, to spend the night)," "to arrange lodging for him."

9.53 TEV	RSV
But the people there would not receive him, because it was clear that he was on his way to Jerusalem.	but the people would not receive him, because his face was set toward Jerusalem.

The reason the Samaritans would not receive Jesus was that they knew he was on his way to Jerusalem to take part in one of the religious festivals at the Temple. They were unwilling to help people going to celebrate a festival at a place they themselves did not regard as the true place of worship.

9.54 TEV	RSV
When the disciples James and John saw this, they said, "Lord, do you want us to call fire down from heaven to destroy them?"*j*	And when his disciples James and John saw it, they said, "Lord, do you want us to bid fire come down from heaven and consume them?"*e*

*j*Some manuscripts add as Elijah did. *e*Other ancient authorities add as Elijah did

James and John: see 5.10.
saw this: or "heard about this," "learned about this."
Lord: see 5.8.
call fire down from heaven: or "ask God to send fire down from heaven."

Textual Note: as the RSV and TEV footnotes show, many Greek manuscripts and early versions add "as Elijah did" (a reference to the incident narrated in 2 Kgs 1.9-12). The older translations (such as KJV)

included these words, but it is quite certain that they were not part of
the original text of Luke.

9.55   TEV   RSV
    Jesus turned and rebuked them.^{k} But he turned and rebuked them.^{f}

^{k}*Some manuscripts add* and said, ^{f}Other ancient authorities add *and*
"You don't know what kind of a   *he said, "You do not know what*
Spirit you belong to; for the Son   *manner of spirit you are of; for*
of Man did not come to destroy   *the Son of man came not to destroy*
men's lives, but to save them."   *men's lives but to save them"*

    rebuked: see 4.35.
    Textual Note: as the RSV and TEV footnotes show, some Greek manu-
scripts and early versions add, "and said, 'You don't know what kind of
Spirit you belong to; for the Son of Man did not come to destroy men's
lives but to save them.'" The older translations included this material,
but recent translations, based on better editions of the Greek New Testament, omit it. It is difficult to be certain of the exact meaning of the
word "spirit" in this passage. TEV (in footnote) takes it to be the divine Spirit: "You don't know the nature of God's Spirit, to whom you belong"—that is, that the Spirit which controlled them was not one of
vengeance and destruction. The second saying is similar to 19.10.

9.56   TEV   RSV
Then Jesus and his disciples went   And they went on to another village.
on to another village.

    Jesus and his disciples went: the literal translation "they went"
(RSV) would mean (1) James and John, or (2) Jesus, James, and John, or
(3) Jesus and all the disciples. It seems obvious that the text means
Jesus and all the disciples, and a translation should make this clear.

SECTION HEADING

    The Would-Be Followers of Jesus: "Some Who Wanted to Follow Jesus,"
"Conditions of Discipleship." The English expression Would-Be implies an
unaccomplished goal; they expressed a desire but did not act on it.

    Jesus is on his way to his death in Jerusalem, and this section
shows what is required of those who want to follow him. Complete dedica-
tion to Jesus and to the principles of the Kingdom of God is required.

9.57   TEV   RSV
    As they went on their way, a   As they were going along the
man said to Jesus, "I will follow   road, a man said to him, "I will
you wherever you go."   follow you wherever you go."

[169]

As they went on their way: since this begins a new section it may be better to say "As Jesus and his disciples went...."

I will follow you: "I will go with you," "I will be your disciple."

wherever you go: "to all places (or, any place) you go to." This man volunteers to follow Jesus.

9.58	TEV	RSV
	Jesus said to him, "Foxes have holes, and birds have nests, but the Son of Man has no place to lie down and rest."	And Jesus said to him, "Foxes have holes, and birds of the air have nests; but the Son of man has nowhere to lay his head."

Foxes have holes: there may be a specific term for the place where foxes live: "burrows," or "lairs," or "dens."

birds have nests: these are wild birds (Greek "the birds of the air"), not domesticated fowl. Jesus is saying that wild animals, both beasts and birds, have a place to call their own, where they can rest and be safe from their natural enemies.

the Son of Man: see 5.24. Since Jesus is talking about himself, it may be necessary to say "but I, the Son of Man, have no place...."

to lie down and rest: this translates the Greek "to lay his head" (RSV). Jesus points out to the man that he, Jesus, has no fixed place to stay, and any follower must be willing to share his homelessness.

9.59	TEV	RSV
	He said to another man, "Follow me." But that man said, "Sir, first let me go back and bury my father."	To another he said, "Follow me." But he said, "Lord, let me first go and bury my father."

In this case, Jesus commands a man to become his disciple.

Sir: see 5.12.

first let me go back: it may be necessary to expand somewhat, as follows: "I will (follow you), but first let me go back...."

go back: go back home.

bury my father: there seem to be two possible meanings: (1) this is meant literally; that is, the man's father is already dead, or is near death, and the man wants to take care of his father's funeral before going with Jesus; or (2) the expression may be an idiom which means that the father is an old man, and he, the son, wants to stay home and provide for his father as long as the father lives; then the son will go with Jesus. In view of the uncertainty, it is recommended that the translation say quite clearly "and bury my father," as though the father had already died.

9.60	TEV		RSV

9.60   TEV   RSV

Jesus answered, "Let the dead bury their own dead. You go and proclaim the Kingdom of God."

But he said to him, "Leave the dead to bury their own dead; but as for you, go and proclaim the kingdom of God."

Let the dead bury their own dead: there is an obvious play on words here, for no dead person can bury another dead person. The first the dead is quite clearly used in the figurative sense, "people who are not spiritually alive," that is, people whose lives are not measured in terms of the Kingdom of God and its demands. The second their own dead means dead people who are members of a person's family. The answer seems rather cruel, for Jesus is demanding that this man not perform one of the most important duties of a pious Jew, that is, provide a proper funeral for the dead father and thus show proper respect. But Jesus' command "Follow me" takes precedence over all family obligations. "The task of burying dead people belongs to those who are spiritually dead; if you want true life, follow me!" This is the meaning of Jesus' statement.

proclaim the Kingdom of God: "announce the message about the Kingdom of God" (see 9.2). For Kingdom of God see 4.43.

9.61   TEV   RSV

Another man said, "I will follow you, sir; but first let me go and say good-bye to my family."

Another said, "I will follow you, Lord; but let me first say farewell to those at my home."

This man is a volunteer, but asks that he be allowed to do something else before following Jesus.

sir: as in verse 59.

say good-bye to my family: this is a reasonable request, from this man's point of view. But it shows some hesitation on his part in acting immediately and decisively on his offer.

9.62   TEV   RSV

Jesus said to him, "Anyone who starts to plow and then keeps looking back is of no use for the Kingdom of God."

Jesus said to him, "No one who puts his hand to the plow and looks back is fit for the kingdom of God."

starts to plow: plowing at that time was done by having an animal pull a plow; its sharp point dug into the soil, while the man would hold the handles of the plow and guide it in order to make a straight furrow. He had to keep a close look at the ground in front of him to avoid any stones or roots that might break the point of the plow. If he kept looking back he would not be able to do a good job of plowing. Where plowing is not practiced, an expression for preparing the ground or otherwise working in the fields might be used; or else a footnote might provide the necessary information.

is of no use for the Kingdom of God: that is, does not measure up to its requirements. To follow Jesus in the Kingdom of God requires single-minded devotion to the task; a person who wants to be a citizen of the Kingdom cannot be distracted by other matters.

Chapter 10

SECTION HEADING

<u>Jesus Sends Out the Seventy-Two</u>: "The Mission of Seventy-Two Follow-ers of Jesus."

This incident is similar to the sending out of the twelve apostles (9.1-6), and some of the instructions are the same. The thirty-six pairs of disciples are sent ahead to places where Jesus himself planned to go, and so they prepare the way for him. A sense of urgency dominates the account; there is not much time, and the messengers must concentrate on doing their job without distraction or interference. The return of the disciples is reported in verses 17-20, after the account of Jesus' con-demnation of towns whose people did not repent and believe (verses 13-16).

10.1

TEV

After this the Lord chose an-other seventy-two^l men and sent them out two by two, to go ahead of him to every town and place where he himself was about to go.

RSV

After this the Lord appointed seventy^g others, and sent them on ahead of him, two by two, into every town and place where he himself was about to come.

^{l}seventy-two; *some manuscripts have* seventy.

^{g}Other ancient authorities read *seventy-two*

<u>the Lord</u>: see 5.8.
<u>chose</u>: "selected," "appointed" (RSV), "designated."
<u>seventy-two</u>: as the RSV and TEV texts and footnotes show, there is uncertainty here (and in verse 17) whether the original text of Luke had the number seventy or seventy-two. The witness of the Greek manuscripts and early versions is fairly evenly divided and does not settle the question. Most modern translations have seventy-two in the text and seventy in the footnote.
<u>seventy-two men</u>: the Greek text says only "seventy-two others" (that is, other than the twelve apostles). The presumption is that they were all men, but this is not necessarily so; there could have been women in the group, especially wives of some of the men. If possible a neutral term "seventy-two other disciples (or, followers)" is preferable to <u>sev-enty-two men</u>.
<u>every town and place</u>: the word for <u>place</u> in Greek is just as vague as the English word.
<u>where he himself was about to go</u>: Jesus is on the road, on the way to Jerusalem (9.51-52).

[173]

10.2

10.2 TEV	RSV
He said to them, "There is a large harvest, but few workers to gather it in. Pray to the owner of the harvest that he will send out workers to gather in his harvest.	And he said to them, "The harvest is plentiful, but the laborers are few; pray therefore the Lord of the harvest to send out laborers into his harvest.

harvest: this figure of speech is used of people; they are ready to be persuaded, or won over to accept Jesus' message. They are ready to be "gathered in" into the Kingdom of God, as harvest is gathered into a barn. There are various ways of speaking about harvest: "crop," "ripe grain," "what is ready to be reaped."

the owner of the harvest: this refers to God; owner translates the word "lord" (see 5.12, Sir).

workers: in this context the intended meaning is probably "more workers"; there are already a few, and more are needed. The Greek word translated workers is a general term; a specific term such as "reapers," "harvesters," may be used.

If the figurative language of this saying does not carry much meaning in a given language, it can be changed to a simile: "The people you will go to are like a harvest that is ready to be gathered, but there are few people to go out and win them. So pray to God, who is like the owner of a crop, that he will send out more of his servants to gather these people into the Kingdom of God."

10.3 TEV	RSV
Go! I am sending you like lambs among wolves.	Go your way; behold, I send you out as lambs in the midst of wolves.

like lambs among wolves: as a lamb is weak and defenseless against ravaging wolves, so the followers of Jesus would be defenseless against their enemies.

10.4 TEV	RSV
Don't take a purse or a beggar's bag or shoes; don't stop to greet anyone on the road.	Carry no purse, no bag, no sandals; and salute no one on the road.

purse: "money bag" or whatever may be a portable container for metal money.

beggar's bag: see 9.3.

shoes: "sandals" (RSV). The text seems to mean that they were not to wear sandals at all; but the meaning could be that they were not to carry an extra pair with them.

don't stop to greet: "don't take the time to greet." There is urgency in their mission, and they are to hurry on to their destinations without wasting any time. The English word "salute" (RSV) should not be taken to mean just to wave the hand as one goes by without stopping.

10.5   TEV   RSV

Whenever you go into a house, first   Whatever house you enter, first say,
say, 'Peace be with this house.'   'Peace be to this house!'

Whenever you go into a house, first say: "Before you go into someone's home, say."
Peace be with this house: this is the Jewish greeting. Peace is not
just lack of hostility but a condition of well-being, health, prosperity:
"May all be well with you." Here the word house stands for "family"; so
the translation could be " Peace be with all of you," "I wish peace to
all this family," "May God give peace to you."

10.6   TEV   RSV

If a peace-loving man lives there,   And if a son of peace is there, your
let your greeting of peace remain   peace shall rest upon him; but if
on him; if not, take back your   not, it shall return to you.
greeting of peace.

a peace-loving man: this translates the idiom "a son of peace" (RSV).
Here peace-loving is used in the general sense of "friendly," "hospita-
ble."
your greeting of peace: "your greeting, 'Peace be with you.'"
let...remain on him: this can be expressed negatively, "don't take
it back," "don't withdraw it."
take back: "revoke," "annul," "withdraw." This instruction reflects
the belief that a greeting of peace would actually confer peace, well-
being, to the ones to whom it was extended; to retract it meant to cancel
the blessings.

10.7   TEV   RSV

Stay in that same house, eating and   And remain in the same house, eat-
drinking whatever they offer you,   ing and drinking what they provide,
for a worker should be given his   for the laborer deserves his wages;
pay. Don't move around from one   do not go from house to house.
house to another.

Stay in that same house: see the similar instruction in 9.4.
a worker should be given his pay: "a worker deserves his salary."
This is a general statement (perhaps proverbial) and is added to justify
the instruction that the disciples are to receive free hospitality from
their hosts, and not have to carry provisions with them.
Don't move around from one house to another: they were to be satisfied with what they received from their hosts, and not seek more lavish
accommodations and food with some other family in that town.

10.8 TEV	RSV
Whenever you go into a town and are made welcome, eat what is set before you,	Whenever you enter a town and they receive you, eat what is set before you;

are made welcome: "the people there welcome (or, receive) you."
eat what is set before you: "eat whatever they give you," "be satisfied with whatever food they provide you."

10.9 TEV	RSV
heal the sick in that town, and say to the people there, 'The Kingdom of God has come near you.'	heal the sick in it and say to them, 'The kingdom of God has come near to you.'

heal the sick: see 9.2.
say to the people there: RSV "say to them" makes it appear that the disciples were to say this only to the sick; what is meant is all the people in that town.
Kingdom of God: see 4.43.
has come near you: both RSV and TEV translate the Greek verb "has come near." But it could mean "has arrived," "is here," and that is how some translate it. (For further comments see Mark Handbook on 1.15.)

10.10-11 TEV	RSV
But whenever you go into a town and are not welcomed, go out in the streets and say, 11 'Even the dust from your town that sticks to our feet we wipe off against you. But remember that the Kingdom of God has come near you!'	But whenever you enter a town and they do not receive you, go into its streets and say, 11 'Even the dust of your town that clings to our feet, we wipe off against you; nevertheless know this, that the kingdom of God has come near.'

Here is the opposite case of the friendly reception in verses 6-8.
Even the dust: see the same instruction in 9.5. Here the verb wipe off is used, whereas in 9.5 it is shake off; but the action is the same, that is, taking off the sandals and removing the dust.
we wipe off against you: "we wipe off to show that what you are doing is wrong."
remember: "know" (RSV), "be aware of the fact."
the Kingdom of God has come near you: as RSV shows, the Greek text does not have the pronoun "you." There may be an intentional difference between this and what is said in verse 9b; but it seems quite likely that the two are parallel, so that TEV you is justified.

10.12 TEV	RSV
I assure you that on the Judgment Day God will show more mercy to Sodom than to that town!	I tell you, it shall be more tolerable on that day for Sodom than for that town.

I assure you: "I tell you the truth," "Believe me," "You may be sure."
the Judgment Day: "the day when God will judge the world," "the day
when God will judge all the people of the world." This is what Greek "on
that day" (RSV) means.
show more mercy to: or "be less severe with," or "punish (the people
of) Sodom less...."
Sodom: a city near the Dead Sea which God had destroyed by fire because of the great wickedness of its people (see Gen 19.24-28).

SECTION HEADING

The Unbelieving Towns: "The Towns Whose People Would Not Believe
Jesus" or "...Jesus' Message."

Jesus denounces two Galilean towns where he had proclaimed his message and performed miracles, and warns them that God will punish them.
These verses (13-15) are not connected chronologically with what precedes
or follows, but are placed here in order to emphasize the importance of
the mission of the disciples, and of the need of people to repent and believe. The final verse of the section (verse 16) fits into the immediate
context of Jesus' sending out his followers on their mission of preaching
and healing.

10.13   TEV   RSV
   "How terrible it will be for   "Woe to you, Chorazin! woe to
you, Chorazin! How terrible for you   you Bethsaida! for if the mighty
too, Bethsaida! If the miracles   works done in you had been done in
which were performed in you had   Tyre and Sidon, they would have re-
been performed in Tyre and Sidon,   pented long ago, sitting in sack-
the people there would have long   cloth and ashes.
ago sat down, put on sackcloth, and
sprinkled ashes on themselves, to
show that they had turned from
their sins!

How terrible: "Too bad," "How bad are the things that will happen
to you." Jesus is talking about God's punishment; he is not talking about
disasters, either natural or man-made.
Chorazin: a town north of Capernaum, on the west side of Lake Galilee; Bethsaida is probably on the northeast corner of the lake.
Tyre and Sidon: see 6.17.
sackcloth: a coarse black cloth which people wore to express sorrow
or repentance (see particularly Jonah 3.6-9).
ashes: they were sprinkled on the head. If these two cultural items
(sackcloth and ashes) are difficult or impossible to represent in translation, the meaning may be expressed by an emphatic statement such as
"the people there long ago would have declared (or, confessed) publicly
that they had turned from their sins."

[177]

10.14 TEV	RSV
God will show more mercy on the Judgment Day to Tyre and Sidon than to you.	But it shall be more tolerable in the judgment for Tyre and Sidon than for you.

See verse 12.

10.15 TEV	RSV
And as for you, Capernaum! Did you want to lift yourself up to heaven? You will be thrown down to hell!"	And you, Capernaum, will you be exalted to heaven? You shall be brought down to Hades.

Capernaum: see 4.23.
lift yourself up to heaven...be thrown down to hell: the language is taken from Isaiah 14.13,15, where the prophet denounces the king of Babylonia. The figure lift yourself up to heaven means "become the greatest (or, most powerful) of all towns," while be thrown down to hell means "be completely destroyed." The Greek word translated hell is "Hades" (see RSV), the equivalent of the Hebrew Sheol, the world of the dead. The passive be thrown down has God as the actor: "God will throw you down," "God will destroy you."

10.16 TEV	RSV
Jesus said to his disciples, "Whoever listens to you listens to me; whoever rejects you rejects me; and whoever rejects me rejects the one who sent me."	"He who hears you hears me, and he who rejects you rejects me, and he who rejects me rejects him who sent me."

This verse reflects the attitude that a messenger, such as these disciples were, represented the one who sent them. So in welcoming them, people would be welcoming the one who sent them; in rejecting them, they were rejecting the one who sent them.
listens: that is, "accepts" or "believes" (your message).
rejects: "turns away from," "refuses to listen to."
the one who sent me: that is, God. To welcome an apostle means to welcome Jesus, which means to welcome God.

SECTION HEADING

The Return of the Seventy-Two: "The Seventy-Two Disciples Return to Jesus."

This completes the story of the seventy-two commissioned messengers (10.1-12).

10.17 TEV

The seventy-two[m] men came back in great joy. "Lord," they said, "even the demons obeyed us when we gave them a command in your name!"

[m] seventy-two; *some manuscripts have* seventy *(see verse 1).*

RSV

The seventy[g] returned with joy, saying, "Lord, even the demons are subject to us in your name!"

[g] Other ancient authorities read *seventy-two*

The seventy-two men: see 10.1.
demons: see 4.33.
we gave them a command: that is, to go out of people.
in your name: "using your name," "calling out your name"; or "invoking your power (or, authority)," or "acting on your behalf," "acting as your representatives."

10.18 TEV

Jesus answered them, "I saw Satan fall like lightning from heaven.

RSV

And he said to them, "I saw Satan fall like lightning from heaven.

I saw Satan fall: "I was watching and saw when Satan fell." There is no indication as to when Jesus saw Satan fall. The statement is in answer to the disciples' power over the demons. Satan (the name of the Devil; it means "the opponent") was regarded as the chief of the demons, who got their power from him. The disciples' power over the demons was evidence that Satan, the lord of the demons, had already lost his power.
like lightning: the comparison here is with the suddenness and speed with which lightning comes down from the sky.
from heaven: this may be taken with lightning, as part of the simile: "I saw Satan when he fell, like lightning falls from the sky"; or else it may go with Satan, that is, "I saw when Satan fell from heaven, like lightning." Probably the latter is intended: the symbolism here seems to reflect the language of Isaiah 14.12, where the prophet speaks of the downfall of the king of Babylonia.

10.19 TEV

Listen! I have given you authority, so that you can walk on snakes and scorpions and overcome all the power of the Enemy, and nothing will hurt you.

RSV

Behold, I have given you authority to tread upon serpents and scorpions, and over all the power of the enemy; and nothing shall hurt you.

Listen!: this translates a form of the Greek verb "to see" (RSV "Behold"), which is an attention getter, serving to emphasize the importance of what follows.
authority: here in the sense of "power."
walk on snakes and scorpions: the language is figurative, and the translation should retain the figures, if possible. Here snakes are clearly "poisonous snakes"; and the sting of scorpions is very painful

[179]

and may occasionally be fatal. Where scorpions are unknown, the name of some dangerous reptile may be used, such as a poisonous lizard.
In the Greek text the verb "walk upon" governs the two objects, snakes and scorpions and all the power of the Enemy (see RSV); TEV uses another verb, overcome, for the latter phrase, since in English "to walk on" does not go naturally with "power."
the Enemy: the Devil (or, Satan).
hurt: "harm," "injure," "damage."
Jesus' statement is that he shares his authority with them; they are his commissioned representatives and so have his authority and power to defeat the forces of evil.

10.20 TEV	RSV
But don't be glad because the evil spirits obey you; rather be glad because your names are written in heaven."	Nevertheless do not rejoice in this, that the spirits are subject to you; but rejoice that your names are written in heaven."

don't be glad...rather be glad: this is stated absolutely, but in effect it is a comparison: "You should be happier over the fact that your names are written in heaven than you are that the evil spirits obey you."
the evil spirits: Greek says only "the spirits" (RSV); see 4.33.
your names are written in heaven: this refers to the concept of a book kept by God in which the names of the righteous, his people, are all recorded.

SECTION HEADING

Jesus Rejoices: "Jesus Praises God."

This section in TEV (verses 21-24) includes three different sayings, whose original setting may only be surmised. The first one (verse 21) is a prayer introduced by the words "In that same hour" (RSV), and so may be related to what immediately precedes; but the content of the verse argues against any such connection. The second saying (verse 22) focuses on Jesus and his relation to the Father, while the third one (verses 23-24) is addressed to the disciples.

10.21 TEV	RSV
At that time Jesus was filled with joy by the Holy Spirit[n] and said, "Father, Lord of heaven and earth! I thank you because you have shown to the unlearned what you have hidden from the wise and	In that same hour he rejoiced in the Holy Spirit and said, "I thank thee, Father, Lord of heaven and earth, that thou hast hidden these things from the wise and understanding and revealed them to

learned. Yes, Father, this was how you were pleased to have it happen.

babes; yea, Father, for such was thy gracious will.[h]

[n]by the Holy Spirit; *some manuscripts have* by the Spirit; *others have* in his spirit.

[h]Or *so it was well-pleasing before thee*

At that time: formally, with reference to what has preceded; but probably used in a rather vague and general way.

filled with joy by the Holy Spirit: this translates the Greek "rejoiced in the Holy Spirit" (RSV), which seems to mean that because of the power or influence of the Holy Spirit Jesus was joyful. The translation could be "Because of the Holy Spirit, Jesus was glad and said" or "The Holy Spirit made Jesus happy, and he said."

As TEV footnote indicates, other Greek manuscripts and early versions have different texts which may mean "Jesus was glad in his spirit"; those that have "by the Spirit" mean the same as the text translated here.

Father: "my Father."

Lord of heaven and earth: "Lord of the universe," "Master of all creation."

I thank you: or "I praise you."

A comparison between TEV and RSV shows that TEV has changed the order of the Greek, particularly because of a different understanding of the Greek demonstrative pronoun "these (things)." As translated by RSV, it would appear that this is a direct and specific reference to the power over evil that Jesus had given the disciples. TEV understands that the pronoun refers to some other specific matter, not now known, or else it refers generally to the whole teaching about the Kingdom of God (see 8.10).

shown: "revealed" (RSV), "made known."

the unlearned: "the simple," "the uninstructed people"; the Greek word "children" or "babies" (see RSV) is used here in a figurative sense of unsophisticated, inexperienced, immature people.

what: "the things that," "the truth that," "the understanding that."

the wise and learned: "the wise and intelligent": the two words mean the same, and it is not necessary to have two different words in translation, if it is not natural to use synonyms in a given language. Whatever terms are chosen, the contrast should not be between "schooled" (that is, possessing an academic degree) and "unschooled" (that is, illiterate). The contrast is not between those who have gone to school and those who haven't, but between different attitudes or perceptions: those who believe they are wise and those who admit their ignorance.

this was how you were pleased to have it happen: or, more simply, "this is what you chose to do" or "this happened in accordance with your will."

The statement may be restructured as follows: "...and said, 'I praise you, Father, Lord of the universe! I thank you because you revealed to simple people the truths you have hidden from those who are wise and intelligent. Yes, Father, I thank you that this is what you chose to do.'"

10.22 TEV	RSV
"My Father has given me all things. No one knows who the Son is except the Father, and no one knows who the Father is except the Son and those to whom the Son chooses to reveal him."	All things have been delivered to me by my Father; and no one knows who the Son is except the Father, or who the Father is except the Son and any one to whom the Son chooses to reveal him."

Here Jesus is talking, but it is no longer a prayer to God. It may be that for this reason many Greek manuscripts and early versions begin the verse, "Then Jesus turned to the disciples and said."

has given me all things: this may mean either (1) authority over all creation or (2) all knowledge. Whatever may have been the meaning in the original context, in the present context the adjective "all" probably means "all knowledge." In either case, it is the close relationship between Father and Son that is emphasized; only they truly know each other. Only the Father truly knows the Son, and only the Son truly knows the Father.

But the second part of the statement has an added element: people can truly know who God is, but only those who have been given this knowledge by the Son himself.

10.23 TEV	RSV
Then Jesus turned to the disciples and said to them privately, "How fortunate you are to see the things you see!	Then turning to the disciples he said privately, "Blessed are the eyes which see what you see!

This third saying specifies that it was addressed privately to the disciples. All these sayings emphasize the privileged situation of the followers of Jesus: they are "the simple ones" who have received truths barred from the wise and learned; they have received from Jesus the revelation about the Father; and they have seen the truth about the Kingdom of God that others had wanted to see but didn't.

fortunate: this translates the same word elsewhere translated "happy" (see 6.20).

to see the things you see: here the verb "to see" probably has a wider meaning than physical sight; it means to perceive the truths about God and his Kingdom.

10.24 TEV	RSV
I tell you that many prophets and kings wanted to see what you see, but they could not, and to hear what you hear, but they did not."	For I tell you that many prophets and kings desired to see what you see, and did not see it, and to hear what you hear, and did not hear it."

prophets (see 1.70): here these are the Hebrew prophets who spoke about the future actions of God and his Messiah.

kings: kings of the people of Israel.

they could not...they did not: "they didn't see...they didn't hear."

SECTION HEADING

The Parable of the Good Samaritan: "The Story about a Kind (or, Compassionate) Samaritan."

This parable is told in response to a question posed by an authorized
interpreter of the Law of Moses. The teacher of the Law wanted to put Jesus to the test; his motive may not have been as sinister as the TEV
translation implies. Whatever the man's motivation, the incident is designed to show not only Jesus' understanding of the Law of Moses, but how
that Law is to be put into practice by his followers. True life, eternal
life, is given to those whose love for others is a matter of deeds, not
of words.

10.25   TEV   RSV
     A teacher of the Law came up   And behold, a lawyer stood up
and tried to trap Jesus. "Teacher,"   to put him to the test, saying,
he asked, "what must I do to re-   "Teacher, what shall I do to in-
ceive eternal life?"   herit eternal life?"

     teacher of the Law: see 5.17.
     came up: or "stood up" (RSV). If the latter is meant, it implies a
teaching situation, perhaps in a synagogue.
     tried to trap Jesus: or "put Jesus to the test" (see RSV). The Greek
verb (also used in 4.12) may have the neutral sense, meaning only that
the teacher of the Law wanted to engage Jesus in a learned dispute over
the Law of Moses.
     Teacher: this translates the Greek equivalent of "Rabbi," a title of
respect.
     receive: this translates the Greek verb "to inherit" (see RSV), used
in the biblical sense of being given by God the blessings he confers upon
his people. The English word "inherit" normally implies the death of the
one from whom the gift is received, and so is not an appropriate word.
     eternal life: this is life hereafter, the life at the end of the
present age, life in the future Messianic age.

10.26   TEV   RSV
     Jesus answered him, "What do   He said to him, "What is written in
the Scriptures say? How do you in-   the law? How do you read?"
terpret them?"

     Jesus tests the teacher of the Law, asking him how he understands
the Law of Moses.
     What do the Scriptures say?: this translates "What is written in the
law?" (RSV). For "written" see 2.23; for the Scriptures see 4.16. "The
Law" refers to the first five books of the Old Testament, the Torah.
     How do you interpret them?: literally "How do you read?" (RSV), or
"How do you understand them?" Or else the translation can be "What do you
read in them?" That is, what do you learn when you read them?

[183]

10.27 TEV	RSV
The man answered, "'Love the Lord your God with all your heart, with all your soul, with all your strength, and with all your mind'; and 'Love your neighbor as you love yourself.'"	And he answered, "You shall love the Lord your God with all your heart, and with all your soul, and with all your strength, and with all your mind; and your neighbor as yourself."

The teacher of the Law answers by quoting Deuteronomy 6.5 and Leviticus 19.18.

The first command cited (Deut 6.5) is addressed to Israel as a whole, and so the singular "your" in the Lord your God indicates that the Lord is the God of Israel. As the man recites the commandment, "You shall love the Lord your God" (RSV), the pronoun "you" and the adjective "your" do not refer to Jesus but are part of the language of Deuteronomy 6.5. If there is a problem with the pronoun referent, the translation could be "We must love the Lord our God," in which "we" and "our" are inclusive; or else the indefinite "One is to love the Lord his God"—but the personal forms are better.

the Lord your God: "the Lord, who is the God you (or, we) worship." heart...soul...strength...mind: these are ways of describing the total self; it means to love with all one's being, unreservedly, totally, unconditionally. It is to be noticed that the Hebrew text of Deuteronomy 6.5 has only "heart...soul...strength."

The second command (Lev 19.18) speaks of the attitude a Jew was to have toward a fellow Jew; neighbor here is a generic term, meaning one of the same country (or race); it does not refer to someone who lives next door. To say "fellow human being" or "fellow-man" is to go beyond the limited meaning of the word in its biblical context; "fellow countrymen" or "fellow Jews" would be the most faithful representation of the meaning of the original. Or else, in a vaguer sense, of those who belong to one's group: "Love those who belong to your group as you love yourself." The whole point of the story here is the definition of "neighbor": in Leviticus 19.18 it meant one thing; Jesus is about to redefine the word more broadly.

as you love yourself: "just as much as you love yourself."

Here again the you and yourself do not refer to Jesus; so it may be better to translate the commandment, "We must love our fellow countrymen as we love ourselves."

10.28 TEV	RSV
"You are right," Jesus replied; "do this and you will live."	And he said to him, "You have answered right; do this, and you will live."

Jesus approves of the answer given by the teacher of the Law.

You are right: "You have answered correctly."

do this: that is, put into practice these two commandments you have just cited. A conditional form may be useful: "If you do this you will live."

live: that is, in terms of the man's question (verse 25), "live eternally."

10.29

TEV	RSV
But the teacher of the Law wanted to justify himself, so he asked Jesus, "Who is my neighbor?"	But he, desiring to justify himself, said to Jesus, "And who is my neighbor?"

justify himself: "put himself in the right," "vindicate himself." The sense seems to be that since the teacher of the Law knew the answer to his own question, his question was pointless; so he wants to justify his question, to show that his question was a valid one.

Who is my neighbor?: the question he now asks implies that the meaning of "neighbor" is not certain; the commandment is not clear. It should be quite clear in translation that the singular neighbor is a generic term; it is not a reference to one person only.

10.30

TEV	RSV
Jesus answered, "There was once a man who was going down from Jerusalem to Jericho when robbers attacked him, stripped him, and beat him up, leaving him half dead.	Jesus replied, "A man was going down from Jerusalem to Jericho, and he fell among robbers, who stripped him and beat him, and departed, leaving him half dead.

There was once a man: this is a conventional way in English of beginning a story.

going down from Jerusalem to Jericho: Jericho was some 24 kilometers northeast of Jerusalem and some 1,100 meters lower in altitude.

robbers attacked him: the literal "he fell among robbers" (RSV) could be misleading. These are "bandits" or "outlaws."

stripped him: "took off his clothes"; here the idea could be "took away everything he had."

beat him up: probably with clubs or sticks.

10.31

TEV	RSV
It so happened that a priest was going down that road; but when he saw the man, he walked on by on the other side.	Now by chance a priest was going down that road; and when he saw him he passed by on the other side.

It so happened: "by chance" (RSV), "by coincidence."

going down: from Jerusalem to Jericho.

on the other side: that is, on the opposite side of the road so as to avoid any possibility of ritual defilement.

10.32 TEV	RSV
In the same way a Levite also came there, went over and looked at the man, and then walked on by on the other side.	So likewise a Levite, when he came to the place and saw him, passed by on the other side.

Levite: a member of the priestly tribe of Levi, who had the duty of helping in the services in the Temple (see Num 3.1-13; 1 Chr 23.27-32). In many translations it will be helpful to explain this title either in a footnote or else in a Word List in an appendix.
came...went over and looked: it is possible that the text means simply "when he came...and saw" (RSV); but the Greek New Testament text followed by TEV appears to say what TEV says.

10.33 TEV	RSV
But a Samaritan who was traveling that way came upon the man, and when he saw him, his heart was filled with pity.	But a Samaritan, as he journeyed, came to where he was; and when he saw him, he had compassion,

Samaritan: see 9.52.
who was traveling that way: the text does not say in which direction the Samaritan was going.
his heart was filled with pity: "he felt very sorry," "he had compassion on him" (see 7.13).

10.34 TEV	RSV
He went over to him, poured oil and wine on his wounds and bandaged them; then he put the man on his own animal and took him to an inn, where he took care of him.	and went to him and bound up his wounds, pouring on oil and wine; then he set him on his own beast and brought him to an inn, and took care of him.

oil and wine: the olive oil and wine served as remedies, the olive oil to soothe the pain and the wine to disinfect the wounds.
animal: either a donkey or a mule.
inn: a place where lodging (and food, usually) is available for pay.
he took care of him: "he provided for his needs."

10.35 TEV	RSV
The next day he took out two silver coins and gave them to the innkeeper. 'Take care of him,' he told the inkeeper, 'and when I come back this way, I will pay you whatever else you spend on him.'"	And the next day he took out two denarii^i and gave them to the innkeeper, saying, 'Take care of him; and whatever more you spend, I will repay you when I come back.' ^{i}The denarius was a day's wage for a laborer

took out: of his purse, or pocket.

two silver coins: this translates the Greek "two denarii" (see RSV); as the RSV footnote shows, a denarius was the daily wage of a common laborer (see Matt 20.2). In many languages the general term two silver coins will be understood much better than the specific "two denarii."

innkeeper: "the man who owned (or, managed) the inn."

when I come back this way: the Samaritan's instructions make clear that he plans to return that way.

10.36 TEV	RSV
And Jesus concluded, "In your opinion, which one of these three acted like a neighbor toward the man attacked by the robbers?"	Which of these three, do you think, proved neighbor to the man who fell among the robbers?"

And Jesus concluded: TEV adds this to make clear that the story is ended, and that what follows is a question to the teacher of the Law.

acted like a neighbor: "was a neighbor," "did what a neighbor should do."

10.37 TEV	RSV
The teacher of the Law answered, "The one who was kind to him." Jesus replied, "You go, then, and do the same."	He said, "The one who showed mercy on him." And Jesus said to him, "Go and do likewise."

The one who was kind to him: "The one who helped (or, took care of) him."

do the same: referring to the kindness that the Samaritan did; "act in the same way he did," "be helpful to others as he was."

SECTION HEADING

Jesus Visits Martha and Mary: "Jesus in the Home of Martha and Mary."

This short story emphasizes the prominent place given women by this Gospel.

10.38 TEV	RSV
As Jesus and his disciples went on their way, he came to a village where a woman named Martha welcomed him in her home.	Now as they went on their way, he entered a village; and a woman named Martha received him into her house.

on their way: to Jerusalem (see 9.51).

he came: this follows the text literally. The disciples are not mentioned further in this story, but it seems probable that they were still
with Jesus.

welcomed him: "received him as a guest."

10.39   TEV   RSV
She had a sister named Mary, who   And she had a sister called Mary,
sat down at the feet of the Lord   who sat at the Lord's feet and lis-
and listened to his teaching.   tened to his teaching.

a sister named Mary: it appears that Martha was the mistress of the
house, so it is probable that Mary was the younger sister.

sat down at the feet: in the position of a learner, or follower.

the Lord: see 5.8.

his teaching: or "his message," "what he said."

10.40   TEV   RSV
Martha was upset over all the work   But Martha was distracted with much
she had to do, so she came and   serving; and she went to him and
said, "Lord, don't you care that my   said, "Lord, do you not care that
sister has left me to do all the   my sister has left me to serve
work by myself? Tell her to come   alone? Tell her then to help me."
and help me!"

upset: "worried," "exasperated." Or else "Martha was very busy with
all the work."

don't you care that...?: this is a rhetorical question, expressing
Martha's exasperation. She felt she was being exploited, and she is ac-
cusing Jesus of being insensitive to her situation. "Doesn't it bother
you that...?" "Aren't you concerned over the fact that...?"

10.41-42   TEV   RSV
    The Lord answered her, "Mar-   But the Lord answered her, "Martha,
tha, Martha! You are worried and   Martha, you are anxious and troubled
troubled over so many things, 42 but about many things; 42 one thing is
just one is needed. Mary has chosen   needful.ʲ Mary has chosen the good
the right thing, and it will not be   portion, which shall not be taken
taken away from her."   away from her."

                                      ʲOther ancient authorities read *few*
                                      things are needful, or only one

Jesus' answer has been variously understood. He gently rebukes Martha for being worried and troubled over so many things, an obvious reference to all the trouble she was going to in getting the meal ready.
(This becomes even more obvious if the disciples—or some of them—are
there with Jesus.) But, he adds, just one is needed. What this refers to

is uncertain; perhaps just one dish, a simple meal, not an elaborate feast. Or else, this may be a reference to what Mary was doing: listening to his teaching was the one necessary thing.

the right thing: or "the better part." This means that Mary's choice of listening to Jesus' teaching is hers by right and should not be regarded as a selfish action for which she should be punished.

it will not be taken away from her: or "no one will ever take it away from her."

As RSV footnote shows, instead of just one is needed, some Greek manuscripts and early versions have "only a few things are needed, or just one." The text translated by RSV and TEV is the one that should be preferred.

Chapter 11

Jesus' Teaching on Prayer: "Jesus Teaches how His Followers Should Pray."

As usual in the various incidents reported in this long middle section of the Gospel (9.51—19.27), no precise time or place is given, nor is any connection made with what precedes or what follows. In response to the disciples' request, Jesus gives them a model prayer (verses 2-4), after which he tells them a story which illustrates the need for persistence in prayer.

11.1   TEV   RSV
    One day Jesus was praying in   He was praying in a certain
a certain place. When he had fin-   place, and when he ceased, one of
ished, one of his disciples said to   his disciples said to him, "Lord,
him, "Lord, teach us to pray, just   teach us to pray, as John taught
as John taught his disciples."   his disciples."

One day...a certain place: a general statement of time and place.
Lord: see 5.8.
teach us to pray: "teach us what we should say when we pray," "tell us what words to use when we pray."
John: John the Baptist; in 5.33, reference is made to the regular practice of John's disciples of fasting and praying.

11.2   TEV   RSV
    Jesus said to them, "When you   And he said to them, "When you pray,
pray, say this: say:
        'Father: "Father, hallowed be thy name.
            May your holy name be   Thy kingdom come.
                honored;
            may your Kingdom come.

This version of what is usually called "The Lord's Prayer" differs from the better-known version in Matthew 6.9-13. Early copyists of the manuscripts added to this Gospel the various words and phrases from Matthew to make the two identical (see KJV), but a modern translation should follow the best Greek text, as represented in RSV and TEV.
Father: where this is obligatorily possessed, "Our Father" (since this is a corporate prayer).

May your holy name be honored: "We pray that people will honor your holy name." It may be that in some languages name has no real relation to the person, so it may be best to translate "May people honor you as being holy," "We pray that people will honor you as God" or "...acknowledge that you are the true God."

may your Kingdom come: "we pray that you will (soon) rule over all humanity (or, all the world)." For Kingdom see 4.43.

11.3	TEV	RSV
	Give us day by day the food we need.^{o}	Give us each day our daily bread;^{k}

^{k}Or our bread for the morrow

^{o}the food we need; or food for the next day.

Give: care should be taken not to choose a verb which means "to dole out"; in some languages the appropriate equivalent will be "make it possible for us to have."

day by day: "every day," "each day" (RSV).

the food we need: "enough food to satisfy our needs"; food translates the Greek word for "bread" (RSV), which means here food in general and not just bread as such. As RSV and TEV footnotes show, there is uncertainty over the precise meaning of the Greek word translated we need; it may be taken to mean "the food we need for this very day" or "the food we need for the next day."

11.4	TEV	RSV
	Forgive us our sins, for we forgive everyone who does us wrong. And do not bring us to hard testing.'"	and forgive us our sins, for we ourselves forgive every one who is indebted to us; and lead us not into temptation."

Forgive: in some languages there are idiomatic expressions available (see 5.20).

sins: "wrongs," "bad things," "actions which are against your will."

everyone who does us wrong: this translates "everyone who is in debt to us" (see RSV), which is one of the biblical ways of speaking about sins and transgressions. A literal translation may make it appear that financial obligations are meant, so it is better to translate as TEV has done, or else, "everyone who sins against us."

do not bring us to hard testing: the Greek word translated hard testing may be understood in the morally neutral sense of "test" or the negative sense of "temptation," depending on the purpose of such an event. If the purpose is good (as it must be if God is the author), then something like testing seems appropriate; if the purpose is evil, that is, to lead one into sin, then the proper translation would be "temptation." The petition reflects the belief that God governs all circumstances of our lives, so that temptations from the Devil are understood as testing sent by God. The verb bring may be better represented by "take," "lead" (RSV), "make us go." Some languages may prefer to use a causative expression such as "Please do not cause us to meet hard testing."

11.5-6 TEV	RSV
And Jesus said to his disciples, "Suppose one of you should go to a friend's house at midnight and say to him, 'Friend, let me borrow three loaves of bread. 6 A friend of mine who is on a trip has just come to my house, and I don't have any food for him!'	And he said to them, "Which of you who has a friend will go to him at midnight and say to him, 'Friend, lend me three loaves; 6 for a friend of mine has arrived on a journey, and I have nothing to set before him';

In the story that follows it is easy to get the pronominal referents confused, so care must be taken that the reader know throughout the story that: (1) Jesus is speaking; (2) one of you (disciples) is the main actor in this make-believe story; and (3) there are two friends, one who comes to spend the night with the main actor, and the other one to whose house the main actor goes in order to get food. Another factor to be considered is that the form of the main part of the story is that of a question (verses 5-7; see RSV), with an implied answer that is not at all clear. So a translator should clearly understand the story before translating it, and should make sure that the various participants are clearly defined and easily identified.

Suppose: this is a way of beginning a made-up story. "Let's make believe that...."

midnight: "late at night," "the middle of the night."

let me borrow: "lend me" (RSV), "I need to borrow."

loaves of bread: at that time a loaf was fairly small, round, and hard.

who is on a trip: "who has been traveling," "who is passing through."

11.7 TEV	RSV
And suppose your friend should answer from inside, 'Don't bother me! The door is already locked, and my children and I are in bed. I can't get up and give you anything.'	and he will answer from within, 'Do not bother me; the door is now shut, and my children are with me in bed; I cannot get up and give you anything'?

And suppose: this is added by TEV in order to keep clear the flow of the story.

your friend: to make clear who is the speaker and to whom he is speaking.

door is already locked...my children and I are in bed: the friend refuses the request because of the trouble involved. The setting is that of a rather humble Palestinian home, with only one large room, in which at night mats were spread on the floor for the family to sleep.

11.8　　　　　TEV

Well, what then? I tell you that
even if he will not get up and give
you the bread because you are his
friend, yet he will get up and give
you everything you need because you
are not ashamed to keep on asking.

RSV

I tell you, though he will not get
up and give him anything because
he is his friend, yet because of
his importunity he will rise and
give him whatever he needs.

Well, what then?: another TEV device to carry on the story. The
story has been told, and now Jesus is bringing it to a rather surprising
conclusion. Another possibility would be "What do you think he will do?"
　　even if he will not...yet he will: this rather elaborate structure
may need to be simplified; for example, "I tell you, it may be true that
he won't get up and give you the bread just because you are his friend
(or, you and he are friends). But he will get up and give you all you
need because you are not ashamed to keep on asking." Or else, "Even
though he doesn't want to, he will at last get up and give you everything
you need. He will do it, not because you are his friend, but because you
keep on asking."
　　(you are) not ashamed to keep on asking: this translates the Greek
"(his) bold persistence," "shameless insistence."

11.9　　　　　TEV

And so I say to you: Ask, and you
will receive; seek, and you will
find; knock, and the door will be
opened to you.

RSV

And I tell you, Ask, and it will be
given you; seek, and you will find;
knock, and it will be opened to you.

　　Ask, and you will receive: "Ask God (for what you need) and he will
give it to you." It should be noticed that here Ask means to ask for
something, not to ask a question.
　　seek...knock: as with Ask, God is the one from whom something is
sought. There is a progression from the general to the particular: simply
to Ask is general; to seek is to try to find a particular thing; to knock
is to go to the place where one believes that particular thing will be
found.
　　find: not accidentally but on purpose. The translation may be "you
will obtain (or, get) it," "you will have it."
　　knock: this is a way of asking permission to enter a place. It may
be better to say "knock on God's door and he will open it for you"; care,
however, must be taken not to imply that the one doing the knocking is
seeking permission to enter heaven. In a number of languages a person
makes his presence known by coughing, or calling out, or clapping his
hands, and not by knocking. So appropriate adjustments must be made; in
some tribes in East Africa only thieves will knock, and they do so to
find out whether there is anyone at home.
　　the door will be opened: "God will open the door." There may be some
difficulty in preserving the figure, but it should be kept, if at all
possible. It may be possible to use the idea of "help": "if you ask for
God's help, he will give it to you."

11.10	TEV	RSV

For everyone who asks will receive, and he who seeks will find, and the door will be opened to anyone who knocks.

For every one who asks receives, and he who seeks finds, and to him who knocks it will be opened.

The same expressions should be used in this verse as in the previous verse.

will receive: as it stands, this implies that God will give anything that a person asks for; but as verse 13 shows, God is concerned to give good things to those who ask him. The absolute language of this verse, however, should not be qualified, as it is characteristic of much of Jesus' teaching.

will be opened to anyone: it may be necessary to say "will be opened for him to enter," to avoid giving the impression that the door will be opened only momentarily and be closed soon after.

11.11-12	TEV	RSV

Would any of you who are fathers give your son a snake when he asks for fish? 12 Or would you give him a scorpion when he asks for an egg?

What father among you, if his son asks for^l a fish, will instead of a fish give him a serpent; 12 or if he asks for an egg, will give him a scorpion?

^{l}Other ancient authorities insert bread, will give him a stone; or if he asks for

Would any of you who are fathers...?: this rhetorical question may be transformed into a statement: "None of you who are fathers would...," "No father would...," or "A father would not...." Or the saying may be reversed: "When a son asks his father for a fish, will his father give him a snake?" or "...his father will not give him a snake."

snake: if this animal is regularly eaten (which it wasn't by the Jews in the time of Jesus), it will be necessary to refer to a snake that is not eaten, or else to an animal that is not used for food.

a scorpion: see 10.19. It is said that a scorpion with its limbs closed around it looks like a small egg.

The saying may be restructured as follows: "Suppose one of you has a son who comes and asks you for a fish. Would you give him a snake? (Or, ...You wouldn't give him a snake!) Or if he asks for an egg, would you give him a scorpion? (Or, ...you wouldn't give him a scorpion!)"

As the RSV footnote shows, some Greek manuscripts and early versions insert in verse 11 the addition "if he asks for bread, will you give him a stone?" (as in Matt 7.9). This is not part of the original text of Luke and should not be included in translation.

11.13	TEV	RSV

As bad as you are, you know how to give good things to your children.

If you then, who are evil, know how to give good gifts to your children,

How much more, then, will the Father in heaven give the Holy Spirit to those who ask him!"	how much more will the heavenly Father give the Holy Spirit to those who ask him!"

TEV has restructured the material in this verse, giving first the statement of fact about how a human father acts, and then the declaration of how the heavenly Father acts.

As bad as you are: a statement of the fact that all human beings are sinful. "Even though you are bad, you know how...."

How much more, then: the generosity and goodness of the heavenly Father is much greater than that of an earthly father.

the Father in heaven: "your heavenly Father," or "your Father who lives in heaven."

the Holy Spirit: here regarded as the greatest gift the heavenly Father can bestow on his children.

SECTION HEADING

Jesus and Beelzebul: "Jesus Is Accused of Being Allied with Beelzebul."

Jesus is pictured here engaged in his mission of expelling demons, which gives rise to a controversy. The theme of increased criticism of and opposition to Jesus on the part of the religious leaders becomes more and more prominent from now on, but does not come to a head until the last week in Jerusalem.

11.14 TEV	RSV
Jesus was driving out a demon that could not talk; and when the demon went out, the man began to talk. The crowds were amazed,	Now he was casting out a demon that was dumb; when the demon had gone out, the dumb man spoke, and the people marveled.

driving out a demon: see 4.33.

that could not talk: since the demon-possessed man could not talk, it was concluded that the demon itself was dumb; when the demon was expelled, the man was able to talk.

The crowds: "The large crowd," "all the people there."

amazed: see 2.18.

11.15 TEV	RSV
but some of the people said, "It is Beelzebul, the chief of the demons, who gives him the power to drive them out."	But some of them said, "He casts out demons by Beelzebul, the prince of demons";

Beelzebul: the name given to the Devil as the ruler of evil spirits.

the chief of the demons: "the ruler (or, king) of the demons."

gives him the power to drive them out: the phrase in Greek "in (the name of) Beelzebul" indicates that Jesus is seen not just as an ally of but as a subordinate to Beelzebul; it is the greater one who gives authority or power to someone else.

11.16	TEV	RSV
	Others wanted to trap Jesus, so they asked him to perform a miracle to show that God approved of him.	while others, to test him, sought from him a sign from heaven.

It is to be noticed that RSV closely joins this verse to the preceding one, while TEV begins a separate paragraph here. The verse deals with a different subject (which will be taken up only in verses 29-32); verses 17-20 have to do with the accusation of being in league with Beelzebul.

wanted to trap: this verb is the same one used in 4.2, and is also closely related to the one used in 10.25. Here the purpose is clearly evil, so TEV has to trap. The trap is this: if Jesus performs a miracle, he does it for his own benefit (something Jesus always refused to do); if he doesn't, this proves (so they thought) that God isn't with him.

a miracle to show that God approved of him: this translates the Greek "a sign from heaven" (RSV), which indicates proof of God's approval in the form of a miracle. The miracle would show that God's power was really at work in Jesus. The translation may say "a miracle as proof (or, evidence) that he possessed God's power (or, authority)." The direct form of address may be used, "...so they asked him, 'Perform a miracle and that will show us that God approves of you (or, ...that you really have God's power).'"

11.17	TEV	RSV
But Jesus knew what they were thinking, so he said to them, "Any country that divides itself into groups which fight each other will not last very long; a family divided against itself falls apart.		But he, knowing their thoughts, said to them, "Every kingdom divided against itself is laid waste, and a divided household falls.

knew what they were thinking: this would seem to refer to the people in verse 16; but the statement of Jesus answers the accusation of the people in verse 15, who had not spoken directly to Jesus.

Any country: Jesus makes a comparison, pointing out what happens to any organized group, whether a country (Greek "kingdom") or a family, whenever there is controversy and fighting. Internal revolt brings ruin. The comparison with Satan's kingdom in the next verse is obvious.

will not last very long: "is ruined," "falls into chaos," "collapses."

falls apart: "does not survive," "comes to an end."

11.18	TEV	RSV

So if Satan's kingdom has groups fighting each other, how can it last? You say that I drive out demons because Beelzebul gives me the power to do so.

And if Satan also is divided against himself, how will his kingdom stand? For you say that I cast out demons by Beelzebul.

For the literal form of the Greek text see RSV.

how can it last?: "it will not survive," "it will come to an end."

You say that: Jesus cites their own words to show how stupid their accusation is. If he were fighting Beelzebul's servants by the power that Beelzebul gave him, the result would be civil war in Beelzebul's kingdom. For Satan see 10.18.

11.19	TEV	RSV

If this is how I drive them out, how do your followers drive them out? Your own followers prove that you are wrong!

And if I cast out demons by Beelzebul, by whom do your sons cast them out? Therefore they shall be your judges.

Here Jesus uses another argument to show how stupid their accusation is.

your followers: "people belonging to your group"; this is what the Greek "your sons" (RSV) means.

prove that you are wrong: in the context, this is what "they will be your judges" means (see RSV). The fact that the followers of Jesus' accusers had the power to expel demons was proof that the accusation made against him was frivolous and baseless.

The statement may be restructured: "If I drive out demons by means of the power that Beelzebul gives, then who gives your followers the power to drive them out?"

11.20	TEV	RSV

No, it is rather by means of God's power that I drive out demons, and this proves that the Kingdom of God has already come to you.

But if it is by the finger of God that I cast out demons, then the kingdom of God has come upon you.

it is rather by means of God's power: this translates what in Greek is formally a conditional statement, "if it is..." (RSV). This kind of conditional statement assumes that the condition is true, so a translation should not make it appear that there is some doubt about it.

God's power: this translates "the finger of God" (RSV), by which God's power in action is meant (see Exo 8.19).

the Kingdom of God: see 4.43.

has already come to you: "has arrived upon you," "is already here with (or, among) you." The activity of Jesus in driving out demons is evidence that the Kingdom of God has arrived. Instead of speaking of the coming of the Kingdom of God, it may be better to translate "...that God has already begun to rule among (or, over) you."

	TEV	RSV
11.21	"When a strong man, with all his weapons ready, guards his own house, all his belongings are safe.	When a strong man, fully armed, guards his own palace, his goods are in peace;

In verses 21-22 the figure changes somewhat; the picture here is of a house guarded by its owner, who is strong and well armed. Only someone stronger will be able to plunder the house. It seems better to do as TEV has done and begin a new paragraph. This is a short parable in which a strong man stands for Satan, while a stronger man is Jesus, who has the power of God. A translation should retain the figures, without trying to interpret them; in the context, the meaning is quite clear.

house: the Greek word is not the usual one for "house"; it could mean "courtyard," "farm," "dwelling," or "palace" (RSV). Here the more general term house seems preferable.

	TEV	RSV
11.22	But when a stronger man attacks him and defeats him, he carries away all the weapons the owner was depending on and divides up what he stole.	but when one stronger than he assails him and overcomes him, he takes away his armor in which he trusted and divides his spoil.

the weapons the owner was depending on: "the weapons the owner trusted to keep him safe" or "...to repel the enemy."

divides up: that is, with his companions or friends.

what he stole: this translates "his booty," "his spoil" (RSV). This could mean: (1) the things the strong man had previously stolen and which now had been taken from him; or (2) the things the stronger man took from the strong man. In either case the "spoil" or booty is the same, but it is probable that meaning (1) is intended by the Greek.

	TEV	RSV
11.23	"Anyone who is not for me is really against me; anyone who does not help me gather is really scattering.	He who is not with me is against me, and he who does not gather with me scatters.

This verse seems to be an independent saying which has been placed in this context. Here the meaning is that there are no neutral spectators in the fight between the forces of the Kingdom of God and the forces of Satan. TEV says really in both instances in order to make the paradox less strange.

for me: "with me" (RSV), "on my side."

help me gather...scattering: this is a figure taken from harvest; whoever does not help Jesus gather in people, that is, bring people to him, is scattering them. Or the figure could be that of a flock of sheep: a shepherd tries to keep the sheep together and not to scatter them. In either case, the point of the saying is the same.

SECTION HEADING

The Return of the Evil Spirit: "From Bad to Worse."

This saying about evil spirits is placed here, since the subject of the whole preceding section has been that of demons and Beelzebul.

11.24 TEV	RSV
"When an evil spirit goes out of a person, it travels over dry country looking for a place to rest. If it can't find one, it says to itself, 'I will go back to my house.'	"When the unclean spirit has gone out of a man, he passes through waterless places seeking rest; and finding none he says, 'I will return to my house from which I came.'

an evil spirit: see 4.33; here evil translates the Greek "unclean" (RSV).

goes out: "is driven out," "is expelled."

dry country: "land without any water," "country where there are no rivers or springs." The desert was thought to be the place where demons liked to live.

a place to rest: "a place to live," "a home."

it says to itself, 'I will go back to my house': "it decides to go back to its house," "...go back home."

my house: the evil spirit considers the person it had possessed as belonging to it.

11.25 TEV	RSV
So it goes back and finds the house clean and all fixed up.	And when he comes he finds it swept and put in order.

clean and all fixed up: this simply says what the house is now like; there is no indication that someone cleaned it and fixed it up. The assumption is that the house is like it was when the demon left it.

fixed up: not in the sense of "repaired," but "tidied up," "neat," "everything in place."

11.26 TEV	RSV
Then it goes out and brings seven other spirits even worse than itself, and they come and live there. So when it is all over, that person is in worse shape than he was at the beginning."	Then he goes and brings seven other spirits more evil than himself, and they enter and dwell there; and the last state of that man becomes worse than the first."

they come: or "they go."

when it is all over: "in the end"; or "the final condition of that person is worse than his original condition," because now he has eight evil spirits, not just one.

[199]

11.27

SECTION HEADING

True Happiness: "Jesus Teaches Who Is Truly Happy."

This brief incident emphasizes the importance of obeying God's message as proclaimed by Jesus.

11.27 TEV	RSV
When Jesus had said this, a woman spoke up from the crowd and said to him, "How happy is the woman who bore you and nursed you!"	As he said this, a woman in the crowd raised her voice and said to him, "Blessed is the womb that bore you, and the breasts that you sucked!"

a woman spoke up from the crowd: or "a woman in the crowd spoke up."
spoke up...and said: or "called out to him," "shouted at him."
How happy: see 6.20.
the woman who bore you and nursed you: that is, your mother. In some circumstances it may be indelicate to speak of "the womb...and the breasts that you sucked" (RSV), and the most appropriate way to phrase this should be used; for example, "the woman who gave birth to you and brought you up."

11.28 TEV	RSV
But Jesus answered, "Rather, how happy are those who hear the word of God and obey it!"	But he said, "Blessed rather are those who hear the word of God and keep it!"

Jesus' answer is that obeying God's word counts more for true happiness than being his (that is, Jesus') mother.
the word of God: "God's message" (see 5.1).

SECTION HEADING

The Demand for a Miracle: "Jesus Refuses to Perform a Miracle."

The setting for this statement of Jesus goes back to verse 16 (see verse 16). Jesus refuses to perform a miracle designed to prove that he is God's authorized spokesman.

11.29 TEV	RSV
As the people crowded around Jesus, he went on to say, "How evil are the people of this day! They ask for a miracle, but none will be given them except the miracle of Jonah.	When the crowds were increasing, he began to say, "This generation is an evil generation; it seeks a sign, but no sign shall be given to it except the sign of Jonah.

the people of this day: "the people living now," "This generation" (RSV).

a miracle: this translates the word "sign" (as in verse 16).

miracle of Jonah: "the sign of Jonah" (RSV). As the following verse makes clear, what is meant here is not Jonah's three days and nights in the fish (as in Matt 12.39-40), but Jonah's mission to the people of Nineveh. Here, then, miracle might be out of place, and something different might be attempted, such as "...but none (or, no miracle) will be performed for them. The only thing they will be given is the example of Jonah." And then what comes in verse 30 follows quite naturally.

11.30   TEV

In the same way that the prophet Jonah was a sign for the people of Nineveh, so the Son of Man will be a sign for the people of this day.

RSV

For as Jonah became a sign to the men of Nineveh, so will the Son of man be to this generation.

the prophet Jonah was a sign for the people of Nineveh: here Jesus explains what a sign is: not an amazing miracle performed by Jonah, but the message that he, as a prophet, announced to the people of Nineveh, the capital of the mighty empire of Assyria (see Jonah 3). Jonah's message was that God's punishment would soon fall upon the city unless the people confessed their sins and repented. Jonah's message was the sign. In the same way the Son of Man is a sign for the people of his day. For Son of Man see 5.24.

the people of Nineveh: "the Ninevites." RSV "the men of Nineveh" is wrong.

11.31   TEV

On the Judgment Day the Queen of Sheba will stand up and accuse the people of today, because she traveled all the way from her country to listen to King Solomon's wise teaching; and there is something here, I tell you, greater than Solomon.

RSV

The queen of the South will arise at the judgment with the men of this generation and condemn them; for she came from the ends of the earth to hear the wisdom of Solomon, and behold, something greater than Solomon is here.

the Queen of Sheba: the story is told in 1 Kings 10.1-10. TEV has used the Old Testament name Sheba; RSV translates the Greek word used here, "the South."

will stand up and accuse: she will act as witness against the people living in Jesus' day. Both here and in the next verse will stand up (two different but synonymous verbs in Greek) could be taken to mean "will rise," "will be resurrected"; while possible, this interpretation is not very likely. But if this meaning is chosen, it could be represented: "The Queen of Sheba will be raised together with the people living now, and she will accuse you."

all the way from her country: the Greek says "from the ends of the earth"; this could be represented by "a very long distance," or with a modern idiom, "halfway around the world."

something...greater: the Greek text does not say "someone greater," as though referring to Jesus himself, but something...greater. The emphasis is on Solomon's wisdom: he was the wisest person of his time (see 1 Kgs 4.29-31); and the something...greater here is the wisdom of the teachings about the Kingdom of God.

11.32   TEV   RSV

| On the Judgment Day the people of Nineveh will stand up and accuse you, because they turned from their sins when they heard Jonah preach; and I assure you that there is something here greater than Jonah! | The men of Nineveh will arise at the judgment with this generation and condemn it; for they repented at the preaching of Jonah, and behold, something greater than Jonah is here. |

the people of Nineveh: here the Greek says "the men of Nineveh," a reference to those who lived in Nineveh when Jonah went there.
they turned from their sins: see 3.3.
something...greater: here, again, not a person, "someone greater." In this case it is the message of Jonah, which caused a whole city to repent and so save itself from destruction. This something...greater is the message about the Kingdom of God, which is greater than the message proclaimed by Jonah.

SECTION HEADING

The Light of the Body: "The Eyes as the Light for the Body."

In this section two different sayings have been brought together. The first one (verse 33) has to do with the proclamation of the Kingdom of God, which is likened to a lamp that, when lit, should be put where its light can be seen by all. The second saying (verses 34-36) has to do with spiritual perception, that is, understanding of spiritual truths, which are compared to light.

11.33   TEV   RSV

| "No one lights a lamp and then hides it or puts it under a bowl;[p] instead, he puts it on the lampstand, so that people may see the light as they come in. | "No one after lighting a lamp puts it in a cellar or under a bushel, but on a stand that those who enter may see the light. |

[p]*Some manuscripts do not have* or puts it under a bowl.

No one lights...or puts: "People do not light...and put." If the plural "people" is used, it may be necessary to say "lamps," in which case the singular it (three times) must become "them."
a lamp: see 8.16.
hides it: "puts it in a hidden place."

bowl: the Greek word refers to a dry measure of about two gallons
(over eight liters), and such a bowl was used to measure and to hold
grain; it would be big enough so that a lamp could be placed under it.
lampstand: "the place where the lamp is placed."
as they come in: to the house, probably a small one-room house common in Jesus' day.

11.34   TEV   RSV
Your eyes are like a lamp for the   Your eye is the lamp of your body;
body. When your eyes are sound,   when your eye is sound, your whole
your whole body is full of light;   body is full of light; but when it
but when your eyes are no good,   is not sound, your body is full of
your whole body will be in darkness. darkness.

Your eyes: "The eyes," "A person's eyes." Throughout all three verses
(34-36) you and your are singular but are used to refer to anyone in general.
are like a lamp: the Greek text uses a metaphor, "are a lamp," which
TEV has represented by a simile (the Greek also uses the singular "eye"—
see RSV). The figure seems strange, for the eyes are spoken of as a source
of light, so that healthy eyes provide the body with lots of light while
poor eyes provide the body with no light. If the figure is difficult to
retain, a translation may say 'Your eyes provide light for the body (or,
the whole person)," "Your eyes let in light for the body."
Some have interpreted the Greek word translated sound as a reference
to generosity, and the Greek word translated no good as a reference to
stinginess. This is possible, but most translations follow the interpretation adopted in TEV and others.

11.35   TEV   RSV
Make certain, then, that the light   Therefore be careful lest the light
in you is not darkness.   in you be darkness.

the light in you is not darkness: another paradoxical statement,
since darkness cannot be light. Another possible translation would be
'Make sure that you have light in yourself and not darkness," "Be certain
that instead of darkness, you have light in you."

11.36   TEV   RSV
If your whole body is full of   If then your whole body is full of
light, with no part of it in dark-   light, having no part dark, it will
ness, it will be bright all over,   be wholly bright, as when a lamp
as when a lamp shines on you with   with its rays gives you light."
its brightness."

The contrasting light and darkness are figures for life and death.
To be completely possessed by (God's) light, inside and out, is to have
life, full life, real life.

11.37

SECTION HEADING

Jesus Accuses the Pharisees and the Teachers of the Law: "Jesus Condemns the Religious Leaders."

Here the hostility between Jesus and the religious leaders is shown to be intensifying. Jesus' accusations are very sharp and seem rather unprovoked. In this Gospel there have been few instances of opposition on the part of the religious leaders, and it is to be noticed that in the other Gospels this extended criticism of them comes later, during the last week in Jerusalem (see Matt 23.1-36; Mark 12.38-40).

11.37 TEV	RSV
When Jesus finished speaking, a Pharisee invited him to eat with him; so he went in and sat down to eat.	While he was speaking, a Pharisee asked him to dine with him; so he went in and sat at table.

When Jesus finished speaking: this better represents the meaning of the Greek than RSV "While he was speaking."
Pharisee: see 5.17.
eat with him: that is, at his house. It is not certain which meal this is; perhaps it is the main meal of the day (see 7.36).
sat down to eat: see 5.29; 7.36.

11.38 TEV	RSV
The Pharisee was surprised when he noticed that Jesus had not washed before eating.	The Pharisee was astonished to see that he did not first wash before dinner.

was surprised: the same verb as in verse 14.
washed: or "bathed." The verb means "to dip," and here it may mean "to dip the hands" or else "to dip the body"; probably the former is meant. The washing was as much a ritual as a hygienic measure; it was done not only to get rid of dirt but also to rid a person of ritual defilement caused by being in contact with Gentiles or with ritually unclean objects.

11.39 TEV	RSV
So the Lord said to him, "Now then, you Pharisees clean the outside of your cup and plate, but inside you are full of violence and evil.	And the Lord said to him, "Now you Pharisees cleanse the outside of the cup and of the dish, but inside you are full of extortion and wickedness.

the Lord: see 5.8.
clean the outside of your cup and plate: not a hygienic measure, but a ritual action. Here the outside is stressed, to contrast with the inside that follows; it is the contrast between external (ceremonial) matters and internal (ethical) matters.

[204]

inside you are full: this is precisely what the Greek text seems to
say (literally "but your [plural] inside is full"). But in light of the
fact that in the next two verses the "inside" and "outside" refer quite
specifically to dishes and not to the person, it is possible that here
the Greek "your inside" means "the inside of your cups and plates" (as
it clearly is in Matt 23.25). But very few translations have so rendered
it.

violence and evil: that is, you cherish, or harbor, ideas of violence and evil in your hearts.

11.40	TEV	RSV
Fools! Did not God, who made the outside, also make the inside?	You fools! Did not he who made the outside make the inside also?

This saying makes more sense if in verse 39 "your inside" means "the
inside of your cups and plates." For here the meaning is clearly that the
inside (of the cups and plates) is just as sacred in God's sight as is
the outside.

The rhetorical question expects "Yes" for an answer; a statement may
be more appropriate: "God made both the outside and the inside," "God
made the inside as well as the outside."

11.41	TEV	RSV
But give what is in your cups and plates to the poor, and everything will be ritually clean for you.	But give for alms those things which are within; and behold, everything is clean for you.

give...to the poor: "give as alms," "presents of love," "gifts of
pity (or, compassion)."

what is in your cups and plates: this translates "the things inside
referring to the food. Acts of love and compassion count more than ritual
cleanliness; they really make something acceptable to God, fit for his use
(that is, "clean").

everything will be ritually clean for you: in the context, all cups
and plates, but perhaps in a broader sense, "everything you have." All
you have will become ritually clean if you perform deeds of charity.

11.42	TEV	RSV
"How terrible for you Phari⁻ sees! You give to God one tenth of the seasoning herbs, such as mint and rue and all the other herbs, but you neglect justice and love for God. These you should practice, without neglecting the others.	"But woe to you Pharisees! for you tithe mint and rue and every herb, and neglect justice and the love of God; these you ought to have done, without neglecting the others.

How terrible for you: see 6.24. This refers to God's punishment.
You give to God one tenth: Leviticus 27.30 and Deuteronomy 14.22
specify that one tenth of all the produce of the land, whether grain or

fruit, must be given to God; the Pharisees were so strict in obeying this command that they gave one tenth even of the seasoning herbs.

mint and rue: these are herbs used for seasoning food, so TEV has added the qualifier the seasoning herbs. The stems and leaves of mint and the leaves of rue were sprinkled on food. (See *Fauna and Flora of the Bible* for a description of these plants.) Where these herbs are unknown, one may say "little scented plants used for seasoning food" or "cheap seasoning plants," "small plants of little value."

neglect: "fail to practice," "don't follow."

justice: "doing the right thing to others."

love for God: that is, to obey the commandment to love God (see 10.27).

These you should practice, without neglecting the others: "These are the really important things you should do; but this does not mean that you should fail to do the other things."

11.43   TEV   RSV

"How terrible for you Phari-   Woe to you Pharisees! for you love
sees! You love the reserved seats   the best seat in the synagogues and
in the synagogues and to be greeted salutations in the market places.
with respect in the marketplaces.

reserved seats in the synagogues: for synagogues see 4.15. The reserved seats were in front of the wooden chest which contained the sacred scrolls; they were reserved for important people.

to be greeted with respect: "to have people greet you respectfully," "to have people bow to you when they meet you."

11.44   TEV   RSV

How terrible for you! You are like Woe to you! for you are like graves
unmarked graves which people walk   which are not seen, and men walk
on without knowing it."   over them without knowing it."

The point of this saying is that graves were regarded as ritually unclean because of the decomposing bodies inside; so they were carefully marked so people would not defile themselves by walking on them. But if the grave was unmarked, someone might walk on it without knowing it, and so become ritually unclean. So the Pharisees, with their hearts full of violence and evil (verse 39), were sources of defilement, for their exterior did not reveal the filthy condition of their interior. Without knowing it, people would become defiled by coming in contact with them.

It may be necessary either to put some information in a footnote, or else fill out the text here; for example, "You are like unmarked graves that people don't see; they walk on them and become ritually unclean."

11.45-46   TEV   RSV

One of the teachers of the Law   One of the lawyers answered
said to him, "Teacher, when you say   him, "Teacher, in saying this you
this, you insult us too!"   reproach us also." 46 And he said,

46 Jesus answered, "How terrible also for you teachers of the Law! You put onto people's backs loads which are hard to carry, but you yourselves will not stretch out a finger to help them carry those loads.

"Woe to you lawyers also! for you load men with burdens hard to bear, and you yourselves do not touch the burdens with one of your fingers.

teachers of the Law: see 5.17.
insult: "speak rude words," "say bad things."
You put...loads which are hard to carry: this is a figure of speech for the duties that the teachers of the Law, on the basis of their interpretation of the Law of Moses, imposed on the people. There were many laws in the oral tradition that had grown around the written Law, and which the teachers of the Law said should be obeyed also. The figure may be abandoned: "You impose heavy obligations that are difficult to obey," "There are many difficult obligations (or, laws) which you say people must follow."
The following figure (stretch out a finger) may also be expressed literally: "but you yourselves will not do anything to make it easier for people to obey those laws." Jesus is condemning their lack of compassion in their unwillingness to interpret and apply the laws in such a way as to make them easier to obey.

11.47-48   TEV
How terrible for you! You make fine tombs for the prophets—the very prophets your ancestors murdered. 48 You yourselves admit, then, that you approve of what your ancestors did; they murdered the prophets, and you build their tombs.

RSV
Woe to you! for you build the tombs of the prophets whom your fathers killed. 48 So you are witnesses and consent to the deeds of your fathers; for they killed them, and you build their tombs.

You make fine tombs: "You build the tombs in which the prophets are buried." For prophets see 1.70.
You yourselves admit: this translates "you are witnesses" (RSV). The meaning is "Your actions show (or, prove) that...."

11.49   TEV
For this reason the Wisdom of God said, 'I will send them prophets and messengers; they will kill some of them and persecute others.'

RSV
Therefore also the Wisdom of God said, 'I will send them prophets and apostles, some of whom they will kill and persecute,'

the Wisdom of God: it is impossible to tell what this refers to, whether to a book by that title, or to a passage in a book in which Wisdom is personified and speaks (as she does in Prov 8). In any case, it does not seem that this phrase means "God, in his wisdom, says"—although many so translate it. For the personalized use of Wisdom see also 7.35.

them...they: in this context, the people of the time of Jesus.
messengers: probably "apostles" (RSV) represents better the meaning of the word (see 6.13).
and persecute others: it does not seem likely that the Greek text means, as RSV has it, "some of whom they will kill and persecute."

11.50   TEV

TEV	RSV
So the people of this time will be punished for the murder of all the prophets killed since the creation of the world,	that the blood of all the prophets, shed from the foundation of the world, may be required of this generation,

the people of this time: literally "this generation."
will be punished for the murder of all the prophets killed: this represents the meaning of "the blood of all the prophets...may be required" (RSV).
The passive will be punished may be changed to an active, "God will punish (the people of this time)." Or else, the Greek idiom may be taken to mean "so the people of this time will be charged with (or, held responsible for; or, found guilty of) the murder of all the prophets."

11.51   TEV

TEV	RSV
from the murder of Abel to the murder of Zechariah, who was killed between the altar and the Holy Place. Yes, I tell you, the people of this time will be punished for them all!	from the blood of Abel to the blood of Zechariah, who perished between the altar and the sanctuary. Yes, I tell you, it shall be required of this generation.

Abel: the first one to be murdered (Gen 4.8).
Zechariah: son of Jehoiada the priest, of the late ninth century B.C., whose murder is reported in 2 Chronicles 24.20-22. In the Hebrew arrangement of the Old Testament books, 2 Chronicles is the last book, so that Zechariah's murder is the last one to be reported in the Hebrew Bible, as Abel's is the first one.
between the altar and the Holy Place: the altar was the one that stood in the court at the east side of the Temple; the Holy Place is the Temple.
will be punished: the same as in verse 50.

11.52   TEV

TEV	RSV
"How terrible for you teachers of the Law! You have kept the key that opens the door to the house of knowledge; you yourselves will not go in, and you stop those who are trying to go in!"	Woe to you lawyers! for you have taken away the key of knowledge; you did not enter yourselves, and you hindered those who were entering."

the key that opens the door to the house of knowledge: this translates "the key of knowledge" (RSV). In view of the following go in, TEV
took the figure to represent knowledge as a house (or school, or synagogue). In any case, the language is figurative, and knowledge here is
not scientific or academic knowledge, but knowledge of God's will as revealed in the Torah.

11.53-54	TEV	RSV
	When Jesus left that place, the teachers of the Law and the Pharisees began to criticize him bitterly and ask him questions about many things, 54 trying to lay traps for him and catch him saying something wrong.	As he went away from there, the scribes and the Pharisees began to press him hard, and to provoke him to speak of many things, 54 lying in wait for him, to catch at something he might say.

When Jesus left: and not "As Jesus left" (see RSV).
criticize him bitterly: "accuse him angrily," "be very hostile to
him."
trying to lay traps: the language is figurative. They were trying to
get Jesus to say something that would lay him open to the charge of disobeying the Law of Moses or of offending the holy name of God.

Chapter 12

A Warning against Hypocrisy: "Jesus Warns against Hypocrisy."

Verses 1-12 contain a series of warnings and assurances that Jesus directs to his disciples. Most translations divide them into three sections, as TEV has done.

12.1

TEV	RSV
As thousands of people crowded together, so that they were stepping on each other, Jesus said first to his disciples, "Be on guard against the yeast of the Pharisees—I mean their hypocrisy.	In the meantime, when so many thousands of the multitude had gathered together that they trod upon one another, he began to say to his disciples first, "Beware of the leaven of the Pharisees, which is hypocrisy.

thousands of people: the language is not precise, and the figure in the Greek text, "tens of thousands of the crowd," is meant to indicate a very large group of people.

stepping on each other: "getting in one another's way," "pushed one another."

said first to his disciples: logically, Jesus should then have spoken to the crowd, but this does not happen. The adverb may mean "spoke primarily to his disciples."

Be on guard against: "Watch out for," "Keep yourselves from," "Have nothing to do with."

the yeast of the Pharisees: yeast (or, leaven) is a substance used in the making of bread, to cause the dough to rise. In some languages it is called "that which causes bread to swell (or, to rise)" or "that which causes bread to be sour." Here Jesus uses the word in a figurative sense, which is immediately explained: the yeast used by the Pharisees is their hypocrisy (see 6.42), their appearing to be what they really were not.

12.2

TEV	RSV
Whatever is covered up will be uncovered, and every secret will be made known.	Nothing is covered up that will not be revealed, or hidden that will not be known.

Whatever is covered up...every secret: this is an example of poetic parallelism, in which the same thing is said in two different ways. If

[210]

necessary the two can be expressed by one statement: "Everything that is not known," "Every secret action (or, word)," "Everything that people do (or, say) in private."

will be uncovered...will be made known: "will become known," "everyone will know about it." The time when this will happen is the Day of Judgment, and the uncovering or revelation will be God's judgment. So it may be preferable to use an active form of the verb: "God will uncover... God will make known."

As RSV shows, the form of the statement is a double negative ("Nothing...will not be revealed"), which TEV has represented by a positive. In connection with verse 1, the meaning is that hypocrisy is useless; hidden motives and desires will at last become known.

12.3   TEV   RSV

TEV	RSV
So then, whatever you have said in the dark will be heard in broad daylight, and whatever you have whispered in private in a closed room will be shouted from the housetops.	Therefore whatever you have said in the dark shall be heard in the light, and what you have whispered in private rooms shall be proclaimed upon the housetops.

This verse also uses parallelism; the same truth is expressed in two different ways.

in the dark: "in secret," "in private," "in hiding."

in broad daylight: "publicly," "openly," "where everyone can hear."

the housetops: the roofs of the houses were flat, and people would go up there for rest and conversation at the end of the day's work. The houses were quite close to one another, and so it was possible for people on one roof to talk to the people on the roof of the next house. If this cultural item makes no sense or gives the wrong sense in some language, it is possible to say "will be proclaimed publicly," "will be told in the public squares (or, out in the streets)."

SECTION HEADING

Whom to Fear: "You Should Fear God," "Don't Fear People; Fear God."

This saying is directed to Jesus' disciples and teaches the need to trust in God, who has the power of death and life over all creation.

12.4   TEV   RSV

TEV	RSV
"I tell you, my friends, do not be afraid of those who kill the body but cannot afterward do anything worse.	"I tell you, my friends, do not fear those who kill the body, and after that have no more that they can do.

of those who kill the body: "of people, who can only kill the body," or "...kill you physically," or "...cause you to die physically."

do anything worse: or "do anything else."

12.5 TEV	RSV
I will show you whom to fear: fear God, who, after killing, has the authority to throw into hell. Believe me, he is the one you must fear!	But I will warn you whom to fear: fear him who, after he has killed, has power to cast into hell;[m] yes, I tell you, fear him!

[m]Greek *Gehenna*

fear God: the Greek has "fear him who..." (RSV), a reference to God, who as Judge of all has the right and power to throw into hell.

after killing: this may be wrongly understood to mean that God has the power to throw into hell only after he kills someone. So the translation may be "fear God, who not only has the authority (or, power) to kill a person, but also to throw that person into hell (or, cause that person to go to hell)."

hell: "place of destruction," "place of punishment of the wicked"; it was thought of as an abyss in the depths of the earth. The Greek word *geenna* has been transliterated "Gehenna" in English (see the RSV footnote); the Greek word represents the Hebrew phrase "valley of Hinnom," which was to the south and southwest of Jerusalem, where the city's refuse was dumped.

12.6 TEV	RSV
"Aren't five sparrows sold for two pennies? Yet not one sparrow is forgotten by God.	Are not five sparrows sold for two pennies? And not one of them is forgotten before God.

sparrows: common and worthless birds.

two pennies: the smallest unit of currency; "very little money."

not one...is forgotten: or, stated positively, "God remembers them all," "God cares for each and every sparrow."

12.7 TEV	RSV
Even the hairs of your head have all been counted. So do not be afraid; you are worth much more than many sparrows!	Why, even the hairs of your head are all numbered. Fear not; you are of more value than many sparrows.

have all been counted: another way of referring to God. It would seem rather odd to say "God has counted them all"; it would be more appropriate to say something like "God knows how many they are." The whole saying could be rendered, "God even knows how many hairs you have on your head."

do not be afraid: of people, that is; or, of anything that might happen to you.

worth much more: in God's sight. "You are worth much more to God," "you are much more precious to God."

SECTION HEADING

Confessing and Rejecting Christ: "Being for Christ or Being against Christ."

There are three sayings in this section: the first one (verses 8-9) and the third one (verses 11-12) encourage faithfulness; the second one (verse 10) warns against blaspheming the Holy Spirit. Jesus is still speaking to his disciples.

12.8-9 TEV	RSV
"I assure you that whoever declares publicly that he belongs to me, the Son of Man will do the same for him before the angels of God. 9 But whoever rejects me publicly, the Son of Man will also reject him before the angels of God.	"And I tell you, every one who acknowledges me before men, the Son of man also will acknowledge before the angels of God; 9 but he who denies me before men will be denied before the angels of God.

declares publicly that he belongs to me: "declares openly that he is my follower," "says, 'I am a follower (or, disciple) of the Son of Man.'" A rather complete statement must be made here in order to make clear what the following "denies me" (RSV) means.

publicly: "in front of everybody," "where everyone can hear."

the Son of Man: see 5.24. Since Jesus is speaking about himself, it may be necessary to say "I, the Son of Man."

before the angels of God: this represents the Day of Judgment.

rejects me: here the opposite of "acknowledges me" of verse 8 (RSV); "denies that he is my follower," "says, 'I am not a follower of the Son of Man.'"

12.10 TEV	RSV
"Anyone who says a word against the Son of Man can be forgiven; but whoever says evil things against the Holy Spirit will not be forgiven.	And every one who speaks a word against the Son of man will be forgiven; but he who blasphemes against the Holy Spirit will not be forgiven.

says a word against: "says wrong (or, bad) things about." The language is vague, and the expression is a general one which includes any kind of hostile or disrespectful statement. It is something deliberately said, however, not a casual slip of the tongue.

can be forgiven: or "will be forgiven" (RSV), that is, by God on Judgment Day; "God will forgive him."

says evil things: this translates the verb "to blaspheme" (see RSV), which applies specifically to unworthy statements made against God (for which, in the Old Testament, punishment was death).

will not be forgiven: by God on Judgment Day.

12.11-12   TEV   RSV

"When they bring you to be   And when they bring you before the
tried in the synagogues or before   synagogues and the rulers and the
governors or rulers, do not be wor- authorities, do not be anxious how
ried about how you will defend   or what you are to answer or what
yourself or what you will say.   you are to say; 12 for the Holy
12 For the Holy Spirit will teach   Spirit will teach you in that very
you at that time what you should   hour what you ought to say."
say."

These two verses forsee a time of persecution, when the followers
of Jesus will be put on trial because of their commitment to him.
     they bring you: "you are brought (or, taken)," "the authorities take
you."
     synagogues: see 4.15. This indicates persecution from Jews. Local
trials were held in the synagogue.
     governors or rulers: this indicates Gentile persecution. The two
Greek words mean the same and do not intend to designate two different
kinds of authorities.
     defend: that is, in the setting of a trial, an oral defense, not a
physical one, against false charges brought against them.
     yourself: this should be "yourselves"; the second person pronoun in
these two verses is always plural.

SECTION HEADING

     The Parable of the Rich Fool: "The Story about a Foolish Rich Man,"
"Jesus Warns against Love of Riches."

     The setting is still the one described in verse 1, and Jesus' par-
able is prompted by the request made by a man in the crowd.

12.13   TEV   RSV

     A man in the crowd said to   One of the multitude said to
Jesus, "Teacher, tell my brother   him, "Teacher, bid my brother divide
to divide with me the property our the inheritance with me."
father left us."

     A man in the crowd: the Greek says only "Someone in the crowd," who
is identified in verse 14 as a man.
     Teacher: see 3.12.
     the property our father left us: this translates "the inheritance"
(RSV). According to Deuteronomy 21.17, the older brother received double
the share of the younger. It seems clear that here my brother is "my
older brother."

12.14   TEV   RSV

     Jesus answered him, "Man, who But he said to him, "Man, who made
gave me the right to judge or to di- me a judge or divider over you?"
vide the property between you two?"

Man: a form of address should be chosen that is devoid of emotional content, that is, it should be neither hostile nor particularly friendly, and so be fitting for strangers. For example, in some situations in the United States, "Mister" would be appropriate; in other places, on a more informal level, "Buddy."

who gave me the right...?: I don't have the right (or, authority)," "I haven't been given the authority."

to judge or to divide the property: here, because of the nature of the case, the two functions are the same. "No one has made me a judge with the authority to divide the property between you two," "I don't have the right to decide how the property should be divided between you and your brother."

12.15   TEV   RSV
And he went on to say to them all,   And he said to them, "Take heed,
"Watch out and guard yourselves   and beware of all covetousness; for
from every kind of greed; because   a man's life does not consist in
a person's true life is not made   the abundance of his possessions."
up of the things he owns, no mat-
ter how rich he may be."

every kind of greed: greed is the strong desire to possess things; so every kind of greed is "greed for anything (or, everything)," "the desire to possess (or, own) all sorts of things."

a person's true life: as the following parable shows, Jesus is not talking about mere physical existence, that is, mortal life; he is talking of true life, which is not to be measured according to the amount of possessions.

is not made up of: "does not consist of," "is not to be measured by."

12.16-17   TEV   RSV
    Then Jesus told them this par-   And he told them a parable, saying,
able: "There was once a rich man   "The land of a rich man brought
who had land which bore good crops.   forth plentifully; 17 and he thought
17 He began to think to himself, 'I   to himself, 'What shall I do, for I
don't have a place to keep all my   have nowhere to store my crops?'
crops. What can I do?

parable: see 5.36.
There was once: see 8.5.
bore good crops: "produced (or, yielded) abundant harvests."
The man's dialogue with himself (verses 17-19) may have to be expressed in indirect form instead of the direct form used in RSV and TEV. For example, "He realized that he didn't have a place big enough in which to keep all his crops, and wondered what he could do." But, as is plain, the direct form is much more effective.

12.18 TEV	RSV
This is what I will do,' he told himself; 'I will tear down my barns and build bigger ones, where I will store the grain and all my other goods.	And he said, 'I will do this: I will pull down my barns, and build larger ones; and there I will store all my grain and my goods.

tear down: it is very likely that this does not mean the complete destruction of the materials used in his barns, but means that he would dismantle them. "I will pull down."

barns: "sheds," "bins," "storehouses."

all my other goods: "all my other possessions."

12.19 TEV	RSV
Then I will say to myself, Lucky man! You have all the good things you need for many years. Take life easy, eat, drink, and enjoy yourself!'	And I will say to my soul, Soul, you have ample goods laid up for many years; take your ease, eat, drink, be merry.'

Then I will say to myself: here myself translates "my soul" (RSV); in English, at least, myself is more natural than "my soul."

Lucky man!: this is an attempt to get the flavor of the situation; "Soul" (RSV) is a most unnatural way of addressing oneself. It is to be noticed that in verse 20 the same word occurs again, and there will be few languages in which one word will be adequate and natural in all three contexts.

If it is strange to represent a man talking to himself in the second person form of address, it is possible to translate verse 19: "And then I will tell myself what a lucky man I am! I have all the good things I need for many years. I will take life easy, eat, drink, and have a good time."

12.20 TEV	RSV
But God said to him, 'You fool! This very night you will have to give up your life; then who will get all these things you have kept for yourself?'"	But God said to him, 'Fool! This night your soul is required of you; and the things you have prepared, whose will they be?'

you will have to give up your life: "you are going to die." RSV shows that the Greek text reflects the Aramaic impersonal third person plural form, "they demand your life from you." This is a special use of the plural form that indicates God as the actor, but without mentioning God's name. "Tonight I am taking your life from you," "Tonight I am demanding that you surrender your life."

kept for yourself: "accumulated," "laid up," "stored."

12.21   TEV   RSV
    And Jesus concluded, "This is   So is he who lays up treasure for
how it is with those who pile up   himself, and is not rich toward
riches for themselves but are not   God."
rich in God's sight."

    And Jesus concluded: TEV does this to show that the story is over,
and Jesus now makes the application.
    in God's sight: "from God's point of view." Or, "This is what hap-
pens to someone who accumulates riches for himself, but whom God does
not consider rich."

SECTION HEADING

    Trust in God: "The Heavenly Father Takes Care of His Children."

    This section follows naturally upon what precedes, continuing the
theme of material possessions. Jesus teaches his followers that worry
over bodily needs is an indication of little faith in God, who knows
their needs and will provide for them.

12.22   TEV   RSV
    Then Jesus said to the disci-   And he said to his disciples,
ples, "And so I tell you not to   "Therefore I tell you, do not be
worry about the food you need to   anxious about your life, what you
stay alive or about the clothes   shall eat, nor about your body,
you need for your body.   what you shall put on.

    And so: in light of what he has just said about false wealth.
    not to worry: in some languages worry is expressed idiomatically as
"that which eats you" or "that which is killing your mind." So a translation may say "Do not let your thoughts about what you will eat or wear
kill you."
    the clothes you need for your body: "the clothes you need"; in some
languages the phrase for your body may appear ridiculous, since clothes
are obviously for the body.

12.23   TEV   RSV
Life is much more important than   For life is more than food, and the
food, and the body much more impor- body more than clothing.
tant than clothes.

    Life...the body: Jesus is making the point again that life consists
of more than satisfaction of physical needs, and that clothing is not
the most important thing so far as one's body is concerned.
    Life: "your life"; in some languages one must use a verb: "It is
more important to live than to be concerned about food."

[217]

12.24 TEV	RSV
Loot at the crows: they don't plant seeds or gather a harvest; they don't have storage rooms or barns; God feeds them! You are worth so much more than birds!	Consider the ravens: they neither sow nor reap, they have neither storehouse nor barn, and yet God feeds them. Of how much more value are you than the birds!

Look at: this might imply that as Jesus spoke there were crows flying around, which is quite possible. But it might be better to say "Think about the crows," "Take the crows as an example." This example concerns worrying about food.

crows: see *Fauna and Flora of the Bible* under the entry "Raven."

plant seeds: "plant (or, sow) crops."

gather a harvest: "bring in the grain when it is ripe."

storage rooms or barns: "places to keep their crops"; it is not necessary to have two different words.

12.25 TEV	RSV
Can any of you live a bit longer^q by worrying about it?	And which of you by being anxious can add a cubit to his span of life?^{n}
^{q}live a bit longer; *or* grow a bit taller.	^{n}Or *to his stature*

Can any of you...?: another rhetorical question which may be represented by a statement, "No one can live...."

As the TEV and RSV footnotes show, the Greek expression may be understood to refer to height, not to longevity. So the translation may say "No one can grow a bit taller...." RSV's literal "add a cubit to his span of life" does not make sense in English, except in the footnote variant "add a cubit to his stature"; a cubit was a measure of nearly half a meter (or eighteen inches).

12.26 TEV	RSV
If you can't manage even such a small thing, why worry about the other things?	If then you are not able to do as small a thing as that, why are you anxious about the rest?

such a small thing: it seems strange that to live a bit longer (verse 25) should be considered a small thing; but it would appear that the figure used ("cubit") indicates a small amount of time, as compared with the biblical seventy years as the normal life span.

12.27 TEV	RSV
Look how the wild flowers grow: they don't work or make clothes for themselves. But I tell you that not	Consider the lilies, how they grow; they neither toil nor spin;^{o} yet I tell you, even Solomon in all his

even King Solomon with all his wealth had clothes as beautiful as one of these flowers.

glory was not arrayed like one of these.

O Other ancient authorities read *Consider the lilies; they neither spin nor weave*

wild flowers: see *Fauna and Flora of the Bible* under the entry "Lily." This example concerns worrying about clothes. In translation, any brightly colored wild flower may serve to represent the meaning of the text.

As RSV footnote shows, instead of grow: they don't work or make clothes for themselves, one Greek manuscript and some early versions have "neither weave cloth nor make clothes for themselves."

with all his wealth: literally "in all his glory" (RSV), which may be translated "splendor," "luxury." In his time King Solomon was the richest of all kings (1 Kgs 10.23).

as beautiful as one of these flowers: the Greek says literally "as beautiful as the clothes one of these flowers wears." Where appropriate, the translation can say this.

12.28   TEV
It is God who clothes the wild grass—grass that is here today and gone tomorrow, burned up in the oven. Won't he be all the more sure to clothe you? What little faith you have!

RSV
But if God so clothes the grass which is alive in the field today and tomorrow is thrown into the oven, how much more will he clothe you, O men of little faith!

It is God who clothes: "God is the one who gives clothes to." The vivid expression should be preserved in translation.

wild grass: "wild (or, uncultivated) plants," "wild growth."

is here today and gone tomorrow: "is alive one day but is destroyed the next day."

burned up in the oven: the kind of growth or plants to which Jesus was referring were useful in heating up the clay ovens in which bread was baked. It is not to be implied in translation that people burned up the plants in their ovens just in order to get rid of them.

Won't he be all the more sure...?: "Certainly he will take greater care," "Certainly he will be more concerned."

What little faith you have!: "Your faith in God is so weak!" "You do not trust God as you should." This is an exclamation of surprise and at the same time a rebuke.

12.29-30   TEV
"So don't be all upset, always concerned about what you will eat and drink. 30 (For the pagans of this world are always concerned

RSV
And do not seek what you are to eat and what you are to drink, nor be of anxious mind. 30 For all the nations of the world seek these

about all these things.) Your Father knows that you need these
things.

things; and your Father knows that
you need them.

all upset: "worried," "distracted."
TEV encloses the first part of verse 30 in parentheses since it
interrupts the sequence; the second part of the verse relates directly
to verse 29.
the pagans of this world: "the heathen," "the people who do not believe in the true God," "those who do not believe in the true God are
always worried about such things."
you need these things: "you should have these things," "it is necessary for you to have food, drink, and clothing."

12.31 TEV	RSV
Instead, be concerned with his Kingdom, and he will provide you with these things.	Instead, seek his^p kingdom, and these things shall be yours as well.
	^{p}Other ancient authorities read *God's*

be concerned with his Kingdom: "be concerned with the values that
matter in the Kingdom of God," or "be concerned with living the way you
should in the Kingdom of God." For Kingdom see 4.43.
he will provide: as the RSV shows, the Greek text uses a passive
form of the verb, which points to divine activity.
As the RSV footnote shows, instead of his Kingdom many Greek manuscripts and early versions have "the Kingdom of God."

SECTION HEADING

Riches in Heaven: "Jesus Teaches how People (or, We) Can Have Riches
in Heaven."

The same subject continues: material possessions and faith in God's
goodness. Jesus is still talking with his disciples, and these verses
(32-34) may be joined to the preceding section, if it seems better to do
so.

12.32 TEV	RSV
"Do not be afraid, little flock, for your Father is pleased to give you the Kingdom.	"Fear not, little flock, for it is your Father's good pleasure to give you the kingdom.

little flock: Jesus compares his followers to a small flock of
sheep: he is their shepherd. Where this figure is unsuitable, something
like "small group" or "few people" may be said.
your Father is pleased: "your Father has decided."

give you the Kingdom: here the Kingdom of God is seen as something that will happen at the end of the world. The idea may be that of sharing in the Father's rule (see 22.29-30); so "to rule with him in his Kingdom" might be said.

12.33 TEV	RSV
Sell all your belongings and give the money to the poor. Provide for yourselves purses that don't wear out, and save your riches in heaven, where they will never decrease, because no thief can get to them, and no moth can destroy them.	Sell your possessions, and give alms; provide yourselves with purses that do not grow old, with a treasure in the heavens that does not fail, where no thief approaches and no moth destroys.

give the money to the poor: as in 11.41.
purses that don't wear out...riches in heaven: spiritual wealth, not material.
where they will never decrease: or "...never run out," "...never disappear."
thief: one who steals when the owner isn't looking; in some languages there is a distinction made between a thief and a robber; a robber uses threats or violence to take people's belongings. Here, then, thief is preferable.
moth: much of the wealth of that time consisted of expensive garments and rugs, which could be ruined by moths.

12.34 TEV	RSV
For your heart will always be where your riches are.	For where your treasure is, there will your heart be also.

your heart: this represents feelings, concern, interest. If a literal translation is misleading, something like the following may be said: "Do this (that is, accumulate riches in heaven) because your concern (or, interest) is always directed toward the place where your riches are," or "...because you are always mindful of (or, thinking about) the place where your riches are stored." Or else something quite different might be said: "If you do this, you will never be worried that your riches might disappear."

SECTION HEADING

Watchful Servants: "Jesus Tells His Disciples to Be Always Watchful."

The subject matter changes here, and Jesus begins to talk about the need for being ever alert for the unexpected and unpredictable coming of the Son of Man.

12.35   TEV   RSV
  "Be ready for whatever comes,   "Let your loins be girded and
dressed for action and with your   your lamps burning,
lamps lit,

     Be ready...dressed for action: this represents the meaning of "Your
loins are to be girded (see RSV), that is, have your clothes fastened
tightly at the waist. To prepare for action the long outer garment was
pulled up and kept tight at the waist by the belt, so as not to get in
the way. "Be ready for action, with your belts tight around your waists."
Or else, "Always be ready for whatever might happen."
     lamps: see 8.16.

12.36   TEV   RSV
like servants who are waiting for   and be like men who are waiting for
their master to come back from a   their master to come home from the
wedding feast. When he comes and   marriage feast, so that they may
knocks, they will open the door   open to him at once when he comes
for him at once.   and knocks.

     a wedding feast: this would go on for seven days, so the servants
wouldn't know exactly when their master would return.
     When he comes: in order to make the connection clearer, the trans-
lation might be "If they are ready, they will be able to open the door
for him as soon as he returns and knocks."
     knocks: see 11.9.

12.37   TEV   RSV
How happy are those servants whose   Blessed are those servants whom the
master finds them awake and ready   master finds awake when he comes;
when he returns! I tell you, he   truly, I say to you, he will gird
will take off his coat, have them   himself and have them sit at table
sit down, and will wait on them.   and he will come and serve them.

     How happy: see 6.20. Here perhaps "How fortunate" is better; or else
"How good it will be for them."
     take off his coat: or "put on an apron" or whatever is appropriate
for a man to do who is going to serve food to others.
     sit down: see 5.29.
     wait on them: "serve them food" (as in 4.39).

12.38   TEV   RSV
How happy they are if he finds them If he comes in the second watch, or
ready, even if he should come at   in the third, and finds them so,
midnight or even later!   blessed are those servants!

     at midnight or even later: this translates "even in the second watch
or the third watch" (see RSV). The twelve hours of night were divided

into four three-hour periods: the second one went from 9:00 p.m. to midnight, and the third one from midnight to 3:00 a.m.

12.39 TEV	RSV
And you can be sure that if the owner of a house knew the time when the thief would come, he would not let the thief break into his house.	But know this, that if the householder had known at what hour the thief was coming, he^q would not have left his house to be broken into.

^{q}Other ancient authorities add *would have watched and*

Here another short parabolic saying is used to teach the need for watchfulness.

the owner of a house: "the head of a family."

the thief: or "a thief" (any thief, not a specific one).

would not let: that is, he would take all the precautions necessary: locking the door securely and probably staying awake.

As the RSV footnote shows, many Greek manuscripts and early versions add "he would stay awake and" (as in Matt 24.43).

12.40 TEV	RSV
And you, too, must be ready, because the Son of Man will come at an hour when you are not expecting him."	You also must be ready; for the Son of man is coming at an unexpected hour."

In the same way that a homeowner stays on watch, the followers of Jesus must always be ready, so as not to be taken by surprise.

the Son of Man will come: or "I, the Son of Man, will come."

at an hour when you are not expecting him: "at an hour when you say, 'He isn't coming now.'"

SECTION HEADING

The Faithful or the Unfaithful Servant: "A Servant Must Be Obedient."

This section arises naturally from the preceding one, and some translations may wish to join the two sections into one. The theme that runs through this section is that of being a faithful servant during the master's absence, so as to receive an appropriate reward when he returns.

12.41 TEV	RSV
Peter said, "Lord, does this parable apply to us, or do you mean it for everyone?"	Peter said, "Lord, are you telling this parable for us or for all?"

parable: see 5.36.

apply to us: this translates "are you telling...for us" (RSV). Peter wants to know if the lesson of the parable is meant for all the listeners or in particular for the disciples.

12.42	TEV	RSV

TEV	RSV
The Lord answered, "Who, then, is the faithful and wise servant? He is the one that his master will put in charge, to run the household and give the other servants their share of the food at the proper time.	And the Lord said, "Who then is the faithful and wise steward, whom his master will set over his household, to give them their portion of food at the proper time?

The question Who, then, is...? is a way of introducing the story that is coming. It is a matter of describing such a servant. "What kind of person is a faithful and wise servant?" "How does a faithful and wise servant act (or, behave)?" As RSV shows, the question goes on to the end of the verse, but this makes for a rather complex sentence. Another possibility (besides the one TEV offers) is to turn the relative clause into another question: "Who is the servant whom the master will put in charge...?" Though formally closer to the Greek text, in effect this makes two (parallel) questions which are not answered, and the statement in verse 43 makes little sense.

faithful: "trustworthy," "obedient," "dependable."

servant: as RSV shows, the Greek word here is "steward" (RSV), that is, manager, administrator, overseer.

run the household: "manage the affairs of the house." The fact that there are several servants, supervised by a general manager, shows that this is a rather affluent household.

the other servants: or "all the people in the house" (including the members of the family).

Implicit in this verse (see the next verse) is the fact that the master is leaving home for a while, and that is why he gives this servant such a responsibility. It may be necessary to make this explicit: "I will tell you what a faithful and wise servant is like. He is the one that his master, when he is about to leave home on a trip, puts in charge of the household. The master tells him to give the other servants their food at the proper time."

12.43	TEV	RSV

TEV	RSV
How happy that servant is if his master finds him doing this when he comes home!	Blessed is that servant whom his master when he comes will find so doing.

How happy: "How fortunate"; see 6.20.

doing this: "carrying out his duties," "doing what his master had told him to do."

comes home: "returns," "comes back home."

12.44 TEV	RSV
Indeed, I tell you, the master will put that servant in charge of all his property.	Truly, I say to you, he will set him over all his possessions.

put...in charge of all his property: "put in charge of everything he owns," "make him the manager of all his affairs."

12.45-46 TEV	RSV
But if that servant says to himself that his master is taking a long time to come back and if he begins to beat the other servants, both the men and the women, and eats and drinks and gets drunk, 46 then the master will come back one day when the servant does not expect him and at a time he does not know. The master will cut him in pieces[r] and make him share the fate of the disobedient.	But if that servant says to himself, 'My master is delayed in coming,' and begins to beat the menservants and the maidservants, and to eat and drink and get drunk, 46 the master of that servant will come on a day when he does not expect him and at an hour he does not know, and will punish[r] him, and put him with the unfaithful.

[r] cut him in pieces; *or* throw him out.

[r] Or *cut him in pieces*

says to himself: TEV uses the indirect form; but RSV follows the Greek, using the direct form, which may be preferable: "...he will say to himself, 'My master is taking a long time to return.'"

beat: mistreat, abuse.

It should be noticed that the construction of verses 45-46 is rather involved: But if...and if...then the master will come back. As it stands it says that the master's return is the result of the servant's bad conduct; actually it is the punishment that the master will inflict on the servant that is the result of the bad conduct. So it may be better to restructure as follows:

45 But that servant may say to himself that his master won't come back for a long time. So he begins to beat the other servants, both the men and the women, and eats, drinks, and gets drunk. 46 One day the master will come back when the servant does not expect him and at a time he does not know, and he will punish that servant. He will cut him in pieces and make him share the fate of the disobedient.

It is to be noticed that one day and a time are two synonymous clauses, which both RSV and TEV represent formally. But it is not necessary to do so, and the translation can be "One day, at a time when the servant least expects him (or, does not expect him), the master will come back...."

12.45-46

cut him in pieces: as both TEV and RSV show, there is some uncertainty over the meaning of the Greek word, which occurs only here and in the parallel passage in Matthew 24.51. The literal meaning of the Greek is "to cut in two." In light of the uncertainty, it may be best to use a general term, "punish him severely."

share the fate of the disobedient: "be punished with the disobedient (or, the unbelievers)," "be punished as the disobedient are punished."

12.47

TEV	RSV
"The servant who knows what his master wants him to do, but does not get himself ready and do it, will be punished with a heavy whipping.	And that servant who knew his master's will, but did not make ready or act according to his will, shall receive a severe beating.

These two verses (47-48) point up the responsibility that goes with privilege: to know and disobey is a worse offense than to be ignorant and disobey.

The servant who knows...but does not: or "If a servant knows...but he does not...."

a heavy whipping: "a severe punishment," "will be heavily flogged."

12.48

TEV	RSV
But the servant who does not know what his master wants, and yet does something for which he deserves a whipping, will be punished with a light whipping. Much is required from the person to whom much is given; much more is required from the person to whom much more is given.	But he who did not know, and did what deserved a beating, shall receive a light beating. Every one to whom much is given, of him will much be required; and of him to whom men commit much they will demand the more.

"But if a servant does not know what his master wants (him to do), and yet does something for which he should be punished, he will receive a light punishment."

The final conclusion is stated in the second part of verse 48: privilege brings responsibility. The two passive phrases much is given and much more is given refer to God's action in giving abilities or opportunities to his servants. "God expects much (or, a lot) from the person to whom he gives much (or, a lot); and he expects even more from the person to whom he gives more."

SECTION HEADING

Jesus the Cause of Division: "Jesus Causes Disagreement among People," "Not Concord, but Discord."

It is not clear what provoked this statement from Jesus. He seems to be speaking to his followers (verse 51, Do you suppose...?); in verse 54 the mention of the people seems to imply that what has come before was not addressed to the people.

12.49   TEV   RSV

| "I came to set the earth on fire, and how I wish it were already kindled! | "I came to cast fire upon the earth; and would that it were already kindled! |

I came: as God's messenger, or as the Messiah, to bring God's judgment on his people. "My mission (or, task) is...."
to set the earth on fire: literally "to throw fire on the earth." This fire is the symbol of God's punishment. The figure should be retained (see 3.16-17), but it may have to be transformed into a simile in order not to be taken literally: "I have come to bring God's punishment upon people, which will be like a fire that will burn them."
how I wish it were already kindled!: "how I wish it had already started burning!" This is an expression of frustration, of impatience, of the desire to see God's judgment at work.

12.50   TEV   RSV

| I have a baptism to receive, and how distressed I am until it is over! | I have a baptism to be baptized with; and how I am constrained until it is accomplished! |

Here baptism is used as a figure of difficulties and sufferings which "drown" a person, as a plunge into the water will drown. The figure was not uncommon. If the metaphor is difficult for the reader, a translation can say something like "I am to be plunged into suffering, as a person is plunged into water at baptism"; or, abandoning the figure if absolutely necessary: "I have to experience (or, undergo) severe suffering."
how distressed I am: "what anguish I feel," "how disturbed I am." Jesus would prefer that his "baptism" happen soon; the prospect of the suffering it will bring is deeply disturbing, and Jesus wants to get it over with.

12.51   TEV   RSV

| Do you suppose that I came to bring peace to the world? No, not peace, but division. | Do you think that I have come to give peace on earth? No, I tell you, but rather division; |

I came: or "I have come" (as in verse 49).
to bring peace to the world: as the following verses show, peace here is social harmony, concord, agreement: "to bring peace to people," or "to eliminate discord from the world," "to cause all disagreement to stop."

12.52 TEV	RSV
From now on a family of five will be divided, three against two and two against three.	for henceforth in one house there will be five divided, three against two and two against three;

The division is caused by the way in which members of the same family respond to Jesus' claims: some will accept, others will reject. And so there will be a split, and family members will be against one another.

three against two and two against three: this repetitious style need not be imitated: "three on one side and two on the other."

12.53 TEV	RSV
Fathers will be against their sons, and sons against their fathers; mothers will be against their daughters, and daughters against their mothers; mothers-in-law will be against their daughters-in-law, and daughters-in-law against their mothers-in-law."	they will be divided, father against son and son against father, mother against daughter and daughter against her mother, mother-in-law against her daughter-in-law and daughter-in-law against her mother-in-law."

The language of this verse reflects Micah 7.6.

The different family relationships specified here will have to be handled in a way that accurately reflects familial patterns in the society a particular language represents. In some instances it may not be necessary to repeat the two groups each time, as the Greek text does. Perhaps "Fathers and sons will be against each other; mothers and daughters will fight each other; and mothers-in-law and daughters-in-law will do the same."

SECTION HEADING

Understanding the Time: "Jesus Warns His Listeners."

This section follows logically from the previous one, in which Jesus had warned his disciples of the divisions his message would cause. Such local conflicts were to be seen as part of a larger pattern, and they pointed to the sudden arrival of God's judgment. The people should be able to see this clearly, but they do not.

12.54-55 TEV	RSV
Jesus said also to the people, "When you see a cloud coming up in the west, at once you say that it is going to rain—and it does. 55 And when you feel the south wind blowing, you say that it is going to get hot—and it does.	He also said to the multitudes, "When you see a cloud rising in the west, you say at once, 'A shower is coming'; and so it happens. 55 And when you see the south wind blowing, you say, 'There will be scorching heat'; and it happens.

Jesus said also to the people: the Greek seems to imply that here
Jesus speaks to the crowd, in contrast to speaking to his disciples.
This is more clearly represented by "Then Jesus said to the people."
    a cloud coming up in the west: rain clouds came in from the Medi-
terranean Sea, from the west.
    As RSV shows, the Greek text uses the direct form of address in re-
porting what people say; TEV uses the indirect form, you say that. Either
is possible, and a translation should use the form that best suits that
particular language.
    south wind blowing: from the desert south of Judea.

12.56	TEV	RSV
	Hypocrites! You can look at the earth and the sky and predict the weather; why, then, don't you know the meaning of this present time?	You hypocrites! You know how to interpret the appearance of earth and sky; but why do you not know how to interpret the present time?

Hypocrites!: see 6.42. This sounds rather strange here; more in
keeping with the situation would be "Fools!" or "How stupid you are!"
The implication is that these people pretend not to understand what is
happening at the present time.
    the earth and the sky: here in the sense of certain matters that
indicate a change in the weather: the appearance of clouds in the west,
the blowing of wind from the south, and other such weather signals.
    predict the weather: or "tell what's going to happen," "tell what it
means."
    why, then, don't you know...?: this is not a request for information.
The initial Hypocrites! implies that these people deliberately refuse to
recognize the meaning of certain things happening at this time, specifically, the mission and message of Jesus (see 11.30).

SECTION HEADING

    Settle with Your Opponent: "Jesus Teaches about Settling Disputes."

    These three verses in Greek follow without a break from the preceding
section (verses 54-56) and would seem to be directed to the people in
general, not to the disciples in particular. Yet the content seems to
apply to the followers of Jesus rather than to all people.

12.57	TEV	RSV
	"Why do you not judge for your- selves the right thing to do?	"And why do you not judge for yourselves what is right?

    Another rhetorical question, in which Jesus accuses them of being
unwilling to decide what is the right thing to do. In the following verses
Jesus gives a specific instance of what should be done.

12.58 TEV	RSV
If someone brings a lawsuit against you and takes you to court, do your best to settle the dispute with him before you get to court. If you don't, he will drag you before the judge, who will hand you over to the police, and you will be put in jail.	As you go with your accuser before the magistrate, make an effort to settle with him on the way, lest he drag you to the judge, and the judge hand you over to the officer, and the officer put you in prison.

In verses 58-59 the second person pronoun you is singular.

brings a lawsuit against you and takes you to court: this translates the Greek "your opponent (at law)"; the meaning may be expressed more concisely: "If someone takes you to court," "...before a judge in order to accuse you." Or it may be that technical terms may be used, like the English, "If anyone sues you" or "If someone hales you into court."

settle the dispute: "come to an agreement with," "resolve your differences with."

drag you: this verb means to use force in taking the person before the judge.

police: "law officer," "court officer."

you will be put in jail: "he (or, the law officer) will put you in jail."

12.59 TEV	RSV
There you will stay, I tell you, until you pay the last penny of your fine."	I tell you, you will never get out till you have paid the very last copper."

the last penny of your fine: "the complete amount the judge orders you to pay," "all that you must pay before you will be set free." The English word penny translates the Greek word for the smallest coin in circulation at that time.

Chapter 13

Turn from Your Sins or Die: "The Need for Repentance."

In this section Jesus uses a current incident as a lesson on the need of people to repent in order to avoid divine punishment. The parable that follows in the next section (verses 6-9) also teaches the need for repentance.

13.1   TEV

At that time some people were there who told Jesus about the Galileans whom Pilate had killed while they were offering sacrifices to God.

13.1   RSV

There were some present at that very time who told him of the Galileans whose blood Pilate had mingled with their sacrifices.

At that time: a general designation of time. The setting is still the same one described in 12.1.

were there: or "arrived," "got there," "came up."

The people tell Jesus of some Galileans who had been killed by Pilate's soldiers while they, the Galileans, were offering their animal sacrifices in the Temple. (A literal translation of the Greek, as in RSV, hardly makes sense.)

Pilate had killed: "Pilate had ordered killed." Pilate (see 3.1) did not do this personally. It is assumed that Pilate had ordered them killed because they were nationalists, plotting the overthrow of the Roman domination of Palestine. They were killed just as they were slaughtering their animals to offer as a sacrifice in the Temple, and their blood got mixed with that of the animals (see RSV).

13.2   TEV

Jesus answered them, "Because those Galileans were killed in that way, do you think it proves that they were worse sinners than all other Galileans?

13.2   RSV

And he answered them, "Do you think that these Galileans were worse sinners than all the other Galileans, because they suffered thus?

The verse may be restructured as follows: "Do you think that the way those Galileans were killed (or, died) proves that they were worse sinners than all other Galileans?" The question form should be retained in translation, since Jesus himself provides the answer in the next verse.

[231]

killed in that way: the literal translation "suffered" (RSV) might indicate that the Galileans were wounded, not killed.

13.3

TEV	RSV
No indeed' And I tell you that if you do not turn from your sins, you will all die as they did.	I tell you, No; but unless you repent you will all likewise perish.

turn from your sins: see 3.3.

you will all: not just the people who told Jesus what had happened, but all of the people there.

you will all die as they did: or "you will all die also." Jesus is not referring to death as the natural end to life, but violent death.

13.4

TEV	RSV
What about those eighteen people in Siloam who were killed when the tower fell on them? Do you suppose this proves that they were worse than all the other people living in Jerusalem?	Or those eighteen upon whom the tower in Siloam fell and killed them, do you think that they were worse offenders than all the others who dwelt in Jerusalem?

Jesus refers to another tragedy, which had apparently happened rather recently.

Siloam: a suburb of Jerusalem.

the tower: it is not certain what this was; perhaps the tower was part of the fortifications in the wall that surrounded Jerusalem. Some adaptation must be made in some languages: "house (or, building) one looks from," "a high building."

RSV keeps the material in one sentence (a question) for the whole verse; it seems simpler to divide into two sentences, or perhaps even three: "You remember the eighteen people in Siloam who were killed when the tower fell on them. What does that prove? Do you think it proves that they were greater sinners than all the other people in Jerusalem?"

worse: the Greek says "greater debtors," a way of speaking about sinners (see 11.4).

13.5

TEV	RSV
No indeed! And I tell you that if you do not turn from your sins, you will all die as they did."	I tell you, No; but unless you repent you will all likewise perish."

This is the same as verse 3; the only difference is the adverb "likewise" (RSV), which in verse 3 translates a different (but synonymous) adverb.

SECTION HEADING

The Parable of the Unfruitful Fig Tree: "Jesus Tells a Story about a Barren Fig Tree."

Since this parable illustrates the result of not repenting, this section may be joined to the preceding one.

13.6 TEV	RSV
Then Jesus told them this parable: "There was once a man who had a fig tree growing in his vineyard. He went looking for figs on it but found none.	And he told this parable: "A man had a fig tree planted in his vineyard; and he came seeking fruit on it and found none.

parable: see 5.36.
There was once: see 8.5.
vineyard: the fact that it was among grapevines that the fig tree was growing is not important in this story; so, if necessary, the more general "garden" or "orchard" or "field" may be used.
He went looking: "From time to time he looked," "Every now and then he went and looked." As the next verse shows, he did this more than once.

13.7 TEV	RSV
So he said to his gardener, 'Look, for three years I have been coming here looking for figs on this fig tree, and I haven't found any. Cut it down! Why should it go on using up the soil?'	And he said to the vinedresser, 'Lo, these three years I have come seeking fruit on this fig tree, and I find none. Cut it down; why should it use up the ground?'

gardener: "the man who took care of his vineyard (or, garden)."
for three years: "during the last three years." Fig trees normally produce figs twice a year, in May (early crop) and in late August (late crop).
using up the soil: or 'wasting (valuable) space." Another tree that would produce fruit could be planted in that spot.

13.8 TEV	RSV
But the gardener answered, 'Leave it alone, sir, just one more year; I will dig around it and put in some fertilizer.	And he answered him, 'Let it alone, sir, this year also, till I dig about it and put on manure.

Leave it alone: "Let it stand (or, live)," "Don't cut it down now."
dig around it: "break up the soil around it," "hoe the ground around it."
fertilizer: "manure" (RSV), "dung." Where no such methods are used, the more general statement may be used, "take good care of it," "do for it all that I can."

[233]

13.9

13.9 TEV	RSV
Then if the tree bears figs next year, so much the better; if not, then you can have it cut down.'"	And if it bears fruit next year, well and good; but if not, you can cut it down.'"

so much the better: "well and good" (RSV), "that's fine." Or else the sentence could be "Maybe that will make the tree bear figs next year. If it doesn't...."

SECTION HEADING

Jesus Heals a Crippled Woman on the Sabbath: "Another Dispute about the Sabbath."

This cure on the Sabbath brings Jesus into conflict once more with the religious authorities; see the similar incident in 6.6-11.

13.10-11 TEV	RSV
One Sabbath Jesus was teaching in a synagogue. 11 A woman there had an evil spirit that had kept her sick for eighteen years; she was bent over and could not straighten up at all.	Now he was teaching in one of the synagogues on the sabbath. 11 And there was a woman who had had a spirit of infirmity for eighteen years; she was bent over and could not fully straighten herself.

Sabbath: see 4.16.
teaching in a synagogue: see 4.15.
had an evil spirit: "was possessed (or, controlled) by an evil spirit." For evil spirit see 4.23. The effect of the spirit's possession was that the woman could not stand up straight. The Greek "a spirit of weakness" means "a spirit that made the woman weak (or, ill)."
straighten up at all: the Greek may mean "straighten up in the least" or "straighten up completely." The former seems preferable.

13.12 TEV	RSV
When Jesus saw her, he called out to her, "Woman, you are free from your sickness!"	And when Jesus saw her, he called her and said to her, "Woman, you are freed from your infirmity."

Woman: in the context this is a proper mode of address. In some languages other terms will be used by a man speaking to a woman he has not met before. In some instances, the best way to handle this is not to represent it formally at all: "When Jesus saw her, he said to her, 'I tell you, you are free from your sickness.'"
you are free: "you are set free," "you are no longer held by your illness." The declaration of Jesus frees her from the evil spirit.

13.13   TEV

He placed his hands on her, and at once she straightened herself up and praised God.

      RSV

And he laid his hands upon her, and immediately she was made straight, and she praised God.

placed his hands on her: see 4.40; it would be either on her head or on her shoulders.

straightened herself up: "stood up straight," "straightened her back."

praised God: "gave thanks to God," "said to God, 'I thank you.'"

13.14   TEV

The official of the synagogue was angry that Jesus had healed on the Sabbath, so he spoke up and said to the people, "There are six days in which we should work; so come during those days and be healed, but not on the Sabbath!"

      RSV

But the ruler of the synagogue, indignant because Jesus had healed on the sabbath, said to the people, "There are six days on which work ought to be done; come on those days and be healed, and not on the sabbath day."

The official of the synagogue: the same position held by Jairus (see 8.41, 49).

was angry: "was indignant." The religious authorities permitted such deeds of mercy on the Sabbath if the sick person's life was in danger. The woman needed help, but obviously it was not an emergency.

in which we should work: in a general sense, "in which work can be done" (see RSV), "in which one is allowed (by the Law) to work," "in which the Law says we are to work."

but not: "but don't come."

13.15   TEV

The Lord answered him, "You hypocrites! Any one of you would untie his ox or his donkey from the stall and take it out to give it water on the Sabbath.

      RSV

Then the Lord answered him, "You hypocrites! Does not each of you on the sabbath untie his ox or his ass from the manger, and lead it away to water it?

Lord: see 5.8.

hypocrites: see 6.42. Jesus here speaks not to the synagogue official alone, but to him as a representative of religious authorities; it seems there were others there (see verse 17) who shared the official's attitude.

As RSV shows, Jesus replies with a rhetorical question, which TEV has represented as a statement.

untie...from the stall: the Greek text says "untie...from the manger" (RSV); for "manger" see 2.7. Since the place where the animal is tied is not significant, it may be better simply to say "untie his ox or his donkey and lead (or, take) it to give it water...."

ox: the word is meant generically of a bovine animal; the specific "castrated bull" need not be said. (See *Fauna and Flora of the Bible*, under the entry "Ox.")

13.16   TEV   RSV

Now here is this descendant of Abraham whom Satan has kept in bonds for eighteen years; should she not be released on the Sabbath?"

And ought not this woman, a daughter of Abraham whom Satan bound for eighteen years, be loosed from this bond on the sabbath day?"

descendant of Abraham: "daughter of Abraham" (RSV), that is, a member of the covenant people, Israel, the people of God.

Satan: see 10.18.

Satan has kept in bonds: the figurative language is vivid: "Satan has kept her sick, as though he had tied her up."

kept in bonds: "kept prisoner," "kept enslaved."

The rhetorical question should she not...? may be represented by a statement: "certainly she should be released on the Sabbath!"

13.17   TEV   RSV

His answer made his enemies ashamed of themselves, while the people rejoiced over all the wonderful things that he did.

As he said this, all his adversaries were put to shame; and all the people rejoiced at all the glorious things that were done by him.

his enemies: "his opponents," "those who were against him."

ashamed: there are various idiomatic and expressive ways of talking about shame: "the eyes are ashamed," "the body is cold," "lose face," "have to sell face."

the people: the people there in the synagogue.

SECTION HEADING

The Parable of the Mustard Seed: "Jesus Tells a Story about the Mustard Seed," "Jesus Compares the Kingdom of God to a Mustard Seed."

Jesus tells two parables (verses 18-21) to illustrate what the Kingdom of God is like. It is unlikely that the setting for these parables was the synagogue where he healed the crippled woman (verse 13). It may be better to combine the two sections into one: "Two Parables about the Kingdom of God."

13.18   TEV   RSV

Jesus asked, "What is the Kingdom of God like? What shall I campare it with?

He said therefore, "What is the kingdom of God like? And to what shall I compare it?

The two questions are a way of gaining the attention of the listeners. If the double question is unnatural, one will be enough: "How shall I describe the Kingdom of God?" or "What shall I say the Kingdom of God is like?"

13.19   TEV

It is like this. A man takes a mustard seed and plants it in his
field. The plant grows and becomes
a tree, and the birds make their
nests in its branches."

                              RSV

It is like a grain of mustard seed
which a man took and sowed in his
garden; and it grew and became a
tree, and the birds of the air made
nests in its branches."

It is like this: the comparison applies to the whole story and not
simply to the initial a mustard seed. The comparison is the difference
in size between the seed and the plant that grows from it. "It is like
what happens when a man takes a mustard seed and plants it in his field."

mustard: see *Fauna and Flora of the Bible*, under the entry "Mustard." The shrub grows taller than a person's height; its exceptional
height is emphasized by and becomes a tree.

make: "build," "construct," or whatever word is appropriate for a
bird's activity in building a nest.

SECTION HEADING

The Parable of the Yeast: "Jesus Compares the Kingdom of God to
Yeast."

13.20-21   TEV

Again Jesus asked, "What shall
I compare the Kingdom of God with?
21 It is like this. A woman takes
some yeast and mixes it with a
bushel of flour until the whole
batch of dough rises."

                              RSV

And again he said, "To what
shall I compare the kingdom of God?
21 It is like leaven which a woman
took and hid in three measures of
flour, till it was all leavened."

The comparison here is the effect that a small bit of yeast has upon a large mass of dough.

yeast: or "leaven" (see 12.1).

mixes: the literal translation of the Greek verb "hid" (RSV) does
not make sense in the context of making bread.

a bushel of flour: this translates the Greek "three *sata*," the Greek
word (singular *saton*) being the equivalent of the Hebrew measure *seah*,
which was about 1 1/2 pecks. Three *sata* are equivalent to 35.25 liters;
in terms of weight, this would be 25 kilograms or 55 pounds.

the whole batch of dough rises: "the batch of dough is completely
leavened."

SECTION HEADING

The Narrow Door: "The Narrow Entrance to Life."

This section makes clear again that Jesus is on his way to Jerusalem,
where suffering and death await him (see 9.51). Entrance into the Kingdom

[237]

of God requires persistence and a relationship to Jesus other than belonging to the people of Israel.

13.22   TEV   RSV

Jesus went through towns and   He went on his way through
villages, teaching the people and   towns and villages, teaching, and
making his way toward Jerusalem.   journeying toward Jerusalem.

The verse may be restructured as follows: "As Jesus continued on his way to Jerusalem, he passed through many towns and villages, where he taught the people (about the Kingdom of God)."

13.23-24   TEV   RSV

Someone asked him, "Sir, will just   And some one said to him, "Lord,
a few people be saved?"   will those who are saved be few?"
    Jesus answered them, 24 "Do   And he said to them, 24 "Strive to
your best to go in through the   enter by the narrow door; for many,
narrow door; because many people   I tell you, will seek to enter and
will surely try to go in but will   will not be able.
not be able.

Sir: see 5.12.
be saved: from God's punishment, on Judgment Day.
them: here Jesus speaks to the people with him, and not only to the person who asks him the question.
to go in: if necessary, "to go into the Kingdom of God."
will not be able: "will not succeed."
All that is said here is that the entrance to the Kingdom of God is like a narrow door, and that not everyone who tries to go in will be able to.

13.25   TEV   RSV

The master of the house will get   When once the householder has risen
up and close the door; then when   up and shut the door, you will begin
you stand outside and begin to   to stand outside and to knock at the
knock on the door and say, 'Open   door, saying, 'Lord, open to us.' He
the door for us, sir!' he will an-   will answer you, 'I do not know
swer you, 'I don't know where you   where you come from.'
come from!'

The master of the house: see 12.39.
What follows is a long and complex sentence, and it may be better to divide it into two sentences:

The time will come when the master of the house will get up and lock the door. Then as you stand outside, you will begin to knock on the door and say, 'Let us in, sir!' But he will answer, 'I don't know where you are from!'

get up: at the end of the evening meal, when it is time to go to bed.

where you come from: this is what the Greek text says, but it appears to say that entrance to the Kingdom will depend on where one lives. As the next two verses make clear, however, it is a matter of relationship with the master of the house. So a translation would be justified in saying "I don't know you," "I have never met you before," or "You are not my friends."

13.26-27 TEV

Then you will answer, 'We ate and drank with you; you taught in our town!' 27 But he will say again, I don't know where you come from. Get away from me, all you wicked people!'

13.26-27 RSV

Then you will begin to say, 'We ate and drank in your presence, and you taught in our streets.' 27 But he will say, 'I tell you, I do not know where you come from; depart from me, all you workers of iniquity!'

The people outside answer that they are friends of the master of the house: They had eaten meals with him and had heard him teach. They had been his table companions and his students.

13.28 TEV

How you will cry and gnash your teeth when you see Abraham, Isaac, and Jacob, and all the prophets in the Kingdom of God, while you are thrown out!

13.28 RSV

There you will weep and gnash your teeth, when you see Abraham and Isaac and Jacob and all the prophets in the kingdom of God and you yourselves thrust out.

cry and gnash your teeth: in pain and despair. It may be impossible to use the figure gnash your teeth; so a translation may say "weep and wail," "cry out in pain and despair."

when you see: the Kingdom of God at the end of time, with the Hebrew patriarchs and prophets inside, while these people are outside.

prophets: see 1.70.

Kingdom of God: here the Kingdom is pictured as a future event in terms of a banquet at which all God's people will be present. It was sometimes referred to as "the Messianic banquet" (see also 16.22).

thrown out: this implies a previous admittance, so it is better to translate "barred," "excluded," "not allowed to go in," "kept out."

13.29 TEV

People will come from the east and the west, from the north and the south, and sit down at the feast in the Kingdom of God.

13.29 RSV

And men will come from east and west, and from north and south, and sit at table in the kingdom of God.

from the east...west...north...south: "from all over the world," "from all foreign countries."

sit down: see 5.29 for the way in which meals were eaten.

13.30

13.30 TEV	SV
Then those who are now last will be first, and those who are now first will be last."	And behold, some are last who will be first, and some are first who will be last."

The saying in this verse does not seem appropriate here; but in the context it appears to mean that Jesus' listeners, who are supposed to rank first (Jews), will be excluded from the Kingdom, while people from all over the world, who are supposed to rank last (Gentiles), will be inside. So their position is reversed: first and last refer not to time but to rank, position, status.

SECTION HEADING

Jesus' Love for Jerusalem: this section (and the parallel in Matt 23.37-39) is usually called "Jesus' Lament over Jerusalem"—but it should be noticed that the text says nothing about his weeping over the city; this is found in Luke 19.41-44.

This curious incident begins with the friendly warning on the part of some Pharisees that Jesus leave Galilee, the territory governed by Herod Antipas, and go elsewhere. Jesus' caustic reply leads into a statement of love and concern for Jerusalem, the city he is going to, and where he, like the prophets, will be put to death.

13.31 TEV	RSV
At that same time some Pharisees came to Jesus and said to him, "You must get out of here and go somewhere else, because Herod wants to kill you."	At that very hour some Pharisees came, and said to him, "Get away from here, for Herod wants to kill you."

Pharisees: see 5.17.
came: "went."
here: Galilee; somewhere else: outside Galilee.
Herod: Herod Antipas, ruler of Galilee (see 3.1).
wants to kill you: "intends to have you killed" or "...put to death."

13.32 TEV	RSV
Jesus answered them, "Go and tell that fox: 'I am driving out demons and performing cures today and tomorrow, and on the third day I shall finish my work.'	And he said to them, "Go and tell that fox, 'Behold, I cast out demons and perform cures today and tomorrow, and the third day I finish my course.

tell that fox: "tell that fox for me," or "deliver this message from me to that fox." It may not be appropriate to have quotes within quotes, so it is possible to say "go and tell that fox that I am driving out demons...."

fox: a symbol of craftiness or cunning. In some places the animal may be a jackal, a wolverine, a hare, or a spider. If no appropriate animal exists, the figure may be abandoned: "tricky person," "cunning man," "one who deceives." Or else the figure may represent lack of worth: "insignificant," "of no account."

driving out demons: see 4.33.

today and tomorrow, and on the third day: these are not meant literally; Jesus is not saying, "I will stop working the day after tomorrow." It is a statement that he will continue his normal activities, but only for a limited period of time.

I shall finish my work: the Greek says only "I am finished." "I will be through," "I will reach my goal."

13.33 TEV	RSV
Yet I must be on my way today, tomorrow, and the next day; it is not right for a prophet to be killed anywhere except in Jerusalem.	Nevertheless I must go on my way today and tomorrow and the day following; for it cannot be that a prophet should perish away from Jerusalem.'

Here Jesus is no longer talking about the message for Herod; he is speaking to his listeners, the Pharisees.

What Jesus here affirms is that despite his intention not to flee, he must continue on his way to Jerusalem, which is not under Herod's control.

it is not right: words of irony. Jerusalem must live up to her fame as a killer of prophets. A translation may say "it isn't fitting (or, appropriate)." Or else, "Jerusalem is the only fitting place where a prophet should be killed," or "A prophet should be put to death only in Jerusalem."

Here, by implication, Jesus classifies himself as a prophet.

13.34 TEV	RSV
"Jerusalem, Jerusalem! You kill the prophets, you stone the messengers God has sent you! How many times I wanted to put my arms around all your people, just as a hen gathers her chicks under her wings, but you would not let me!	O Jerusalem, Jerusalem, killing the prophets and stoning those who are sent to you! How often would I have gathered your children together as a hen gathers her brood under her wings, and you would not!

Jesus here speaks to Jerusalem. If it seems strange to address a city, a translation may say "People of Jerusalem[" But it is more effective to have Jesus address the city itself, if possible.

the prophets...the messengers: no particular distinction between the two is intended. A prophet is one who speaks God's message, and a messenger is one whom God sends to proclaim his message.

the messengers God has sent you: this translates the Greek passive "those who have been sent to you" (literally "to her," but it is better

to keep to the second person of address in translation, since Jesus is
speaking directly to the city).

How many times I wanted: "many times I have wanted" or "...I have
tried."

put my arms around all your people: this translates "gather together
your children" (see RSV). The following simile (just as a hen) indicates
what kind of "gathering" this is, so put my arms around expresses the
meaning; or else one can say "gather you around me" or "bring you all together to me."

a hen...her chicks: "a mother hen...her little chickens." Many languages have collective terms, and one may be used (as RSV "brood" has
done).

you would not let me: this translates the plural pronoun "you,"
which refers to the people of Jerusalem; so the translation could be "but
your people (or, citizens) would not let me."

13.35   TEV   RSV
And so your Temple will be aban-   Behold, your house is forsaken. And
doned. I assure you that you will   I tell you, you will not see me un-
not see me until the time comes   til you say, 'Blessed is he who
when you say, 'God bless him who   comes in the name of the Lord!'"
comes in the name of the Lord.'"

your Temple: the Greek is "your house" (RSV). This could be taken
to mean "your city," that is, the city is the place where Jerusalem lives.
The Greek uses the present form of the verb "is abandoned" (see RSV).
But Jesus is not describing Jerusalem as it was at the time he spoke these
words; this is a prophecy of what is going to happen, so it is better to
use the future tense, will be abandoned. There is the question of the
actor implied in the passive abandoned: it could be "people," that is,
there will not be any people in the Temple; or, more probably, God is the
actor: "God will abandon the Temple (or, the city)."

the time comes when you say: see 19.38. The words that follow use
the language of Psalm 118.26.

God bless him: this translates the Greek passive "Blessed be," which
may be understood as a request, "May he be blessed," or as a statement,
"He is blessed." In the context it seems better to understand it as a
request.

in the name of the Lord: here the Lord is God. The statement may
mean: (1) as a representative of God, "the servant (or messenger, or
spokesman) of the Lord"; or (2) "with the authority (or, power) of the
Lord." The first one seems preferable.

Chapter 14

Jesus Heals a Sick Man: "Another Cure on the Sabbath," "Jesus Heals Another Person on the Sabbath."

This cure again brings Jesus into conflict with the religious leaders. In this incident they are passive and quiet, unable to respond to Jesus' action or words.

14.1   TEV   RSV
One Sabbath Jesus went to eat   One sabbath when he went to
a meal at the home of one of the   dine at the house of a ruler who
leading Pharisees; and people were   belonged to the Pharisees, they
watching Jesus closely.   were watching him.

Sabbath: see 4.16.
to eat a meal: it is assumed that Jesus went by invitation (see similar instance in 7.36), so it should not appear that Jesus entered into the Pharisee's house uninvited.
one of the leading Pharisees: "one of the more important (or, influential) Pharisees"; for Pharisees see 5.17.
people: "the people there," "all who were present."
were watching Jesus closely: if necessary, the meaning may be filled out, "were watching Jesus closely to see what he would do" (see the same situation in 6.7).

14.2-3   TEV   RSV
A man whose legs and arms were   And behold, there was a man before
swollen came to Jesus, 3 and Jesus   him who had dropsy. 3 And Jesus
spoke up and asked the teachers of   spoke to the lawyers and Pharisees,
the Law and the Pharisees, "Does   saying, "Is it lawful to heal on the
our Law allow healing on the Sab-   sabbath, or not?"
bath or not?"

legs and arms were swollen: this is an attempt to describe the man's condition without using the medical term "dropsy"; this is an illness caused by the accumulation of body fluids in tissues or cavities of the body, thus causing the legs and arms to swell. If the technical term is used, either in a footnote or a Word List, the term should be explained. Otherwise, a description of the illness may be attempted: "A man who suffered from an illness that made his legs and arms swell."

[243]

14.2-3

came to Jesus: obviously wanting to be cured; the text, however,
does not explicitly say so.
the teachers of the Law: see 5.17.
our Law: see 6.2,9. The question closely resembles the one asked in
6.9.

14.4   TEV   RSV
But they would not say a   But they were silent. Then he took
thing. Jesus took the man, healed   him and healed him, and let him go.
him, and sent him away.

took the man: either in the sense of taking him aside, or else meaning that Jesus placed his hands on him.
sent him away: "told him to go (home)."

14.5   TEV   RSV
Then he said to them, "If any one   And he said to them, "Which of you,
of you had a son or an ox that hap-   having a son^8 or an ox that has fall-
pened to fall in a well on a Sab-   en into a well, will not immediately
bath, would you not pull him out at   pull him out on a sabbath day?"
once on the Sabbath itself?"

                                       ^{8}Other ancient authorities read *an
                                       ass*

The rhetorical question is a way of making a strong statement: "If
any one of you had..., at once you would pull him out, even though it was
the Sabbath!" Jesus makes a similar statement in 13.15.
The sentence may be too long and complex, and it may be necessary
to restructure as follows: "Suppose one of you had a son or an ox that
fell in a well on the Sabbath—what would you do? You would go at once
and pull him out, even though it was a Sabbath."
As the RSV footnote shows, instead of son, many Greek manuscripts
and early versions have "donkey" (as in 13.15). Actually "donkey" better
fits the context, and its manuscript support is quite strong; some translations prefer "donkey."

14.6   TEV   RSV
But they were not able to an-   And they could not reply to this.
swer him about this.

The people there could not say anything, because they knew that the
Law allowed such deeds of mercy on the Sabbath.

SECTION HEADING

Humility and Hospitality: "A Lesson for Guests and for Hosts."

[244]

This incident arises naturally from the preceding one. Here Jesus talks about humility as opposed to pride, and about genuine hospitality, which expects no returns, as opposed to conventional social obligations.

14.7	TEV	RSV
	Jesus noticed how some of the guests were choosing the best places, so he told this parable to all of them:	Now he told a parable to those who were invited, when he marked how they chose the places of honor, saying to them,

the best places: probably the ones nearest to the host. For seating arrangements at a meal see 5.29; also 16.22-23 (the poor man seated next to Abraham).

parable: see 5.36. What follows is not a parable as such, but actually a piece of advice. So the translation may say "he gave them this advice," "he taught them this lesson," "he gave them this illustration."

to all of them: or "to them" (RSV).

14.8	TEV	RSV
	"When someone invites you to a wedding feast, do not sit down in the best place. It could happen that someone more important than you has been invited,	"When you are invited by any one to a marriage feast, do not sit down in a place of honor, lest a more eminent man than you be invited by him;

you: here it is singular.

a wedding feast: the festivities would last seven days.

best place: in most cultures there are more desirable and less desirable places at meals. A guest will be seated according to his social standing.

more important: "of higher social standing."

14.9	TEV	RSV
	and your host, who invited both of you, would have to come and say to you, 'Let him have this place.' Then you would be embarrassed and have to sit in the lowest place.	and he who invited you both will come and say to you, 'Give place to this man,' and then you will begin with shame to take the lowest place.

would have to come: this necessity is imposed by the situation; a person of higher rank must have the more desirable place.

say to you, 'Let him have this place': or, to avoid quotes within quotes, "and tell you to let the other guest sit in that place."

embarrassed: "ashamed," "humiliated," "with loss of face."

the lowest place: "the least desirable (or, worst) place"; "the place farthest away from the host" or "the place where ordinary people sit."

14.10 TEV	RSV
Instead, when you are invited, go and sit in the lowest place, so that your host will come to you and say, 'Come on up, my friend, to a better place.' This will bring you honor in the presence of all the other guests.	But when you are invited, go and sit in the lowest place, so that when your host comes he may say to you, 'Friend, go up higher'; then you will be honored in the presence of all who sit at table with you.

The exact reverse is given here of the situation in verses 8-9: the lowest place...a better place...bring you honor.

14.11 TEV	RSV
For everyone who makes himself great will be humbled, and everyone who humbles himself will be made great."	For every one who exalts himself will be humbled, and he who humbles himself will be exalted."

makes himself great: "tries to be the most important one," "wants to rule the others."
will be humbled: "will be made unimportant," "will be brought down." Both passive forms, will be humbled and will be made great, have God as the implied actor: "God will humble him...God will make him important."

14.12 TEV	RSV
Then Jesus said to his host, "When you give a lunch or a dinner, do not invite your friends or your brothers or your relatives or your rich neighbors—for they will invite you back, and in this way you will be paid for what you did.	He said also to the man who had invited him, "When you give a dinner or a banquet, do not invite your friends or your brothers or your kinsmen or rich neighbors, lest they also invite you in return, and you be repaid.

give: here in the sense of inviting people to come to one's house for a meal.
lunch...dinner: the noon and the evening meals.
your brothers or your relatives: here brothers may be used in the restricted sense of blood brothers, or else in the extended sense of close family members, as contrasted with the more distant relatives.
paid: or "repaid" (RSV), "paid back." The host at such occasions feels certain that his guests will invite him to a meal, and so he will not have lost anything. There has been no giving, but only a trade; no real generosity is involved.

14.13-14 TEV	RSV
When you give a feast, invite the poor, the crippled, the lame, and the blind; 14 and you will be	But when you give a feast, invite the poor, the maimed, the lame, the blind, 14 and you will be blessed,

blessed, because they are not able   because they cannot repay you. You
to pay you back. God will repay   will be repaid at the resurrection
you on the day the good people rise of the just."
from death."

feast: "banquet," "reception," "party."
you will be blessed: that is, by God.
because: care must be taken that the causal relationship be made
clear. Jesus is saying that such a person will be blessed by God, who
will reward him on Resurrection Day. So it might be better to restructure
the saying by placing a period at the end of verse 13 and translating
verse 14 as follows: "They are not able to pay you back, but God will
bless you and reward you...."
the day the good people rise from death: here the Last Judgment is
spoken of in terms only of the resurrection of "the just" (RSV). It might
be preferable to use the passive voice, "are raised from death," or to
supply the agent, "God will raise from death." As for the good, it might
be better to translate "those who obey (or, please) God" (see 1.6). So
the last part of the verse might be translated, "...and reward you on the
day he brings to life (or, causes to live again) the people who obey him
(or, who please him)."

SECTION HEADING

The Parable of the Great Feast: "Those Who Are Invited to the Kingdom of God."
This parable is told at the same occasion described in 14.1, and is
told in response to a statement by one of those present at the meal in
the Pharisee's house.

14.15   TEV   RSV
When one of the men sitting at   When one of those who sat at
the table heard this, he said to   table with him heard this, he said
Jesus, "How happy are those who   to him, "Blessed is he who shall
will sit down at the feast in the   eat bread in the kingdom of God!"
Kingdom of God!"

How happy: see 6.20.
the feast in the Kingdom of God: the future Kingdom of God is here
pictured as a banquet at which all God's people will be present (see also
16.22).
The Greek text uses the singular form "he who" (RSV), which is a way
of referring to all in general who will be present at the Messianic banquet.

14.16   TEV   RSV
Jesus said to him, "There was   But he said to him, "A man once gave
once a man who was giving a great   a great banquet, and invited many;
feast to which he invited many peo-
ple.

[247]

The story Jesus tells is simple, the participants are clearly marked, the dialogue is direct, and the conclusion arises naturally from the situation described. The implication of the man's statement in verse 15 was that the feast of the Kingdom is of such a nature that no one would turn down an invitation to come; the parable Jesus tells teaches that it's not that simple.

feast: "banquet" (RSV), "party" (same word as in verse 13).

14.17 TEV	RSV
When it was time for the feast, he sent his servant to tell his guests, 'Come, everything is ready!'	and at the time for the banquet he sent his servant to say to those who had been invited, 'Come; for all is now ready.'

to tell his guests: or "to tell each one of those who had been invited." The servant would have to go around to the homes of all the guests and deliver the message.

everything is ready: or "it's time for the feast (or, banquet)."

In this story it will be better to keep the direct form of the dialogue, as TEV and RSV have done, rather than use the indirect form.

14.18 TEV	RSV
But they all began, one after another, to make excuses. The first one told the servant, 'I have bought a field and must go and look at it; please accept my apologies.'	But they all alike began to make excuses. The first said to him, 'I have bought a field, and I must go out and see it; I pray you, have me excused.'

one after another: "one by one," "each and every one."

a field: to be used for planting.

must go: 'must go out" (of town).

look at it: "inspect it."

please accept my apologies: "please excuse me," "please present my regrets," or whatever form of a polite refusal is used. "Please tell your master I'm sorry that I can't come."

14.19 TEV	RSV
Another one said, 'I have bought five pairs of oxen and am on my way to try them out; please accept my apologies.'	And another said, 'I have bought five yoke of oxen, and I go to examine them; I pray you, have me excused.'

five pairs of oxen: RSV uses the appropriate English expression "five yoke of oxen." Where animals are not used in pairs to plow, the translation may be "ten oxen (or, farming bulls)." And where animals are not used to work the fields it may be necessary to say "ten cows," or something similar.

try them out: that is, hitch each yoke to a plow and find out if the two oxen work well together. The translation "examine" (RSV) does not seem to do justice to the Greek verb, which means "to test." "I am going to find out if they work well."

14.20   TEV   RSV
Another one said, 'I have just got-   And another said, 'I have married a
ten married, and for that reason I   wife, and therefore I cannot come.'
cannot come.'

It is not clear why this man's recent marriage made it impossible
for him to be present at the banquet; it makes sense only if his wife
was not to be included (see verse 24), and he would rather be with her
than go to the banquet.

14.21   TEV   RSV
The servant went back and told all   So the servant came and reported
this to his master. The master was   this to his master. Then the house-
furious and said to his servant,   holder in anger said to his servant,
'Hurry out to the streets and al-   'Go out quickly to the streets and
leys of the town, and bring back   lanes of the city, and bring in the
the poor, the crippled, the blind,   poor and maimed and blind and lame.'
and the lame.'

his master: see 5.12. For the term "householder" (RSV) see 12.39.
the streets and alleys: there are different ways of speaking of the
main thoroughfare of a town or city, and the secondary roads: "the main
street (or, road) and the side streets."
The four classes of people to be invited are the same as those listed
in verse 13.

14.22   TEV   RSV
Soon the servant said, 'Your order   And the servant said, 'Sir, what
has been carried out, sir, but   you commanded has been done, and
there is room for more.'   still there is room.'

In the Greek, the servant appears to reply that he has already done
what the master told him to do (see RSV). But the sense seems clear that
the servant follows his master's instructions, and then comes back to
report what he has done. So something like TEV Soon, or "Soon afterward";
or "The servant obeyed, and reported back to his master."
Your order has been carried out: "I have done what you told me to
do."

14.23   TEV   RSV
So the master said to the servant,   And the master said to the servant,
'Go out to the country roads and   'Go out to the highways and hedges,
lanes and make people come in, so   and compel people to come in, that
that my house will be full.   my house may be filled.

Here small villages or rural areas are referred to: <u>country roads</u> <u>and lanes</u>. The Greek word translated <u>lanes</u> means "hedgerows" or "hedges" (RSV), which are rows of bushes, shrubs, or small trees which formed a fence or boundary, and where tramps or beggars were to be found.

<u>make people come in</u>: "force the people you find there to come in."

14.24 TEV	RSV
I tell you all that none of those men who were invited will taste my dinner!'"	For I tell you,[8] none of those men who were invited shall taste my banquet.'"
	[8]The Greek word for *you* here is plural

<u>I tell you</u>: here <u>you</u> is plural and indicates that the master is speaking not only to his servant but to the guests already assembled for the banquet.

<u>men</u>: here the specific word for males is used, which seems to indicate that only men had been invited.

<u>who were invited</u>: that is, the original group: "who were first invited."

<u>taste</u>: "eat," "partake of."

SECTION HEADING

<u>The Cost of Being a Disciple</u>: "What It Means to Be a Disciple of Jesus."

In this section Jesus is back on the road, making his way toward Jerusalem (see 9.51). It is in light of what awaits him there that he tells these people what it means to follow him, and urges them carefully to consider the cost of doing so.

14.25-26 TEV	RSV
Once when large crowds of people were going along with Jesus, he turned and said to them, 26 "Whoever comes to me cannot be my disciple unless he loves me more than he loves his father and his mother, his wife and his children, his brothers and his sisters, and himself as well.	Now great multitudes accompanied him; and he turned and said to them, 26 "If any one comes to me and does not hate his own father and mother and wife and children and brothers and sisters, yes, and even his own life, he cannot be my disciple.

<u>he turned</u>: Jesus is ahead, and the people are following behind him. It is to be noticed that RSV translates "hate his own father and mother and wife and children and brothers and sisters, yes, and even his own life," whereas TEV has used the form <u>loves me more than he loves his</u>

father.... TEV and other dynamic equivalent translations have done this
because the language of the Greek text reflects the Semitic way of speaking in absolute contrast of love as opposed to hate, when it really means
to indicate a greater or lesser degree of love, as the parallel in Matthew 10.37 shows. Jesus was not ordering his would-be followers to hate the
members of their family, but rather to give preference to him over those
who were nearest and dearest to them. Only in this way can Jesus' requirement be clearly understood. On the basis of the parallel Matthew 10.37, a
translator is justified in translating as TEV and others have done.

and himself as well: "and his own life." Loyalty to Jesus takes precedence over all human ties, over all personal desires.

14.27   TEV   RSV
Whoever does not carry his own   Whoever does not bear his own cross
cross and come after me cannot be   and come after me, cannot be my dis-
my disciple.   ciple.

carry his own cross: this figure obviously has reference to Jesus'
own experience. It means that his followers must be prepared to share
his fate, to be persecuted and to die as he was about to. It should not
mean some petty irritation or inconvenience, as the phrase "to bear a
cross" often means in English.

carry: if the manner of carrying must be specified, it would be
"carry on his shoulder."

come after me: "follow me," "go with me (to where I go)."

14.28   TEV   RSV
If one of you is planning to build   For which of you, desiring to build
a tower, he sits down first and   a tower, does not first sit down
figures out what it will cost, to   and count the cost, whether he has
see if he has enough money to fin-   enough to complete it?
ish the job.

As RSV shows, the verse is in the form of a question: "Which one of
you...does not...?" The answer is obviously "None," that is, anyone will
calculate the costs before beginning to build a tower. It is easier to
represent the meaning in the form of a statement, as TEV has done.

If one of you: it is not necessary to keep the personal form, and
something more general may be said: "Anyone who," "Whoever," "A man who."

tower: this is probably a watchtower for a vineyard. It is not necessary in translation to be so specific, particularly if such a construction is unknown; so "building" or "house" may be said.

14.29-30   TEV   RSV
If he doesn't, he will not be able   Otherwise, when he has laid a foun-
to finish the tower after laying   dation, and is not able to finish,
the foundation; and all who see what all who see it begin to mock him,

happened will make fun of him.
30 'This man began to build but
can't finish the job!' they will
say.

30 saying, 'This man began to build,
and was not able to finish.'

If he doesn't: what follows is the result when a man starts to build
without first finding out whether he has enough money to finish the job.
It may be better to restructure verse 29: "If he doesn't, it may be that
he will lay the foundation and then discover he cannot finish the tower
(or, building). If this happens, then all who see what happened will make
fun of him."
This man: in a mocking, contemptuous way: "This fellow."

14.31 TEV	RSV
If a king goes out with ten thousand men to fight another king who comes against him with twenty thousand men, he will sit down first and decide if he is strong enough to face that other king.	Or what king, going to encounter another king in war, will not sit down first and take counsel whether he is able with ten thousand to meet him who comes against him with twenty thousand?

Another hypothetical case, in the form of a question, which TEV has
represented as a conditional statement.
If in some languages the numbers ten thousand and twenty thousand
are a problem, it may be necessary to say something like "If a king (or,
chief) goes with his soldiers (or, army) to fight another king who has
twice as many men (or, soldiers) as he has...."
decide: from the next verse, it seems quite obvious that no king
would actually decide that he can successfully wage war against an armed
force twice the size of his.
if he is strong enough: "if he has enough soldiers (or, men)."
to face: "to fight against," "to meet in battle."

14.32 TEV	RSV
If he isn't, he will send messengers to meet the other king to ask for terms of peace while he is still a long way off.	And if not, while the other is yet a great way off, he sends an embassy and asks terms of peace.

to ask for terms of peace: it may be better to represent this in the
form of a direct proposal or question, such as "...he will send messengers to meet the other king and ask him, 'What can we (exclusive) do to
keep from war?'" or "What are your conditions for not fighting us?" Or
else "We want to be friends with you," "We don't want to fight against
you."
while he is still a long way off: that is, the other king, with his
twenty thousand men. In case of restructuring, this clause will have to
come first, for example, "If he isn't, he will send messengers to the
other king while he (or, that king) is still a long way off (or, before

he has come too near), to say, 'What are the conditions for stopping the
fighting?'"

14.33   TEV   RSV
In the same way," concluded Jesus,   So therefore, whoever of you does
"none of you can be my disciple un- not renounce all that he has cannot
less he gives up everything he has. be my disciple.

TEV adds the words concluded Jesus to make clear that this is Jesus'
remark, and not part of the story.
The application actually goes back to verses 26-27, which discuss
the need for placing loyalty to Jesus above all other relationships.
gives up: "leaves behind," "lets go," "says good-bye to." Instead
of a statement with two negatives (none of you...unless) it may be better
to have an affirmation: "In the same way, if any one of you wants to be
my disciple he must give up everything he has."

SECTION HEADING

Worthless Salt: "What Is Worthless Is Thrown Away."

This saying does not obviously relate to what precedes, except in a
general way with respect to genuineness. A follower of Jesus who does not
fulfill the function of a disciple is worthless and will be discarded.
Some translations include these two verses in the preceding section;
most keep it as a separate section, with references under the heading
giving the parallel passages.

14.34   TEV   RSV
"Salt is good, but if it loses   "Salt is good; but if salt has
its saltiness, there is no way to   lost its taste, how shall its salti-
make it salty again.   ness be restored?

loses its saltiness: pure salt does not lose its saltiness, but in
ancient times much of the salt was impure and would dissolve from exces-
sive dampness, leaving only flavorless salt-like crystals. So the translation can be "If the salt no longer tastes (or, acts) like salt," "If
what looks like salt is really no longer salt."
there is no way to make it salty again: this translates the rhetorical question, "how can its saltiness be restored?" It may be better to
say "there is no way people (or, we) can make it salty again."

14.35   TEV   RSV
It is no good for the soil or for   It is fit neither for the land nor
the manure pile; it is thrown away. for the dunghill; men throw it away.
Listen, then, if you have ears!   He who has ears to hear, let him
                                      hear."

for the <u>soil</u>: that is, to make the soil more fertile.
<u>the manure pile</u>: "the pile of fertilizer."
<u>it is thrown away</u>: "people throw it away."
<u>Listen, then, if you have ears</u>: see 8.8.

Chapter 15

SECTION HEADING

The Lost Sheep: "Joy over a Lost Sheep that Was Found."

The three parables in this chapter all have a common theme: God's love for those who do not seem worthy of his love. They are told by Jesus in response to the criticism made by the religious leaders because he was associating with people who, in their opinion, weren't of much value in God's sight.

15.1   TEV

One day when many tax collectors and other outcasts came to listen to Jesus,

RSV

Now the tax collectors and sinners were all drawing near to hear him.

One day: a way in English to begin a story.
tax collectors: see 3.12. Since they worked for the pagan Roman government, they were despised by most Jews.
other outcasts: see 5.30.

15.2   TEV

the Pharisees and the teachers of the Law started grumbling, "This man welcomes outcasts and even eats with them!"

RSV

And the Pharisees and the scribes murmured, saying, "This man receives sinners and eats with them."

Pharisees and the teachers of the Law: see 5.17.
grumbling: "complaining," "criticizing."
This man: as in 14.30.

15.3-4   TEV

So Jesus told them this parable:
4 "Suppose one of you has a hundred sheep and loses one of them—what does he do? He leaves the other ninety-nine sheep in the pasture and goes looking for the one that got lost until he finds it.

RSV

So he told them this parable:
4 "What man of you, having a hundred sheep, if he has lost one of them, does not leave the ninety-nine in the wilderness, and go after the one which is lost, until he finds it?

[255]

parable: see 5.36.

As RSV shows, the whole of verse 4 is one rhetorical question, which TEV has broken up into a hypothetical question and the answer.

loses: care must be taken to use a word that applies naturally to a sheep that strays away from the flock. It should not appear that the fault lies with the shepherd. So it might be better to translate "...has a hundred sheep and one of them gets lost (or, wanders away)."

the pasture: the Greek word (which RSV translates "wilderness") means here open fields where sheep would graze.

15.5-6 TEV	RSV
When he finds it, he is so happy that he puts it on his shoulders 6 and carries it back home. Then he calls his friends and neighbors together and says to them, 'I am so happy I found my lost sheep. Let us celebrate!'	And when he has found it, he lays it on his shoulders, rejoicing. 6 And when he comes home, he calls together his friends and his neighbors, saying to them, 'Rejoice with me, for I have found my sheep which was lost.'

TEV says explicitly that the shepherd carries the sheep back home rather than back to the flock. The Greek may not mean precisely this, and a translation could be "...he puts it on his shoulders 6 and carries it back. And when he gets home, he calls...." Here, by implication at least, the shepherd carries the lost sheep back to the flock. But what TEV says is also a possible understanding of the Greek.

I am so happy...Let us celebrate: TEV uses the two expressions to translate what in Greek is one expression, "Rejoice with me" (RSV)—as in 1.58.

15.7 TEV	RSV
In the same way, I tell you, there will be more joy in heaven over one sinner who repents than over ninety-nine respectable people who do not need to repent.	Just so, I tell you, there will be more joy in heaven over one sinner who repents than over ninety-nine righteous persons who need no repentance.

Here, if necessary, the verse could begin "And Jesus concluded: 'In the same way...'" to show that this is Jesus' comment and not part of the parable.

sinner...respectable people: the application is evident; the one sinner who repents stands for those who came to listen to Jesus' teachings, while the respectable people who do not need to repent stand for the religious leaders. It is quite probable that the statement is ironical. Jesus was not saying that such people as the Pharisees and the teachers of the Law didn't need to repent, but he was simply reflecting their opinion about themselves. So it might be necessary to say "ninety-nine good people who think they do not need to repent."

repent: see 3.3.

The key word in this parable is joy: the participle of the verb "rejoice" in verse 5 (when the shepherd finds the sheep); the imperative of the verb "rejoice together" in verse 6 (the shepherd's invitation to his friends and neighbors); and the noun "joy" in verse 7 (joy in heaven).

SECTION HEADING

The Lost Coin: "Joy over a Lost Coin that Was Found."

15.8   TEV   RSV

"Or suppose a woman who has ten silver coins loses one of them—what does she do? She lights a lamp, sweeps her house, and looks carefully everywhere until she finds it.

"Or what woman, having ten silver coins, ^{t} if she loses one coin, does not light a lamp and sweep the house and seek diligently until she finds it?

^{t}The drachma, rendered here by *silver coin*, was about a day's wage for a laborer

Or: this shows that this parable is a companion to the preceding one. Again the question form is used, which TEV has represented as it does in verse 4.

silver coins: as RSV footnote shows, the Greek drachma was a coin worth a day's wage for a field worker.

lamp: see 8.16.

15.9   TEV   RSV

When she finds it, she calls her friends and neighbors together, and says to them, 'I am so happy I found the coin I lost. Let us celebrate!'

And when she has found it, she calls together her friends and neighbors, saying, 'Rejoice with me, for I have found the coin which I had lost.'

This verse follows closely the action of verse 6. Here in Greek friends and neighbors are feminine. Languages that have different forms for the two genders (such as Portuguese, Spanish, French) will naturally use the feminine forms here.

15.10   TEV   RSV

In the same way, I tell you, the angels of God rejoice over one sinner who repents."

Just so, I tell you, there is joy before the angels of God over one sinner who repents."

Here the phrase the angels of God performs the same function as heaven does in verse 7. The literal translation "before the angels of God" (RSV) makes it appear that someone other than the angels is rejoicing; the meaning here is rather "among the angels of God."

[257]

15.11-12

SECTION HEADING

The Lost Son: "Joy over a Son Who Returned Home."

Here the connection with the preceding parables is not quite so close. The theme is the same, but besides the younger son who leaves home and returns, there is also the older son who does not leave home. The traditional title "Prodigal Son" reflects the statement in verse 13 about how spendthrift and wasteful the younger son was.

15.11-12	TEV	RSV
	Jesus went on to say, "There was once a man who had two sons. 12 The younger one said to him, 'Father, give me my share of the property now.' So the man divided his property between his two sons.	And he said, "There was a man who had two sons; 12 and the younger of them said to his father, 'Father, give me the share of property that falls to me.' And he divided his living between them.

There was once: a way of beginning a story.
my share of the property now: instead of waiting until his father's death. By Jewish Law the older son was given twice the amount given the younger son. The translation may be "my share of the inheritance"; "Give me now what I am due to receive when you die."

15.13	TEV	RSV
	After a few days the younger son sold his part of the property and left home with the money. He went to a country far away, where he wasted his money in reckless living.	Not many days later, the younger son gathered all he had and took his journey into a far country, and there he squandered his property in loose living.

sold...the money: this is the meaning of the Greek verb which RSV translates "gathered."
wasted his money in reckless living: "spent all his money recklessly," "wasted all his money in dissolute living" or "...in wasteful extravagance."

15.14	TEV	RSV
	He spent everything he had. Then a severe famine spread over that country, and he was left without a thing.	And when he had spent everything, a great famine arose in that country, and he began to be in want.

a severe famine: "a shortage of food."
he was left without a thing: "he was in desperate need," or, more specifically, "he had nothing to eat" or "he was about to starve."

[258]

15.15 TEV

So he went to work for one of the
citizens of that country, who sent
him out to his farm to take care
of the pigs.

RSV

So he went and joined himself to
one of the citizens of that country,
who sent him into his fields to feed
swine.

went to work for: this translates the Greek expression "joined himself to" (RSV). In this context it refers to his action in doing something that would provide him food. Some translations have "hired himself
out to," or something similar that describes a system almost like slavery, in which a man works only for his food.

pigs: animals considered unclean by Jews (see Deut 14.8); this is a
vivid description of a very desperate situation.

15.16 TEV

He wished he could fill himself
with the bean pods the pigs ate,
but no one gave him anything to
eat.

RSV

And he would gladly have fed on^u
the pods that the swine ate; and
no one gave him anything.

^{u}Other ancient authorities read
filled his belly with

he could fill himself: "kill his hunger," "satisfy his hunger." (The
alternative words in some Greek texts indicated in the RSV footnote mean
basically the same thing as the expression translated in the TEV text.)

the bean pods: the fruit of the carob tree (see *Fauna and Flora of
the Bible*, under the entry "Carob"). In a given language, whatever pigs
eat may be used here; or else, in a more general way, "the food the pigs
were given to eat." If possible it should be something (like the carob
pods) that human beings would also be willing to eat.

anything to eat: or "any of it (that is, of the bean pods) to eat."
The text may mean that he was not allowed to eat even what was fed the
pigs.

15.17 TEV

At last he came to his senses and
said, 'All my father's hired workers have more than they can eat,
and here I am about to starve!

RSV

But when he came to himself he said,
'How many of my father's hired servants have bread enough and to spare,
but I perish here with hunger!

he came to his senses: there are idiomatic ways of saying this, such
as "his self came back," "his heart arrived," "he understood himself,"
"his heart came to life again."

and said: "and thought," "and said to himself." Here through verse
19 the young man is talking to himself and is saying to himself what he
will say to his father once he returns home. It may not be very natural
to imitate the Greek style here (see the similar passage in 12.17-19).

15.17

    All...workers: the literal translation "How many..." (RSV) may make it appear that many, but not all, of his father's hired servants have enough to eat.
    about to starve: "dying of hunger," "starving to death."

15.18-19 TEV	RSV
I will get up and go to my father and say, "Father, I have sinned against God and against you. 19 I am no longer fit to be called your son; treat me as one of your hired workers."ᵗ	I will arise and go to my father, and I will say to him, "Father, I have sinned against heaven and before you; 19 I am no longer worthy to be called your son; treat me as one of your hired servants."ˡ

    In these verses the young man rehearses what he will say to his father. It is more effective if the direct form of RSV and TEV can be maintained. But if not, something like the following may be said: "I will get up, go back home, and tell my father that I have sinned against God and against him, and so am no longer fit to be treated as his son. I will tell my father to treat me as one of his hired servants."
    against God: this translates the Greek "against heaven" (RSV), a way of speaking about God.
    I am no longer fit: "I do not deserve," "I am not worthy," "I don't merit the honor."

15.20 TEV	RSV
So he got up and started back to his father.	And he arose and came to his father.
"He was still a long way from home when his father saw him; his heart was filled with pity, and he ran, threw his arms around his son, and kissed him.	But while he was yet at a distance, his father saw him and had compassion, and ran and embraced him and kissed him.

    started back: this is said in order to prepare for the following a long way from home.
    his father saw him: the implication seems to be that the father was watching for his son's return.
    his heart was filled with pity: "he felt sorry for him," "he was moved with compassion for him."
    threw his arms around his son: "hugged him," "embraced him" (RSV).
    kissed him: on the cheeks, in oriental fashion (see 7.45). Where both hugging and kissing by men is not practiced, it may be better to say "greeted him warmly (or, affectionately)."

15.21 TEV	RSV
'Father,' the son said, 'I have sinned against God and against you.	And the son said to him, 'Father, I have sinned against heaven and

I am no longer fit to be called   before you; I am no longer worthy
your son.'   to be called your son.'*v*

> *v*Other ancient authorities add *treat
> me as one of your hired servants*

The son tells his father what he had planned to say (verses 18-19);
but he is not allowed to say "treat me as one of your hired workers." (As
the RSV footnote shows, this was added by some Greek manuscripts and
early versions, but it is not part of the original text here.)

15.22   TEV   RSV
But the father called to his serv-   But the father said to his servants,
ants. 'Hurry!' he said. 'Bring the   'Bring quickly the best robe, and
best robe and put it on him. Put a   put it on him; and put a ring on his
ring on his finger and shoes on his   hand, and shoes on his feet;
feet.

the best robe: a long outer garment. Or "the best clothes."
on his finger: the Greek word is normally translated "hand" (RSV);
obviously it doesn't mean "hand" here. The ring was a sign of status or
authority.
shoes: "sandals" would be better. Sandals were a sign of a free man
(a slave went about barefoot).

15.23   TEV   RSV
Then go and get the prize calf and   and bring the fatted calf and kill
kill it, and let us celebrate with   it, and let us eat and make merry;
a feast!

the prize calf: in English this is traditionally "the fatted calf"
(RSV), that is, the calf that was being given extra food to fatten it
for eating. The translation could be "the fattest calf," "the best calf."
If in some culture no animal is kept this way in order to be eaten, it
will be necessary to say "the best food there is" or something similar.
let us celebrate with a feast: "let's have a banquet," "we will have
a feast and a party."

15.24   TEV   RSV
For this son of mine was dead, but   for this my son was dead, and is
now he is alive; he was lost, but   alive again; he was lost, and is
now he has been found.' And so the   found.' And they began to make
feasting began.   merry.

Here the father gives the reason for the feasting. Both expressions,
was dead and was lost (and the opposites is alive and has been found),
are used figuratively, since the son had neither died nor had he gotten

[261]

lost. But he was, so to speak, as though he were dead, as though he had lost himself.

15.25	TEV	RSV

TEV	RSV
"In the meantime the older son was out in the field. On his way back, when he came close to the house, he heard the music and dancing.	"Now his elder son was in the field; and as he came and drew near to the house, he heard music and dancing.

In keeping with the two first parables, this third one should have ended with verse 24. What follows is a new development, and shows that the father loves not only the younger son but the older one as well.

On his way back: presumably after the day's work was done; and he is coming back to the house for dinner.

the music: of instruments.

dancing: or "people dancing."

15.26	TEV	RSV

TEV	RSV
So he called one of the servants and asked him, 'What's going on?'	And he called one of the servants and asked what this meant.

servants: this may have been a house servant (as opposed to field workers).

'What's going on?': TEV puts into direct form what in Greek is indirect (see RSV). Either is acceptable; the direct form is a bit more vivid: "What's happening?" "What does this (noise) mean?" "What are they doing in there?"

15.27	TEV	RSV

TEV	RSV
'Your brother has come back home,' the servant answered, 'and your father has killed the prize calf, because he got him back safe and sound.'	And he said to him, 'Your brother has come, and your father has killed the fatted calf, because he has received him safe and sound.'

has killed the prize calf, because: this is an abbreviated way of saying "has killed the prize calf in order to have a banquet, because...."

he got him back: some translations have difficulty with this and so translate simply "he (that is, the younger son) came back." But this obscures an important element: the father has his son back with him at home, where he belongs. "He has his son back with him (or, back at home)" or something similar might be said.

15.28-29	TEV	RSV

TEV	RSV
The older brother was so angry that he would not go into the house; so his father came out and begged him	But he was angry and refused to go in. His father came out and entreated him, 29 but he answered his

to come in. 29 But he spoke back to his father, 'Look, all these years I have worked for you like a slave, and I have never disobeyed your orders. What have you given me? Not even a goat for me to have a feast with my friends!

father, 'Lo, these many years I have served you, and I never disobeyed your command; yet you never gave me a kid, that I might make merry with my friends.

begged him to come in: or "and begged him, 'Please come in.'" The Greek form of the verb "to beg" indicates that the father kept asking his son to go in.

spoke back: in English this may indicate a certain lack of respect, which in the context is natural.

I have worked...like a slave: "I have worked like a servant." The Greek verb "to be a slave (or, servant)" appropriately fits the son's mood.

TEV, in order to bring out the emphatic position of "to me" in Greek, has a question, What have you given me? and the answer, Not even a goat....

even a goat: a cheap animal, in comparison with the fat calf.

have a feast: the same verb used in verse 24.

15.30   TEV
But this son of yours wasted all your property on prostitutes, and when he comes back home, you kill the prize calf for him!'

               RSV
But when this son of yours came, who has devoured your living with harlots, you killed for him the fatted calf!'

this son of yours: a tone of contempt is intended.

wasted all your property: of course the younger son had spent what was rightfully his.

prostitutes: there are appropriate and inappropriate terms for such women. Some idiomatic expressions are: "ten pence women," "women who live like dogs," "women who walk."

15.31-32   TEV
'My son,' the father answered, 'you are always here with me, and everything I have is yours. 32 But we had to celebrate and be happy, because your brother was dead, but now he is alive; he was lost, but now he has been found.'"

               RSV
And he said to him, 'Son, you are always with me, and all that is mine is yours. 32 It was fitting to make merry and be glad, for this your brother was dead, and is alive; he was lost, and is found.'"

everything I have is yours: since the younger son had already claimed his share of the estate, all the rest would go to the older brother.

we had to: "it was right." In some instances a rhetorical question will be natural: "How could we not celebrate and be happy?" or "How could we keep from celebrating and being happy?"

be happy: the same Greek verb discussed in verse 7 as a key word.
your brother: or "this brother of yours" (RSV), which is more emphatic.
was dead...is alive: see verse 24.

Chapter 16

The Shrewd Manager: "A Dishonest Administrator."

No specific setting is given for this parable, which Jesus tells his disciples. The parable has to do with prudent use of opportunities and responsibilities; the point of the parable comes in verse 8, and Jesus makes the application in verse 9. Verses 10-12 form one unit, which may not necessarily be related to the parable; and verse 13 is another independent saying which is placed here, perhaps because of the word "mammon" (RSV) in verse 13 (see "mammon" in verse 11, RSV).

16.1   TEV

Jesus said to his disciples, "There was once a rich man who had a servant who managed his property. The rich man was told that the manager was wasting his master's money,

16.1   RSV

He also said to the disciples, "There was a rich man who had a steward, and charges were brought to him that this man was wasting his goods.

There was once: see 15.11.
a servant who managed his property: this translates the Greek noun "steward" (RSV), "manager," "administrator" (see 12.42).
The rich man was told: "The rich man heard," or "It was reported," "People were saying."

16.2   TEV

so he called him in and said, 'What is this I hear about you? Turn in a complete account of your handling of my property, because you cannot be my manager any longer.'

16.2   RSV

And he called him and said to him, 'What is this that I hear about you? Turn in the account of your stewardship, for you can no longer be steward.'

What is this I hear about you?: "How do you explain what I have heard about you?" or "Is it true what they're saying about you?"
Turn in a complete account: "Write down a full statement."
It may be better to reverse the order of the two clauses: "You cannot be my manager any longer, so turn in a complete account of your handling of my property."
you cannot be: or, in a more direct fashion, "I'm firing you," "I am letting you go," "I am forced to dismiss you." The steward's report will be the last thing he will do as a steward.

[265]

16.3 TEV	RSV
The servant said to himself, 'My master is going to dismiss me from my job. What shall I do? I am not strong enough to dig ditches, and I am ashamed to beg.	And the steward said to himself, 'What shall I do, since my master is taking the stewardship away from me? I am not strong enough to dig, and I am ashamed to beg.

said to himself: "thought."

dig ditches: TEV thus represents the verb "dig" with the direct object ditches, because in English an object for "dig" is almost indispensable. Or else "to work the soil," "to till the ground." Or else an expression for heavy manual labor could be used.

I am ashamed to beg: "I am too proud to beg." There seemed to be no other alternative. Losing his job under these circumstances made it improbable that he could get another job as a steward.

16.4 TEV	RSV
Now I know what I will do! Then when my job is gone, I shall have friends who will welcome me in their homes.'	I have decided what to do, so that people may receive me into their houses when I am put out of the stewardship.'

Now I know: the thought comes to him suddenly, and he makes a decision.

when my job is gone: "when I have lost my job," "after my master fires me."

friends who will welcome me: the man is certain that his plan will gain him friends who will take care of him after he loses his job.

16.5-6 TEV	RSV
So he called in all the people who were in debt to his master. He asked the first one, 'How much do you owe my master?' 6 'One hundred barrels of olive oil,' he answered. 'Here is your account,' the manager told him; 'sit down and write fifty.'	So, summoning his master's debtors one by one, he said to the first, 'How much do you owe my master?' 6 He said, 'A hundred measures of oil.' And he said to him, 'Take your bill, and sit down quickly and write fifty.'

all the people: or, similar to RSV, "he called them all in one by one."

barrels: the Greek has the equivalent of the Hebrew measure *bath*, which was about 37 liters (8 gallons). It is not necessary to have the exact amounts, only the proportion between the old and the new accounts. In some places instead of barrels a word such as "jars," or "bottles," or "vats," or "jugs," will be appropriate.

sit down and write: or "sit down quickly and write." It may be necessary to say "sit down quickly and write that you owe (my master) fifty barrels of olive oil."

16.7

TEV	RSV
Then he asked another one, 'And you—how much do you owe?' 'A thousand bushels of wheat,' he answered. 'Here is your account,' the manager told him; 'write eight hundred.'	Then he said to another, 'And how much do you owe?' He said, 'A hundred measures of wheat.' He said to him, 'Take your bill, and write eighty.'

The Greek word for "measures" (RSV) here is the Greek equivalent of the Hebrew dry measure *cor*, which was about 370 liters (or 10 bushels). If weight is preferable, the totals for "one hundred measures" would be 21,000 kilograms (44,000 pounds) and 16,800 kilograms (35,200 pounds). Again, it is the proportion between the two amounts that is important.

16.8

TEV	RSV
As a result the master of this dishonest manager praised him for doing such a shrewd thing; because the people of this world are much more shrewd in handling their affairs than the people who belong to the light."	The master commended the dishonest steward for his shrewdness; for the sons of this world^w are more shrewd in dealing with their own generation than the sons of light.

^{w}Greek *age*

The key word in this verse is shrewd, which may also be translated "prudent," or translated as the nouns "common sense," "forethought."
the people of this world: "people who are concerned with worldly matters," in contrast with the people who belong to the light, that is, people who are concerned with the values of the Kingdom of God.
handling their affairs: RSV translates "in dealing with their own generation," which is taken to mean "in dealing with people of their own kind." Either translation is justified; the context would seem to favor TEV.

16.9

TEV	RSV
And Jesus went on to say, "And so I tell you: make friends for yourselves with worldly wealth, so that when it gives out, you will be welcomed in the eternal home.	And I tell you, make friends for yourselves by means of unrighteous mammon,^{a} so that when it fails they may receive you into the eternal habitations.

^{a}*Mammon* is a Semitic word for money or riches

And Jesus went on to say: here Jesus applies the moral of the parable to his followers.
worldly wealth: "wealth of this wicked (or, sinful) world." It would seem that the Greek phrase means money or wealth that is gained in a world which is by nature wicked, or sinful. It does not seem likely that the phrase means "money earned by dishonest (or, fraudulent) means," as some have interpreted it. "Use your material (or, worldly) wealth to make

16.9

friends for yourselves": this sounds like bribing, or at least like deliberately buying friendship, and something of this shade of meaning
cannot be avoided.

when it gives out: "when your wealth disappears" or "when your
wealth is no longer of any value," "when your money can do you no good."

you will be welcomed: this translates the active third person plural
"they will welcome you" (see RSV), referring to the friends one has made
(which parallels precisely with "they will welcome you" in the parable,
in verse 4). But it may well be that this active form is used to refer
to God (see the similar "they demand" in 12.20): "God will welcome you."
If possible a passive expression, like the one that TEV uses, will do.

the eternal home: a reference to heaven.

16.10 TEV	RSV
Whoever is faithful in small mat-ters will be faithful in large ones; whoever is dishonest in small matters will be dishonest in large ones.	"He who is faithful in a very little is faithful also in much; and he who is dishonest in a very little is dishonest also in much.

It might be better to start a separate paragraph here, which will
include verses 10-12.

faithful: "honest," "trustworthy," "dependable," as opposed to dishonest.

in small matters: "in handling (or, managing) a small amount." The
essential element is still that of being a steward, an administrator of
the property of the master.

16.11 TEV	RSV
If, then, you have not been faith-ful in handling worldly wealth, how can you be trusted with true wealth?	If then you have not been faithful in the unrighteous mammon,[a] who will entrust to you the true riches?

[a]*Mammon* is a Semitic word for money
or riches

The rhetorical question in this verse expects the answer, "You cannot be trusted with true wealth." It may be that a statement will be
better: "If, then, you have not been faithful..., you cannot be trusted
with true wealth." Here worldly wealth, that is, material riches (same
phrase as in verse 9), is contrasted with true wealth, that is, spiritual
riches. You is plural.

16.12 TEV	RSV
And if you have not been faithful with what belongs to someone else, who will give you what belongs to you?	And if you have not been faithful in that which is another's, who will give you that which is your own?

The rhetorical question in verse 12 is like the one in verse 11, with the implied answer, "No one will give you what belongs to you." The explicit referents of what belongs to someone else, and of what belongs to you are not clear. In connection with the preceding verse, the implication seems to be that managing someone else's property, that is, the job of a steward, serves to show whether or not a person can be trusted to handle faithfully his own (spiritual) possessions. But this is not at all evident.

16.13 TEV	RSV
"No servant can be the slave of two masters; he will hate one and love the other; he will be loyal to one and despise the other. You cannot serve both God and money."	No servant can serve two masters; for either he will hate the one and love the other, or he will be devoted to the one and despise the other. You cannot serve God and mammon."*a*

*a*Mammon is a Semitic word for money or riches

This is an independent saying and should be placed in a separate paragraph.

can be the slave of: or, simply, "serve" (RSV). This reflects the situation at that time when a servant, or slave, worked for only one master, or owner.

Here, as in verse 26, it seems likely that the contrasts hate and love, be loyal to and despise, are to be understood as comparatives (see 14.26), and that the meaning is "he will love one more than he loves the other, he will be more loyal to one than to the other." But in light of the concluding application, where God and money are the two masters, it seems better to use the absolute forms of the Greek.

serve: here "worship," "be loyal to," "be a slave of," may be used. It may be necessary to use two verbs, one for God and the other for money. The order may be reversed: "You cannot (or, One can't) have both God and money as masters."

SECTION HEADING

Some Sayings of Jesus: "Jesus Teaches about Other Matters."

There is no obvious relation between the previous verses and verses 14-18. Some translations include verses 14-15 in the preceding section, which is probably better than what TEV does. In this case, a new section can begin with verse 16, with the same heading, Some Sayings of Jesus.

Or else, verses 16-18 can be divided into two sections: (1) "The Law and the Kingdom of God," verses 16-17; and (2) "Jesus Teaches about Divorce," verse 18. This seems to be the best way to divide the material.

16.14   TEV   RSV
      When the Pharisees heard all   The Pharisees, who were lovers
this, they made fun of Jesus, be-   of money, heard all this, and they
cause they loved money.   scoffed at him.

      Pharisees: see 5.17.
      heard all this: in the context, this refers to what Jesus told his
disciples in verses 1-13.
      TEV makes clear that the Pharisees made fun of Jesus because they
loved money.

16.15   TEV   RSV
Jesus said to them, "You are the   But he said to them, "You are those
ones who make yourselves look right who justify yourselves before men,
in other people's sight, but God   but God knows your hearts; for what
knows your hearts. For the things   is exalted among men is an abomina-
that are considered of great value   tion in the sight of God.
by man are worth nothing in God's
sight.

      make yourselves look right: or "make yourselves look good," "try to
appear as good people."
      God knows your hearts: "God knows what you really are like," "God
knows what you think and feel."
      by man: "by people." Or "For the things that people think so highly
of are worth nothing in God's sight," or "People may think some things
are valuable which God considers worthless."

16.16   TEV   RSV
      "The Law of Moses and the writ-   "The law and the prophets were
ings of the prophets were in effect until John; since then the good news
up to the time of John the Baptist; of the kingdom of God is preached,
since then the Good News about the   and every one enters it violently.
Kingdom of God is being told, and
everyone forces his way in.

      The Law of Moses and the writings of the prophets: these are, re-
spectively, the first five books of the Hebrew Scriptures (the Torah)
and the second division of the Hebrew Scriptures (the Prophets). The
phrase means here the Hebrew Bible, the teachings of the Hebrew faith,
the Jewish religion. It may be necessary to say "What is written in the
Law of Moses and the books of the prophets."
      were in effect: it is difficult to decide the exact meaning of the
verb "were" (RSV). Something like "were in force," "were valid," or "had
authority" seems to be meant. Simply to say "existed" is not sufficient,
because they did continue to exist after the time of John the Baptist.
      With John the Baptist began a new era, the time of the proclamation
of the Kingdom of God.

everyone forces his way in: or "everyone tries hard to get into the Kingdom of God." This is a difficult saying, and it is hard to decide exactly how the words are meant.

16.17 TEV	RSV
But it is easier for heaven and earth to disappear than for the smallest detail of the Law to be done away with.	But it is easier for heaven and earth to pass away, than for one dot of the law to become void.

This verse should appear as a separate paragraph. Its connection with what precedes is very weak. This verse emphasizes the permanent validity of the Law: everything in it will be fulfilled.

By use of the comparative construction, it is easier for...than for, an absolute statement is being made: "Heaven and earth will not disappear, nor will the most insignificant requirement of the Law become invalid."

smallest detail: literally "one stroke," a reference to a small projection ("horn") that distinguished certain Hebrew consonants from others (for example, the *beth* from the *kaph*). Translations use a variety of idiomatic expressions: "comma," "period," "tilde," "dash," "one dotting of an 'i.'"

16.18 TEV	RSV
"Any man who divorces his wife and marries another woman commits adultery; and the man who marries a divorced woman commits adultery.	"Every one who divorces his wife and marries another commits adultery, and he who marries a woman divorced from her husband commits adultery.

A saying on divorce. The statement is absolute and admits of no exceptions. Only the first marriage is valid; subsequent marriages are not valid.

SECTION HEADING

The Rich Man and Lazarus: "The Parable about Lazarus and the Rich Man."

No setting is given for this parable; it is not even called a parable in the text. Its placement here seems to be due to the statements in verses 16-17 about the Law and the Prophets, and the concluding reference to them in verses 29-31.

16.19 TEV	RSV
"There was once a rich man who dressed in the most expensive clothes and lived in great luxury every day.	"There was a rich man, who was clothed in purple and fine linen and who feasted sumptuously every day.

the most expensive clothes: this translates "purple robes and fine linen clothes" (see RSV). The "purple" would be the outer garment; the "linen" would be the inner garment.

lived in great luxury: or "had splendid banquets" (the same verb used in 15.24).

16.20	TEV	RSV
	There was also a poor man named Lazarus, covered with sores, who used to be brought to the rich man's door,	And at his gate lay a poor man named Lazarus, full of sores,

Lazarus: the name (an abbreviation of "Eleazar") means "God helps." This is the only time a person in a parable is given a name.

covered with sores: "who was covered with sores," "who had sores all over his body."

used to be brought: this is said to bring out the repetitive aspect of the verb.

door: "to the door (or, gate) of the rich man's house."

It may be better to end verse 20 with a full stop and begin verse 21: "He hoped he would get to eat...."

16.21	TEV	RSV
	hoping to eat the bits of food that fell from the rich man's table. Even the dogs would come and lick his sores.	who desired to be fed with what fell from the rich man's table; moreover the dogs came and licked his sores.

the bits of food that fell: or perhaps, "the food that was left over and thrown away after the rich man got through eating."

Even the dogs: a final detail showing the miserable condition of Lazarus.

16.22	TEV	RSV
	The poor man died and was carried by the angels to sit beside Abraham at the feast in heaven. The rich man died and was buried,	The poor man died and was carried by the angels to Abraham's bosom. The rich man also died and was buried;

and was carried: in some languages it may be necessary to say "and his soul (or, spirit) was carried."

to sit beside Abraham at the feast in heaven: here heaven is pictured as a banquet, with Abraham as the host of all God's people (see 13.28-29; 14.15). Lazarus is given the place of honor right next to Abraham (see 5.29). Simply to translate "to Abraham's bosom" hardly makes sense and sounds ridiculous. Another possible translation: "to be with Abraham in Paradise (or, heaven)." For the phrase "to be in someone's bosom" see John 13.23.

16.23   TEV
and in Hades,[8] where he was in
great pain, he looked up and saw
Abraham, far away, with Lazarus at
his side.

16.23   RSV
and in Hades, being in torment, he
lifted up his eyes, and saw Abraham
far off and Lazarus in his bosom.

[8]HADES: *The world of the dead.*

 Hades: the Hebrew "Sheol," the world of the dead. Here it is practically equivalent to hell.
 he looked up: Hades was thought to be in the depths of the earth;
Paradise was thought to be in the heights above earth.

16.24   TEV
So he called out, 'Father Abraham!
Take pity on me, and send Lazarus
to dip his finger in some water and
cool off my tongue, because I am in
great pain in this fire!'

16.24   RSV
And he called out, 'Father Abraham,
have mercy upon me, and send Lazarus
to dip the end of his finger in
water and cool my tongue; for I am
in anguish in this flame.'

 Father Abraham: see 3.8. The rich man is a Jew, and he speaks to
the father of his race.
 It may be necessary to restructure this verse as follows: "Father
Abraham! I am suffering terribly in this fire! So take pity on me and
tell Lazarus to dip his finger in water and cool off my tongue."

16.25   TEV
But Abraham said, 'Remember, my
son, that in your lifetime you were
given all the good things, while
Lazarus got all the bad things. But
now he is enjoying himself here,
while you are in pain.

16.25   RSV
But Abraham said, 'Son, remember
that you in your lifetime received
your good things, and Lazarus in
like manner evil things; but now
he is comforted here, and you are
in anguish.

 my son: Abraham responds to the rich man and acknowledges the racial
kinship.
 in your lifetime: "while you lived (on earth)."
 you were given: or "you got," "you received."
 enjoying himself: "having a happy time."

16.26   TEV
Besides all that, there is a deep
pit lying between us, so that those
who want to cross over from here to
you cannot do so, nor can anyone
cross over to us from where you
are.'

16.26   RSV
And besides all this, between us
and you a great chasm has been fixed,
in order that those who would pass
from here to you may not be able,
and none may cross from there to us.'

16.26

a deep pit: "a wide chasm," "a huge ditch."

between us: here the us is inclusive; the Greek says "between us (exclusive) and you (plural)," that is, between the place where all the righteous are and the place where the sinners are being punished.

to you: this is plural: "to you who are there."

16.27   TEV   RSV
The rich man said, 'Then I beg you,   And he said, 'Then I beg you, father,
father Abraham, send Lazarus to my   to send him to my father's house,
father's house,

The rich man now pleads for his brothers.

my father's house: the phrase does not necessarily imply that the father is still alive; it means only that the man's five brothers are still living at home.

16.28   TEV   RSV
where I have five brothers. Let him   for I have five brothers, so that
go and warn them so that they, at   he may warn them, lest they also
least, will not come to this place   come into this place of torment.'
of pain.'

warn them: in the context, this means to warn them not to live as he did, but to change their ways (see verse 30).

will not come: this may have to be expanded to "will not have to come, after they die." The rich man wants his brothers to go where Lazarus is.

16.29   TEV   RSV
Abraham said, 'Your brothers have   But Abraham said, 'They have Moses
Moses and the prophets to warn   and the prophets; let them hear
them; your brothers should listen   them.'
to what they say.'

Moses and the prophets: see verse 16. The text should not appear to mean that Moses and the prophets are still alive (on earth) to warn the five brothers. "Your brothers can read what Moses and the prophets wrote; your brothers should pay attention to that!"

listen: this seems to imply the weekly synagogue services, where passages from the Torah and the Prophets were regularly read.

16.30   TEV   RSV
The rich man answered, 'That is not   And he said, 'No, father Abraham;
enough, father Abraham! But if   but if some one goes to them from
someone were to rise from death and   the dead, they will repent.'
go to them, then they would turn
from their sins.'

That is not enough: or "My brothers won't listen to them." The rich man is saying that a stronger warning than the Hebrew Scriptures is needed to get his brothers to repent of their sins. And he is also trying to excuse himself.

turn from their sins: see 3.3.

16.31 TEV	RSV
But Abraham said, 'If they will not listen to Moses and the prophets, they will not be convinced even if someone were to rise from death.'"	He said to him, 'If they do not hear Moses and the prophets, neither will they be convinced if some one should rise from the dead.'"

be convinced: that is, to repent, to change their ways. There is no excuse for the five brothers, nor for the rich man himself.

Chapter 17

SECTION HEADING

Sin: "The Danger of Falling into Sin," "The Danger of Committing
Sin."

Verses 1-10 cover brief sayings of Jesus on three different subjects.
TEV has divided the material into three sections, but it may be better to
have only one section, with the heading "Some Teachings of Jesus." There
is no indication of place and occasion of these sayings, and there is no
logical or topical connection that links them together.

17.1   TEV

Jesus said to his disciples,
"Things that make people fall into
sin are bound to happen, but how
terrible for the one who makes them
happen!

              RSV

And he said to his disciples,
"Temptations to sin^x are sure to
come; but woe to him by whom they
come!

^{x}Greek *stumbling blocks*

Jesus: since this is the beginning of a section, TEV gives the name
and not just the pronoun "he" (RSV).
    disciples: see 5.30.
    Things that make people fall into sin: this translates the Greek
"stumbling blocks." The usage is figurative; appropriate equivalents may
be "pitfalls," "snares," "hidden dangers," or anything else appropriate
to the idea of causing to stray, err, go wrong. Here people seems to refer specifically to followers of Jesus (see one of these little ones in
the next verse). Since the punishment threatened is so severe, it would
seem that the sin here is the worst one possible for a follower of Jesus,
that is, to apostatize, to renounce the faith, to quit following Jesus.
(In the parallel passage Matt 18.6-7, the two sayings of verses 1-2 here
are given in reverse order.)
    are bound to happen: "are inevitable," "are certain to happen."
    how terrible: see 6.24.
    the one who makes them happen: "the person responsible for such
things." It should not appear that the words mean that one person alone
will be responsible for such things. The text means any person who is the
cause of someone falling into sin, of rejecting faith in Jesus.

[276]

17.2	TEV	RSV

It would be better for him if a
large millstone were tied around
his neck and he were thrown into
the sea than for him to cause one
of these little ones to sin.

It would be better for him if a
millstone were hung round his neck
and he were cast into the sea, than
that he should cause one of these
little ones to sin.[y]

[y]Greek *stumble*

It would be better: death by drowning is preferable to the unspecified punishment awaiting such a person. Since two bad things are being
contemplated, neither one of which is "better" in the sense of being
good, it might be better in some languages to translate "It is worse for
a person to cause one of these little ones to sin than it would be if a
large millstone were tied around his neck and he were thrown into the
sea."

if a large millstone were tied: "if someone tied a large millstone."

large millstone: the large top stone which turned on its axis and
thus ground the grain between it and the lower millstone. If millstone is
not known in a given language, the substitution of "a very large stone"
may be required.

one of these little ones: it would appear that these are immature
believers, people who are beginners in the Christian way.

to sin: this is the verb form of the noun in verse 1: "cause to
stumble" (see the RSV text and footnote); "to abandon his faith in me,"
"to stop believing in me."

17.3	TEV	RSV

So watch what you do!
    "If your brother sins, rebuke
him, and if he repents, forgive
him.

Take heed to yourselves; if your
brother sins, rebuke him, and if he
repents, forgive him;

So watch what you do!: TEV and others connect this with the preceding two verses; RSV and others connect it with what follows. Here you is
plural, the disciples. "Be careful how you act," "Keep watch on yourselves."

your brother: see 6.41; here your is singular; Jesus is speaking of
each one individually.

sins: this is the verb "to sin" in a general sense without saying
whom the sin is against. It would make more sense if the meaning were
"sins against you" (or, "offends you"), and the specific sins against you
in verse 4 makes it most likely that the same meaning is intended here.
So it is better to translate here "sins against you." Since here the sin
is against a person, not against God, it might be better to say "if he
wrongs you," "if he does something bad to you."

rebuke: "reprimand," "censure." Or else, "tell him to stop doing
that," "tell him that what he is doing is wrong."

repents: see 3.3. Here it may be better to say "If he says, 'I did
wrong'" or "If he says, 'I am sorry I did that.'"

forgive: see 5.20.

17.4	TEV	RSV

If he sins against you seven times in one day, and each time he comes to you saying, 'I repent,' you must forgive him."

and if he sins against you seven times in the day, and turns to you seven times, and says, 'I repent,' you must forgive him."

This verse repeats, in an expanded and emphatic way, what is said in verse 3. If seven times implies that this is the absolute limit, and that an eighth offense need not be forgiven, it will be better to say "many times."

SECTION HEADING

Faith: "The Power of Faith."

17.5	TEV	RSV

The apostles said to the Lord, "Make our faith greater."

The apostles said to the Lord, "Increase our faith!"

apostles: see 6.13.
the Lord: see 5.8.
Make our faith greater: this is faith in God. It may not be natural to speak of faith in terms of size or quantity; so it may be better to say "stronger, deeper, more genuine" or the like. "Help us to believe more strongly in God" or "Give us more faith."

17.6	TEV	RSV

The Lord answered, "If you had faith as big as a mustard seed, you could say to this mulberry tree, 'Pull yourself up by the roots and plant yourself in the sea,' and it would obey you.

And the Lord said, "If you had faith as a grain of mustard seed, you could say to this sycamine tree, 'Be rooted up, and be planted in the sea,' and it would obey you.

as big as: this is required by the figure that is used; a mustard seed was considered to be the smallest of all seeds (see 13.19). If mustard is unknown, "a very small seed" may be said.
you could say: this is required by the form of the Greek, which pictures the condition as not fulfilled: "If you had (which you don't) faith as big as a mustard seed, you could say (which you cannot) to this mulberry tree...."
mulberry tree: see *Fauna and Flora of the Bible*, under the entry "Mulberry tree."
Pull yourself up by the roots: "Uproot yourself," "Pull yourself out of the ground."
plant yourself: obviously a tree cannot be planted in the sea; so it may be better to say (even though the alternatives are also impossible) "grow in the sea," "stand in the sea."

It may be better to restructure as follows: "If your faith were as large as a mustard seed, you would be able to order this mulberry tree to pull itself out of the ground and go stand in the sea. And the tree would obey you."

SECTION HEADING

A Servant's Duty: "How a Good Servant Behaves."

This saying is not connected in any way with the preceding one. Jesus is talking to his followers; it does not seem likely that he is talking only to the twelve apostles.

17.7 TEV	RSV
"Suppose one of you has a servant who is plowing or looking after the sheep. When he comes in from the field, do you tell him to hurry along and eat his meal?	"Will any one of you, who has a servant plowing or keeping sheep, say to him when he has come in from the field, 'Come at once and sit down at table'?

The form of the Greek is a rhetorical question which goes without a major break to the end of verse 8; RSV has broken the material into two rhetorical questions. TEV has restructured the material differently (see a similar case in 11.5).

a servant: "a slave."

plowing: or, more generally, "working in the field."

looking after: "tending," "taking care of."

When he comes in: as the context shows, this is at the end of the day's work, in time for the evening meal.

the field: a term is needed which applies both to a field where crops grow and to a pasture where sheep graze. It may be better to say "When he comes in after finishing his work," or "When his work is done and he comes to the house."

It is to be noticed that TEV uses indirect discourse in this verse; RSV follows the Greek and uses direct discourse. RSV makes it appear that the master is inviting the servant to sit at the table with him; it seems more likely that TEV better represents the meaning of the text.

eat his meal: this translates "recline (at the table)"—see 5.29.

17.8 TEV	RSV
Of course not! Instead, you say to him, 'Get my supper ready, then put on your apron and wait on me while I eat and drink; after that you may have your meal.'	Will he not rather say to him, "Prepare supper for me, and gird yourself and serve me, till I eat and drink; and afterward you shall eat and drink'?

Of course not! Instead: this makes clear that "Will he not rather" (RSV) is a strong negation. And TEV structure avoids having a complex direct discourse embedded into a rhetorical question.

[279]

17.8

Get my supper ready: "Prepare my food," "Fix my meal."
put on your apron: or whatever is the appropriate language for such a situation; "prepare to serve me," "get ready to wait on me."
you may have your meal: "you can eat," "you can have your supper."

17.9	TEV	RSV

17.9 TEV: The servant does not deserve thanks for obeying orders, does he?

RSV: Does he thank the servant because he did what was commanded?

This is another rhetorical question; in some cases a direct statement may be preferable: "And the servant does not deserve thanks for obeying orders."
does not deseve thanks: or, similar to RSV, "He doesn't thank the servant" or "He doesn't praise the servant"; or else, "The servant does not deserve praise."
obeying orders: or "obeying his master's order."

17.10 TEV: It is the same with you; when you have done all you have been told to do, say, 'We are ordinary servants; we have only done our duty.'"

RSV: So you also, when you have done all that is commanded you, say, 'We are unworthy servants; we have only done what was our duty.'"

Jesus applies the saying to his listeners.
all you have been told to do: in the situation, this probably refers to what Jesus himself commands his followers to do, and not God's laws in general.
We: this is inclusive.
ordinary servants: the Greek adjective translated by RSV "unworthy" here means "unworthy of praise (or, thanks)." The translation may say "We are merely servants and deserve no thanks (or, praise)."

SECTION HEADING

Jesus Heals Ten Men: the language used in the heading should follow the wording of the text.

In this section the author once more sets the incident in the context of the journey from Galilee to Jerusalem (see 9.52). Only Jesus appears in this incident, but it is assumed that the disciples were with him.

17.11 TEV: As Jesus made his way to Jerusalem, he went along the border between Samaria and Galilee.

RSV: On the way to Jerusalem he was passing along between Samaria and Galilee.

[280]

went along the border between Samaria and Galilee: the meaning of the Greek text is not very clear; it would seem to say "he passed through the midst of Samaria and Galilee." But since Samaria is south of Galilee, anyone going to Jerusalem would first go through Galilee and then through Samaria. Instead of the meaning expressed by TEV, some translations have "he was passing through the border regions between Samaria and Galilee."

Samaria was the province south of Galilee and was ruled by the Roman governor Pontius Pilate (see 3.1).

17.12

TEV	RSV
He was going into a village when he was met by ten men suffering from a dreaded skin disease. They stood at a distance	And as he entered a village, he was met by ten lepers, who stood at a distance

he was met: since these men could not live in a village, the scene seems to be that Jesus was met by them outside the village; Jesus had not yet gone into it. So instead of He was going into, it may be better to say "He was about to enter."

17.13

TEV	RSV
and shouted, "Jesus! Master! Have pity on us!"	and lifted up their voices and said, "Jesus, Master, have mercy on us."

Master: see 5.5. Here the term does not mean that they considered themselves his disciples or followers; it is simply a term of respect.
Have pity on us: they want to be healed, and so they appeal to his feeling of compassion.

17.14

TEV	RSV
Jesus saw them and said to them, "Go and let the priests examine you." On the way they were made clean.^{t}	When he saw them he said to them, "Go and show yourselves to the priests." And as they went they were cleansed.

^{t}MADE CLEAN: See 5.12.

let the priests examine you: see 5.14. The priests could certify that the men had been healed of their disease.
On the way: "As they went."
made clean: see 5.12.

17.15-16

TEV	RSV
When one of them saw that he was healed, he came back, praising God in a loud voice. 16 He threw himself to the ground at Jesus' feet	Then one of them, when he saw that he was healed, turned back, praising God with a loud voice; 16 and he fell on his face at Jesus' feet,

[281]

and thanked him. The man was a Samaritan.	giving him thanks. Now he was a Samaritan.

he came back: to Jesus, of course.
threw himself to the ground: "prostrated himself," "knelt down."
Samaritan: see 9.52.

17.17   TEV   RSV
Jesus spoke up, "There were ten men   Then said Jesus, "Were not ten
who were healed; where are the oth-   cleansed? Where are the nine?
er nine?

spoke up: the text does not say to whom he was speaking, whether to
his disciples, or to other people around him.
There were ten men: in Greek this is a rhetorical question (see
RSV); it is not a request for information.
Instead of the passive who were healed it may be better to use the
active: "I healed ten men"; or "I healed ten men, didn't I?"

17.18   TEV   RSV
Why is this foreigner the only one   Was no one found to return and give
who came back to give thanks to   praise to God except this foreign-
God?"   er?"

As RSV shows, the Greek says "Weren't there any others found to return...?" The use of the verb "to find" in Greek does not indicate a
search; in this context it is simply a substitute for "to be."
Why...?: the question indicates surprise on the part of Jesus. He
cannot understand why only the Samaritan returned to express his grati-
tude to God.
foreigner: here, non-Israelite; Jesus here reflects the attitude of
the Jews. It may be necessary to expand as follows: "Why is it that only
this foreigner (or, non-Israelite) returned to give thanks to God? Why
didn't the Israelites do this?"

17.19   TEV   RSV
And Jesus said to him, "Get up and   And he said to him, "Rise and go
go; your faith has made you well."   your way; your faith has made you
                                       well."

your faith has made you well: "you were healed because you believed."
Here faith is faith in Jesus (see 7.50; 8.48).

SECTION HEADING

The Coming of the Kingdom: "How the Kingdom of God Will Come."

[282]

This incident is unrelated to what precedes. There is no way of determining where Jesus was when this discourse took place. After responding to the question posed to him by some Pharisees (verses 20-21), Jesus turns to his disciples and speaks to them about the future coming of God's Kingdom (verses 22-37).

17.20   TEV   RSV

Some Pharisees asked Jesus when the Kingdom of God would come. His answer was, "The Kingdom of God does not come in such a way as to be seen.	Being asked by the Pharisees when the kingdom of God was coming, he answered them, "The kingdom of God is not coming with signs to be observed;

Pharisees: see 5.17.

Kingdom of God: see 4.43. If a noun phrase is unsuitable, the translation could be "...asked Jesus, 'When will God establish his Kingdom (or, rule) on earth?'" or "...'When will God begin to rule over mankind?'"

in such a way as to be seen: or "the coming of the Kingdom of God is not an event that will be seen" or "...an event preceded by signs that can be seen" (see RSV). The Pharisees wanted a timetable, and they thought that there would be unusual signs that would indicate that the Kingdom was about to come. A possible translation would be "The coming of the Kingdom of God will not be preceded by visible signs."

17.21   TEV   RSV

No one will say, 'Look, here it is!' or, 'There it is!'; because the Kingdom of God is within you."[u]	nor will they say, 'Lo, here it is!' or 'There!' for behold, the kingdom of God is in the midst of you."[z]

[u] within you; or among you, or will suddenly appear among you. [z] Or *within you*

The order in this verse may be changed to "The Kingdom of God is within you, and so no one will say, 'Look, here it is!' or 'There it is!'"

As the TEV footnote shows, the Greek phrase which it translates within you may be taken to mean "among you" (RSV "in the midst of you") or "will suddenly appear among you." The rendering within you indicates that the rule of God is an internal matter, the reign of God in the human heart; "among you" means the Kingdom was already there, as Jesus spoke, which is an oblique reference to himself and his message. The third possibility is that the Kingdom is a future event.

17.22   TEV   RSV

Then he said to the disciples, "The time will come when you will wish you could see one of the days of the Son of Man, but you will not see it.	And he said to the disciples, "The days are coming when you will desire to see one of the days of the Son of man, and you will not see it.

see one of the days of the Son of Man: this rather enigmatic phrase seems to mean "see at least one of the days when the Son of Man will be present in all his power and glory." The title Son of Man (see 5.24) refers to Jesus himself, and the days of the Son of Man will be his future glorious return (see verse 24). The coming of the Son of Man is not the coming of the Kingdom.

you will not see it: in the context, this means that the coming of the Son of Man will not be preceded by signs—no one will be able to predict when it will take place. When it finally comes, it will be unexpected but will be clearly seen by all.

17.23 TEV	RSV
There will be those who will say to you, 'Look, over there!' or, 'Look, over here!' But don't go out looking for it.	And they will say to you, 'Lo, there!' or 'Lo, here!' Do not go, do not follow them.

Look, over there...Look, over here: this is a way of saying "The Son of Man is over there...The Son of Man is over here." As the following verse shows, the coming of the Son of Man will be visible to everyone; no one will have private knowledge of the event.

don't go out looking for it: or "don't go after those people."

17.24 TEV	RSV
As the lightning flashes across the sky and lights it up from one side to the other, so will the Son of Man be in his day.	For as the lightning flashes and lights up the sky from one side to the other, so will the Son of man be in his day.[a]

[a]Other ancient authorities omit *in his day*

As the lightning: this saying may need to be restructured as follows: "The coming of the Son of Man will be as visible as lightning which flashes across the sky and lights up the whole earth." The comparison is not with the speed of lightning but with its visibility.

lights it up: that is, the sky; but it may be more appropriate to say "lights up the earth."

so will the Son of Man be in his day: "so will it be on the day the Son of Man appears."

In these verses, as elsewhere, the title the Son of Man is a reference to Jesus, and it may be necessary in every instance to say quite explicitly "I, the Son of Man."

As the RSV footnote shows, a few of the older Greek manuscripts and early versions omit in his day. Whether retained or omitted, the meaning is the same: the reference is to the coming of the Son of Man.

17.25   TEV
But first he must suffer much and
be rejected by the people of this
day.

RSV
But first he must suffer many things
and be rejected by this generation.

first: "before he comes."
This saying resembles closely the saying in 9.22. Here the people of this day (see 7.31) takes the place of the religious leaders named in 9.22.

17.26-27   TEV
As it was in the time of Noah so
shall it be in the days of the Son
of man. 27 Everybody kept on eating
and drinking, and men and women
married, up to the very day Noah
went into the boat and the flood
came and killed them all.

RSV
As it was in the days of Noah, so
will it be in the days of the Son
of man. 27 They ate, they drank,
they married, they were given in
marriage, until the day when Noah
entered the ark, and the flood came
and destroyed them all.

the time of Noah: that is, before Noah and his family entered the boat.
the days of the Son of Man: "the time before the Son of Man comes (or, appears)."
Verse 27 indicates that people kept on living normal lives up to the day the flood started; they did not take seriously the possibility, clearly indicated by what Noah was doing, that something catastrophic was about to take place.
In Greek "they married" (RSV) refers to men, while "they were given in marriage" (RSV) refers to women; so TEV has men and women married; or else, "they married."
the boat: an appropriate term whould be used of a vessel that was 450 feet long, 75 feet wide, and 45 feet high; or in metric measurements: 165 meters, 27.5 meters, 16.5 meters (see Gen 6.15).
flood: the biblical narrative (Gen 7.11-23) describes the heavy rains for 40 days (and the overflow from springs and rivers) as the cause of the destructive mass of water that covered the earth.

17.28-29   TEV
It will be as it was in the time of
Lot. Everybody kept on eating and
drinking, buying and selling,
planting and building. 29 On the
day Lot left Sodom, fire and sulfur
rained down from heaven and killed
them all.

RSV
Likewise as it was in the days of
Lot—they ate, they drank, they
bought, they sold, they planted,
they built, 29 but on the day when
Lot went out from Sodom fire and
sulphur rained from heaven and destroyed them all—

The same normal conditions of living prevailed in Sodom (and Gomorrah) up to the day it was destroyed by fire from heaven (see Gen 19.23-25).

sulfur: a yellow substance which burns with intense heat and produces an unpleasant smell. The phrase fire and sulfur may be represented
by "burning sulfur" or "burning pieces (or, stones) of sulfur."
   rained down: "came down," "poured down." Or else, God may be named
as the subject: "God caused burning sulfur to come down from heaven."

17.30	TEV	RSV
	That is how it will be on the day the Son of Man is revealed.	so will it be on the day when the Son of man is revealed.

That is how it will be: that is, normal human activity will prevail
until the great day.
   is revealed: here in the sense of "appears (in glory)."

17.31-32	TEV	RSV
	"On that day the man who is on the roof of his house must not go down into the house to get his belongings; in the same way the man who is out in the field must not go back to the house. 32 Remember Lot's wife!	On that day, let him who is on the housetop, with his goods in the house, not come down to take them away; and likewise let him who is in the field not turn back. 32 Remember Lot's wife.

On that day: the day of the glorious coming of the Son of Man. But
what follows in verses 31-32 seems hardly to fit the context of the final
day, since on that day no flight will be possible. So it appears likely
that verses 31-32 refer to some temporal catastrophe, such as the fall of
Jerusalem. But verses 34-35 refer to the final day.
   the roof: flat, reached by outside steps (see 5.19), a place where
people went to rest and to have conversation after the day's work was
done. The language is condensed (see RSV); the meaning is that a man on
the roof must flee at once without wasting time to go into the house and
gather up his belongings to take with him.
   in the field: that is, working. Such a man should not go back to
the house to retrieve some of his belongings, but must flee at once.
   Remember Lot's wife!: "Remember what happened to Lot's wife!" (see
Gen 19.26). This is added as a warning of what will happen to those who
do not flee at once.

17.33	TEV	RSV
	Whoever tries to save his own life will lose it; whoever loses his life will save it.	Whoever seeks to gain his life will lose it, but whoever loses his life will preserve it.

This verse is almost identical with 9.24. In this context the saying
is strange. The best course for a translator to take is to follow closely
the language of 9.24.

17.34 TEV	RSV
On that night, I tell you, there will be two people sleeping in the same bed: one will be taken away, the other will be left behind.	I tell you, in that night there will be two in one bed; one will be taken and the other left.

that night: here the coming of the Son of Man is spoken of as taking place at night.

two people: in Greek the pronouns that follow (one...the other) are masculine, but it is not necessary to say "two men sleeping in the same bed"—a statement which could be objectionable.

be taken away...be left behind: this seems to imply the work of the angels taking God's people (see Mark 13.27; Matt 24.31). The one taken away is one of the chosen people.

17.35 TEV	RSV
Two women will be grinding meal to-gether: one will be taken away, the other will be left behind."v	There will be two women grinding together; one will be taken and the other left."b

grinding meal together: the small hand mill consisted of two flat stones, one on top of the other. The top stone was turned on the lower stone (which was fixed), and the grain between the stones was ground in-to meal (see verse 2).

[17.36] TEV	RSV
v*Some manuscripts add verse 36:* Two men will be working in a field: one will be taken away, the other will be left behind *(see Mt 24.40).*	bOther ancient authorities add verse 36, *"Two men will be in the field; one will be taken and the other left"*

The evidence for the inclusion of this verse is much weaker than the evidence for its omission. It was added by copyists from Matthew 24.40. If a translator feels the omission of the verse will cause diffi-culty, it may be included in the text; but a footnote similar to the one used in TEV should be added.

17.37 TEV	RSV
The disciples asked him, "Where, Lord?" Jesus answered, "Wherever there is a dead body, the vultures will gather."	And they said to him, "Where, Lord?" He said to them, "Where the body is, there the eagles$c$ will be gathered together." cOr *vultures*

Where, Lord?: "Where will this happen?" This must be a reference back to what is described in verses 31-32; it hardly fits the context of the final coming of the Son of Man (verses 34-35).

17.37

Jesus' answer is probably a current proverb of his time, similar to today's proverbial saying, "Where there's smoke there's fire." The presence of vultures is a sure sign of a dead body. There will be unmistakable evidence of where the event will take place; no one will have to be told about it.

Chapter 18

The Parable of the Widow and the Judge: "The Need for Insistence in Prayer."

In this parable Jesus again uses a real-life situation in order to teach a spiritual truth. In this instance, however, the parable focuses on human conduct which illustrates what God is not like. God is not like the corrupt judge; God will respond to his people's cries and will save them.

18.1	TEV	RSV
	Then Jesus told his disciples a parable to teach them that they should always pray and never become discouraged.	And he told them a parable, to the effect that they ought always to pray and not lose heart.

his disciples: as RSV shows, the Greek says only "them"; here the disciples are meant (see 17.37).
parable: see 5.36.
never become discouraged: or "never give up," "never stop believing that God will answer."

18.2	TEV	RSV
	"In a certain town there was a judge who neither feared God nor respected man.	He said, "In a certain city there was a judge who neither feared God nor regarded man;

neither feared God: as seen in 1.50, the verb "to fear" with God as object means to respect, honor, have reverence for; it does not mean primarily to be afraid of God or of his anger, although this may be an element. Here the judge is described as an irreverent, irreligious person, who disregarded God's laws.
nor respected man: "nor had respect for others"; this describes the judge as one who did not care for people's rights; he is a callous, insensitive person.

[289]

18.3   TEV

And there was a widow in that same town who kept coming to him and pleading for her rights, saying, 'Help me against my opponent!'

RSV

and there was a widow in that city who kept coming to him and saying, 'Vindicate me against my adversary.'

pleading for her rights, saying, 'Help me against my opponent!': TEV has used both indirect and direct discourse to bring out the meaning of the Greek "Give me revenge against," "Vindicate me against" (RSV). The widow wants the judge to rule in her favor and against her opponent in the lawsuit. The implication is that her demand is a just one. Some translations use indirect discourse altogether: "...coming to him and demanding that he rule in her favor and against her opponent."

Here opponent is used in a legal sense; it may be necessary to expand somewhat: "the person who is against me" or "the person with whom I have a legal dispute."

18.4-5   TEV

For a long time the judge refused to act, but at last he said to himself, 'Even though I don't fear God or respect man, 5 yet because of all the trouble this widow is giving me, I will see to it that she gets her rights. If I don't, she will keep on coming and finally wear me out!'"

RSV

For a while he refused; but afterward he said to himself, 'Though I neither fear God nor regard man, 5 yet because this widow bothers me, I will vindicate her, or she will wear me out by her continual coming.'"

refused to act: "didn't give a decision," "didn't decide the case"; or, more simply, "For a long time the judge did nothing."

The judge's words to himself (in verse 4) repeat what is said about him in verse 2.

It may be preferable to restructure as follows: "I don't fear God or respect man. But this widow is causing me so much trouble that I will give her her rights (or, rule in her favor)."

I will see to it that she gets her rights: this translates the same Greek verb used in the widow's plea (RSV "vindicate").

wear me out: the verb is not used here in a physical sense, but in terms of the judge's peace of mind, his patience.

18.6-7   TEV

And the Lord continued, "Listen to what that corrupt judge said. 7 Now, will God not judge in favor of his own people who cry to him day and night for help? Will he be slow to help them?

RSV

And the Lord said, "Hear what the unrighteous judge says. 7 And will not God vindicate his elect, who cry to him day and night? Will he delay long over them?

the Lord: see 5.8.
that corrupt judge: the adjective may be translated "crooked," "dishonest," "venal."

In verse 7 the two rhetorical questions contrast the judge's attitude with that of God: God will judge in favor of his people and will do it speedily. Since Jesus himself answers the rhetorical questions (verse 8), it is essential to keep the question form in verse 7.

his own people: "the people who belong to him," "the people he has made his own."

Will he be slow to help them?: "Will he delay in answering their cries?"

18.8 TEV	RSV
I tell you, he will judge in their favor and do it quickly. But will the Son of Man find faith on earth when he comes?"	I tell you, he will vindicate them speedily. Nevertheless, when the Son of man comes, will he find faith on earth?"

The final question does not expect a definite answer but expresses uncertainty and perhaps anxiety about the matter. The form of the question should not imply either a positive or a negative answer, but should leave the question unanswered.

Son of Man: see 5.24.

faith: in the context, the faith (or assurance) that God does answer his people's cries and does not delay in saving them. The implication is that the coming of the Son of Man is God's way of answering his people's cries for help.

Instead of find faith on earth when he comes it may be better to say "find people who have faith (or, who believe) when he comes (or, returns) to earth."

SECTION HEADING

The Parable of the Pharisee and the Tax Collector: "True Righteousness."

This parable speaks about prayer also, but here the emphasis is upon the different attitudes shown by the two men as they prayed. The preceding parable emphasized God's attitude in responding to his people's cries; this one emphasizes the human attitude.

18.9 TEV	RSV
Jesus also told this parable to people who were sure of their own goodness and despised everybody else.	He also told this parable to some who trusted in themselves that they were righteous and despised others:

also: this implies that this parable was told at the same time the preceding one was told. However, this one is not addressed specifically to his disciples but to self-righteous people in general.

18.9

goodness: this represents the Greek "righteous" (RSV), which carries the idea of obeying God's laws—the commandments and rules in the Torah. One way of representing the meaning of the word would be "people who were certain they were religious (or, they obeyed the Law of Moses)."

18.10   TEV

"Once there were two men who went up to the Temple to pray: one was a Pharisee, the other a tax collector.

RSV

"Two men went up into the temple to pray, one a Pharisee and the other a tax collector.

Once: this is a way of beginning a story in English.
went up: the Temple stood on top of Mount Moriah. In the Bible it is always referred to as Mount Zion.
Pharisee: see 5.17.
tax collector: see 5.27.

18.11   TEV

The Pharisee stood apart by himself and prayed,^{w} 'I thank you, God, that I am not greedy, dishonest, or an adulterer, like everybody else. I thank you that I am not like that tax collector over there.

RSV

The Pharisee stood and prayed thus with himself, 'God, I thank thee that I am not like other men, extortioners, unjust, adulterers, or even like this tax collector.

^{w}stood apart by himself and prayed;
  some manuscripts have stood up and
  prayed to himself.

stood apart by himself and prayed: this translates a Greek text slightly different from the one translated by RSV (and the TEV footnote). In the TEV text the emphasis is on the Pharisee's separating himself from others while he prayed; in the RSV text the emphasis is on the Pharisee's praying silently. RSV "prayed thus with himself" is not intended to mean that the Pharisee prayed to himself and not to God; it means he prayed silently or in a soft voice.
greedy: or "swindler."
dishonest: or "lawbreaker," "criminal."
The Pharisee says everybody else is greedy, dishonest, adulterer. Obviously he would not mean that all other people were like that; but the exaggerated language should be retained.
that tax collector over there: or, more simply, "that tax collector." TEV says over there, since in verse 11 it says that the Pharisee stood apart by himself.

18.12   TEV

I fast two days a week, and I give you one tenth of all my income.'

RSV

I fast twice a week, I give tithes of all that I get.'

[292]

fast two days a week: see 5.33.
give you: the tithe (one tenth of all my income) was an offering to
God and was usually given at the Temple.

18.13   TEV   RSV
But the tax collector stood at a   But the tax collector, standing far
distance and would not even raise   off, would not even lift up his eyes
his face to heaven, but beat on his   to heaven, but beat his breast, say-
breast and said, 'God, have pity on   ing, 'God, be merciful to me a sin-
me, a sinner!'   ner!'

     at a distance: from other people; or, specifically, from the Phari-
see.
     raise his face to heaven: this was the normal attitude in prayer.
     beat on his breast: a sign of sorrow and repentance.
     have pity: "have compassion," "be merciful" (RSV).
     It may be preferable to restructure as follows: "O God, I am a sin-
ner. Have compassion on me!"

18.14   TEV   RSV
I tell you," said Jesus, "the tax   I tell you, this man went down to
collector, and not the Pharisee,   his house justified rather than the
was in the right with God when he   other; for every one who exalts him-
went home. For everyone who makes   self will be humbled, but he who
himself great will be humbled, and   humbles himself will be exalted."
everyone who humbles himself will
be made great."

     was in the right with God: this represents the Greek passive parti-
ciple which RSV translates "justified." In this context the meaning may
be (as several translations have) "had his sins forgiven," "was forgiven
by God." Or else, "had God's approval," "had done what God considers good
(or, right)."
     The last part of verse 14 is almost completely identical with 14.11.

SECTION HEADING

     Jesus Blesses Little Children: "Jesus and Children," "Children and
the Kingdom of God."

     In this section, the incident concludes with a saying which does not
quite fit the babies of verse 15. It is instructive to notice that Matthew
has placed this saying in a different context (Matt 18.13).

18.15   TEV   RSV
     Some people brought their ba-   Now they were bringing even in-
bies to Jesus for him to place his   fants to him that he might touch

hands on them. The disciples saw   them; and when the disciples saw
them and scolded them for doing so,   it, they rebuked them.

    babies: the Greek word is different from the one used in verses
16-17, and is generally used of a young child who still needs to be carried (see 2.12,16).
    place his hands on them: probably on the head, a gesture accompany-
ing a prayer or a blessing.
    scolded: "reprimanded," "rebuked" (RSV); or else, "told them not to
do that." This is the same verb used in 17.3 (see also 4.35).
    them: that is, the people carrying the babies. It does not seem that
them could refer to the babies themselves.

18.16   TEV   RSV
but Jesus called the children to   But Jesus called them to him, say-
him and said, "Let the children   ing, "Let the children come to me,
come to me and do not stop them,   and do not hinder them; for to such
because the Kingdom of God belongs   belongs the kingdom of God.
to such as these.

    called the children to him: here another word in Greek is used which
ordinarily refers to a child old enough to walk; but in 1.59,66,76 it is
used of the eight-day-old John the Baptist; and in 2.27 it is used of the
forty-day-old Jesus. Jesus' action and words in this verse seem to imply
that the children can come to him on their own.
    Let the children come to me and do not stop them: the double command
is an emphatic way of saying "Don't stop the children from coming to me,"
"You must not keep the children from being brought to me."
    the Kingdom of God belongs to such as these: it may be impossible to
use the verb belongs with Kingdom of God; so it may be necessary to say
"It is people who are like these children who are in the Kingdom of God"
or "...who have God as their King."
    to such as these: Jesus is not saying that children, as such, are of
the Kingdom, but that people who are like children are of the Kingdom; "to
people who are like (these) children."

18.17   TEV   RSV
Remember this! Whoever does not re- Truly, I say to you, whoever does
ceive the Kingdom of God like a   not receive the kingdom of God like
child will never enter it."   a child shall not enter it."

    Remember this!: an emphatic way of calling attention to what follows
(see 4.24).
    It may be difficult, if not impossible, to speak of "receiving" the
Kingdom of God; so it may be necessary and much more desirable to speak
of "whoever does not accept God as King" or "whoever does not submit himself to the rule of God."
    To receive...like a child means to have the same attitude a child
has when a gift is offered, that is, to accept promptly and gladly.

enter it: this does not mean to go to heaven after death, but to become a citizen of the Kingdom of God now, that is, to enjoy the blessings of having God as King.

SECTION HEADING

The Rich Man: "Rich People and the Kingdom of God."

This incident, like the preceding one, has no indication of time and place. Only from verse 35 on does the Gospel indicate precisely where Jesus was. In placing this incident immediately after the one about children, Luke follows the same order found in Mark (10.13-31) and Matthew (19.13-30).

18.18 TEV	RSV
A Jewish leader asked Jesus, "Good Teacher, what must I do to receive eternal life?"	And a ruler asked him, "Good Teacher, what shall I do to inherit eternal life?"

A Jewish leader: the Greek word is the same one used of Jairus in 8.41.

Teacher: "Rabbi," a title of respect.

to receive eternal life: "so that God will give me eternal life." The translation of the Greek verb "to inherit" (RSV) should be done with care to avoid the idea inherent in the verb of someone dying before someone else is given what the dead person owned. So something like "to receive," "to have," or "to be given" will be better (see 10.25).

eternal life: "life that never ends," "life everlasting." This is life with God, after death (see 10.25).

18.19 TEV	RSV
"Why do you call me good?" Jesus asked him. "No one is good except God alone.	And Jesus said to him, "Why do you call me good? No one is good but God alone.

Jesus rejects the use of the adjective good, saying that only God can be called (absolutely) good. The rhetorical question Why...? is a mild rebuke: "You shouldn't call me good." And then the comment would follow: "Only God is good; no one else is good," or, more simply, "God is the only one who is good."

18.20 TEV	RSV
You know the commandments: 'Do not commit adultery; do not commit murder; do not steal; do not accuse anyone falsely; respect your father and your mother.'"	You know the commandments: 'Do not commit adultery, Do not kill, Do not steal, Do not bear false witness, Honor your father and mother.'"

You know the commandments: "You know what the Law of Moses requires (or, demands)." Jesus then cites several of the Ten Commandments, from Exodus 20.12-16. Each of them, in Greek, as in the Hebrew of Exodus, has the verb in the second person singular of the imperative mood.

Do not commit adultery (Exo 20.14): "Do not sleep with another man's wife," "Do not have sexual relations with another man's wife."

do not commit murder (Exo 20.13): this prohibits one person from killing another without proper authority; it is not (in the context in Exodus) a commandment against all killing, such as killing in war or capital punishment.

do not steal (Exo 20.15): "do not take what belongs to someone else."

do not accuse anyone falsely (Exo 20.16): this commandment has to do with testimony presented at a trial in court; "do not lie when you testify about someone."

respect your father and your mother (Exo 20.12): the verb means "show respect for," "honor." This is not merely a matter of words but of conduct as well; it comes close to saying "obey your father and your mother."

18.21   TEV   RSV
     The man replied, "Ever since   And he said, "All these I have ob-
I was young, I have obeyed all   served from my youth."
these commandments."

Ever since I was young: "From the time I was a boy." This probably means from the time he was twelve or thirteen years old, when he became "a son of the Law."

18.22   TEV   RSV
     When Jesus heard this, he said And when Jesus heard it, he said to
to him, "There is still one more   him, "One thing you still lack. Sell
thing you need to do. Sell all you all that you have and distribute to
have and give the money to the poor, the poor, and you will have treasure
and you will have riches in heaven; in heaven; and come, follow me."
then come and follow me."

There is still one more thing you need to do: in addition to obeying the commandments, the man had to do one more thing.

Jesus' instructions are concise and direct: Sell all you have, "Sell all your possessions"; give the money to the poor, the man was to give away everything to needy people; follow me, "become my disciple." The promise you will have riches in heaven is given to assure the man that though he would not have any wealth here on earth, that is, any material possessions, he would be rich in spiritual, eternal possessions. The sentence may be restructured as follows: "Go back home, sell all your possessions, and give the money to poor people. If you do this, you will have riches in heaven. Then come back and be my disciple."

18.23   TEV   RSV
But when the man heard this, he   But when he heard this he became
became very sad, because he was   sad, for he was very rich.
very rich.

It may be better to restructure this sentence and place the reason
for the man's reaction first: "The man was extremely rich, and so he became very sad when he heard Jesus' words."

18.24   TEV   RSV
     Jesus saw that he was sad and   Jesus looking at him said, "How hard
said, "How hard it is for rich peo- it is for those who have riches to
ple to enter the Kingdom of God!   enter the kingdom of God!

RSV translates a Greek text that says "Looking at him, Jesus said";
TEV translates a Greek text that says "Seeing that he was very sad, Jesus said." The manuscript evidence is not decisive, and a translator may
feel free to translate either text.
     to enter the Kingdom of God: "to become citizens of the Kingdom of
God," "to submit themselves to the rule of God."

18.25   TEV   RSV
It is much harder for a rich person For it is easier for a camel to go
to enter the Kingdom of God than   through the eye of a needle than
for a camel to go through the eye   for a rich man to enter the kingdom
of a needle."   of God."

In Greek the text says "It is easier for a camel to go through the
eye of a needle than for a rich person to enter the Kingdom of God." TEV
has used the reverse comparison (It is much harder...than), since the
preceding verse speaks of the difficulty of entering the Kingdom. But
other translations may prefer to use the form of the Greek.
     a camel to go through the eye of a needle: the camel was the largest
animal known in Palestine and the eye of a needle the smallest opening.
This metaphor is a vivid way of saying that it is impossible for a rich
person to enter the Kingdom of God.
     In many languages the comparative form may be difficult, and so it
may be necessary to say "It is very difficult for a camel...needle; it is
more difficult for a rich person...Kingdom of God."
     Where camel is unknown, a classifier may be needed such as "a large
animal called camel," or else a descriptive phrase, "a large animal with
a humped back." Unless absolutely unavoidable, it is not recommended that
some other animal replace the camel.
     There are various idioms for what in English is called "eye of a
needle": "ear of a needle," "mouth of a needle," "nose of a needle."

18.26   TEV   RSV
     The people who heard him   Those who heard it said, "Then who
asked, "Who, then, can be saved?"   can be saved?"

18.26

Who, then, can be saved?: this is equivalent to a statement, "If that is true, then nobody can be saved!" But the form of a question should be used in translation since Jesus' words in the next verse are a reply.

18.27	TEV	RSV
	Jesus answered, "What is impossible for man is possible for God."	But he said, "What is impossible with men is possible with God."

Jesus' reply may be represented as follows: "It is impossible for a person to save himself; but God can save him." Or, "God is able to do what a person (or, human being) cannot do."

18.28	TEV	RSV
	Then Peter said, "Look! We have left our homes to follow you."	And Peter said, "Lo, we have left our homes and followed you."

Peter's remark is in reaction to Jesus' command to the rich man to sell all his possessions and follow Jesus (verse 22). Peter reminds Jesus that he and the other disciples have left everything to follow him. Obviously he wants to know if they have riches in heaven (verse 22).

18.29-30	TEV	RSV
	"Yes," Jesus said to them, "and I assure you that anyone who leaves home or wife or brothers or parents or children for the sake of the Kingdom of God 30 will receive much more in this present age and eternal life in the age to come."	And he said to them, "Truly, I say to you, there is no man who has left house or wife or brothers or parents or children, for the sake of the kingdom of God, 30 who will not receive manifold more in this time, and in the age to come eternal life."

Jesus' answer is addressed not only to Peter but to the other disciples as well.

I assure you: see 4.24.

It is to be noticed that the Greek employs a double negative, "no one who...who will not receive" (see RSV). TEV has the simpler and more natural positive form anyone who...will receive.

leaves: "gives up," "abandons." This is a deliberate action.

for the sake of the Kingdom of God: "in order to become a citizen of the Kingdom of God," "in order to submit himself to the rule of God."

will receive: that is, from God. So it may be better to make this explicit: "will receive from God" or "will be given by God."

this present age: "the age (or, time) we are now living in"; this contrasts with the age to come, after the Day of Judgment.

eternal life: as in verse 18.

SECTION HEADING

Jesus Speaks a Third Time about His Death: see the section headings at 9.22 and 9.43b.

This is the third time that Jesus tells his disciples about his death in Jerusalem. From here on the focus of the narrative is upon the last week in Jerusalem.

18.31	TEV	RSV

Jesus took the twelve disciples aside and said to them, "Listen! We are going to Jerusalem where everything the prophets wrote about the Son of Man will come true.

And taking the twelve, he said to them, "Behold, we are going up to Jerusalem, and everything that is written of the Son of man by the prophets will be accomplished.

took...aside: to tell them privately, away from the crowd.
going to Jerusalem: preferably, "going up to Jerusalem" (RSV), as in verse 10.
the prophets: see 1.70. The reference here is to the passages in the prophetic books of the Hebrew Scriptures.
Son of Man: see 5.24.
will come true: "will be fulfilled," "will be done."

18.32	TEV	RSV

He will be handed over to the Gentiles, who will make fun of him, insult him, and spit on him.

For he will be delivered to the Gentiles, and will be mocked and shamefully treated and spit upon;

handed over: see 9.44.
the Gentiles: the Roman authorities in Jerusalem.
make fun of him: see 22.63; 23.11.
insult him: see 22.65.

18.33	TEV	RSV

They will whip him and kill him, but three days later he will rise to life."

they will scourge him and kill him, and on the third day he will rise."

whip him: "flog him"; the punishment inflicted on those who were condemned to death.
three days later he will rise to life: see 9.22.

18.34	TEV	RSV

But the disciples did not understand any of these things; the

But they understood none of these things; this saying was hid from

meaning of the words was hidden from them, and they did not know what Jesus was talking about.

them, and they did not grasp what was said.

The verse uses three expressions to portray the disciples' complete lack of understanding.

was hidden: the passive form here should not be taken to indicate divine activity; it is simply another way of emphasizing the disciples' inability to understand what Jesus was talking about.

SECTION HEADING

Jesus Heals a Blind Beggar: "Jesus Restores the Sight of a Blind Beggar."

Jesus and his disciples are now near Jericho as they make their way to Jerusalem, which is in the Judean hills 24 kilometers southwest of Jericho. In this section no mention is made of the disciples, but it is assumed that they are with Jesus.

18.35-36   TEV

As Jesus was coming near Jericho, there was a blind man sitting by the road, begging. 36 When he heard the crowd passing by, he asked, "What is this?"

RSV

As he drew near to Jericho, a blind man was sitting by the roadside begging; 36 and hearing a multitude going by, he inquired what this meant.

sitting by the road: where he would beg from the passers-by.
he asked: if a personal object is required, the translation can say "he asked the people close to him."
What is this?: 'What's happening?' The indirect form may be preferred: "...he asked what was happening."

18.37-38   TEV

"Jesus of Nazareth is passing by," they told him.
38 He cried out, "Jesus! Son of David! Have mercy on me!"

RSV

They told him, "Jesus of Nazareth is passing by." 38 And he cried, "Jesus, Son of David, have mercy on me!"

Jesus of Nazareth: see 4.34.
Son of David: a title for the Messiah. In order to avoid the misunderstanding that Jesus' father was named David, it may be better to say "Descendant of King David." But it is better to have Son of David in the text, and in a footnote explain that this expression was used by Jews at that time as a title for the Messiah.
Have mercy on me: as in 17.13, a way of asking Jesus to cure him.

18.39   TEV   RSV
    The people in front scolded   And those who were in front rebuked
him and told him to be quiet. But   him, telling him to be silent; but
he shouted even more loudly, "Son   he cried out all the more, "Son of
of David! Have mercy on me!"   David, have mercy on me!"

The people in front: those who were leading the crowd as it walked
by.
    scolded him and told him to be quiet: "ordered him to be quiet,"
"told him to shut up." For scolded see 18.15.

18.40-41   TEV   RSV
    So Jesus stopped and ordered   And Jesus stopped, and commanded
the blind man to be brought to him.   him to be brought to him; and when
When he came near, Jesus asked him,   he came near, he asked him, 41 "What
41 "What do you want me to do for   do you want me to do for you?" He
you?"   said, "Lord, let me receive my
    "Sir," he answered, "I want to   sight."
see again."

    ordered the blind man to be brought to him: or "ordered, 'Bring the
blind man to me.'"
    Sir: see 5.12.
    see again: it is not possible to say whether the Greek verb implies
that the man at one time had had normal vision, but then had lost his
sight. The TEV translation implies this is the case; RSV "let me receive
my sight" does not. The same verb is used in Jesus' reply in verse 42,
and also in verse 43.

18.42-43   TEV   RSV
    Jesus said to him, "Then see!   And Jesus said to him, "Receive your
Your faith has made you well."   sight; your faith has made you well."
    43 At once he was able to see,   43 And immediately he received his
and he followed Jesus, giving   sight and followed him, glorifying
thanks to God. When the crowd saw   God; and all the people, when they
it, they all praised God.   saw it, gave praise to God.

    Then see!: this is the imperative of the verb: "See again!" or "Re-
ceive your sight" (RSV).
    Your faith has made you well: see 17.19.
    he was able to see: or "he saw again" (the same verb as in verses
41,42).

Chapter 19

Jesus and Zacchaeus: "Seeking the Lost."

The conversion of Zacchaeus is another instance of the importance in this Gospel of people who were considered of little worth by the more orthodox elements in the Jewish community. The use of the words Salvation and descendant of Abraham in verse 9 is significant; the tax collector is as much one of God's people as the strictest observer of the Law. No mention is made of Jesus' disciples in this incident.

19.1-2 TEV	RSV
Jesus went on into Jericho and was passing through. 2 There was a chief tax collector there named Zacchaeus, who was rich.	He entered Jericho and was passing through. 2 And there was a man named Zacchaeus; he was a chief tax collector, and rich.

was passing through: Jesus did not stop in Jericho but kept on going toward Jerusalem.

chief tax collector: presumably he was one who oversaw the activities of a number of tax collectors (see 3.12).

19.3-4 TEV	RSV
He was trying to see who Jesus was, but he was a little man and could not see Jesus because of the crowd. 4 So he ran ahead of the crowd and climbed a sycamore tree to see Jesus, who was going to pass that way.	And he sought to see who Jesus was, but could not, on account of the crowd, because he was small of stature. 4 So he ran on ahead and climbed up into a sycamore tree to see him, for he was to pass that way.

who Jesus was: that is, which one in the crowd was Jesus. It is enough simply to say "He was trying to see (or, get a look at) Jesus."

because of the crowd: there were many people with Jesus (see 18.36), and this kept Zacchaeus from seeing him because he (Zacchaeus) was a short man.

It may be better to restructure the material as follows: "He kept trying to get a look at Jesus, but couldn't because he was a short man and couldn't see over the crowd which surrounded Jesus."

sycamore tree: see *Fauna and Flora of the Bible*, under the entry "sycamore." If this particular kind of tree is unknown it will be enough to say "a tree," "a tall tree."

19.5	TEV	RSV

When Jesus came to that place, he looked up and said to Zacchaeus, "Hurry down, Zacchaeus, because I must stay in your house today."

And when Jesus came to the place, he looked up and said to him, "Zacchaeus, make haste and come down; for I must stay at your house today."

came to that place: "came to the place where the tree was" or "came to the tree."

I must: this may sound strange in translation, as though Jesus had no choice in the matter. In many places in the New Testament this expression indicates necessity resulting from the divine will, and something of that may be present here.

stay in your house today: "be a guest today in your home." Presumably this would include an overnight stay.

19.6	TEV	RSV

Zacchaeus hurried down and welcomed him with great joy.

So he made haste and came down, and received him joyfully.

welcomed him: here Zacchaeus is already at home, so it may be necessary to expand somewhat: "Zacchaeus hurried down the tree and took Jesus to his home, where he welcomed him gladly."

19.7	TEV	RSV

All the people who saw it started grumbling, "This man has gone as a guest to the home of a sinner!"

And when they saw it they all murmured, "He has gone in to be the guest of a man who is a sinner."

who saw it: that is, Jesus being welcomed into Zacchaeus' house.

as a guest: see the same verb in 9.12 (where it is translated lodging).

sinner: here in the specialized sense noted in 5.30. It would be possible here to translate "...a guest in the home of a man who does not keep the Law of Moses!"

19.8	TEV	RSV

Zacchaeus stood up and said to the Lord, "Listen, sir! I will give half my belongings to the poor, and if I have cheated anyone, I will pay him back four times as much."

And Zacchaeus stood and said to the Lord, "Behold, Lord, the half of my goods I give to the poor; and if I have defrauded any one of anything, I restore it fourfold."

stood up: presumably at the meal.

Lord: see 5.8; sir: see 5.12.

19.8

if I have cheated: the form of the Greek indicates that Zacchaeus
is admitting having cheated, and is promising to repay fourfold. As a tax
collector he would have opportunities to charge more duties on goods and
produce than required by the law (see 3.12-13).

19.9-10   TEV   RSV
    Jesus said to him, "Salvation   And Jesus said to him, "Today sal-
has come to this house today, for   vation has come to this house, since
this man, also, is a descendant of   he also is a son of Abraham. 10 For
Abraham. 10 The Son of Man came to   the Son of man came to seek and to
seek and to save the lost."   save the lost."

It is a bit strange that Jesus addresses Zacchaeus, yet uses the
third person: this house and this man. But Jesus' words were intended for
all who were there.
    Salvation has come: it may be difficult to use a verb of motion (come)
with salvation, a noun that expresses an action, which is often more
adequately represented by a verb. So it may be necessary to say something
like "Today God has saved this family" or "Today this family has been
saved by God." In the context, Salvation here refers specifically to the
forgiveness of sins.
    this house: "this home," "this family."
    also: besides the religious leaders present, who knew they were de-
scendants of Abraham.
    descendant of Abraham: not simply that Zacchaeus was racially a Jew,
but that he was also a member of the covenant people, the people of God
(see 13.16).
    the Son of Man came: or, as always, "I, the Son of Man, have come."
    the lost: the Greek singular is not a specific individual, but is
generic, "people who are lost."

SECTION HEADING

The Parable of the Gold Coins: "Faithful and Unfaithful Servants."

The setting for this parable is stated clearly (verse 11). The climax
of the Gospel story is about to be reached, and in light of what is going
to happen in Jerusalem, Jesus tells this parable in order to impress upon
his listeners what the coming of the Kingdom of God means. The disciples
are not mentioned in this incident.

19.11   TEV
    While the people were listen-   As they heard these things, he
ing to this, Jesus continued and   proceeded to tell a parable, because
told them a parable. He was now   he was near to Jerusalem, and be-
almost at Jerusalem, and they sup-   cause they supposed that the kingdom
posed that the Kingdom of God was   of God was to appear immediately.
just about to appear.

[304]

The opening words in Greek "As they listened to this" are vague. They hardly fit the context of Jesus' words to Zacchaeus (verses 9-10), and the statement "because he was close to Jerusalem" (see RSV) is strange when Jerusalem is still 24 kilometers away. But the meaning of the words is clear enough and a translator should faithfully represent it.

parable: see 5.36.

just about to appear: that is, as soon as Jesus entered Jerusalem. The people believed that the "appearance" or "arrival" of the Kingdom of God would be a visible event (see 17.20).

It may be better to indicate specifically the causal relationship as follows: "The people listened to what Jesus said. He was now so close to Jerusalem that they were expecting that the Kingdom of God was about to appear; so he continued talking and told them this parable."

19.12 TEV	RSV
So he said, "There was once a man of high rank who was going to a country far away to be made king, after which he planned to come back home.	He said therefore, "A nobleman went into a far country to receive a kingdom and then return.

There was once: see 15.11.

a man of high rank: "a nobleman" (RSV).

to be made king: "to be named (or, appointed) king," that is, of the region or province where he lived. The situation is that of a local man of high rank (or noble birth) who went to Rome to receive from the Roman Emperor the title of "king" as ruler of his own region, or country (as verse 14 makes clear).

19.13 TEV	RSV
Before he left, he called his ten servants and gave them each a gold coin and told them, 'See what you can earn with this while I am gone.'	Calling ten of his servants, he gave them ten pounds,[e] and said to them, 'Trade with these till I come.'
	[e]The mina, rendered here by *pound*, was about three months' wages for a laborer

Before he left: TEV makes clear that the man didn't call his servants to him after he left.

his ten servants: or "ten of his servants" (RSV).

gave them each a gold coin: as the RSV footnote shows, the coin mentioned was worth about three months' wages; a *mina* was equivalent to 100 denarii (see 10.35). The exact purchasing power is not important; a fairly considerable amount should be indicated. (TEV has a gold coin because in certain areas of the English-speaking world "a silver coin" is regarded as having little value.)

See what you can earn with this: or "Do business with this money," "Invest this money," "Put this money to work."

19.14   TEV

Now, his countrymen hated him, and
so they sent messengers after him
to say, 'We don't want this man to
be our king.'

RSV

But his citizens hated him and sent
an embassy after him, saying, 'We
do not want this man to reign over
us.'

    his countrymen: "his fellow citizens."
messengers: "some representatives," "a delegation" (as in 14.32).
to say: that is, to the Emperor.

19.15   TEV

    "The man was made king and
came back. At once he ordered his
servants to appear before him, in
order to find out how much they
had earned.

RSV

When he returned, having received
the kingdom, he commanded these
servants, to whom he had given the
money, to be called to him, that
he might know what they had gained
by trading.

    was made king: "was named (or, appointed) king" (as in verse 12).
    to appear before him, in order to find out: or, more succinctly,
"He ordered his (ten) servants to report to him how much they had earned."
TEV omits "to whom he had given the money" (RSV) as being redundant.
    how much they had earned: or "how much profit they had made."

19.16   TEV

The first one came and said, 'Sir,
I have earned ten gold coins with
the one you gave me.'

RSV

The first came before him, saying,
'Lord, your pound has made ten pounds
more.'

    The first one: for the purposes of the parable, it is not necessary
to have the reports of all ten servants.
    Sir: see 5.12.
    I have earned: as RSV shows, the Greek says "Your *mina* has pro-
duced...." If this is a natural way of speaking, then it can be easily
stated.
    ten gold coins: he has now ten times the original amount.
with the one you gave me: or "with your gold coin."

19.17   TEV

'Well done,' he said; 'you are a
good servant! Since you were faithful in small matters, I will put
you in charge of ten cities.'

RSV

And he said to him, 'Well done, good
servant! Because you have been
faithful in a very little, you shall
have authority over ten cities.'

    Well done: "Very good," "That's fine," "Excellent."
    small matters: "a small job." "a small responsibility."
    in charge of ten cities: the master is now king, and so he is able
to reward his servant with a position of considerable prestige and
authority.

19.18-19   TEV   RSV
The second servant came and said,   And the second came, saying, 'Lord,
'Sir, I have earned five gold   your pound has made five pounds.'
coins with the one you gave me.'   19 And he said to him, 'And you are
19 To this one he said, 'You will   to be over five cities.'
be in charge of five cities.'

The language of these two verses is quite similar to that of verses
16-17. The Greek has a different verb (although synonymous, as RSV shows):
"Your *mina* has produced...."

19.20   TEV   RSV
Another servant came and said,   Then another came, saying, 'Lord,
'Sir, here is your gold coin; I   here is your pound, which I kept
kept it hidden in a handkerchief.   laid away in a napkin;

I kept it hidden: or "I saved it," "I kept it safe."
handkerchief: or "cloth." RSV "napkin" is not quite correct.

19.21   TEV   RSV
I was afraid of you, because you   for I was afraid of you, because
are a hard man. You take what is   you are a severe man; you take up
not yours and reap what you did   what you did not lay down, and
not plant.'   reap what you did not sow.'

a hard man: "severe" (RSV), "strict," "ruthless." The master is
shown to be a ruthless businessman. The two charges made against him are
similar: the master, by whatever means, legal or illegal, profits from
the work of others.
You take what is not yours: RSV, "you take up what you did not lay
down," seems to understand the text to mean the picking up of a bag of
threshed grain from the threshing floor when one has not brought those
heads of grain to be threshed. But the language could refer to withdraw-
ing from a bank what one has not deposited. It is sufficient here to use
a general statement in parallel with what follows, as TEV has done; or
else something like "You get something for nothing."

19.22   TEV   RSV
He said to him, 'You bad servant!   He said to him, "I will condemn you
I will use your own words to con-   out of your own mouth, you wicked
demn you! You know that I am a   servant! You knew that I was a se-
hard man, taking what is not mine   vere man, taking up what I did not
and reaping what I have not plant-   lay down and reaping what I did not
ed.   sow?

bad: here in the sense of irresponsible, inefficient, or lazy.
I will use your own words: or "Your own words are all I need in
order to condemn you." The servant, knowing what kind of man his master
was, should have taken some action.

[307]

19.23 TEV	RSV
Well, then, why didn't you put my money in the bank? Then I would have received it back with interest when I returned.'	Why then did you not put my money into the bank, and at my coming I should have collected it with interest?'

Why didn't you...?: this is a rhetorical question that could be translated as a statement, "You should have...."

put my money in the bank: or "deposited my money in the bank."

It may be necessary to do some restructuring as follows: "You should have deposited my gold coin in the bank, where it would draw (or, earn) interest. Then, when I returned home, I would have received the coin, plus the interest."

There are idiomatic expressions for interest: "flower" or "child" of money; or else "what money produces."

19.24 TEV	RSV
Then he said to those who were standing there, 'Take the gold coin away from him and give it to the servant who has ten coins.'	And he said to those who stood by, 'Take the pound from him, and give it to him who has the ten pounds.'

those who were standing there: this probably refers to his personal attendants, or guards. As a king he would have a number of attendants present at all times.

19.25 TEV	RSV
But they said to him, 'Sir, he already has ten coins!'	(And they said to him, 'Lord, he has ten pounds!')

The text does not mean to imply that the attendants did not obey the king's command; it simply registers their amazement that he would give the coin to the servant who had earned the most.

Textual Note: a few Greek manuscripts and early versions omit this verse. Most modern translations include it.

19.26 TEV	RSV
'I tell you,' he replied, 'that to every person who has something, even more will be given; but the person who has nothing, even the little that he has will be taken away from him.	'I tell you, that to every one who has will more be given; but from him who has not, even what he has will be taken away.

This verse states the same truth that is found in 8.18, where the saying is applied to the ability, or desire, to learn about the Kingdom of God. Here it is applied to the willingness to work for the master's good.

The king in the parable is the speaker; but he is addressing the application to the followers of Jesus.

more will be given: since God is the giver, it may be better to say "God will give more."

has nothing...the little that he has: see 8.18. The sense of the saying is that whoever does not use what he has been given will have it taken away by God.

19.27	TEV	RSV
	Now, as for those enemies of mine who did not want me to be their king, bring them here and kill them in my presence!'"	But as for these enemies of mine, who did not want me to reign over them, bring them here and slay them before me.'"

The king, still speaking to his attendants, orders the execution of his rebellious subjects. In verse 14 it is said that his countrymen hated him; it would not seem that he ordered the death of them all, but of the leaders of the movement against him.

kill them: "put them to death," "execute them," "slaughter them."

Here ends the long travel narrative that began at 9.51 in this Gospel.

SECTION HEADING

The Triumphant Approach to Jerusalem: TEV has divided verses 28-44 into two sections, labeling the first one (verses 28-40) Jesus' approach to the city; however, it is to be noticed that in verse 41 he has not yet entered Jerusalem. But a translation may prefer to have only one section for verses 28-44 and label it "Jesus Arrives in Jerusalem."

19.28	TEV	RSV
	Jesus said this and then went on to Jerusalem ahead of them.	And when he had said this, he went on ahead, going up to Jerusalem.

went on to Jerusalem ahead of them: this might make it appear that Jesus left the others behind and entered the city alone. It would be better to translate "Jesus said this, and then went on in front of them toward Jerusalem." It should be quite clear that the others are following him.

In the context them refers to the people who had heard him tell the parable (verse 11).

19.29	TEV	RSV
	As he came near Bethphage and Bethany at the Mount of Olives, he sent two disciples ahead	When he drew near to Bethphage and Bethany, at the mount that is called Olivet, he sent two of the disciples,

Bethphage: near the Mount of Olives; it was practically a suburb of Jerusalem.

Bethany: about three kilometers east of Jerusalem.

Mount of Olives: just to the east of the city, across Kidron Valley. It would be better to translate "Mount of Olive Trees"; and the word for Mount should indicate a hill, not a mountain.

19.30   TEV   RSV

| with these instructions: "Go to the village there ahead of you; as you go in, you will find a colt tied up that has never been ridden. Untie it and bring it here. | saying, "Go into the village opposite, where on entering you will find a colt tied, on which no one has ever yet sat; untie it and bring it here. |

the village: presumably Bethphage.
a colt: the young of a donkey.
tied up: "tied to a post," "tethered."

19.31   TEV   RSV

| If someone asks you why you are untying it, tell him that the Master^x needs it." | If any one asks you, 'Why are you untying it?' you shall say this, 'The Lord has need of it.'" |

^{x}the Master; or its owner.

why you are untying it: TEV uses indirect discourse; RSV, following the form of the Greek, uses direct discourse. A translator should use whichever form is more natural in the language.

the Master: RSV translates "the Lord," which is the Christian title often applied to Jesus in this Gospel (see 5.8). It is difficult to think that Jesus would have used it in that sense to refer to himself. As the TEV footnote indicates, the meaning may be "its owner." In some instances, translators have attempted to meet the problem posed by the use of the title by saying "...tell him that I, whom you (or, people) call the Lord, need it." If the TEV interpretation is followed, it may be necessary to use the possessive form, "Our Master" (here and in verse 34).

19.32-33   TEV   RSV

| They went on their way and found everything just as Jesus had told them. 33 As they were untying the colt, its owners said to them, "Why are you untying it?" | So those who were sent went away and found it as he had told them. 33 And as they were untying the colt, its owners said to them, "Why are you untying the colt?" |

its owners: this translates the same Greek word (plural) which in verse 31 TEV translates 'Master' (see 5.12).

19.34-35 TEV

"The Master needs it," they answered, 35 and they took the colt to Jesus. Then they threw their cloaks over the animal and helped Jesus get on.

RSV

And they said, "The Lord has need of it." 35 And they brought it to Jesus, and throwing their garments on the colt they set Jesus upon it.

they threw...and helped: as the text stands, the subject is the two disciples (verse 29) sent by Jesus to get the animal.
cloaks: the outer garments (see 6.29).

19.36 TEV

As he rode on, people spread their cloaks on the road.

RSV

And as he rode along, they spread their garments on the road.

people spread: as RSV shows, the Greek says only "they spread," but the subject cannot be the same one of verse 35, that is, the two disciples. The gesture of spreading their cloaks on the road in front of Jesus as he rode to Jerusalem was a way of honoring him, as triumphant conquerors were honored.

19.37 TEV

When he came near Jerusalem, at the place where the road went down the Mount of Olives, the large crowd of his disciples began to thank God and praise him in loud voices for all the great things that they had seen:

RSV

As he was now drawing near, at the descent of the Mount of Olives, the whole multitude of the disciples began to rejoice and praise God with a loud voice for all the mighty works that they had seen,

the road went down the Mount of Olives: Jesus was now on the western slope of the Mount of Olives; the road led down to Kidron Valley, on the other side of which was the city of Jerusalem.
the large crowd of his disciples: since more than the twelve apostles are meant, it would be better to say "the large crowd of his followers."
the great things: or "the miracles," or "the mighty deeds" (that Jesus had performed).

19.38 TEV

"God bless the king who comes in the name of the Lord! Peace in heaven and glory to God!"

RSV

saying, "Blessed is the King who comes in the name of the Lord! Peace in heaven and glory in the highest!"

The first part of the praise uses language that reflects Psalm 118.26.
God bless: this translates the Greek passive "blessed," which may be understood as a request, "Blessed be," or as a statement, "Blessed is" (RSV). In the context it seems better to understand it as a request.

[311]

in the name of the Lord: either (1) as a representative of the Lord (that is, God), and thus "as the servant (or, messenger, or, spokesman) of the Lord"; or (2) "with the authority (or, power) of the Lord."

Peace in heaven: as a shout of praise, these words express thanks to God for giving his people peace, that is, salvation.

glory to God: this translates "glory in the highest places" (see 2.14). It is an exhortation for people to praise God for his goodness.

19.39-40 TEV	RSV
Then some of the Pharisees in the crowd spoke to Jesus. "Teacher," they said, "command your disciples to be quiet!"	And some of the Pharisees in the multitude said to him, "Teacher, rebuke your disciples." 40 He answered, "I tell you, if these were silent, the very stones would cry out."
40 Jesus answered, "I tell you that if they keep quiet, the stones themselves will start shouting."	

Pharisees: see 5.17.
Teacher: see 18.18.
command...to be quiet: this translates the Greek verb "rebuke" (RSV; see 18.15).
your disciples: as in verse 37, "your followers."

SECTION HEADING

Jesus Weeps over Jerusalem: "Jesus Predicts the Destruction of Jerusalem."

As noted at the beginning of the preceding section (verse 28), this section may be joined to it.

19.41 TEV	RSV
He came closer to the city, and when he saw it, he wept over it,	And when he drew near and saw the city he wept over it,

closer: perhaps after crossing Kidron Valley and starting up the hill on which the city was built.
wept over it: "he wept out of compassion for it" or "...because he felt sorry for it." The city is addressed as though it were a person; the reference is to the inhabitants of the city, and it may be necessary to make this explicit. But in light of verse 44 (which speaks of you and the people within your walls) it is better to maintain the form of the Greek, if possible.

19.42	TEV	RSV

saying, "If you only knew today what is needed for peace! But now you cannot see it!   saying, "Would that even today you knew the things that make for peace! But now they are hid from your eyes.

If you only knew: this expresses sorrow over the city's ignorance. It may be better to render "How I wish that you knew today what you need in order to have peace!"

what is needed: that is, the conditions that produce peace, which here is not merely the absence of armed conflict but the gift of God's salvation to his people.

you cannot see it: this translates the passive "hidden from your eyes." As in the similar case of 18.34, this does not seem to be a reference to divine activity.

19.43	TEV	RSV

The time will come when your enemies will surround you with barricades, blockade you, and close in on you from every side.   For the days shall come upon you, when your enemies will cast up a bank about you and surround you, and hem you in on every side,

The destruction of Jerusalem is predicted.

The rather technical language used in this verse to describe the siege of the city may pose a problem in some languages, and it may be necessary to use more general terms: "The time will come when your enemies will surround you completely; they will stop all traffic in and out of the city, and keep on attacking you from every side."

19.44	TEV	RSV

They will completely destroy you and the people within your walls; not a single stone will they leave in its place, because you did not recognize the time when God came to save you!"   and dash you to the ground, you and your children within you, and they will not leave one stone upon another in you; because you did not know the time of your visitation."

In this verse in Greek (see RSV) the city is spoken of as having children, which is a way of speaking of the inhabitants of the city (TEV the people within your walls). It may not be possible to use one verb (destroy) for both the city and its inhabitants; so it may be necessary to say "They will destroy you completely and will kill all your inhabitants."

not a single stone will they leave in its place: this is a vivid statement of complete destruction.

because: this introduces the reason for Jerusalem's destruction by its enemies, and it may be better to have a complete stop after walls and begin a new sentence: "All these things will happen to you because...."

you did not recognize the time when God came to save you: this translates the Greek "you did not know the time (or, occasion) of your visitation" (see RSV). This abstract noun "visitation" is a way of speaking of God coming to the aid of his people (see 1,68). If the TEV form is followed, it should not appear that Jesus is referring to himself as God. Jesus was God's representative, offering salvation to God's people, but they refused to accept it.

recognize: the meaning is a willful refusal to acknowledge that God came to save them, and not just ignorance of this fact; so it might be well to translate "you were not willing to recognize the occasion...."

SECTION HEADING

Jesus Goes to the Temple: "Jesus Expels the Merchants from the Temple."

This is Jesus' first act after he arrives in the capital city, and at once he displays the power and authority which characterize his activities in Jerusalem (20.1—21.38).

19.45 TEV	RSV
Then Jesus went into the Temple and began to drive out the merchants,	And he entered the temple and began to drive out those who sold,

the Temple: the Jerusalem Temple was a very large construction, with many buildings and various open courts on different levels. It was in one of these courts, known as the Court of the Gentiles, where the merchants would be carrying on their business; this was one of the outer courts, not inside the sanctuary itself. For the convenience of the worshipers, many of whom came from faraway places, the merchants sold birds (such as pigeons or doves), animals (such as rams, goats, and sheep), and salt, wine, and olive oil, which were to be used in the sacrifices.

drive out: the text does not say how Jesus expelled the merchants, whether by use of physical force or simply by an authoritative command.

19.46 TEV	RSV
saying to them, "It is written in the Scriptures that God said, 'My Temple will be called a house of prayer.' But you have turned it into a hideout for thieves!"	saying to them, "It is written, 'My house shall be a house of prayer'; but you have made it a den of robbers."

that God said: TEV adds this in order to make clear that in the following quotation from Isaiah 56.7 the speaker is God, not Jesus.

My Temple: this translates "My house" (RSV), which may also be translated "My house of worship," "The Temple (or, house) where I am worshiped."

will be called a house of prayer: TEV wrongly has will be called; the Greek has only "will be" (see RSV). In the Isaiah passage this is a prophecy about the future and is addressed to the foreigners who will come to worship the God of Israel.

a house of prayer: "a house (or, place) where people will pray to me," "a place where people worship."

But you: these are Jesus' words, addressed to the merchants.

a hideout for thieves: this recalls the language of Jeremiah 7.11; hideout translates "cave," a place where theives would hide from the authorities. Some translate "a den of theives" or "a robbers' cave."

19.47	TEV	RSV

19.47   TEV

Every day Jesus taught in the Temple. The chief priests, the teachers of the Law, and the leaders of the people wanted to kill him,

RSV

And he was teaching daily in the temple. The chief priests and the scribes and the principal men of the people sought to destroy him;

chief priests: see 9.22.

teachers of the Law: see 5.17.

the leaders of the people: it is not clear who these people are; "leading citizens," "important people in Jerusalem."

wanted to kill him: preferably, "kept trying to kill him."

19.48   TEV

but they could not find a way to do it, because all the people kept listening to him, not wanting to miss a single word.

RSV

but they did not find anything they could do, for all the people hung upon his words.

could not find a way to do it: "were unable to kill him."

all the people: this portrays Jesus as constantly surrounded by a large group of listeners, thus making it impossible for the religious authorities to do away with him.

Chapter 20

The Question about Jesus' Authority: "Jesus' Authority Is Challenged," "Jesus' Authority."

This incident follows from the preceding one, but it is not pictured as having taken place the same day. It is the first of a series of encounters with several different groups; in all the encounters Jesus displays complete authority.

20.1 TEV	RSV
One day when Jesus was in the Temple teaching the people and preaching the Good News, the chief priests and the teachers of the Law, together with the elders, came	One day, as he was teaching the people in the temple and preaching the gospel, the chief priests and the scribes with the elders came up

preaching the Good News: "announcing (or, proclaiming) the Good News"; see 3.18.
chief priests: see 9.22; teachers of the Law: see 5.17; elders: see 7.3.

20.2 TEV	RSV
and said to him, "Tell us, what right do you have to do these things? Who gave you such right?"	and said to him, "Tell us by what authority you do these things, or who it is that gave you this authority."

what right: "what authority (or, power)."
these things: or "this." The reference is to his action against the merchants in the Temple court (19.45-46).
Who gave you such right?: "Who gave you this authority?"

20.3-4 TEV	RSV
Jesus answered them, "Now let me ask you a question. Tell me, 4 did John's right to baptize come from God or from man?"	He answered them, "I also will ask you a question; now tell me, 4 Was the baptism of John from heaven or from men?"

[316]

In Greek, Jesus' question in verse 4 is "Was John's baptism from heaven or from men?" This refers to John's authority to baptize, and the question asks whether his authority was given him by God or by man. The question can be stated more simply: "Tell me: did John's authority to baptize come from God or from some person?" or "Tell me: who gave John the authority to baptize? Was it God or was it some person?"

20.5

TEV	RSV
They started to argue among themselves, "What shall we say? If we say, 'From God,' he will say, 'Why, then, did you not believe John?'	And they discussed it with one another, saying, "If we say, 'From heaven,' he will say, 'Why did you not believe him?'

to argue: "to discuss the matter," "to debate," "to question."
The rest of the verse may be translated by putting the questions in indirect speech: "If we say that God gave John the authority to baptize, then Jesus will ask us why we didn't believe John's message" or "...then Jesus will tell us that we should have believed John's message." But the direct form is more vivid and better portrays the situation that the religious leaders found themselves in.

20.6

TEV	RSV
But if we say, 'From man,' this whole crowd here will stone us, because they are convinced that John was a prophet."	But if we say, 'From men,' all the people will stone us; for they are convinced that John was a prophet."

But if we say: again the indirect form may be used, "But if we say that John's authority to baptize was given him by some person, this whole crowd..." or "But this whole crowd here will stone us if we say that John's authority to baptize was not given him by God but by some person. For they are all convinced that John was a prophet."
are convinced: "are certain," "are sure," "believe."
prophet: see 1.76.

20.7-8

TEV	RSV
So they answered, "We don't know where it came from."	So they answered that they did not know whence it was. 8 And Jesus
8 And Jesus said to them, "Neither will I tell you, then, by what right I do these things."	said to them, "Neither will I tell you by what authority I do these things."

We don't know where it came from: "We don't know who gave John the authority to baptize." For the language of Jesus' final answer see verse 2b.

20.9

SECTION HEADING

The Parable of the Tenants in the Vineyard: "Jesus Tells a Story
about Some Evil Tenants." The word used for Tenants will follow the
translation of the word in verse 9.

After having shown that the religious authorities were unwilling to
acknowledge the divine authority present in John the Baptist and in Jesus himself, Jesus goes on to tell a parable which accuses them of fail-
ing in their duty as the overseers of God's people, Israel.

20.9 TEV	RSV
Then Jesus told the people this parable: "There was once a man who planted a vineyard, rented it out to tenants, and then left home for a long time.	And he began to tell the people this parable: "A man planted a vineyard, and let it out to tenants, and went into another country for a long while.

parable: see 5.36.
planted a vineyard: in the Old Testament (see Isa 5.1-2) a vineyard
was a figure of Israel, and God is the owner of the vineyard. It may be
better to say "planted some grapevines," or "planted some grapevines in
his vineyard," since the idea of the vineyard as the people of Israel is
important. Where grapevines and grapes are unknown, it may be possible
to say "planted some vines which give a fruit called grape."
    rented it out to tenants: generally there is no difficulty in rep-
resenting this meaning, since this kind of arrangement is fairly wide-
spread. But the meaning may be expressed, "hired some men to take care
of the vineyard while he was gone," "arranged for some men to take care
of the vineyard in exchange for some of the fruit (or, produce)."
    left home for a long time: or "took a long trip away from home."
The TEV language is intended to show that the move was not meant to be
permanent (see verse 16).

20.10 TEV	RSV
When the time came to gather the grapes, he sent a slave to the tenants to receive from them his share of the harvest. But the tenants beat the slave and sent him back without a thing.	When the time came, he sent a servant to the tenants, that they should give him some of the fruit of the vineyard; but the tenants beat him, and sent him away empty-handed.

When the time came to gather the grapes: "At the time of harvest,"
"When the grapes were ripe," "When the grapes were ready to be gathered."
The time between planting and the first grape harvest was five years.
    to receive from them his share of the harvest: under the contract
the tenants would have a share, and the owner would also have a share.
This share would not be in the form of grapes but would be part of the
money earned from the sale of the wine.
    without a thing: "without any of the owner's share of the harvest."

[318]

20.11-12   TEV   RSV

So he sent another slave; but the   And he sent another servant; him
tenants beat him also, treated him   also they beat and treated shame-
shamefully, and sent him back   fully, and sent him away empty-
without a thing. 12 Then he sent a   handed. 12 And he sent yet a third;
third slave; the tenants wounded   this one they wounded and cast out.
him, too, and threw him out.

treated him shamefully: it is not clear what this shameful treatment consisted of; whatever it was, it was humiliating to the slave.
wounded: by beating him.

20.13   TEV   RSV

Then the owner of the vineyard   Then the owner of the vineyard said,
said, 'What shall I do? I will   'What shall I do? I will send my be-
send my own dear son; surely they   loved son; it may be they will re-
will respect him!'   spect him.'

said: the man said this to himself; "thought to himself."
my own dear son: "my only son, whom I love"; see similar language
in 3.22; 9.35. It seems fairly certain that this was his only son.
will respect him: "will honor him" or "will have respect for him."
A negative form may be used: "they will not mistreat my son," "they will
not disrespect my son."

20.14   TEV   RSV

But when the tenants saw him, they   But when the tenants saw him, they
said to one another, 'This is the   said to themselves, 'This is the
owner's son. Let's kill him, and   heir; let us kill him, that the in-
his property will be ours!'   heritance may be ours.'

the owner's son: "the heir" (RSV); or, "He will inherit the property," "The vineyard will some day belong to him."
his property will be ours: "we will have the vineyard," "we will
get what he would have received"; this translates the Greek "the inheritance will be ours," that is, what he would inherit from his father. In
the context this refers to the vineyard. Whether wrongly or rightly, the
tenants reasoned that if there were no other heir, the property would
become theirs at the death of the owner. This reinforces the idea that
my own dear son in verse 13 means the only son.

20.15   TEV   RSV

So they threw him out of the vine-   And they cast him out of the vineyard and killed him.   yard and killed him. What then will
     "What, then, will the owner   the owner of the vineyard do to
of the vineyard do to the tenants?"   them?
Jesus asked.

threw him out of the vineyard: or "took him outside the vineyard."
What, then, will the owner...?: TEV begins a new paragraph here in
order to show that the parable is ended and what follows is the application; for this reason also TEV adds Jesus asked. The order may be reversed: "Then Jesus asked them, 'What will the owner of the vineyard do
to those tenants?'"

20.16 TEV	RSV
"He will come and kill those men, and turn the vineyard over to oth-er tenants."	He will come and destroy those tenants, and give the vineyard to others." When they heard this,
When the people heard this, they said, "Surely not!"	they said, "God forbid!"

Jesus himself answers his question.
turn the vineyard over: the Greek verb is "he will give" (see RSV).
In terms of the parable, however, it seems likely that the vineyard will
be placed under the supervision of other tenants; the phrase does not
mean that the owner will make a gift of it to other people and so not
own the vineyard any longer.
Surely not!: this translates "May it not be!"—a strong statement
of disagreement.

20.17 TEV	RSV
Jesus looked at them and asked, "What, then, does this scripture mean?	But he looked at them and said, "What then is this that is written:
'The stone which the builders rejected as worthless turned out to be the most important of all.'	'The very stone which the build-ers rejected has become the head of the cor-ner'?

What, then, does this scripture mean?: Jesus quotes Psalm 118.22.
The question is a way of saying that, obviously, the passage quoted
proves that Jesus' concluding statement is true. At first sight the
scripture quoted doesn't seem to apply very exactly to the teaching of
the parable. In terms of the readers of the Gospel, however, the lesson
is quite clear: the owner of the vineyard is God; the tenants are the
religious leaders, who had been placed in charge of God's vineyard (that
is, his people); the slaves were the prophets, who had been rejected;
and the son, who had been killed, was Jesus himself. In the passage from
the psalm, the most important stone for the building of the Temple had
been rejected by the builders; it was the same with Jesus, who was rejected by the people of Israel, and he was the most important part of
God's dwelling place with his people.
the builders: "the men who were putting up the building." It may be
preferable to restructure as follows: "There was a stone which the
builders rejected as worthless, but it was this very stone which turned
out to be the most important one (for the building)."

rejected as worthless: "decided was not a good stone," "decided that it could not be used."

turned out to be: "was discovered to be" or "was actually," "was all the time."

the most important of all: this translates the Greek "the head of the corner," which means either the cornerstone, which is the stone placed at the corner of the foundation where two rows of stone come together, or else the keystone ("capstone"), which completes the arch of the structure. In either case, it is a stone which is absolutely indispensable. In translating this, it may be necessary to make considerable cultural adjustments, such as "the post of the corner," "the root of the house at the corner," "stone heavy pole," "the main pole." Or else a descriptive phrase, such as "the thing joining the walls."

20.18 TEV	RSV
Everyone who falls on that stone will be cut to pieces; and if that stone falls on someone, it will crush him to dust."	Every one who falls on that stone will be broken to pieces; but when it falls on any one it will crush him."

Here the figure changes, and the stone is one on which people can fall, and which can fall on people. In either case, the result is fatal: both will cut to pieces and crush him to dust imply the death of the person.

SECTION HEADING

The Question about Paying Taxes: "Concerning Obligations to the Ruler and to God."

Even though the disputed question appeared to be of a political nature, it was actually a religious one. The Romans were pagan Gentiles, and to pay taxes to them was believed by some to be a betrayal of the Jewish faith, a lessening of the loyalty that belongs only to the God of Israel. Jesus' opponents, defeated in the two previous encounters, now use deceit in their attempt to catch Jesus saying something treasonable.

20.19 TEV	RSV
The teachers of the Law and the chief priests tried to arrest Jesus on the spot, because they knew that he had told this parable against them; but they were afraid of the people.	The scribes and the chief priests tried to lay hands on him at that very hour, but they feared the people; for they perceived that he had told this parable against them.

RSV, by following the literal order of the Greek, makes it appear that the religious authorities were afraid of the people because the people perceived that Jesus had told this parable against the people.

they knew: "they realized," "they understood."
afraid of the people: see the similar situation in 20.6.

20.20   TEV   RSV

So they looked for an opportunity. They bribed some men to pretend they were sincere, and they sent them to trap Jesus with questions, so that they could hand him over to the authority and power of the Roman Governor.	So they watched him, and sent spies, who pretended to be sincere, that they might take hold of what he said, so as to deliver him up to the authority and jurisdiction of the governor.

they looked for an opportunity: this seems to be the meaning of the Greek (which RSV translates "they watched him"); there is no direct object in Greek.

bribed some men to pretend they were sincere: these men were paid to play the part of honest inquirers. In the context the word spies (verse 21) means they were disguising their true intentions; they were pretending to be something they were not. Perhaps something like "impostors" would be better than spies.

trap Jesus with questions: they were trying to get Jesus to say something for which they could accuse him to the Roman governor; "catch Jesus saying something wrong" (see similar language in 11.54).

the authority and power: the two terms mean practically the same thing.

the Roman Governor: Pontius Pilate (see 3.1). Here he stands for the Roman authorities in general.

It might be better to restructure the verse as follows: "They paid some men to go to Jesus and pretend they were sincere in asking him questions. But their real purpose was to try to catch Jesus saying something for which the Jewish leaders could hand him over to the Roman authorities, to be tried and punished (or, executed)."

20.21   TEV   RSV

These spies said to Jesus, "Teacher, we know that what you say and teach is right. We know that you pay no attention to a man's status, but teach the truth about God's will for man.	They asked him, "Teacher, we know that you speak and teach rightly, and show no partiality, but truly teach the way of God.

is right: "is true," "agrees with true teaching."
you pay no attention to a man's status: this translates "you do not look at a face," which is a Semitic phrase meaning "you are impartial (or, unbiased)," "you pay no regard to outward appearances," "your opinion is not determined by external factors" (such as a person's social standing).

teach the truth about God's will for man: this translates the Greek "teach the way of God truly." Here "the way of God" may be taken to mean "the Jewish faith" or "the Jewish religion" or "the Law of Moses." They are complimenting Jesus for being a good teacher of their religious beliefs.

20.22   TEV

Tell us, is it against our Law for us to pay taxes to the Roman Emperor, or not?"

20.22   RSV

Is it lawful for us to give tribute to Caesar, or not?"

is it against our Law...?: this translates the Greek "is it permitted...?" The question refers to the Mosaic Law in general; more specifically, it refers to the way some teachers of the Law interpreted the Mosaic Law. Another translation would be "does the Law of Moses allow us...?" Here our is inclusive: Jesus and all the other Jews are included.

to pay taxes: these were taxes imposed on the Jews by the pagan power, the Roman Empire. The trap that Jesus' enemies wanted to get him into is obvious: if he answered that the Jews should not pay taxes to Rome, then he would be in trouble with the Roman authorities; but if he said that the Jews should pay taxes, he would be in trouble with the people, especially the extremists, who believed that paying taxes to a pagan power was against the will of God.

the Roman Emperor: this is traditionally translated "Caesar," but here it is not the name of a person as such, but the ruling Emperor—at that time Tiberius (who ruled A.D. 14-37).

20.23-24   TEV

But Jesus saw through their trick and said to them, 24 "Show me a silver coin. Whose face and name are these on it?"

"The Emperor's," they answered.

20.23-24   RSV

But he perceived their craftiness, and said to them, 24 "Show me a coin.ᶠ Whose likeness and inscription has it?" They said, "Caesar's."

ᶠ Greek *denarius*

saw through their trick: "was aware of their craftiness"; Jesus knew at once that this was not an honest question, but a trick to try to get him into trouble.

silver coin: the denarius, a Roman silver coin.

face: "likeness" (RSV), "image." The question may be phrased, "Whose likeness and name are on this coin?" On one side of the denarius the emperor's head was sketched, and his name surrounded the head: "Tiberius Caesar Augustus, son of the divine Augustus."

The Emperor's: or "They belong to the Emperor" or "They are the name and face of the Emperor."

20.25   TEV

So Jesus said, "Well, then, pay to the Emperor what belongs to the Emperor, and pay to God what belongs to God."

20.25   RSV

He said to them, "Then render to Caesar the things that are Caesar's, and to God the things that are God's."

pay: "return," "give back," "render" (RSV).

what belongs to the Emperor: the point Jesus is making is that the name and face on the denarius showed that it belonged to the Emperor and so he had the right to collect taxes from them.

It may be better to structure the saying differently: "The things that belong to the Emperor are to be paid to the Emperor, and the things that belong to God are to be paid to God." Of course the verb "paid" is used in a literal sense the first time, but not the second time. But whatever construction and vocabulary are used, the form of both halves of the answer should be the same, if possible.

20.26	TEV	RSV
	There before the people they could not catch him in a thing, so they kept quiet, amazed at his answer.	And they were not able in the presence of the people to catch him by what he said; but marveling at his answer they were silent.

catch him in a thing: this translates a phrase similar in form and identical in meaning to the phrase in verse 20, trap Jesus with questions.

so they kept quiet, amazed at his answer: or "they were so amazed at his answer that they kept quiet."

SECTION HEADING

The Question about Rising from Death: "Jesus Teaches about the Resurrection."

Here Jesus confronts another group, the Sadducees, and decisively defeats them in a debate about the resurrection, a belief accepted by most Jews of that time. Once more Jesus demonstrates his authority.

20.27	TEV	RSV
	Then some Sadducees, who say that people will not rise from death, came to Jesus and said,	There came to him some Sadducees, those who say that there is no resurrection,

Sadducees: a small but influential religious party, composed largely of priests. They claimed to base their beliefs exclusively on the first five books of the Old Testament, the Torah.

say that people will not rise from death: "do not believe in the resurrection of the dead." This was one matter on which they differed from the more numerous Pharisees, who did believe in the resurrection.

came to: or "went to," "approached."

20.28	TEV	RSV
	"Teacher, Moses wrote this law for us: 'If a man dies and leaves a wife but no children, that man's	and they asked him a question, saying, "Teacher, Moses wrote for us that if a man's brother dies, having

brother must marry the widow so
that they can have children who
will be considered the dead man's
children.'

a wife but no children, the man[g]
must take the wife and raise up
children for his brother.

[g]Greek *his brother*

Moses wrote this law for us: the us is inclusive, that is, all the
Jews, including Jesus. The passage cited is Deuteronomy 25.5-6. For us
means "for us to obey." The regulation was given in order to keep alive
in the community of Israel the family name of a man who died without
having any children. A boy born to the widow and the dead man's brother
would be legally considered the dead man's son and would bear his name.

The statement of the law is a long one, and it may be advisable to
break it into two sentences, with a full stop after the widow. Then the
next sentence can begin: "He will do this so that they will have children,
who will be considered the dead man's children."

20.29-32   TEV   RSV
Once there were seven brothers; the   Now there were seven brothers; the
oldest got married and died without   first took a wife, and died without
having children. 30 Then the second   children; 30 and the second 31 and
one married the woman, 31 and then   the third took her, and likewise all
the third. The same thing happened   seven left no children and died.
to all seven—they died without   32 Afterward the woman also died.
having children. 32 Last of all,
the woman died.

The story is told as though this actually happened; it would seem,
however, that this was a made-up story, told in order to show (from the
point of view of the Sadducees) how foolish was the belief in the resurrection.

In each instance, from the first to the sixth brother of the dead
man, the brother married the widow and died without producing an heir
for the woman's first husband.

Last of all: "After all the seven brothers had died," "Finally,"
"At last."

20.33   TEV   RSV
Now, on the day when the dead rise   In the resurrection, therefore,
to life, whose wife will she be?   whose wife will the woman be? For
All seven of them had married her."   the seven had her as wife."

It may be better to restructure the verse: "Since all seven brothers
had married her, whose wife will she be when the dead rise to life?" or
"She was married to all seven brothers. On the day of resurrection, then,
whose wife will she be?"

rise to life: this translates the Greek noun "resurrection"; it may
be preferable to say "are raised to life."

[325]

20.34-35 TEV	RSV
Jesus answered them, "The men and women of this age marry, 35 but the men and women who are worthy to rise from death and live in the age to come will not then marry.	And Jesus said to them, "The sons of this age marry and are given in marriage; 35 but those who are accounted worthy to attain to that age and to the resurrection from the dead neither marry nor are given in marriage,

The men and women of this age: as RSV shows, the Greek phrase is "The sons of this age," which means people in their physical existence on earth (see 16.8) as contrasted with existence after death, in the age to come (see 18.30).

marry: see 17.27 for the same use of the two verbs "they (men) marry" and "they (women) are given in marriage."

It may be better to restructure Jesus' statement as follows: "In this life people get married, but those people whom God will judge worthy to rise from death will not get married in the age to come."

who are worthy: the Greek passive participle means "are judged (or, found) worthy" by God.

20.36 TEV	RSV
They will be like angels and cannot die. They are the sons of God, because they have risen from death.	for they cannot die any more, because they are equal to angels and are sons of God, being sons of the resurrection.

The same truth is stated in two different ways. The emphasis is on their immortality in the age to come: They will be like angels and They are the sons of God. Jesus is saying that marriage is needed only for mortals; immortal beings need no descendants.

20.37 TEV	RSV
And Moses clearly proves that the dead are raised to life. In the passage about the burning bush he speaks of the Lord as 'the God of Abraham, the God of Isaac, and the God of Jacob.'	But that the dead are raised, even Moses showed, in the passage about the bush, where he calls the Lord the God of Abraham and the God of Isaac and the God of Jacob.

Moses clearly proves: Jesus quotes from the Torah as he argues with the Sadducees (see verse 27).

the passage about the burning bush: in some way the passage must be identified succinctly; simply to say "about the bush" (RSV) is probably not sufficient. It may be necessary to say "the passage about the bush that was on fire but didn't burn up."

the God of: in some languages the repetition of the God of might give the impression of three gods; so it may be better to say "the God of Abraham, Isaac, and Jacob" or "the God whom Abraham, Isaac, and Jacob worship."

[326]

20.38	TEV	RSV

He is the God of the living, not of the dead, for to him all are alive."

Now he is not God of the dead, but of the living; for all live to him."

The conclusion is based on the reasoning that since Moses spoke of the Lord as the God of Abraham, Isaac, and Jacob, and since God is the God of living people, not of dead people, then this shows that those three patriarchs of long ago are still living.

for to him all are alive: this would seem to mean that in relationship to him all human beings are alive.

20.39-40	TEV	RSV

Some of the teachers of the Law spoke up, "A good answer, Teacher!" 40 For they did not dare ask him any more questions.

And some of the scribes answered, "Teacher, you have spoken well." 40 For they no longer dared to ask him any question.

teachers of the Law: see 5.17.

They are naturally happy with Jesus' answer because they disagreed with the Sadducees on the subject of resurrection.

they did not dare: this makes it appear that the teachers of the Law are the subject of the verb. But this verb (whose subject is not given in Greek) must refer either to the Sadducees, or to people in general. Following the latter interpretation, the translation would be "After that no one dared ask Jesus any more questions."

SECTION HEADING

The Question about the Messiah: "Who is the Messiah?" "Is the Messiah a Descendant of David?"

Here Jesus himself takes the initiative and criticizes the popular belief that the Messiah would be David's descendant. Jesus does not deny that physically the Messiah would be David's descendant, but he makes the point that the Messiah will be different from the superior to King David. Jesus needs to explain this because the title "Son of David" carries the implication that the Messiah would be a lesser figure than King David.

20.41	TEV	RSV

Jesus asked them, "How can it be said that the Messiah will be the descendant of David?

But he said to them, "How can they say that the Christ is David's son?

them: the people; or, the teachers of the Law.
it be said: "people say."
the Messiah: see 2.11; the descendant of David: see 18.38.

[327]

20.42-43 TEV	RSV

For David himself says in the book of Psalms,
  'The Lord said to my Lord:
    Sit here at my right side
  43 until I put your enemies
      as a footstool under
      your feet.'
	For David himself says in the Book of Psalms,
	  'The Lord said to my Lord,
	    Sit at my right hand,
	  43 till I make thy enemies a stool
	      for thy feet.'

The quotation is from Psalm 110.1. In the psalm, The Lord is Yahweh, the God of the Hebrews; and my Lord is the king of Israel, the one chosen by God. In the context of this Gospel, my Lord is the Messiah. If possible, the translation should stay with the wording of the text; if not, it may be necessary to say "The Lord God said to the Messiah" or "God said to my Lord."

at my right side: "at the place of honor at my side." The right side was the place of honor and authority.

until I put: or "while I put (or, place)."

put your enemies...under your feet: this is a figure of complete defeat and humiliation. If the figure is not appropriate in some languages, it may be abandoned and the meaning expressed by "until I defeat your enemies and humiliate them in your presence."

20.44 TEV	RSV
David called him 'Lord'; how, then, can the Messiah be David's descendant?"	David thus calls him Lord; so how is he his son?"

Jesus' conclusion explains that in the psalm David was talking about the Messiah when he said my Lord; that being so, the Messiah cannot be David's descendant, since the title "David's descendant" implies that David is more important than the Messiah. It may be better to rephrase the verse as follows: "David called the Messiah 'Lord'; so how can the Messiah be David's descendant?" or "Since David called the Messiah his Lord, it follows that the Messiah is not David's descendant."

SECTION HEADING

Jesus Warns against the Teachers of the Law: "Pride and Punishment."

With this final incident, the verbal encounters between Jesus and the religious authorities are ended. Jesus denounces their hypocrisy and their insistence on being treated with respect, and he promises that their punishment will be severe.

20.45-46 TEV	RSV
As all the people listened to him, Jesus said to his disciples, 46 "Be on your guard against the	And in the hearing of all the people he said to his disciples, 46 "Beware of the scribes, who like

teachers of the Law, who like to walk around in their long robes and love to be greeted with respect in the marketplace; who choose the reserved seats in the synagogues and the best places at feasts;	to go about in long robes, and love salutations in the market places and the best seats in the synagogues and the places of honor at feasts,

Be on your guard against: "Watch out for" (see 12.1).

TEV imitates the form of the Greek, with three clauses, each beginning with the relative pronoun who. It may be better to have a full stop after the teachers of the Law and then have complete sentences: "They like to...," "They choose...," and "They take advantage of...."

long robes: this gives the idea of ostentation and pride.

be greeted with respect: "have people greet them respectfully," "have people bow to them when they meet."

reserved seats: "seats of honor"; these were in front of the wooden chest which contained the sacred scrolls, and were reserved for teachers of the Law and other important people.

synagogues: see 4.15.

the best places: the places closest to the host.

20.47 TEV	RSV
who take advantage of widows and rob them of their homes, and then make a show of saying long prayers! Their punishment will be all the worse!"	who devour widows' houses and for a pretense make long prayers. They will receive the greater condemnation."

take advantage of widows and rob them of their homes: this implies actions which might have been legal but were unethical. The literal "devour widows' houses" (RSV) could be meaningless or misleading. In a broader sense the meaning could be expressed, "They take possession of everything widows have" or "They manage to take over widows' belongings."

make a show of saying long prayers: or "for appearance' sake they make long prayers" or "in order to make themselves look good (or, religious) they make long prayers." The meaning of the phrase "for a pretense" (RSV) could be stated as "and then, in order to cover up what they do, they say long prayers."

Their punishment will be all the worse!: "God will punish them even more severely (than he would otherwise)." The literal "the greater condemnation" (RSV) means "a more severe sentence," which means a worse punishment.

Chapter 21

The Widow's Offering: "True Generosity."

Another incident is registered which shows true spiritual qualities in a lowly person who displays far greater devotion to God than do rich and important people.

21.1-2 TEV	RSV
Jesus looked around and saw rich men dropping their gifts in the Temple treasury, 2 and he also saw a very poor widow dropping in two little copper coins.	He looked up and saw the rich putting their gifts into the treasury; 2 and he saw a poor widow put in two copper coins.

looked around: or "looked closely," "observed." It may be better to begin the verse in a different way: "Jesus was in the Temple (or, the court of the Temple), and he observed rich men dropping...."

the Temple treasury: probably one of the thirteen contribution boxes, or receptacles, placed under the colonnade in the Court of the Women.

two little copper coins: the smallest unit of currency at that time (see 12.59).

21.3-4 TEV	RSV
He said, "I tell you that this poor widow put in more than all the others. 4 For the others offered their gifts from what they had to spare of their riches; but she, poor as she is, gave all she had to live on."	And he said, "Truly I tell you, this poor widow has put in more than all of them; 4 for they all contributed out of their abundance, but she out of her poverty put in all the living that she had."

I tell you: see 9.27.

more: not in terms of the amount of money given; obviously what the rich men gave was much more in quantity than what the poor widow gave. In verse 4 Jesus explains this more: the rich gave only a small part of their wealth; she gave everything she had.

what they had to spare of their riches: "part of their great wealth."

[330]

SECTION HEADING

Jesus Speaks of the Destruction of the Temple: "Jesus Predicts that the Temple Will Be Destroyed."

From verse 5 to verse 36 Jesus talks about future events. He first foretells the destruction of the Temple (verse 6), and then he speaks of world-wide troubles and upheavals during which his followers will be persecuted and put on trial (verses 7-19). He predicts the destruction of Jerusalem (verses 20-24) and talks about the coming of the Son of Man (verses 25-28). The discourse ends with a warning about the need to be on watch (verses 29-36).
Various events are spoken of in this chapter, and sometimes it is not clear whether the subject is the destruction of Jerusalem or the final coming of the Son of Man.
Instead of the division of the material that TEV adopts, some translations prefer to divide the discourse into three parts: (1) The Destruction of the Temple (verses 5-6); (2) Signs Preceding the End (verses 7-24); and (3) The Coming of the Son of Man (verses 25-36).

21.5-6 TEV	RSV
Some of the disciples were talking about the Temple, how beautiful it looked with its fine stones and the gifts offered to God. Jesus said, 6 "All this you see—the time will come when not a single stone here will be left in its place; every one will be thrown down."	And as some spoke of the temple, how it was adorned with noble stones and offerings, he said, 6 "As for these things which you see, the days will come when there shall not be left here one stone upon another that will not be thrown down."

Some of the disciples: the Greek says only "some of them" (see RSV). In verse 7 the subject of they asked is not identified; but it is clear that in verses 10-19 Jesus is speaking to his disciples. Because of the composite nature of this discourse, it might be better to translate in verse 5, "Some people were talking...."
the gifts offered to God: these were objects placed in different places to decorate the Temple.
In verse 6 Jesus uses the same language he used in talking about the destruction of Jerusalem in 19.44.

SECTION HEADING

Troubles and Persecutions: "Jesus Says that His Followers Will Be Persecuted."

21.7 TEV	RSV
"Teacher," they asked, "when will this be? And what will happen	And they asked him, "Teacher, when will this be, and what will be the

in order to show that the time has come for it to take place?"	sign when this is about to take place?"

Teacher: as noted in 5.5, in this Gospel the title Teacher is used by someone who is not a disciple of Jesus; this verse seems to be the only exception.

The double question is really one: when will the Temple be destroyed? TEV has represented the Greek word for "the sign" (RSV) by a phrase what will happen in order to show. Or else the translation could be "what event will indicate that the time has come for this to happen." Or the word "sign" can be represented by "unusual happening," "great event," "miracle."

21.8 TEV	RSV
Jesus said, "Watch out; don't be fooled. Many men, claiming to speak for me, will come and say, 'I am he!' and, 'The time has come!' But don't follow them.	And he said, "Take heed that you are not led astray; for many will come in my name, saying, 'I am he!' and, 'The time is at hand!' Do not go after them.

Watch out: "Take care," "Be on your guard," "Pay attention."
Many men: in this context the "many" (RSV) will be men.
claiming to speak for me: the meaning of "in my name" (RSV) here may be understood to be "using my name" or "with my authority (or, power)."
I am he: that is, I am the Messiah.
The time has come: that is, the time of the end.

21.9 TEV	RSV
Don't be afraid when you hear of wars and revolutions; such things must happen first, but they do not mean that the end is near."	And when you hear of wars and tumults, do not be terrified; for this must first take place, but the end will not be at once."

revolutions: or, in a more general sense, "difficulties," "hard times," "disorders."
that the end is near: "that the end will come soon after." It is clear that in verses 8-9 the subject is the end of the age, when the Messiah will return, and that Jesus is saying that it will not be clearly predictable.

21.10 TEV	RSV
He went on to say, "Countries will fight each other; kingdoms will attack one another.	Then he said to them, "Nation will rise against nation, and kingdom against kingdom;

He went on to say: this marks a new subject, and from here to verse 19 Jesus is talking about the persecutions that his followers will endure. A much larger group than the twelve disciples is implied.

Countries...kingdoms: no clear distinction is intended between the two; it is a way of speaking in poetic style of countries, or nations, in general.

21.11	TEV	RSV

There will be terrible earthquakes, famines, and plagues everywhere; there will be strange and terrifying things coming from the sky.

there will be great earthquakes, and in various places famines and pestilences; and there will be terrors and great signs from heaven.

The first part of verse 11 speaks of natural catastrophic events taking place on earth; the second part speaks of fearful, undefined catastrophes from heaven.

famines: "scarcity of food," "people going hungry."

plagues: "epidemics," "diseases."

everywhere: "in many places," "all over the world."

strange and terrifying things: the nature of these "things" (Greek "signs") is not specified. They are not natural events but cosmic disturbances.

21.12	TEV	RSV

Before all these things take place, however, you will be arrested and persecuted; you will be handed over to be tried in synagogues and be put in prison; you will be brought before kings and rulers for my sake.

But before all this they will lay their hands on you and persecute you, delivering you up to the synagogues and prisons, and you will be brought before kings and governors for my name's sake.

Verses 12-17 describe the troubles and persecutions the followers of Jesus will encounter.

all these things: referred to in verses 10-11.

arrested and persecuted: this seems to refer to systematic, organized persecution of the followers of Jesus by the authorities, and not random or isolated cases.

handed over to be tried in synagogues: TEV thus represents the meaning of "handing (you) over to synagogues." It is not to be implied in translation that the followers of Jesus would be imprisoned in synagogues; rather, they would be tried there by Jewish authorities. The synagogue was the place where local trials were held.

before kings and rulers: this refers to persecution in Gentile countries.

for my sake: or "because you are my disciples," "because you proclaim my message."

21.13	TEV	RSV

This will be your chance to tell the Good News.

This will be a time for you to bear testimony.

[333]

21.13

    <u>This will be your chance</u>: "This will provide you with the opportunity." It should not appear that the persecutions will take place in order to give the followers of Jesus the opportunity to testify.

    <u>tell the Good News</u>: this is the meaning of "testimony" (RSV) or "witness." Or else, "to testify about your relationship to me" or "...your belief in me."

21.14   TEV   RSV

TEV	RSV
Make up your minds ahead of time not to worry about how you will defend yourselves,	Settle it therefore in your minds, not to meditate beforehand how to answer;

    <u>ahead of time</u>: that is, before the trial starts.

    <u>how you will defend yourselves</u>: as the context shows, this is defense at trial, when the followers of Jesus will be accused of crimes.

    The statement may be restructured as follows: "Before you are taken to trial (or, to be tried), don't be concerned about how you will defend yourselves" or "Don't try to prepare your defense before you go to trial."

21.15   TEV   RSV

TEV	RSV
because I will give you such words and wisdom that none of your enemies will be able to refute or contradict what you say.	for I will give you a mouth and wisdom, which none of your adversaries will be able to withstand or contradict.

    <u>I will give you</u>: it may be more appropriate to say "I will teach (or, tell) you." It should not appear that Jesus is saying that he will be physically present at the trial instructing his followers on what they should say. When the time comes for them to defend themselves, they will be guided by their (absent) Master.

    <u>words and wisdom</u>: in Greek, "a mouth and wisdom" (RSV). This may be a way of saying "wise words."

    <u>your enemies</u>: people who take you to court; "opponents" in a lawsuit.

21.16   TEV   RSV

TEV	RSV
You will be handed over by your parents, your brothers, your relatives, and your friends; and some of you will be put to death.	You will be delivered up even by parents and brothers and kinsmen and friends, and some of you they will put to death;

    <u>be handed over</u>: to the authorities, to be tried and punished. Here the verb comes close to meaning "betray":"you will be betrayed by."

    <u>your brothers, your relatives</u>: see 14.12.

    <u>will be put to death</u>: that is, by the authorities, as the result of being found guilty at the trial.

21.17	TEV	RSV
Everyone will hate you because of me.		you will be hated by all for my name's sake.

Everyone: this is obviously an exaggeration, but the author's style should be preserved in translation.

because of me: see **for my sake** in verse 12.

21.18	TEV	RSV
But not a single hair from your heads will be lost.		But not a hair of your head will perish.

This verse may be a proverbial saying that Jesus is repeating. It reads strangely after verse 16b, which states that some of Jesus' followers will be put to death. The meaning may be that spiritually they will be kept safe; no one will be lost. And this fits in well with verse 19.

It may be better to state this verse in a positive form: "You will be completely safe, including all the hairs of your head."

21.19	TEV	RS V
Stand firm, and you will save your-selves.		By your endurance you will gain your lives.

Stand firm: "Don't give up," "Remain faithful."

you will save yourselves: the meaning here is spiritual, not physical. So it may be better to translate "you will gain true (or, eternal) life (for yourselves)."

SECTION HEADING

Jesus Speaks of the Destruction of Jerusalem: "Jesus Predicts that Jerusalem Will Be Destroyed."

In 19.43-44 Jesus had spoken about this, but in this context the emphasis is on the danger that Jesus' followers will experience in the catastrophe.

21.20	TEV	RSV
"When you see Jerusalem sur-rounded by armies, then you will know that she will soon be de-stroyed.		"But when you see Jerusalem surrounded by armies, then know that its desolation has come near.

you: the language means that this will happen in the lifetime of Jesus' listeners.

she: English style allows the use of feminine pronouns to refer to a city. RSV has "it"; another possibility would be "the city."

will...be destroyed: this translates the noun "(complete) devasta-
tion," "destruction."

21.21	TEV	RSV

Then those who are in Judea must
run away to the hills; those who
are in the city must leave, and
those who are out in the country
must not go into the city.

Then let those who are in Judea flee
to the mountains, and let those who
are inside the city depart, and let
not those who are out in the country
enter it;

Judea: the southern province.
the hills: the Judean highlands, where they would be safe from enemy forces invading the country.
the city: Jerusalem itself.

21.22	TEV	RSV

For those will be 'The Days of Punishment,' to make come true all
that the Scriptures say.

for these are days of vengeance,
to fulfil all that is written.

'The days of Punishment': TEV interpretets the Greek phrase "days
of vengeance" (RSV) as a technical term for the time of the end (as in
the other Gospels: The Awful Horror, Matt 24.15; Mark 13.14; and the
first pains of childbirth, Matt 24.8; Mark 13.8).
to make come true: "to fulfil" (RSV). What the Scriptures had fore-
told about the end must be fulfilled. Some translations give a different
sense: "when all that is predicted in the Scriptures will come true."

21.23	TEV	RSV

How terrible it will be in those
days for women who are pregnant
and for mothers with little babies!
Terrible distress will come upon
this land, and God's punishment
will fall on this people.

Alas for those who are with child
and for those who give suck in those
days! For great distress shall be
upon the earth and wrath upon this
people;

How terrible: this is said because it will be difficult for such
women to flee in a hurry.
mothers with little babies: the Greek expression is "those (women)
who give suck," that is, mothers with unweaned infants. If such an expression is used, it must not be vulgar, and it must be appropriate when
spoken by a man.
this land: TEV interprets the Greek to be a reference to Palestine;
RSV takes it to mean "the earth." It may not be natural to speak of distress coming upon this land (or, the earth), so it may be better to restructure as follows: "The people of this land (or, the earth) will be
in great distress."
God's punishment: this translates the Greek noun "anger," which refers to God's anger. The translation could be "God will be angry with,"

but it seems more likely in the context that the reference is not to
God's emotions but to the expression of his anger in terms of judgment
and punishment. Instead of the noun phrase, it might be more natural to
use a verbal phrase, "God will punish this people."
    this people: that is, of Palestine; the Jews. (This seems decisive
in favor of this land in the preceding clause.)

21.24   TEV   RSV

Some will be killed by the sword,   they will fall by the edge of the
and others will be taken as prison-   sword, and be led captive among all
ers to all countries; and the hea-   nations; and Jerusalem will be trod-
then will trample over Jerusalem   den down by the Gentiles, until the
until their time is up.   times of the Gentiles are fulfilled.

    Some...others: TEV thus translates to avoid the idea that the same
people would be killed and be taken as prisoners to foreign countries.
The people referred to are Jews, this people of verse 23.
    killed by the sword: or "killed in battle."
    the heathen: or "the Gentiles" (RSV), "the foreigners."
    will trample over: the more general sense of "will dominate," "will
be in charge of," may be preferable.
    until their time is up: implicit in this phrase is the belief that
God has already determined how long the Gentiles will rule Jerusalem.

SECTION HEADING

    The Coming of the Son of Man: "The Events at the End of the Age."

    This section in Greek continues without a break from the former
section, and does not indicate any period of time between the two. Verse
27 clearly shows that these verses (25-28) describe conditions at the end,
when the Son of Man will appear.

21.25   TEV   RSV
    "There will be strange things   "And there will be signs in sun
happening to the sun, the moon,   and moon and stars, and upon the
and the stars. On earth whole coun-   earth distress of nations in per-
tries will be in despair, afraid of   plexity at the roaring of the sea
the roar of the sea and the raging   and the waves,
tides.

    strange things: this translates "signs" (see verse 7). The text does
not specify what these unusual events will be; they will be of a cosmic
nature. The whole universe will be affected.
    whole countries: or, "the peoples of many countries," "many peoples."
    afraid of the roar of the sea and the raging tides: the language is
none too precise, and it is difficult to understand exactly what phenomena are being described. Perhaps it is a description of violent storms
at sea, with the resulting destruction on land. Instead of the raging
tides something like "the huge waves" might be preferable.

[337]

21.26 TEV	RSV
People will faint from fear as they wait for what is coming over the whole earth, for the powers in space will be driven from their courses.	men fainting with fear and with foreboding of what is coming on the world; for the powers of the heavens will be shaken.

the powers in space: these are either the stars themselves, or else the spirits or angels which were thought to rule the stars. If the RSV phrase "the powers of the heavens" is preferred, care should be taken that the word for "heavens" should not indicate the place where God lives, but rather the sky, where the stars are.

will be driven from their courses: either they will fall or else they will wander erratically through space. The Greek verb "will be shaken" (RSV) describes the event as though a quake will shake the stars, as an earthquake shakes things on earth.

21.27 TEV	RSV
Then the Son of Man will appear, coming in a cloud with great power and glory.	And then they will see the Son of man coming in a cloud with power and great glory.

Son of Man: see 5.24. "I, the Son of Man."

will appear: this translates an impersonal plural form that does not specify the actor: "they will see" (RSV); that is, people (everybody) will see.

coming in a cloud: the cloud is used as a heavenly chariot (see Dan 7.13).

with great power and glory: here glory may be radiance, brightness, or else majesty. It may be necessary to use a complete sentence: "He will be powerful and majestic."

21.28 TEV	RSV
When these things begin to happen, stand up and raise your heads, because your salvation is near."	Now when these things begin to take place, look up and raise your heads, because your redemption is drawing near."

these things: the things described in verses 25-26; they will happen just before the coming of the Son of Man, so they will be signs of the salvation that is coming for Jesus' followers.

stand up and raise your heads: an attitude of confidence and expectation.

your salvation is near: "you will soon be saved," "God will soon save you."

SECTION HEADING

The Lesson of the Fig Tree: "The Truth to Be Learned from a Fig Tree."

[338]

By the use of a comparison, Jesus tells his disciples that the events described in verses 25-26 are sure signs of the coming of the Kingdom of God.

21.29   TEV   RSV

Then Jesus told them this par-   And he told them a parable:
able: "Think of the fig tree and   "Look at the fig tree, and all the
all the other trees.   trees;

them: Jesus' followers.

parable: see 5.36. Here something like "comparison" or "illustration" would fit the context better.

Think of: the Greek says "Look at" (RSV), but the sense "Call to mind" or "Remember" is probably intended.

and all the other trees: or "or any other tree."

21.30   TEV   RSV

When you see their leaves beginning as soon as they come out in leaf,
to appear, you know that summer is you see for yourselves and know that
near.   the summer is already near.

their leaves beginning to appear: in the springtime.

you know that summer is near: "you realize that summer is soon com-ing," "...that before long it will be summertime." Summer is the time of year when plants renew their growth, and the appropriate term for such a season should be used.

21.31   TEV   RSV

In the same way, when you see these So also, when you see these things
things happening, you will know   taking place, you know that the
that the Kingdom of God is about to kingdom of God is near.
come.

these things: as in verse 28, this refers to the events described in verses 25-26.

the Kingdom of God is about to come: in this context, the same event as the coming of the Son of Man in verses 27-28.

21.32   TEV   RSV

"Remember that all these   Truly, I say to you, this generation
things will take place before the   will not pass away till all has
people now living have all died.   taken place.

all these things: the same as in verse 31.

before the people now living have all died: this is the same kind of statement that is made in 9.27. "This generation" (RSV) refers to the contemporaries of Jesus.

21.33   TEV   RSV
Heaven and earth will pass away, Heaven and earth will pass away,
but my words will never pass away. but my words will not pass away.

  Heaven and earth: "The sky and the earth," "The universe," "All creation."
  will pass away: "will disappear," "will cease to exist."
  my words will never pass away: "what I say will endure always" or "...will always be true."

SECTION HEADING

  The Need to Watch: "The End Will Come Unexpectedly."

  It might be better not to begin a new section here but to let these final three verses of the discourse be part of the preceding section. Jesus is still talking to his disciples.

21.34   TEV   RSV
"Be careful not to let your-   "But take heed to yourselves
selves become occupied with too lest your hearts be weighed down
much feasting and drinking and with with dissipation and drunkenness and
the worries of this life, or that cares of this life, and that day
Day may suddenly catch you come upon you suddenly like a snare;

  Be careful: "Watch out," "Be on guard."
  not to let yourselves become occupied with: this translates what is literally "not to let your hearts be weighed down" (see RSV). It would seem that "hearts" here means thoughts, mental processes, or else emotions, and that the warning is against becoming too preoccupied, too distracted, by these other things.
  feasting and drinking: excess in eating and drinking.
  and with the worries: or "or with the worries" (see similar language in 8.14; 12.22).
  that Day: "the day when the Son of Man comes."
  may suddenly catch you: that is, it will come when you least expect it, when you are not ready for it.

21.35   TEV   RSV
like a trap. For it will come upon for it will come upon all who dwell
all people everywhere on earth. upon the face of the whole earth.

  like a trap: TEV translates a Greek text which begins verse 35 here; RSV translates another Greek text which begins verse 35 with "for it will come." (Textual Note: in many Greek manuscripts and early versions the words "like a trap" are linked with what follows: "For it (that is, the Day) will come like a trap upon all people....")
  It may be necessary to expand the comparison somewhat: "that Day may come on you unexpectedly, like a trap that catches a bird (or, an animal)."

21.36   TEV
Be on watch and pray always that
you will have the strength to go
safely through all those things
that will happen and to stand before the Son of Man."

RSV
But watch at all times, praying
that you may have strength to escape all these things that will
take place, and to stand before
the Son of man."

have the strength to go safely through: it would appear that this
is what the text means, that is, that the followers of Jesus will be enabled to endure and survive all the troubles and persecutions; it does
not mean, as RSV implies, "to escape all these things."

those things that will happen: the previously mentioned troubles and
persecutions.

stand before the Son of Man: this seems to imply the Son of Man as
judge; to stand before him means to appear before him for judgment.

21.37-38   TEV
Jesus spent those days teaching in the Temple, and when evening
came, he would go out and spend the
night on the Mount of Olives.
38 Early each morning all the people went to the Temple to listen to
him.

RSV
And every day he was teaching
in the temple, but at night he went
out and lodged on the mount called
Olivet. 38 And early in the morning
all the people came to him in the
temple to hear him.

those days: the days between Jesus' arrival in Jerusalem and his
arrest by the Jewish authorities.

Mount of Olives: see 19.29.

all the people: the crowd that usually gathered.

the people went: or "the people would go," that is, every morning.

Chapter 22

The Plot against Jesus: "The Religious Leaders Make Plans to Kill Jesus."

With this section begin the events of the last week in Jerusalem, which culminate in the death and resurrection of Jesus. Instead of having two sections for verses 1-6, as TEV has, it may be better to have one section, since both deal with the same subject.

22.1   TEV

The time was near for the Festival of Unleavened Bread, which is called the Passover.

22.1   RSV

Now the feast of Unleavened Bread drew near, which is called the Passover.

Festival of Unleavened Bread: a festival lasting seven days, 15-22 of the month Nisan (around the beginning of April), which celebrated the deliverance of the ancient Hebrews from their slavery in Egypt. Its name came from the practice of not using leaven (yeast) in making bread during that week (see Exo 12.15-20).

Passover: a one-day festival held on 14 Nisan, which also celebrated the freedom from Egyptian bondage (Exo 12.1-14). The two festivals, Unleavened Bread and Passover, were celebrated as one. That is why the Gospel writer says that the Unleavened Bread festival was called the Passover.

22.2   TEV

The chief priests and the teachers of the Law were afraid of the people, and so they were trying to find a way of putting Jesus to death secretly.

22.2   RSV

And the chief priests and the scribes were seeking how to put him to death; for they feared the people.

chief priests: see 9.22.
teachers of the Law: see 5.17.
secretly: that is, in such a way that the people would not know it. Even though the Greek does not explicitly say this, something like it must be said in order to make sense of the statement that the religious leaders were afraid of the people (see RSV). Jesus was popular with the people, and the religious leaders were afraid of what the people might do.

[342]

SECTION HEADING

Judas Agrees to Betray Jesus: "Judas Is Paid to Betray Jesus."

The action of Judas in betraying Jesus is seen as the result of the power of Satan over him. No other reason is given for what Judas did.

22.3	TEV	RSV
	Then Satan entered into Judas, called Iscariot, who was one of the twelve disciples.	Then Satan entered into Judas called Iscariot, who was of the number of the twelve;

Satan entered into Judas: although this might be a natural way of speaking in some languages, in others a different expression will have to be used: "Satan took control (or, possession) of Judas," "Satan became the ruler of Judas." For Satan see 10.18.

called Iscariot: there are various conjectures about the significance of this name.

the twelve disciples: or "the twelve apostles"; the Greek says only "the twelve" (RSV).

22.4	TEV	RSV
	So Judas went off and spoke with the chief priests and the officers of the Temple guard about how he could betray Jesus to them.	he went away and conferred with the chief priests and officers how he might betray him to them.

went off: that is, away from Jesus and the other disciples.

officers of the Temple guard: the Temple guards were Levites who had the responsibility for guarding the Temple and maintaining order. They could be called, in translation, "the Temple police." It should be clear, either in the text or by means of a footnote, that these were Jews, not Romans.

betray: or "hand over" (see the same verb in 21.16); see 6.16. The verb betray involves the idea that someone who is trusted as a friend becomes an enemy by helping the enemies of the one who trusts him.

22.5-6	TEV	RSV
	They were pleased and offered to pay him money. 6 Judas agreed to it and started looking for a good chance to hand Jesus over to them without the people knowing about it.	And they were glad, and engaged to give him money. 6 So he agreed, and sought an opportunity to betray him to them in the absence of the multitude.

offered to pay: or, "promised to pay," "agreed to pay."

hand...over: the same Greek verb as the one translated betray in verse 4.

[343]

without the people knowing about it: the same kind of situation
described in verse 2.

SECTION HEADING

Jesus Prepares to Eat the Passover Meal: "Preparations to Celebrate
the Passover Festival."

It is to be noticed that this section (verses 7-13) describes only
the preparations for the meal; only in the next section (verses 14-23)
is there a statement about eating the meal. Jesus' instructions to Peter
and John show that he had already made the necessary arrangements (as he
had done in arranging for the colt, 19.29-35).

22.7 TEV	RSV
The day came during the Festival of Unleavened Bread when the lambs for the Passover meal were to be killed.	Then came the day of Unleavened Bread, on which the passover lamb had to be sacrificed.

The Passover meal was celebrated the evening of 14 Nisan (see verse
1); the lambs for the meal were slain before sundown, that is, on 13
Nisan (in the Jewish system the day began at sunset). The singular "Passover lamb" (see RSV) stands for all the lambs that were slain in order to
be eaten by the families as they celebrated the festival.

22.8-9 TEV	RSV
Jesus sent Peter and John with these instructions: "Go and get the Passover meal ready for us to eat." 9 "Where do you want us to get it ready?" they asked him.	So Jesus^h sent Peter and John, saying, "Go and prepare the passover for us, that we may eat it." 9 They said to him, "Where will you have us prepare it?"

^{h}Greek he

Jesus sent: from the language of verse 10 (go into the city) it is
apparent that Jesus and his disciples are outside the city (see 21.37).
the Passover meal: it was eaten after sundown, just as 14 Nisan began. The meal itself was prepared according to the instructions in Exodus
12.1-11.

22.10 TEV	RSV
He answered, "As you go into the city, a man carrying a jar of water will meet you. Follow him into the house that he enters,	He said to them, "Behold, when you have entered the city, a man carrying a jar of water will meet you; follow him into the house which he enters,

the city: Jerusalem.

a man carrying a jar of water: this man would be easily noticed, since ordinarily women carried the water jars. The verb carrying here is used of carrying on the head or on the shoulder.

will meet you: it is not clear whether this meeting would be accidental or on purpose. With no other details available, the choice of words used in this context would suggest that the man would be waiting for them and they would recognize him from the fact that he would be carrying the jar of water. He would make his way to the house, and the two disciples would follow him.

22.11 TEV	RSV
and say to the owner of the house: 'The Teacher says to you, Where is the room where my disciples and I will eat the Passover meal?'	and tell the householder, 'The Teacher says to you, Where is the guest room, where I am to eat the passover with my disciples?'

owner of the house: see 12.39.

The Teacher: or "Our Teacher." The text has three levels of direct discourse: (1) Jesus to the disciples; (2) the disciples to the owner of the house; (3) Jesus' message for the man. It may be better to restructure so as to eliminate one level of direct discourse, as follows: "...and tell him that the Teacher sends this message to him: 'Where is the room...?'" or else it may be preferable to make the question indirect, as follows: "...and tell him that the Teacher wants to know where the room is where he and his disciples will eat the Passover meal."

the room: RSV "the guest room." The text seems to imply that Jesus had already made the arrangements to use the room for the celebration of the festival.

22.12 TEV	RSV
He will show you a large furnished room upstairs, where you will get everything ready."	And he will show you a large upper room furnished; there make ready."

furnished: "prepared," with the necessary carpets, cushions, and tables, where the group would gather to eat the meal.

upstairs: this would be in America what is called the second floor, but is called the first floor (above the ground floor) in many other countries.

22.13 TEV	RSV
They went off and found everything just as Jesus had told them, and they prepared the Passover meal.	And they went, and found it as he had told them; and they prepared the passover.

They went off: or "They went to the city (or, to Jerusalem)."

found everything just as Jesus had told them: as in 19.32.

22.14

The Lord's Supper: "The Institution of the Lord's Supper."

It seems appropriate to have a separate section for verses 14-23; they could be combined with the previous section under the title "Jesus Eats His Last Meal with His Disciples," but because of the importance of the Lord's Supper it seems better to have two sections.

22.14 TEV	RSV
When the hour came, Jesus took his place at the table with the apostles.	And when the hour came, he sat at table, and the apostles with him.

When the hour came: for the Passover meal, after sundown.
took his place at the table with the apostles: see 5.29.

22.15-16 TEV	RSV
He said to them, "I have wanted so much to eat this Passover meal with you before I suffer! 16 For I tell you, I will never eat it until it is given its full meaning in the Kingdom of God."	And he said to them, "I have earnestly desired to eat this passover with you before I suffer; 16 for I tell you I shall not eat it^i until it is fulfilled in the kingdom of God." ^{i} Other ancient authorities read *never eat it again*

before I suffer: Jesus is referring to what lies ahead: his arrest, mistreatment, and crucifixion. To avoid any misunderstanding, it may be better to translate "before I die," "before I am put to death."
I will never eat it: this is literally what the Greek text says, but it seems to imply that Jesus will eat not even this Passover meal; what Jesus is saying is that this is his last Passover, and that he will not eat another one until....
Textual Note: it should be noted that many Greek manuscripts and early versions have "will not eat it again" instead of "will not eat it."
it is given its full meaning: here the Kingdom of God is spoken of as a future event. Only after it comes will the purpose of the Passover meal be fully realized, that is, the complete freedom of the people of God.
in the Kingdom of God: "when the Kingdom of God comes," "when God rules completely over all."
It may be better to rephrase as follows: "I will never eat it again until (or, I will eat it again only when) the Kingdom of God comes, and what the Passover meal signifies is finally accomplished (or, finally comes true)."

22.17   TEV   RSV
     Then Jesus took a cup, gave   And he took a cup, and when he had
thanks to God, and said, "Take   given thanks he said, "Take this,
this and share it among yourselves. and divide it among yourselves;

     Jesus took: the Greek verb here may mean "Jesus received," that is,
someone handed a cup to him. "Jesus was handed a cup...."
     a cup: "a cup full of wine."
     gave thanks to God: "thanked God for the wine."
     Take this: "Take this cup."
     share it among yourselves: that is, to pass the cup from one man to
the next one, each one drinking a bit of the wine.

22.18   TEV   RSV
I tell you that from now on I will   for I tell you that from now on I
not drink this wine until the King-   shall not drink of the fruit of the
dom of God comes."   vine until the kingdom of God comes."

     from now on: this seems to show that in verse 16 the meaning is "I
will not eat it again." This temporal phrase can be translated "after
this," "after this Passover meal."
     this wine: the Passover wine. RSV "of the fruit of the vine" is a
literal translation of the Greek.
     The statement may be restructured as follows: "I tell you that only
after the Kingdom of God comes will I again drink the Passover wine."

22.19   TEV   RSV
     Then he took a piece of bread,   And he took bread, and when he had
gave thanks to God, broke it, and   given thanks he broke it and gave
gave it to them, saying, "This is   it to them, saying, "This is my body
my body, which is given for you.   which is given for you. Do this in
Do this in memory of me."   remembrance of me."

     took: this is a different verb from the one in verse 17.
     a piece of bread: or "a bread," "a loaf of bread." At that time a
loaf was small and round.
     broke it: "broke it into pieces."
     This is my body: given the use of this verse in the Christian com-
munity in general, it is advisable to translate quite literally "This is
my body" and not "This represents (or, signifies) my body."
     which is given for you: "which is offered as a sacrifice to God on
your behalf (or, for your good)."
     Do this in memory of me: this seems to refer to future celebrations
of the supper, and suggests that the followers of Jesus are to eat the
bread of the supper in order to keep alive his name and teachings in
their group: "in order to remember me."

22.20 TEV	RSV
In the same way, he gave them the cup after the supper, saying, "This cup is God's new covenant sealed with my blood, which is poured out for you.*y*	And likewise the cup after supper, saying, "This cup which is poured out for you is the new covenant in my blood.*j*
y Some manuscripts do not have the words of Jesus after This is my body in verse 19, and all of verse 20.	*j Other authorities omit, in whole or in part, verses 19b-20 (which is given...in my blood).*

the cup: the cup of wine, the same one referred to in verse 17.

after the supper: or "after the Passover meal." This implies that the first cup of wine (verses 17-18) and the bread (verse 19) were distributed among the disciples before the Passover meal.

God's new covenant: "the new covenant (or, agreement) that God makes with his people." This contrasts with the old covenant, made at Mount Sinai (Exo 24.7-8).

sealed with my blood: this translates the Greek "in my blood" (RSV). God's covenant with Israel was ratified, or sealed, by sprinkling on the people the blood of sacrificed animals (Exo 24.7-8); the new covenant is ratified by the blood that Jesus will shed at death.

which is poured out for you: or "which will be poured out for you"—a reference to Jesus' death. The choice of words reflects the Jewish sacrificial system: sacrifices were offered for the forgiveness of sins, and the blood of an animal was offered for sins (see Lev 4.1—5.10).

for you: "on your behalf," "for your benefit."

Textual Note: as the TEV and RSV footnotes show, one Greek manuscript and some early versions omit the words of Jesus from which is given for you in verse 19 to poured out for you in verse 20. Most translations include these words in the text.

22.21 TEV	RSV
"But, look! The one who betrays me is here at the table with me!	But behold the hand of him who betrays me is with me on the table.

But, look!: an expression of surprise and horror.

betrays: see 22.4. Perhaps, "will betray me."

here at the table: "is eating with me"; an expression of close friendship.

22.22 TEV	RSV
The Son of Man will die as God has decided, but how terrible for that man who betrays him!"	For the Son of man goes as it has been determined; but woe to that man by whom he is betrayed!"

The Son of Man: "I, the Son of Man."

will die: this is the meaning of the Greek verb "goes" (RSV).

<u>as God has decided</u>: the Greek passive participle "as it has been decided" refers to the divine will.

<u>how terrible</u>: see 17.1.

22.23   TEV   RSV
     Then they began to ask among   And they began to question one an-
themselves which one of them it   other, which of them it was that
could be who was going to do this.   would do this.

<u>they</u>: "the apostles" (verse 14).
<u>it could be</u>: this is said to represent in indirect form what in direct form would be "Which one of us could it be who will do this?" (or "...who plans to do this?").

SECTION HEADING

     <u>The Argument about Greatness</u>: "The Disciples Argue about Who Is the Greatest."

     This is a rather strange setting for this argument. But Jesus' an-swer seems to indicate that the argument had to do with the coming King-dom of God; the disciples were arguing which one of them would have the highest rank in the Kingdom.

22.24   TEV   RSV
     An argument broke out among   A dispute also arose among them,
the disciples as to which one of   which of them was to be regarded as
them should be thought of as the   the greatest.
greatest.

     <u>An argument broke out</u>: "The disciples began to argue (among them-selves)."
     <u>should be thought of as</u>: "should be considered (or, regarded as)." Here <u>greatest</u> means "the greatest among them." If the passive construc-tion is difficult to represent, the translation may say "...which one among them should people consider (or, regard) as the greatest of them" or "...should people say, 'He's the greatest (or, most important) of the twelve disciples.'"

22.25   TEV   RSV
Jesus said to them, "The kings of   And he said to them, "The kings of
the pagans have power over their   the Gentiles exercise lordship over
people, and the rulers claim the   them; and those in authority over
title 'Friends of the People.'   them are called benefactors.

     <u>the pagans</u>: or "the Gentiles" (see 21.24, <u>the heathen</u>).
     <u>the rulers</u>: this is parallel with <u>The kings</u>. A possible way to han-dle this parallel structure would be "Pagan kings have complete power

over their people, and some of them claim the title 'Friends of the People.'"

claim the title: this takes the form of the Greek verb as middle voice, that is, "call themselves"; if taken as a passive (the two forms are the same in Greek), it can be translated "are called" (RSV), "want people to call them," "tell their subjects to call them."

Friends of the People: "Benefactors" (see RSV), "Generous Rulers," "Protectors."

22.26	TEV	RSV
	But this is not the way it is with you; rather, the greatest one among you must be like the youngest, and the leader must be like the servant.	But not so with you; rather let the greatest among you become as the youngest, and the leader as one who serves.

But this is not the way: or, as an imperative, "But this cannot (or, shall not) be the way"; or "It must not be this way among you."

the greatest...the youngest: the second term, literally "the younger (one)," usually refers to age; but in contrast with "the greater (one)," here it refers to status: "the greatest...the humblest," "the most important...the least important."

must be like: or "must act like," "must be no different from."

22.27	TEV	RSV
	Who is greater, the one who sits down to eat or the one who serves him? The one who sits down, of course. But I am among you as one who serves.	For which is the greater, one who sits at table, or one who serves? Is it not the one who sits at table? But I am among you as one who serves.

The question which Jesus asks, Who is greater...? is answered by another question, "Is it not...?" (RSV). TEV has represented the second question by an affirmative statement.

The one who sits down, of course: for this situation of someone sitting at a meal and someone else waiting on him, see 17.8.

I am among you: "In my dealings (or, relationship) with you, I am like a servant (or, I do the work of a servant)."

22.28-29	TEV	RSV
	"You have stayed with me all through my trials; 29 and just as my Father has given me the right to rule, so I will give you the same right.	"You are those who have continued with me in my trials; 29 and I assign to you, as my Father assigned to me, a kingdom,

You have stayed with me: "You have continued faithful to me," "You have not abandoned me."

my trials: "my difficulties," "the hard times I've had."

the right to rule: this translates the Greek noun "kingdom" (RSV), which here is clearly not an area or a period of time, but the power or right to rule: "the authority (or, power) to rule."

If the verb "to rule" requires a direct object, in verse 30 the object which the disciples are to rule is clearly stated. In the case of Jesus, something like the following could be said: "My Father has given me the authority (or, power) to rule over his people. And I give you the same authority."

22.30 TEV	RSV
You will eat and drink at my table in my Kingdom, and you will sit on thrones to rule over the twelve tribes of Israel.	that you may eat and drink at my table in my kingdom, and sit on thrones judging the twelve tribes of Israel.

This verse shows that Jesus is telling his disciples that they are going to share his authority as King of God's people.

my table in my Kingdom: here the Kingdom is portrayed as a banquet, at which all of God's people will be present (see 16.22).

to rule over: the Greek verb "to judge" (see RSV) in a context like this one does not mean simply to judge in the restricted sense, that is, of determining the guilt or innocence of people, but to govern, to rule.

SECTION HEADING

Jesus Predicts Peter's Denial: "Jesus Tells Peter that He Will Deny Him" or "...Deny that He Knows Him."

This incident (verses 31-34) takes place in the upper room in Jerusalem (verse 14). Together with the next incident (verses 35-38), it serves to set the stage for the reaction of the disciples to Jesus' arrest and trial.

22.31 TEV	RSV
"Simon, Simon! Listen! Satan has received permission to test all of you, to separate the good from the bad, as a farmer separates the wheat from the chaff.	"Simon, Simon, behold, Satan demanded to have you,^{k} that he might sift you^k like wheat,
	^{k}The Greek word for *you* here is plural; in verse 32 it is singular

It may be necessary to begin the section with "Jesus said."

Simon, Simon: Jesus uses Peter's given name (see 6.14). In some languages the repetition of the name may not be natural, or it may carry overtones of censure or anger, which are not intended by the Greek.

Satan: see 10.18.

has received permission: the language implies that God has given
Satan permission to put the disciples to the test. This recalls the situation in The Book of Job (Job 1.9-12; 2.4-6).

to test...chaff: the literal "to sift you like wheat" (see RSV) may
not carry much meaning. TEV has explained the figure in the text itself;
in some cases this could be done by means of a footnote. However it is
done, it should be clear that "you" is plural, referring to all the disciples (TEV all of you).

The Greek "to sift like wheat" refers to the process of shaking the
threshed grain in a sieve, to get rid of stones and other impurities. If
this process is unknown, it may be necessary to abandon the figurative
language altogether, and to simply say "Satan has received permission
from God to put all of you to the test, in order to separate the good
from the bad (or, the faithful from the unfaithful)."

22.32	TEV	RSV
But I have prayed for you, Simon, that your faith will not fail. And when you turn back to me, you must strengthen your brothers."	but I have prayed for you that your faith may not fail; and when you have turned again, strengthen your brethren."

Here Jesus speaks directly to Simon: I have prayed for you.

that your faith will not fail: this is the content of the prayer.
"I have prayed to God, asking him not to let your faith fail."

faith will not fail: here it means "be loyal," "be faithful."

when you turn back to me: this implies that Peter will temporarily
be disloyal.

strengthen: here in the sense of making their faith, or loyalty,
stronger.

brothers: "fellow disciples."

Jesus' statement may be restructured as follows: "After you have
turned back to me, you must help the faith of your fellow disciples" or
"...help your fellow disciples have stronger loyalty."

22.33	TEV	RSV
Peter answered, "Lord, I am ready to go to prison with you and to die with you!"	And he said to him, "Lord, I am ready to go with you to prison and to death."

Peter: it is necessary to identify him, and Jesus addresses him as
Peter in verse 34.

Lord: see 5.8.

I am ready: "I am willing," "I will not hesitate to." Peter understands that Jesus has been talking about Peter's loyalty in time of persecution and danger.

22.34	TEV	RSV
"I tell you, Peter," Jesus said, "the rooster will not crow	He said, "I tell you, Peter, the cock will not crow this day, until

tonight until you have said three
times that you do not know me."

you three times deny that you know
me."

the rooster...crow: some have understood this to refer to the bugle
call known as "the crow of the rooster," which sounded the end of the
third watch of the night (at 3:00 a.m.); it seems preferable, however,
to take it to mean the actual crowing of a rooster (see verse 60).
tonight: it should be remembered that this is nighttime, after the
evening meal.

SECTION HEADING

Purse, Bag, and Sword: "Jesus Warns His Disciples."

It may be preferable to keep this section (verses 35-38) with the
preceding section, under the general title, "Jesus Warns His Disciples."

22.35   TEV   RSV
Then Jesus asked his disci-   And he said to them, "When I
ples, "When I sent you out that   sent you out with no purse or bag
time without purse, bag, or shoes,   or sandals, did you lack anything?"
did you lack anything?"   They said, "Nothing."
"Not a thing," they answered.

that time: TEV adds this to make the reference specific (see 10.3).
purse, bag, or shoes: see 10.4.
It might be better to restructure the material and have a declarative statement followed by a question: "You remember that when I sent
you out (to proclaim the Kingdom of God), I ordered you not to take a
purse or a bag or sandals. Did you lack anything (or, Was there anything
you needed)?"

22.36   TEV   RSV
"But now," Jesus said, "who-   He said to them, "But now, let him
ever has a purse or a bag must   who has a purse take it, and likewise
take it; and whoever does not have   a bag. And let him who has no sword
a sword must sell his coat and buy   sell his mantle and buy one.
one.

In this verse Jesus is telling his disciples that conditions have
changed, and they must take with them purse and bag, and a sword as well.
coat: see 6.29.

22.37   TEV   RSV
For I tell you that the scripture   For I tell you that this scripture
which says, 'He shared the fate of   must be fulfilled in me, 'And he was
criminals,' must come true about   reckoned with transgressors'; for

me, because what was written about
me is coming true."

what is written about me has its
fulfilment."

the scripture: see Isaiah 53.12.
shared the fate of: this translates the passive phrase "was reckoned with" (RSV). This could be taken in the abstract sense of "He was
judged to be a lawbreaker" or "People considered him to be a criminal."
But the concrete sense of "He was treated like a criminal," that is, by
being condemned and executed, seems to fit the context better.
criminals: "lawbreakers," "wicked," "godless."
The verse is fairly long and complex, and it may be that it would
be better to restructure it as follows: "The scripture that says, 'He
shared the fate of criminals' was written about me. And everything the
Scriptures say about me has to come true (or, must be fulfilled)."

22.38   TEV
    The disciples said, "Look!
Here are two swords, Lord!"
"That is enough!"[z] he replied.

RSV
And they said, "Look, Lord, here
are two swords." And he said to
them, "It is enough."

[z]That is enough; or Enough of this.

Here are: or "We have."
That is enough: that is, two swords are sufficient; no more are
needed. But the Greek may mean Enough of this (TEV footnote), that is,
"Drop the subject," "Don't talk about this any more."

SECTION HEADING

    Jesus Prays on the Mount of Olives: "The Agony of Jesus as He
Prays."

    It is still night, after the Passover meal. According to the data
in this Gospel, it was (our) Thursday night; the following morning (our
Friday; 22.66) Jesus is formally tried by the Supreme Council; he is
eventually sentenced to death by Pilate and is crucified before noon
(23.44); he dies and is buried before sundown of that Friday (23.54).

22.39   TEV
    Jesus left the city and went,
as he usually did, to the Mount of
Olives; and the disciples went
with him.

RSV
    And he came out, and went, as
was his custom, to the Mount of
Olives; and the disciples followed
him.

    as he usually did: see 21.37.
Mount of Olives: see 19.29.
It may be better to shift the item about the disciples to the beginning of the verse: "Jesus and his disciples left the city and went,
as usual, to the Mount of Olives."

22.40 TEV

When he arrived at the place, he said to them, "Pray that you will not fall into temptation."

RSV

And when he came to the place he said to them, "Pray that you may not enter into temptation."

the place: what is probably meant is "the place he planned to go to." (It should be noticed that this Gospel does not refer to the Garden of Gethsemane.)

Pray that you will not fall: "Ask God to keep you from being tempted (or, being put to the test)." For temptation see hard testing in 11.4.

22.41 TEV

Then he went off from them about the distance of a stone's throw and knelt down and prayed.

RSV

And he withdrew from them about a stone's throw, and knelt down and prayed,

the distance of a stone's throw: in round figures, about 30 meters, or 100 feet. This might be preferable to the rather elaborate "as far as a person throws a stone."

22.42 TEV

"Father," he said, "if you will, take this cup of suffering away from me. Not my will, however, but your will be done."

RSV

"Father, if thou art willing, remove this cup from me; nevertheless not my will, but thine, be done."^{l}

if you will: "if it is your will," "if you want to."

take this cup of suffering away from me: or "don't let (or, make) me drink from this cup of suffering."

cup of suffering: the Greek says only cup, which here is a figure of suffering. If possible, the figurative language should be kept in translation. In the Old Testament this figure is often used of the punishment that God sends on the wicked (see Psa 75.8; Isa 51.17,22; Jer 25.15).

Not my will, however: or, using verb phrases, "But don't do what I want; do what you want (to do)."

22.43-44 TEV

An angel from heaven appeared to him and strengthened him. 44 In great anguish he prayed even more fervently; his sweat was like drops of blood falling to the ground.^{a}

^{a}*Some manuscripts do not have verses 43-44.*

RSV

^{l}Other ancient authorities add verses 43 and 44: 43 *And there appeared to him an angel from heaven, strengthening him. 44 And being in an agony he prayed more earnestly; and his sweat became like great drops of blood falling down upon the ground.*

RSV omits these two verses from the text; TEV, following the Greek text it translates (United Bible Societies Greek New Testament, third edition), includes the verses. It seems quite clear that these verses were not in the original Gospel of Luke. TEV has done here what it does with the passage John 8.1-11.

appeared to him: or, in the nature of the case, "came to him."

strengthened: "encouraged," "comforted." Moral and spiritual strength is meant.

his sweat was like drops of blood: the text does not say precisely that Jesus "sweated" blood: the comparison like drops of blood probably indicates that the drops of sweat were red, like blood.

22.45-46 TEV	RSV
Rising from his prayer, he went back to the disciples and found them asleep, worn out by their grief. 46 He said to them, "Why are you sleeping? Get up and pray that you will not fall into temptation."	And when he rose from prayer, he came to the disciples and found them sleeping for sorrow, 46 and he said to them, "Why do you sleep? Rise and pray that you may not enter into temptation."

asleep, worn out by their grief: the disciples' grief, or sorrow, is given as the reason why they were asleep. (It is to be remembered that this is probably around midnight.)

Why are you sleeping?: this is a rhetorical question; it means "You shouldn't be sleeping!"

pray that you will not: either this is the content of the prayer (as in verse 40), or else it is the purpose of the prayer: "and pray, so that you will not." But the resultant meaning is much the same in both instances: "and ask God to keep you from falling into temptation."

SECTION HEADING

The Arrest of Jesus: "Jesus Is Arrested by the Religious Authorities."

The arrest takes place there on the Mount of Olives, and Jesus is taken to the High Priest's residence in or near the Temple complex in Jerusalem.

22.47 TEV	RSV
Jesus was still speaking when a crowd arrived, led by Judas, one of the twelve disciples. He came up to Jesus to kiss him.	While he was still speaking, there came a crowd, and the man called Judas, one of the twelve, was leading them. He drew near to Jesus to kiss him;

One of the twelve disciples: as in verse 3.

It may be better to divide the first sentence of this verse into two, as follows: "Jesus was still talking to his disciples when a crowd arrived. Judas, one of the twelve disciples, was leading them."

came up to: or "went to," "approached."

to kiss him: on the cheek (or cheeks), as a man kisses another man.

22.48	TEV	RSV
	But Jesus said, "Judas, is it with a kiss that you betray the Son of Man?"	but Jesus said to him, "Judas, would you betray the Son of man with a kiss?"

is it with a kiss...?: the question reflects surprise and probably sorrow that the disciple would use a gesture of friendship to betray his master.

betray: see verse 4. It may be necessary to specify the ones to whom Judas is betraying Jesus: "Judas, do you kiss me in order to hand the Son of Man over to his enemies?"

Son of Man: see 5.24. It may be necessary here to say "to betray me, the Son of Man?"

22.49	TEV	RSV
	When the disciples who were with Jesus saw what was going to happen, they asked, "Shall we use our swords, Lord?"	And when those who were about him saw what would follow, they said, "Lord, shall we strike with the sword?"

what was going to happen: that is, that Jesus was about to be arrested and taken away.

Shall we use our swords: "Shall we fight them (or, drive them away) with our swords?" The we is exclusive; it refers only to the disciples and does not include Jesus. The question is a genuine one; the disciples' intention is to drive the crowd away.

22.50	TEV	RSV
	And one of them struck the High Priest's slave and cut off his right ear.	And one of them struck the slave of the high priest and cut off his right ear.

High Priest: see 3.2. He is not named; in 3.2 it is reported that Annas and Caiaphas were the high priests when John began his ministry (Matt 26.57 says that Caiaphas was the High Priest at Jesus' trial).

struck...and cut off his right ear: he probably meant to kill, or at least severely wound the man, but succeeded only in cutting off his ear. It seems probable that the slave ducked when he saw the blow coming.

	TEV	RSV
22.51	But Jesus said, "Enough of this!" He touched the man's ear and healed him.	But Jesus said, "No more of this!" And he touched his ear and healed him.

<u>Enough of this!</u>: "No more of this!" (RSV), "Stop it!" This is a strong command, addressed to the disciples. No doubt the others were also getting ready to fight.

<u>touched the man's ear</u>: it is difficult to understand exactly what Jesus did. The language of verse 50 says quite clearly that the unnamed disciple cut off the slave's ear, and one would expect that Jesus would pick it up and attach it to the man's head. But this verse seems to say that Jesus touched the place on the head where the ear had been cut off and healed it, that is, stopped the blood from flowing.

	TEV	RSV
22.52	Then Jesus said to the chief priests and the officers of the Temple guard and the elders who had come there to get him, "Did you have to come with swords and clubs, as though I were an outlaw?	Then Jesus said to the chief priests and officers of the temple and elders, who had come out against him, "Have you come out as against a robber, with swords and clubs?

<u>chief priests</u>: see 9.22.
<u>Temple guard</u>: see 22.4.
<u>elders</u>: see 7.3.
<u>to get him</u>: "to arrest him."
<u>Did you have to come...?</u>: this is put as a question. Jesus is ridiculing them for coming out heavily armed to seize him, as though he were a dangerous outlaw.

<u>as though I were an outlaw</u>: "as though I were a dangerous criminal." The word translated <u>outlaw</u> here is the same one that in 10.30 is translated <u>robber</u>.

	TEV	RSV
22.53	I was with you in the Temple every day, and you did not try to arrest me. But this is your hour to act, when the power of darkness rules."	When I was with you day after day in the temple, you did not lay hands on me. But this is your hour, and the power of darkness."

<u>your hour to act</u>: the Greek "your hour" (RSV) implies that their time to act, that is, to arrest Jesus, has been given them by God.

<u>the power of darkness</u>: this refers to the Devil, as the ruler of evil. In some languages it may be necessary to name him: "when the Devil, the ruler of the kingdom of darkness, is in charge"; or, if <u>darkness</u> is not a metaphor for evil, "when the ruler of evil is at work."

SECTION HEADING

Peter Denies Jesus: "Peter Says Three Times that He Doesn't Know Jesus."

As predicted (verse 34) Peter three times denies Jesus. This is Friday morning, probably near dawn, in the courtyard of the High Priest's house in Jerusalem.

22.54 TEV	RSV
They arrested Jesus and took him away into the house of the High Priest; and Peter followed at a distance.	Then they seized him and led him away, bringing him into the high priest's house. Peter followed at a distance;

They arrested: "They laid hold of" or "They seized" (see RSV); probably the officers of the Temple guard seized Jesus (verse 52).

at a distance: far enough behind where he wouldn't be in danger of being arrested also, but close enough to find out where they were taking Jesus.

22.55 TEV	RSV
A fire had been lit in the center of the courtyard, and Peter joined those who were sitting around it.	and when they had kindled a fire in the middle of the courtyard and sat down together, Peter sat among them.

It may be necessary to restructure this verse and say first that Peter went to the courtyard of the High Priest's house: "Peter went into the courtyard of the High Priest's house. In the center of the courtyard a fire had been lit, and Peter joined those who were sitting around it."

TEV uses the passive had been lit, since it is not certain who lit the fire. The Greek "they lit a fire" does not identify the subject of the verb; it may refer to the people who arrested Jesus (verse 54), or else be an impersonal statement, "people (someone) lit a fire." In this context it was probably the household servants who did it. It was nighttime, and it would be cold.

the courtyard: the inner court, an enclosed area surrounded by buildings or porches, and open to the sky.

22.56-57	RSV
When one of the servant girls saw him sitting there at the fire, she looked straight at him and said, "This man too was with Jesus!" 57 But Peter denied it, "Woman, I don't even know him!"	Then a maid, seeing him as he sat in the light and gazing at him, said, "This man also was with him." 57 But he denied it, saying, "Woman, I do not know him."

22.56-57

at the fire: the Greek says "at the light" (see RSV), but it is the light cast by the fire.

looked straight at him: or "took a hard look at him," "took a closer look" (in order to make sure she recognized him).

This man too was with Jesus: she is speaking to the other people, and the words she uses indicate that she regards Peter as a companion or follower of Jesus: "He also was a companion (or, disciple) of Jesus." The too implies she knows that Jesus habitually had a group of people with him.

I don't even know him: Peter denies not only that he is a follower of Jesus but that he even knows him.

22.58 TEV	RSV
After a little while a man noticed Peter and said, "You are one of them, too!" But Peter answered, "Man, I am not!"	And a little later some one else saw him and said, "You also are one of them." But Peter said, "Man, I am not."

a man: the Greek has only the masculine form of "another (one)," "a different (person)." Peter's answer also identifies this person as a man.

one of them: this may have to be expanded to "one of the followers of that man (or, of Jesus)."

22.59 TEV	RSV
And about an hour later another man insisted strongly, "There isn't any doubt that this man was with Jesus, because he also is a Galilean!"	And after an interval of about an hour still another insisted, saying, "Certainly this man also was with him; for he is a Galilean."

insisted strongly: the verb form indicates that this man spoke more than once: "kept on saying." This man, like the servant girl, talks to the others, not directly to Peter.

was with Jesus: as in verse 56.

he also is a Galilean: that is, Peter is also a Galilean. Perhaps the man knew because of Peter's accent (see Matt 26.73). It may be better to restructure as follows: "This man also is a Galilean, and there is no doubt that he is a follower of Jesus."

22.60 TEV	RSV
But Peter answered, "Man, I don't know what you are talking about!" At once, while he was still speaking, a rooster crowed.	But Peter said, "Man, I do not know what you are saying." And immediately, while he was still speaking, the cock crowed.

I don't know...: a way of denying what someone else has said.
a rooster crowed: see verse 34.

22.61-62   TEV   RSV
The Lord turned around and looked   And the Lord turned and looked at
straight at Peter, and Peter re-   Peter. And Peter remembered the
membered that the Lord had said to   word of the Lord, how he had said
him, "Before the rooster crows to-   to him, "before the cock crows tonight, you will say three times   day, you will deny me three times."
that you do not know me." 62 Peter   62 And he went out and wept bitter-
went out and wept bitterly.   ly.

The Lord: see 5.8.
turned around and looked straight at Peter: verse 54 states that
Jesus had been taken into the High Priest's house; probably he was taken
to a council room. Wherever he was, he was able to see Peter and be seen
by Peter.
Before the rooster crows: see verse 34.
went out: of the courtyard.
wept bitterly: "cried hard," "wept profusely."

SECTION HEADING

Jesus Is Mocked and Beaten: "The Guards Make Fun of Jesus and Beat
Him."

Jesus is being kept under guard by the Jewish Temple guards in the
High Priest's house. It is still night.

22.63   TEV   RSV
The men who were guarding Je-   Now the men who were holding
sus made fun of him and beat him.   Jesus mocked him and beat him;

The men: these are Jewish guards.
beat him: with their hands or fists (as in 20.10-11).

22.64-65   TEV   RSV
They blindfolded him and asked   they also blindfolded him and asked
him, "Who hit you? Guess!" 65 And   him, "Prophesy! Who is it that
they said many other insulting   struck you?" 65 And they spoke many
things to him.   other words against him, reviling
                                         him.

blindfolded him: "tied a cloth around his face," "covered his eyes
with a cloth."

Guess!: this translates the Greek "Prophesy" (RSV), which here has the specific sense of identifying the person without being able to see him.

other insulting things: about his person or his message.

SECTION HEADING

Jesus before the Council: "Jesus Is Tried by the Jewish Supreme Council."

Shortly after sunrise on Friday the Supreme Council of the Jews meets in the High Priest's house and condemns Jesus.

22.66 TEV	RSV
When day came, the elders, the chief priests, and the teachers of the Law met together, and Jesus was brought before the Council.	When day came, the assembly of the elders of the people gathered together, both chief priests and scribes; and they led him away to their council, and they said,

elders: see 7.3.
chief priests: see 9.22.
teachers of the Law: see 5.17.
Jesus was brought: the Greek impersonal plural does not identify the subject of the verb: "they took him." The Temple guards would still be in charge of the prisoner.
Council: the supreme religious court of the Jews, composed of about seventy leaders and presided over by the High Priest.

22.67-68 TEV	RSV
"Tell us," they said, "are you the Messiah?"	"If you are the Christ, tell us." But he said to them, "If I tell you, you will not believe; 68 and if I ask you, you will not answer.
He answered, "If I tell you, you will not believe me; 68 and if I ask you a question, you will not answer.	

TEV has phrased their words as a question, which seems more natural in English than an order.
the Messiah: see 2.11, Christ.
If I tell you: that is, "If I tell you that I am the Messiah."
if I ask you a question: it is not clear from the Greek ("if I ask you") exactly what Jesus had in mind.

22.69 TEV	RSV
But from now on the Son of Man will be seated at the right side of Almighty God."	But from now on the Son of man shall be seated at the right hand of the power of God."

from now on: "in the near future," "before too long." The words of
Jesus reflect the language of Psalm 110.1 (see 20.42-43).
    Son of Man: see 5.24. "I, the Son of Man, will be seated...."
at the right side: see 20.42.
Almighty God: "the Almighty God" or "God, the Almighty One." The
noun "power" (RSV) functions here as an adjective, qualifying God.

22.70 TEV	RSV
They all said, "Are you, then, the Son of God?" He answered them, "You say that I am."	And they all said, "Are you the Son of God, then?" And he said to them, "You say that I am."

The question shows they understood Jesus was talking about himself
when he said the Son of Man (verse 69).
    You say that I am: this answer is a way of avoiding the direct af-
firmation "Yes." Some interpreters take it as an affirmation, "Yes, I
am what you say," but it seems more likely that what is meant is something like "You are the ones who say this, not I."

22.71 TEV	RSV'
And they said, "We don't need any witnesses! We ourselves have heard what he said!"	And they said, "What further testi-mony do we need? We have heard it ourselves from his own lips."

We don't need any witnesses: that is, any people to accuse Jesus of
wrongdoing (this is not a reference to people who were there at the moment and saw what was taking place). "We don't need any other testimony
(or, witness) against him." In their opinion, what Jesus had just said
was enough to convict him.

Chapter 23

Jesus before Pilate: "Pilate Questions Jesus."

It is Friday morning, and the Jewish Supreme Council takes Jesus to Pilate and there accuses him of stirring up a revolution against the Roman government.

23.1 TEV	RSV
The whole group rose up and took Jesus before Pilate,	Then the whole company of them arose, and brought him before Pilate.

The whole group: "All the members of the Council."
took Jesus: the language indicates that the members of the Council themselves took Jesus to Pilate.
Pilate: see 3.1.

23.2 TEV	RSV
where they began to accuse him: "We caught this man misleading our people, telling them not to pay taxes to the Emperor and claiming that he himself is the Messiah, a king."	And they began to accuse him, saying, "We found this man perverting our nation, and forbidding us to give tribute to Caesar, and saying that he himself is Christ a king."

misleading our people: "stirring up a revolution among our people," "causing disorder among our people"; here our is exclusive: these are Jews talking to a Roman.
telling them...and claiming: these are the two specific charges against Jesus; this is how, they say, he is stirring up a revolution.
pay taxes to the Emperor: see 20.22.
the Messiah, a king: they use the Jewish title, the Messiah (see 2.11), and explain to Pilate that this means a king. It might be well to translate "and claiming that he is their Messiah, that is, their king."

23.3   TEV

    Pilate asked him, "Are you the king of the Jews?"
    "So you say," answered Jesus.

23.3   RSV

    And Pilate asked him, "Are you the King of the Jews?" And he answered him, "You have said so."

asked him: or "asked Jesus."
So you say: see 22.70.

23.4   TEV

    Then Pilate said to the chief priests and the crowds, "I find no reason to condemn this man."

23.4   RSV

    And Pilate said to the chief priests and the multitudes, "I find no crime in this man."

chief priests: see 9.22.
the crowds: or better, "the large crowd (that was there)."
I find no reason to condemn this man: or "I don't find this man guilty of any crime."

23.5   TEV

    But they insisted even more strongly, "With his teaching he is starting a riot among the people all through Judea. He began in Galilee and now has come here."

23.5   RSV

    But they were urgent, saying, "He stirs up the people, teaching throughout all Judea, from Galilee even to this place."

they: the same ones referred to in verse 2.
starting a riot: "starting a revolt (or, a revolution)."
Judea: the province ruled by Pilate.
Galilee: the northern province.

SECTION HEADING

Jesus before Herod: "Herod Questions Jesus."

    The text clearly shows that Pilate sent Jesus over to Herod Antipas, ruler of Galilee, because he hoped that Herod would settle this difficult matter.

23.6   TEV

    When Pilate heard this, he asked, "Is this man a Galilean?"

23.6   RSV

    When Pilate heard this, he asked whether the man was a Galilean.

asked: that is, asked the accusers of verse 5.
    It seems better to use the direct form, as TEV has done (Is this man a Galilean?), and not the indirect form (RSV).

23.7 TEV	RSV
When he learned that Jesus was from the region ruled by Herod, he sent him to Herod, who was also in Jerusalem at that time.	And when he learned that he belonged to Herod's jurisdiction, he sent him over to Herod, who was himself in Jerusalem at that time.

the region ruled by Herod: Galilee was ruled by Herod Antipas (see 3.1).

who was also: normally Herod would be in Galilee; and normally Pilate would be in Caesarea.

at that time: during the Passover Festival.

23.8-9 TEV	RSV
Herod was very pleased when he saw Jesus, because he had heard about him and had been wanting to see him for a long time. He was hoping to see Jesus perform some miracle. 9 So Herod asked Jesus many questions, but Jesus made no answer.	When Herod saw Jesus, he was very glad, for he had long desired to see him, because he had heard about him, and he was hoping to see some sign done by him. 9 So he questioned him at some length; but he made no answer.

It may be better in some languages to restructure the material in verse 8 as follows: "Herod had heard about Jesus, and for a long time he had been wanting (or, trying) to see him. He was also hoping to see Jesus perform a miracle. So he was very pleased when he saw Jesus (or, when Jesus was brought to him)."

23.10 TEV	RSV
The chief priests and the teachers of the Law stepped forward and made strong accusations against Jesus.	The chief priests and the scribes stood by, vehemently accusing him.

chief priests: see 9.22.

teachers of the Law: see 5.17.

made strong accusations: "made severe charges against Jesus" or "accused Jesus violently."

23.11 TEV	RSV
Herod and his soldiers made fun of Jesus and treated him with contempt; then they put a fine robe on him and sent him back to Pilate.	And Herod with his soldiers treated him with contempt and mocked him; then, arraying him in gorgeous apparel, he sent him back to Pilate.

and his soldiers: that is, Galilean troops, who would accompany the governor.

made fun of: as in 14.29.

treated him with contempt: this is parallel with made fun of, but implies a greater degree of disrespect.

a fine robe: "a splendid (or, expensive) cloak."

sent him back: TEV has Herod and his soldiers as subject of the
two verbs put and sent. But Herod would be the one to send Jesus back
to Pilate, so it may be better to translate "Herod had his soldiers put
a fine robe on Jesus, and then he sent him back to Pilate."

23.12	TEV	RSV
On that very day Herod and Pilate became friends; before this they had been enemies.	And Herod and Pilate became friends with each other that very day, for before this they had been at enmity with each other.

The Gospel writer explains that before this day Herod and Pilate
had been enemies; but this incident made them friends. If the language
allows, a more complex construction would be effective: "On that day
Herod and Pilate, who before this had been enemies, became friends."

SECTION HEADING

Jesus Is Sentenced to Death: "Pilate Sentences Jesus to Death."

The narrative emphasizes Pilate's reluctance to sentence Jesus. He
could not find Jesus guilty of any crime for which he should be executed,
but he finally gave in to the crowd's clamorous demands.

23.13	TEV	RSV
Pilate called together the chief priests, the leaders, and the people,	Pilate then called together the chief priests and the rulers and the people,

called together: the verb itself implies a gathering; so it is to
be understood that after Herod sent Jesus back to him, Pilate called the
religious authorities and the crowd back together.
   the leaders: members of the Supreme Council.

23.14	TEV	RSV
and said to them, "You brought this man to me and said that he was misleading the people. Now, I have examined him here in your presence, and I have not found him guilty of any of the crimes you accuse him of.	and said to them, "You brought me this man as one who was perverting the people; and after examining him before you, behold, I did not find this man guilty of any of your charges against him;

misleading: this translates a different verb from the one in verse
2, but in this context it has the same meaning.
   I have not found him guilty: he repeats what he said in verse 4.

[367]

23.15 TEV	RSV
Nor did Herod find him guilty, for he sent him back to us. There is nothing this man has done to deserve death.	neither did Herod, for he sent him back to us. Behold, nothing deserving death has been done by him;

he sent him back: if Herod Antipas had found Jesus guilty of a crime, he would have punished him, since Jesus was from Galilee.

to us: by this Pilate means himself and the people he is talking to.

deserve death: "deserve being put to death," "deserve being executed." Or "This man has committed no crime for which I should sentence him to death."

23.16 TEV	RSV
So I will have him whipped and let him go."*b*	I will therefore chastise him and release him."*m*

I will have him whipped: the Roman governor himself would not whip the condemned man; so, either what TEV has done, or else "I will order my soldiers to whip him," represents the meaning of the text. This whipping, or flogging, was a severe punishment; if applied too brutally it could kill the condemned man.

[23.17] TEV	RSV
*b*Some manuscripts add verse 17: At every Passover Festival Pilate had to set free one prisoner for them (see Mk 15.6).	*m*Here, or after verse 19, other ancient authorities add verse 17, Now he was obliged to release one man to them at the festival

As the TEV and RSV footnotes show, this verse does not belong to the original Gospel of Luke. Copyists inserted the verse here (or after verse 19), copying it from Mark 15.6. If the omission of a verse causes difficulties, a translation may wish to include it. But if possible, a footnote should be added which informs the reader that this verse was not part of the original Gospel of Luke.

At every Passover Festival: this was something the Roman governor did every Passover; it was a way of winning favor with the Jews.

Pilate had to: the compulsion reflects a custom which Pilate felt obliged to follow.

for them: "for the people"; or, more specifically, "for the people of Jerusalem."

23.18 TEV	RSV
The whole crowd cried out, "Kill him! Set Barabbas free for us!"	But they all cried out together, "Away with this man, and release to us Barabbas"—

Kill him: "Put him to death," "Execute him."
Set Barabbas free for us: or "We want you to set Barabbas free."
The for us indicates "in answer to our request."

23.19	TEV	RSV

(Barabbas had been put in prison for a riot that had taken place in the city, and for murder.)

a man who had been thrown into prison for an insurrection started in the city, and for murder.

This verse contains a number of items of information: there had been a riot in Jerusalem, during which a murder had occurred for which Barabbas was somehow blamed; so he had been put in prison. All of this took place, of course, before the time the crowd asks Pilate to set Barabbas free. There might be a need to do some restructuring, such as "There had been a riot in the city (or, in Jerusalem), and someone had been murdered. Because of this, Barabbas had been put in prison." But the difficulty with this is that the information is given in order to identify Barabbas, and he should be mentioned first. So it might be better to say "Barabbas was a man who had been put in prison because he was involved in (or, blamed for) a murder that had taken place during a riot in the city." The text does not say precisely that Barabbas had committed the murder or that he was responsible for the riot; it implies that he was somehow involved in both, and for this reason he had been imprisoned. The riot was probably a popular uprising of the Jews against the Roman government.

TEV places this verse within parentheses because it interrupts the narrative.

23.20-21	TEV	RSV

Pilate wanted to set Jesus free, so he appealed to the crowd again. 21 But they shouted back, "Crucify him! Crucify him!"

Pilate addressed them once more, desiring to release Jesus; 21 but they shouted out, "Crucify, crucify him!"

appealed: "called out," "shouted." It is implied by again that Pilate repeated what he had said in verses 14-16.
Crucify: this was a Roman method of execution and was used quite frequently. A translation should use a word or a descriptive phrase that indicates the precise method, and not just a general word for "kill" or "execute."

23.22	TEV	RSV

Pilate said to them the third time, "But what crime has he committed? I cannot find anything he has done to deserve death! I will have him whipped and set him free."

A third time he said to them, "Why, what evil has he done? I have found in him no crime deserving death; I will therefore chastise him and release him."

the third time: the first time occurred in verses 14-16; the second time, in verse 20.

23.22

For Pilate's words, see verses 4,15,16; set him free translates the same Greek verb translated let him go in verse 16.

22.23-24 TEV	RSV
But they kept on shouting at the top of their voices that Jesus should be crucified, and finally their shouting succeeded. 24 So Pilate passed the sentence on Jesus that they were asking for.	But they were urgent, demanding with loud cries that he should be crucified. And their voices prevailed. 24 So Pilate gave sentence that their demand should be granted.

that Jesus should be crucified: "asking Pilate to crucify Jesus" or "...to have Jesus crucified."
succeeded: "prevailed" (RSV), "won."
passed the sentence on Jesus: or "decided to grant their request," "decided to do what they asked for."

23.25 TEV	RSV
He set free the man they wanted, the one who had been put in prison for riot and murder, and he handed Jesus over for them to do as they wished.	He released the man who had been thrown into prison for insurrection and murder, whom they asked for; but Jesus he delivered up to their will.

he handed Jesus over: the verb is the same one used in 22.6. The text seems to say that Pilate turned Jesus over to the crowd, for them to kill him. But Jesus was crucified, and that was the Roman method of execution; the Jewish method was stoning. Therefore the text cannot mean that Jesus was bodily handed over to the mob and that they crucified him. A possible translation would be "and he handed Jesus over to be executed, as they wanted him to do."

SECTION HEADING

Jesus Is Crucified: "The Roman Soldiers Crucify Jesus."

The text does not specifically mention the Roman soldiers until verse 36; in verses 26,32,33,34 the subject of the third person plural verbs is not given. But it seems fairly certain that in all those verses the Roman soldiers are the subject of the verbs.

23.26 TEV	RSV
The soldiers led Jesus away, and as they were going, they met a man from Cyrene named Simon who was coming into the city from the country. They seized him, put the cross on him, and made him carry it behind Jesus.	And as they led him away, they seized one Simon of Cyrene, who was coming in from the country, and laid on him the cross, to carry it behind Jesus.

The soldiers: it may be better to say "The Roman soldiers."
led Jesus away: from Pilate's palace.
Cyrene: the capital of Libya, a country in North Africa.
from the country: "from the countryside," "from the fields outside the city."
seized: "arrested" or "detained."
put the cross on him: here the cross is mentioned for the first time, and the implication is that Jesus had been carrying it until then. A condemned man was forced to carry the horizontal crossbeam, which at the place of execution was fixed to the vertical beam. He would carry it on his back or across his shoulders.

23.27	TEV	RSV
	A large crowd of people followed him; among them were some women who were weeping and wailing for him.	And there followed him a great multitude of the people, and of women who bewailed and lamented him.

weeping and wailing for him: the Greek verb translated weeping means to strike one's breast in sorrow. There is no need to try to use two verbs; such expressions as "were crying loudly for him," "were weeping profusely over him," express the meaning quite well.

23.28-29	TEV	RSV
	Jesus turned to them and said, "Women of Jerusalem! Don't cry for me, but for yourselves and your children. 29 For the days are coming when people will say, 'How lucky are the women who never had children, who never bore babies, who never nursed them!'	But Jesus turning to them said, "Daughters of Jerusalem, do not weep for me, but weep for yourselves and for your children. 29 For behold, the days are coming when they will say, 'Blessed are the barren, and the wombs that never bore, and the breasts that never gave suck!'

Women of Jerusalem: the Greek expression "Daughters of Jerusalem" (RSV) may be natural in some languages.
the days are coming: "the time is coming."
people will say: the Greek has only "they will say" (RSV), which is a way of referring to people in general.
How lucky: see 6.20, Happy.
The three descriptive phrases that follow (RSV "barren...wombs... breasts") are a vivid and emphatic way of saying one thing, that is, "How fortunate are women who do not have children!" A translation must be careful to employ terms that are not indelicate or offensive (see 11.27).

23.30	TEV	RSV
	That will be the time when people will say to the mountains, 'Fall on us!' and to the hills, 'Hide us!'	Then they will begin to say to the mountains, 'Fall on us'; and to the hills, 'Cover us.'

[371]

The language of verse 30 reflects Hosea 10.8. In some languages it may be impossible for people to speak directly to the mountains and the hills. In such a case, a possible translation can be "How we wish the mountains would fall on us and the hills would hide us!"

Fall on us...Hide us: the situation is one of general destruction, and the request may be one for protection, or else for destruction, in order to avoid the awful catastrophe that is coming. It is hard to decide, but it seems that the former (the desire for protection) is the motive for the request.

23.31 TEV	RSV
For if such things as these are done when the wood is green, what will happen when it is dry?"	For if they do this when the wood is green, what will happen when it is dry?"

These are the words of Jesus, and this seems to be a proverbial saying; it means, in the context, that if such a terrible thing as this is done to Jesus, who does not deserve it, far more terrible things will happen in the future to the people of Jerusalem, who will deserve it. Wood of a tree that has just been cut is "green wood"; it is not used for a fire; but dry wood burns very easily, that is, wood that was cut a long time ago.

A statement may be better than a question: "These things are done when the wood is green; much worse things will be done when it is dry."

If the figure of green and dry wood does not make sense, it may be better to abandon the figure altogether: "If such a terrible thing as this happens when the conditions are not right, how much worse will be the things that happen when the conditions are right!" Or, "If an innocent person can be punished like this, how much worse will be the punishment that will come on the wicked!"

23.32 TEV	RSV
Two other men, both of them criminals, were also led out to be put to death with Jesus.	Two others also, who were criminals, were led away to be put to death with him.

led out: that is, out of the city. If the passive were...led out is not natural, the active form may be better: "The soldiers also led out two other men, both of them criminals, to put them to death with Jesus."

23.33 TEV	RSV
When they came to the place called "The Skull," they crucified Jesus there, and the two criminals, one on his right and the other on his left.	And when they came to the place which is called The Skull, there they crucified him, and the criminals, one on the right and one on the left.

the place called "The Skull": it is not known why that particular place had this name; perhaps it was a hill that looked like a human skull.

It may be well in this verse to say explicitly "the Roman soldiers crucified Jesus there." And it may be better to have a complete sentence for the crucifixion of the two criminals: "The soldiers also crucified the two criminals...."

23.34　　　　　TEV
Jesus said, "Forgive them, Father! They don't know what they are doing."[c]

They divided his clothes among themselves by throwing dice.

[c]*Some manuscripts do not have* Jesus said, "Forgive them, Father! They don't know what they are doing."

23.34　　　　　RSV
And Jesus said, "Father, forgive them; for they know not what they do."[n] And they cast lots to divide his garments.

[n]Other ancient authorities omit the sentence *And Jesus...what they do*

As the TEV and RSV footnotes show, the first part of the verse is omitted by some of the oldest Greek manuscripts and early versions. Most modern translations include this sentence.

them: either the Roman soldiers in particular, or else the whole crowd in general.

don't know: "don't realize," "don't understand."

They divided: "The Roman soldiers divided."

by throwing dice: these were either marked pebbles, or else real dice. By such means the soldiers decided which part of Jesus' clothes each one of them would get.

23.35　　　　　TEV
The people stood there watching while the Jewish leaders made fun of him: "He saved others; let him save himself if he is the Messiah whom God has chosen!"

23.35　　　　　RSV
And the people stood by, watching; but the rulers scoffed at him, saying, "He saved others; let him save himself, if he is the Christ of God, his Chosen One!"

the Jewish leaders: members of the Council (see verse 13).

He saved others: a reference to the miracles of Jesus.

the Messiah: see 2.11.

The mocking statement of the leaders may be translated, "He saved other people. If he is the Messiah chosen by God, he should save himself!" The construction let him save himself is a way of expressing an order.

The Greek text has the third person address; it may be better to use the second person and have the words addressed directly to Jesus: "You saved others. So, if you are the Messiah chosen by God, save yourself!"

23.36-37   TEV

The soldiers also made fun of him: they came up to him and offered him cheap wine, 37 and said, "Save yourself if you are the king of the Jews!"

RSV

The soldiers also mocked him, coming up and offering him vinegar, 37 and saying, "If you are the King of the Jews, save yourself!"

cheap wine: there isn't too much difference between cheap wine and "vinegar" (RSV); but vinegar is used as a condiment, and wine is a drink. The Greek word ("sour liquid") here means the common wine (called *posca*) drunk by Roman soldiers. To offer such an ordinary wine to a man who is called a king was an insult.

the king of the Jews: see verse 3.

23.38   TEV

Above him were written these words: "This is the King of the Jews."

RSV

There was also an inscription over him,^o "This is the King of the Jews."

^oOther ancient authorities add *in letters of Greek and Latin and Hebrew*

were written these words: the words were on a slab of wood nailed to the vertical beam of the cross, and contained the charge against the condemned man, so that people would know why he was being executed. The translation may be "Above his head they had put a notice with these words written on it...."

Textual Note: many Greek manuscripts and early versions add after these words the following: "in Greek, Latin, and Hebrew." These words were copied by scribes from John 19.20 and inserted here; they are not part of the original Gospel of Luke.

23.39   TEV

One of the criminals hanging there hurled insults at him: "Aren't you the Messiah? Save yourself and us!"

RSV

One of the criminals who were hanged railed at him, saying, "Are you not the Christ? Save yourself and us!"

hurled insults at him: "insulted him," "reviled him," "spoke evil things at him."

Aren't you the Messiah?: "You are the Messiah, aren't you?" The question is a mocking one; it is not a request for information.

23.40-41   TEV

The other one, however, rebuked him, saying, "Don't you fear God? You received the same sentence he did. 41 Ours, however, is only

RSV

But the other rebuked him, saying, "Do you not fear God, since you are under the same sentence of condemnation? 41 And we indeed justly;

right, because we are getting what we deserve for what we did; but he has done no wrong."	for we are receiving the due reward of our deeds; but this man has done nothing wrong."

rebuked: see 18.15, scolded.

Don't you fear God?: this is a way of rebuking the man's blasphemy. For fear God see 1.50, those who honor him. The question is rhetorical, and the meaning may be expressed directly: "You should respect God."

You received the same sentence he did: obviously the criminal saying this also received the same sentence, so it may be better to say "All three of us received the same sentence (or, were given the same punishment)."

Ours: that is, the sentence the two criminals received.

23.42-43 TEV	RSV
And he said to Jesus, "Remember me, Jesus, when you come as King!"	And he said, "Jesus, remember me when you come into^p your kingdom."
43 Jesus said to him, "I promise you that today you will be in Paradise with me."	43 And he said to him, "Truly, I say to you, today you will be with me in Paradise."

^{p}Other ancient authorities read *in*

Remember me: not just in the sense of thinking about him, but of doing something for him.

when you come as King: this is the meaning of the Greek text that in the RSV footnote is translated "when you come in your kingdom." The slightly different text "...into your kingdom" (RSV text) means "when you are made king" or "when you begin to reign."

I promise: see 4.24, where the same Greek phrase is translated I tell.

Paradise: here Paradise is the equivalent of heaven, the place of the people of God after death; the same as the feast in heaven in 16.22.

SECTION HEADING

The Death of Jesus: "Jesus Dies on the Cross."

Jesus' death is preceded by unusual phenomena and followed by varied reactions from the onlookers.

23.44 TEV	RSV
It was about twelve o'clock when the sun stopped shining and darkness covered the whole country until three o'clock;	It was now about the sixth hour, and there was darkness over the whole land^q until the ninth hour,

^{q}Or *earth*

[375]

twelve o'clock: this translates "the sixth hour" (RSV); the hours of the day were counted from 6:00 a.m.

the sun stopped shining: this translates the phrase (in verse 45 in Greek), "the sun went into an eclipse." The Greek is not to be understood as describing an eclipse as such, but is a general way of saying that the sun stopped shining.

the whole country: or "the whole earth" (see the RSV footnote). As in 21.23, the meaning here is probably "land" or "country," not "earth."

three o'clock: this translates "the ninth hour" (RSV).

23.45 TEV	RSV
and the curtain hanging in the Temple was torn in two.	while the sun's light failed,[r] and the curtain of the temple was torn in two.
	[r]Or *the sun was eclipsed*. Other ancient authorities read *the sun was darkened*

the curtain: this was either the heavy curtain in the Temple, separating the Holy Place from the Most Holy Place (see Exo 26.31-33), or else it was the curtain hanging at the entrance of the Holy Place. The text does not specify when this happened; probably it means to indicate after 3:00 p.m.

23.46 TEV	RSV
Jesus cried out in a loud voice, "Father! In your hands I place my spirit!" He said this and died.	Then Jesus, crying with a loud voice, said, "Father, into thy hands I commit my spirit!" And having said this he breathed his last.

In your hands I place my spirit: these words reflect the language of Psalm 31.5 according to the text of the Septuagint, the ancient Greek translation of the Old Testament. It means "I place myself in your care," "I commit my soul (or, spirit) into your keeping." For spirit a language should use the term that designates what continues to exist after a person's death.

23.47 TEV	RSV
The army officer saw what had happened, and he praised God, saying, "Certainly he was a good man!"	Now when the centurion saw what had taken place, he praised God, and said, "Certainly this man was innocent!"

army officer: see 7.2. He was in command of the squad of soldiers that was given the responsibility of executing Jesus.

a good man: or "an innocent man" (see RSV), that is, not guilty of any crime punishable by death.

23.48-49 TEV	RSV
When the people who had gathered there to watch the spectacle saw what happened, they all went back home, beating their breasts in sorrow. 49 All those who knew Jesus personally, including the women who had followed him from Galilee, stood at a distance to watch.	And all the multitudes who assembled to see the sight, when they saw what had taken place, returned home beating their breasts. 49 And all his acquaintances and the women who had followed him from Galilee stood at a distance and saw these things.

the spectacle: here in the sense of a public affair which everybody can see.

beating their breasts in sorrow: see verse 27.

All those who knew Jesus personally: this indicates a larger group than just the twelve disciples.

followed him from Galilee: or "came with him from Galilee" (see 8.2-3).

stood at a distance: this statement describes what Jesus' friends were doing. It does not appear to mean that they remained there at the place of crucifixion after the crowd had left, but only indicates where they had been all that time.

SECTION HEADING

The Burial of Jesus: "Joseph of Arimathea Buries Jesus."

The burial of Jesus takes place between 3:00 p.m. and sundown, on Friday afternoon (verse 54). Joseph of Arimathea alone takes care of the task; the women who had come with Jesus from Galilee are spectators (verse 55). Nothing is said about the twelve disciples.

23.50-51 TEV	RSV
There was a man named Joseph from Arimathea, a town in Judea. He was a good and honorable man, who was waiting for the coming of the Kingdom of God. Although he was a member of the Council, he had not agreed with their decision and action.	Now there was a man named Joseph from the Jewish town of Arimathea. He was a member of the council, a good and righteous man, 51 who had not consented to their purpose and deed, and he was looking for the kingdom of God.

TEV combines all the various items of information in these two verses into a more logical order. RSV transfers "from the Jewish town of Arimathea" from verse 51 to verse 50. In Greek the text runs without a full stop from the beginning of verse 50 to the end of verse 53.

from Arimathea, a town in Judea: the literal "from Arimathea, a town of the Jews" is rather strange in this context. It may be intended to contrast Joseph with the women, who were from Galilee. Arimathea was about 35 kilometers northwest of Jerusalem.

[377]

a good and honorable man: or "a good and Law-abiding (or, religious) man," "a moral and religious man."

waiting for the coming of the Kingdom of God: "hoping (or, expecting) to see the Kingdom of God come." This characterizes him as a pious, devout Jew, who looked forward to the time when God would establish his Kingdom on earth.

the Council: see 22.66.

their decision and action: that is, in condemning Jesus and handing him over to the Roman authorities.

23.52   TEV   RSV
He went into the presence of Pilate   This man went to Pilate and asked
and asked for the body of Jesus.   for the body of Jesus.

went into the presence of Pilate: this is an appropriate way in English of speaking about an audience with the Roman governor.

asked for: some languages have different verbs to indicate whether the request was successful or unsuccessful. Here, of course, it is a successful request.

22.53   TEV   RSV
Then he took the body down, wrapped   Then he took it down and wrapped it
it in a linen sheet, and placed it   in a linen shroud, and laid him in
in a tomb which had been dug out of   a rock-hewn tomb, where no one had
solid rock and which had never been   ever yet been laid.
used.

took the body down: "off (or, from) the cross" may be added.

a tomb which had been dug out of solid rock: this indicates that the tomb was something like a cave, dug out of solid rock on the side of a hill, not a grave dug below the surface of the ground (see 23.2-4).

23.54   TEV   RSV
It was Friday, and the Sabbath was   It was the day of Preparation, and
about to begin.   the sabbath was beginning.[8]

[8]Greek *was dawning*

Friday: this translates "day of Preparation" (RSV), the day when the Jews made the necessary preparations for the Sabbath, which began at sunset. Some translations may prefer to keep the Jewish name for the day, "Preparation Day," and in a footnote explain the meaning of the name.

23.55-56   TEV   RSV
The women who had followed Je-   The women who had come with him
sus from Galilee went with Joseph   from Galilee followed, and saw the
and saw the tomb and how Jesus'   tomb, and how his body was laid;

body was placed in it. 56 Then they went back home and prepared the spices and perfumes for the body.

On the Sabbath they rested, as the Law commanded.

56 then they returned, and prepared spices and ointments.

On the sabbath they rested according to the commandment.

back home: somewhere in Jerusalem, not in Galilee.

spices and perfumes: aromatic oils, or salves, which were rubbed on the body to prepare it for burial. This was usually done before the body was wrapped in a cloth. But there was no time to do it before sunset, when the Sabbath began.

Sabbath: see 4.16.

they rested: "they did no work."

as the Law commanded: "as required (or, ordered) by the Law of Moses."

Chapter 24

The Resurrection: "Jesus Rises from Death," "Jesus Is Raised to Life."

This account of the resurrection gives the angels' announcement to the women, who find the tomb empty. The women deliver the message to the eleven apostles; they do not believe them, and Peter goes to the tomb and finds it empty. The actual resurrection of Jesus was not seen by anyone.

24.1   TEV   RSV
    Very early on Sunday morning   But on the first day of the
the women went to the tomb, carry-   week, at early dawn, they went to
ing the spices they had prepared.   the tomb, taking the spices which
                                      they had prepared.

Sunday: this translates "the first day of the week" (RSV). Some translations may prefer to use the literal equivalent, and not have the name which is used today for the first day of the week.
the spices they had prepared: see 23.56.

24.2   TEV   RSV
They found the stone rolled away   And they found the stone rolled
from the entrance to the tomb,   away from the tomb,

the stone: nothing has been previously said about the large stone that was rolled across the entrance of the tomb, thus sealing it.
rolled away: it may be preferable to use the active: "that someone had rolled the stone away from the entrance to the tomb."

24.3   TEV   RSV
so they went in; but they did not   but when they went in they did not
find the body of the Lord Jesus.   find the body.^t

                                      ^tOther ancient authorities add *of
                                       the Lord Jesus*

went in: see 23.53.
did not find: they themselves had seen Joseph of Arimathea place
the body there (23.55).
As the RSV footnote shows, one Greek manuscript and some early versions omit "of the Lord Jesus."

24.4	TEV	RSV
	They stood there puzzled about this, when suddenly two men in bright shining clothes stood by them.	While they were perplexed about this, behold, two men stood by them in dazzling apparel;

They stood there puzzled about this: "They didn't know what this
meant," "They were uncertain about what had happened."
two men in bright shining clothes: this is the standard description
of angels (see 24.23).

24.5	TEV	RSV
	Full of fear, the women bowed down to the ground, as the men said to them, "Why are you looking among the dead for one who is alive?	and as they were frightened and bowed their faces to the ground, the men said to them, "Why do you seek the living among the dead?^{u}

^{u}Other ancient authorities add *He
is not here, but has risen*

Full of fear: "Overcome with fear," "Terribly frightened."
the men: the Greek text (verse 4) calls them men; but since they
are angels (see verse 23), it may be better here to say "angels."
Why...?: this is an expression of surprise; "You shouldn't be looking among the dead for one who is alive!" or "You shouldn't come to a
tomb looking for a man who is living!"

24.6	TEV	RSV
	He is not here; he has been raised. Remember what he said to you while he was in Galilee:	Remember how he told you, while he was still in Galilee,

The RSV footnote in verse 5 shows a textual problem. One Greek
manuscript and some versions omit He is not here; he has been raised.
he has been raised: or "he has risen to life."
to you: only in verse 10 are the women identified by name; up until
now all that has been said of them is that they had come with Jesus from
Galilee.

24.7	TEV	RSV
	'The Son of Man must be handed over to sinful men, be crucified,	that the Son of man must be deliv- ered into the hands of sinful men,

24.7

and three days later rise to life.'"	and be crucified, and on the third day rise."

The content of Jesus' statement in this verse refers back to 18.32-33 (see also 9.22). TEV has put the statement in direct form; RSV keeps it in indirect form.

The Son of Man: "I, the Son of Man" (see 5.24).

must: this indicates divine will at work, and modifies all three of the following verbs: be handed over...be crucified...rise to life.

sinful men: the same people who are called the Gentiles of 18.32.

three days later: or "on the third day" (see 9.22).

24.8-9

TEV	RSV
Then the women remembered his words, 9 returned from the tomb, and told all these things to the eleven disciples and all the rest.	And they remembered his words, 9 and returning from the tomb they told all this to the eleven and to all the rest.

the eleven disciples: or "the eleven apostles"; Greek has only "the eleven" (but see apostles in verse 10).

all the rest: "all the other followers of Jesus."

24.10-11

TEV	RSV
The women were Mary Magdalene, Joanna, and Mary the mother of James; they and the other women with them told these things to the apostles. 11 But the apostles thought that what the women said was nonsense, and they did not believe them.	Now it was Mary Magdalene and Joanna and Mary the mother of James and the other women with them who told this to the apostles; 11 but these words seemed to them an idle tale, and they did not believe them.^{v}

Mary Magdalene: see 8.2.

the mother of: the Greek genitive phrase "Mary of James" could mean "Mary the wife of James."

and the other women with them: part of the group referred to in 23.49,55.

apostles: see 6.13.

nonsense: "empty talk," "a foolish tale," "a silly story."

24.12

TEV	RSV
But Peter got up and ran to the tomb; he bent down and saw the grave cloths but nothing else. Then he went back home amazed at what had happened.^{d}	^{v}Other ancient authorities add verse 12, *But Peter rose and ran to the tomb; stooping and looking in, he saw the linen cloths by themselves; and he went home wondering at what had happened*

^{d}Some manuscripts do not have verse 12.

As the TEV and RSV footnotes show, one Greek manuscript and some early versions omit verse 12.

    bent down: to look into the tomb where the body had been placed.

    the grave cloths: the linen cloths used in wrapping the body for burial.

    but nothing else: Peter saw only the grave cloths; this meaning of the text seems intended, rather than RSV "the linen cloths by themselves."

SECTION HEADING

    The Walk to Emmaus: "Two Disciples See the Risen Lord," "The Lord Appears to Two Disciples."

This incident takes place on Sunday, the day that Jesus' tomb is discovered to be empty. At the end of the section, it is also reported that the risen Lord had appeared that same day to Simon.

24.13-14 TEV	RSV
On that same day two of Jesus' followers were going to a village named Emmaus, about seven miles from Jerusalem, 14 and they were talking to each other about all the things that had happened.	That very day two of them were going to a village named Emmaus, about seven miles^w from Jerusalem, 14 and talking with each other about all these things that had happened. ^{w}Greek *sixty stadia;* some ancient authorities read *a hundred and sixty stadia*

    going to: from Jerusalem.

    seven miles: about 11 kilometers. As the RSV footnote shows, some Greek manuscripts and early versions have nineteen miles (about 30 kilometers).

    all the things: this refers to the events connected with the trial and crucifixion of Jesus, and the women's report about the empty tomb.

24.15-16 TEV	RSV
As they talked and discussed, Jesus himself drew near and walked along with them; 16 they saw him, but somehow did not recognize him.	While they were talking and discussing together, Jesus himself drew near and went with them. 16 But their eyes were kept from recognizing him.

    drew near: the picture is that of Jesus coming up from behind and overtaking them as they walked to Emmaus.

    but somehow did not recognize him: the Greek expression "their eyes were prevented from knowing him" indicates that for some reason, perhaps because of God's doing, the two did not recognize Jesus. It would not be advisable, however, to say in translation that God kept them from recognizing Jesus. A possible translation would be "they saw him but did not recognize him" or "...and did not know who he was" or "...did not realize it was Jesus."

24.17-18   TEV   RSV

Jesus said to them, "What are you
talking about to each other, as you
walk along?"
    They stood still, with sad
faces. 18 One of them, named Cleopas, asked him, "Are you the only
visitor in Jerusalem who doesn't
know the things that have been happening there these last few days?"

And he said to them, "What is this
conversation which you are holding
with each other as you walk?" And
they stood still, looking sad.
18 Then one of them, named Cleopas,
answered him, "Are you the only
visitor to Jerusalem who does not
know the things that have happened
there in these days?"

Jesus' question is a way of taking part in the discussion.
with sad faces: "gloomy," "downcast," "looking very sad."
the only visitor in Jerusalem: or "the only person living in Jerusalem." The Greek verb usually means "to live (somewhere) as a visitor,"
"to lodge (temporarily)"; in this context it would be a reference to coming to Jerusalem from elsewhere for the Passover Festival. But the verb
may mean "to live (somewhere) permanently"; here it would be "Are you
the only man living in Jerusalem...?"
    In either case, a statement seems preferable to a question: "You
must be the only visitor to Jerusalem who doesn't know..." (or "You must
be the only citizen of Jerusalem who doesn't know...").
    these last few days: a reference to the events of the previous week.

24.19   TEV   RSV

    "What things?" he asked.
    "The things that happened to
Jesus of Nazareth," they answered.
"This man was a prophet and was
considered by God and by all the
people to be powerful in everything
he said and did.

And he said to them, "What things?"
And they said to him, "Concerning
Jesus of Nazareth, who was a proph-
et mighty in deed and word before
God and all the people,

    Jesus of Nazareth: see 4.34.
    a prophet: see 1.70.
    considered by God and by all the people: it may be unnatural to use
the same verb for God and for all the people having an opinion of Jesus.
The statement, "God considered Jesus to be powerful in everything he
said and did," can only mean that God had shown his approval of Jesus by
enabling him to perform miracles and by giving him a message to proclaim.
It may be necessary to restructure this verse rather radically: "That man
was a great prophet: the great things he did and said showed that God
approved of him. And he also won the approval of all the people."

24.20 TEV	RSV
Our chief priests and rulers handed him over to be sentenced to death, and he was crucified.	and how our chief priests and rulers delivered him up to be condemned to death, and crucified him.

chief priests: see 9.22.

rulers: the members of the Supreme Council.

handed him over to be sentenced to death: it may be necessary to make the participants explicit: "handed him over to the Roman governor for him to sentence him to death."

and he was crucified: the literal "and they crucified him" (see RSV) makes it appear that the chief priests and Jewish rulers crucified Jesus.

24.21 TEV	RSV
And we had hoped that he would be the one who was going to set Israel free! Besides all that, this is now the third day since it happened.	But we had hoped that he was the one to redeem Israel. Yes, and besides all this, it is now the third day since this happened.

we had hoped: this indicates that they no longer held to this hope. The we probably refers not only to the two but to the wider group of Jesus' followers.

to set Israel free: see 2.38.

Besides all that: the time factor explains even more why they had lost hope.

this is now the third day: or "it was two days ago" or "it was the day before yesterday." This is Sunday and they are speaking of what happened the previous Friday, that is, the trial and crucifixion of Jesus.

24.22-23 TEV	RSV
Some of the women of our group surprised us; they went at dawn to the tomb, 23 but could not find his body. They came back saying they had seen a vision of angels who told them that he is alive.	Moreover, some women of our company amazed us. They were at the tomb early in the morning 23 and did not find his body; and they came back saying that they had even seen a vision of angels, who said that he was alive.

surprised: a strong verb, used also in 2.47; 8.56; "completely astounded us."

seen a vision of angels: this is rather redundant; it is enough to say "seen some angels" or "had a vision, in which they saw angels." Vision does not mean that what they saw was not real; rather it means that it was a divine revelation (see 1.22).

24.24 TEV	RSV
Some of our group went to the tomb and found it exactly as the women had said, but they did not see him."	Some of those who were with us went to the tomb, and found it just as the women had said; but him they did not see."

24.24

Some of our group: only Peter is reported to have gone to the tomb (verse 12); nothing has been said of others.

24.25   TEV   RSV

Then Jesus said to them, "How foolish you are, how slow you are to believe everything the prophets said!	And he said to them, "O foolish men, and slow of heart to believe all that the prophets have spoken!

how slow you are to believe: "how reluctant (or, unwilling) you are to believe," "how difficult you find it to believe."
the prophets: the Hebrew prophets; here the phrase is practically equivalent to the Hebrew Scriptures.

24.26   TEV   RSV

Was it not necessary for the Messiah to suffer these things and then to enter his glory?"	Was it not necessary that the Christ should suffer these things and enter into his glory?"

Was it not necessary...?: this question is a way of making a statement about a self-evident truth: "It was necessary for the Messiah to suffer" or "The Messiah had to suffer."
necessary: this implies God's will for the Messiah.
Messiah: see 2.11.
and then to enter his glory: or "and so (or, and as a result) enter his glory." The verbal phrase enter his glory may mean: (1) to receive glory from God, that is, to be designated the Messiah: or (2) to enter the realm of glory, that is, heaven, God's dwelling place, and there to share God's power. This is what is said in 22.69, and it is probably the meaning here. A possible translation would be "The Messiah had to suffer these things and so (or, and as a result) share God's glory (or, power) in heaven."

24.27   TEV   RSV

And Jesus explained to them what was said about himself in all the Scriptures, beginning with the books of Moses and the writings of all the prophets.	And beginning with Moses and all the prophets, he interpreted to them in all the scriptures the things concerning himself.

what was said: or "what was written."
all the Scriptures: "all the books of the (Hebrew) Scriptures."
the books of Moses: the first five books, the Torah, the Pentateuch. This was the first division of the Hebrew Bible.
the writings of all the prophets: this was the second division of the Hebrew Bible.
Instead of beginning with...and the writings, the text may mean "beginning with the books of Moses and going through the writings of all the prophets."

24.28   TEV   RSV

As they came near the village   So they drew near to the village
to which they were going, Jesus to which they were going. He ap-
acted as if he were going farther; peared to be going further,

they were going: strictly speaking, only the two followers of Jesus
were going to Emmaus (verse 13).
Jesus acted as if he were going farther: "Jesus made it seem that
he meant to keep on going," "it seemed that Jesus intended to go on."

24.29   TEV   RSV

but they held him back, saying, but they constrained him, saying,
"Stay with us; the day is almost "Stay with us, for it is toward
over and it is getting dark." So evening and the day is now far
he went in to stay with them.   spent." So he went in to stay with
                                 them.

they held him back: it should not be inferred from this that they
detained him by physical force; "they kept him from going any farther,"
"they got him to change his mind," "they persuaded him to stay."
Stay with us: as a guest, overnight.
almost over: near sundown, when the day would end.
to stay: to spend the night.

24.30   TEV   RSV

He sat down to eat with them, took When he was at table with them, he
the bread, and said the blessing; took the bread and blessed, and
then he broke the bread and gave it broke it, and gave it to them.
to them.

sat down to eat: see 5.29.
took the bread: "took the loaf of bread" (see 22.19). Jesus acts
the part of the host.
said the blessing: or "thanked God for it." The verb is different
from the one used in 22.19, but in the context it means the same—to
offer a prayer of thanks to God.
gave it to them: "gave a piece to each one of them."

24.31   TEV   RSV

Then their eyes were opened and   And their eyes were opened and they
they recognized him, but he disap- recognized him; and he vanished out
peared from their sight.   of their sight.

their eyes were opened and they recognized: this is the reversal of
the condition described in verse 16. The reader should not get the impression that the two had their eyes closed all this time. It may be
necessary to make an adjustment: "Then all at once they recognized him"
or "...they were able to see who he was" or "...they knew that he was
Jesus."

he disappeared from their sight: "he vanished," "he became invisible
to them."

24.32   TEV   RSV
They said to each other, "Wasn't   They said to each other, "Did not
it like a fire burning in us when   our hearts burn within us[c] while
he talked to us on the road and   he talked to us on the road, while
explained the Scriptures to us?"   he opened to us the scriptures?"

                                      [c]Other ancient authorities omit
                                      within us

like a fire burning in us: the figure is one of joy, delight, en-
thusiasm, energy. It should not appear to mean anger or remorse. The
figurative language may have to be abandoned: "Didn't we feel enthusi-
astic (or, excited) while he was talking with us...?" or "Weren't we
filled with emotion (or, delight) when he talked...?"
    It may be better to use a declarative statement: "How delighted (or,
excited) we felt when he talked with us...!"
    on the road: "as we were walking," "as we were coming here."
    Textual Note: as the RSV footnote shows, some early Greek manuscripts
and a few versions omit "within us"; this does not affect the meaning.

24.33-34   TEV   RSV
    They got up at once and went   And they rose that same hour and
back to Jerusalem, where they found   returned to Jerusalem; and they
the eleven disciples gathered to-   found the eleven gathered together
gether with the others 34 and say-   and those who were with them, 34 who
ing, "The Lord is risen indeed! He   said, "The Lord has risen indeed,
has appeared to Simon!"   and has appeared to Simon!"

    the eleven disciples: as in verse 9.
    the others: the larger group of Jesus' followers.
    and saying: in Greek this refers to all, the eleven and the others.
    The Lord is risen: or "The Lord has been raised (to life)."
    appeared to Simon: this Gospel does not record this appearance.

24.35   TEV   RSV
    The two then explained to   Then they told what had happened
them what had happened on the road,   on the road, and how he was known
and how they had recognized the   to them in the breaking of the
Lord when he broke the bread.   bread.

    The two: this is said to identify the subject clearly.
    on the road: or "as they walked to Emmaus."
    the Lord: the Greek has only "he"; but in light of the Lord in
verse 34, it seems proper to use it here.

SECTION HEADING

Jesus Appears to His Disciples.

The appearance of the risen Lord to his followers takes place that same Sunday night. The two followers had reached Emmaus before sundown, and then after eating had returned to Jerusalem, seven miles away. There they reported to the others what had happened, and while they were still talking Jesus appeared to them.

24.36 TEV	RSV
While the two were telling them this, suddenly the Lord himself stood among them and said to them, "Peace be with you."[e]	As they were saying this, Jesus himself stood among them.[x]

[e] Some manuscripts do not have and said to them, "Peace be with you."

[x] Other ancient authorities add and said to them, "Peace to you!"

While the two were telling them this: or 'While they were all talking about this."
the Lord: the Greek text has only "he" (see verse 35).
Peace be with you: this was the customary Jewish greeting (see 10.5).
Textual Note: as the TEV footnote shows (also the RSV text and footnote), one Greek manuscript and some early versions omit and said to them, "Peace be with you." Most translations keep the words in the text.

24.37 TEV	RSV
They were terrified, thinking that they were seeing a ghost.	But they were startled and frightened, and supposed that they saw a spirit.

They: that is, all the people there.
were terrified: as RSV shows, the Greek has two verbs which mean the same thing—a way of expressing great terror.
thinking: "because they thought (or, supposed)."
a ghost: in this context, this is the meaning of the Greek word "spirit" (RSV). (It should be noticed that in 23.46 the Greek "spirit" does not mean ghost.)

24.38 TEV	RSV
But he said to them, "Why are you alarmed? Why are these doubts coming up in your minds?	And he said to them, "Why are you troubled, and why do questionings rise in your hearts?

The two questions are a way of rebuking them. A statement may be preferable: 'You shouldn't be alarmed! You should not have doubts coming up in your minds!"

doubts coming up in your minds: an unnatural expression in English.
It would be better to combine the two questions into one: "Why are you
afraid, and why do you doubt (what you see)?" or "You shouldn't be afraid,
nor should you doubt (what you see)."

24.39 TEV	RSV
Look at my hands and my feet, and see that it is I myself. Feel me, and you will know, for a ghost doesn't have flesh and bones, as you can see I have."	See my hands and my feet, that it is I myself; handle me, and see; for a spirit has not flesh and bones as you see that I have."^{y}

my hands and my feet: possibly these are chosen because they would
show the marks of the crucifixion.
    it is I myself: or in idiomatic English, "it's really me."
    Feel me: care should be taken to use a verb that does not sound im-
proper.
    you will know: "you will realize that it's me."
    The whole statement may be restructured as follows: "Feel me and
you will know (or, find out) that I have flesh and bones. Then you will
be convinced that it's me, not a ghost. For a ghost doesn't have flesh
and bones."

24.40 TEV	RSV
He said this and showed them his hands and his feet.^{f}	^{y}Other ancient authorities add verse 40, *And when he had said this, he showed them his hands and his feet*

^{f}*Some manuscripts do not have verse 40.*

On the basis of one Greek manuscript and some early versions, RSV
omits this verse; TEV includes it. It is better to include it in translation.
    He...showed them: that is, by putting his hands and his feet out in
plain sight.

24.41 TEV	RSV
They still could not believe, they were so full of joy and wonder; so he asked them, "Do you have anything here to eat?"	And while they still disbelieved for joy, and wondered, he said to them, "Have you anything here to eat?"

The description of the disciples' reaction in this verse seems a
bit strange; there is a mixture of disbelief, happiness, and amazement.
The New English Bible effectively combines the various emotions: "They
were still unconvinced, still wondering, for it seemed too good to be
true."
    so he asked them: his purpose was to convince them that it was
really he.

24.42-43 TEV	RSV
They gave him a piece of cooked fish, 43 which he took and ate in their presence.	They gave him a piece of broiled fish, 43 and he took it and ate before them.

cooked: it had been broiled; the important thing is not how it had been prepared, but that it was not raw fish.

Textual Note: many Greek manuscripts and early versions add at the end of verse 42: "and a piece of honeycomb."

in their presence: "as they all watched him."

24.44 TEV	RSV
Then he said to them, "These are the very things I told you about while I was still with you: everything written about me in the Law of Moses, the writings of the prophets, and the Psalms had to come true."	Then he said to them, "These are my words which I spoke to you, while I was still with you, that everything written about me in the law of Moses and the prophets and the psalms must be fulfilled."

Then he said to them: the text implies that all of this takes place at the same place and time, the evening of resurrection Sunday, in Jerusalem.

while I was still with you: a reference to the time they had spent together during his ministry in Galilee, before his death and resurrection.

the Law of Moses, the writings of the prophets: see verse 27.

the Psalms: this may be a way of referring to the third and final division of the Hebrew Bible, called "The Writings," of which Psalms was the first book.

had to: this implies divine will.

come true: "be fulfilled" (RSV), "be accomplished" (see 4.21).

24.45-47 TEV	RSV
Then he opened their minds to understand the Scriptures, 46 and said to them, "This is what is written: the Messiah must suffer and must rise from death three days later, 47 and in his name the message about repentance and the forgiveness of sins must be preached to all nations, beginning in Jerusalem.	Then he opened their minds to understand the scriptures, 46 and said to them, "Thus it is written, that the Christ should suffer and on the third day rise from the dead, 47 and that repentance and forgiveness of sins should be preached in his name to all nations,[z] beginning from Jerusalem.

[z]Or nations. Beginning from Jerusalem you are witnesses |

opened their minds to understand: "enlightened them," "made them able to understand," "gave them the power to understand."

what is written: "what the Scriptures say."

There is a problem with the verbal tenses in reporting what was
said in the past about a future event, part of which has already taken
place. TEV tries to solve the problem by placing a colon after written,
so that what follows is seen to be the content of what is written. It
would be even more effective if (single) quotation marks had been used,
to indicate the precise limits of what is written: the opening mark
would be placed before the Messiah and the closing one at the end of
verse 47. Another way would be "The Scriptures say that the Messiah must
suffer and must rise from death three days later. 47 They also say that
in his name...."

suffer: in the context this means "to die"; so it would be better
to say "die" or "be put to death" (see 22.15).

three days later: see 9.22.

in his name: "as his representatives," "with his authority" (see
21.8).

repentance: see 3.3.

forgiveness: see 5.20.

all nations: "all peoples everywhere."

Considerable restructuring may be needed for verse 47. One way would
be to begin a new sentence as follows: "The Scriptures also say that his
followers (or, disciples) must proclaim this message: 'Repent of your
sins and God will forgive you.' They must proclaim the message first in
Jerusalem and then to all peoples everywhere."

As the RSV footnote shows, the clause "beginning from Jerusalem"
may be connected with "you are (to be) witnesses." This is possible and
makes good sense. Most translations, however, are like the TEV and RSV
text.

24.48	TEV	RSV
	You are witnesses of these things.	You are witnesses of these things.

It would be better to translate "You are to tell (everywhere) what
you have seen." This is not a statement, but a command for them to do
their work as Christian witnesses.

24.49	TEV	RSV
	And I myself will send upon you what my Father has promised. But you must wait in the city until the power from above comes down upon you."	And behold, I send the promise of my Father upon you; but stay in the city, until you are clothed with power from on high."

what my Father has promised: this refers to the Holy Spirit (see
Acts 1.4; 2.33). If necessary, this can be made explicit: "And I myself,
in accordance with my Father's promise, will send the Holy Spirit on
you" or "And I will send the Holy Spirit upon you, as my Father has
promised."

in the city: "here in Jerusalem."

the power from above: a way of speaking about the Holy Spirit.

[392]

comes down upon you: the Greek is "you are clothed with" (RSV). This might not be a natural expression, and it might be preferable to say "you receive" or "you are possessed by."

SECTION HEADING

Jesus Is Taken Up to Heaven: "The Ascension of Jesus."

There is nothing in the text to indicate a lapse of time between the preceding appearance of Jesus (on Sunday evening) and his ascension. The implication is that Jesus was taken up to heaven that same night, after talking with his followers.

24.50   TEV   RSV
    Then he led them out of the   Then he led them out as far
city as far as Bethany, where he   as Bethany, and lifting up his hands
raised his hands and blessed them.   he blessed them.

Bethany: see 19.29.
raised his hands: a gesture accompanying prayer or blessing.
blessed them: or "asked God to bless them."

24.51   TEV   RSV
As he was blessing them, he depart-   While he blessed them, he parted
ed from them and was taken up into   from them, and was carried up into
heaven.^{g} heaven.^{a}

^{g}Some manuscripts do not have and ^{a}Other ancient authorities omit and
was taken up into heaven.   was carried up into heaven

he departed from them: "he left them."
was taken up: by God.
into heaven: the dwelling place of God.
Textual Note: as the TEV and RSV footnotes show, a few Greek manuscripts and early versions omit "and was taken up into heaven."

24.52-53   TEV   RSV
They worshiped him and went back   And they^b returned to Jerusalem
into Jerusalem, filled with great   with great joy, 53 and were contin-
joy, 53 and spent all their time   ually in the temple blessing God.
in the Temple giving thanks to God.
                                      ^{b}Other ancient authorities add wor-
                                      shiped him, and

worshiped him: as the RSV footnote shows, one Greek manuscript and
some early versions omit these words. The word for worshiped is the one
regularly used of God (see 4.7-8).

spent all their time: the language is exaggerated, and it may be better to translate "were constantly in the Temple," "went often to the Temple."

giving thanks to God: see 1.68.

Bibliography

Text

The Greek New Testament, third edition 1975. K. Aland, M. Black, C. M.
    Martini, B. M. Metzger, and A. Wikgren, editors. Stuttgart: United
    Bible Societies.

Commentaries

Creed, J. M. 1953. St. Luke. London: Macmillan and Co.

Gilmour, S. Maclean. 1951. Luke (Interpreter's Bible, volume 8). New
    York: Abingdon-Cokesbury.

Luce, H. K. 1949. St. Luke (Cambridge Greek Testament for Schools and
    Colleges). Cambridge: University Press.

Plummer, A. 1922. St. Luke (International Critical Commentary). Edinburgh:
    T. & T. Clark.

Reiling, J., and Swellengrebel, J. L. 1971. A Translator's Handbook on
    the Gospel of Luke. Leiden: E. J. Brill, for the United Bible
    Societies.

Glossary

This glossary contains terms which are technical from an exegetical or a linguistic viewpoint. Other terms not defined here may be referred to in a Bible dictionary.

active. See voice.

adjective is a word which limits, describes, or qualifies a noun. In English, "red," "tall," "beautiful," "important," etc., are adjectives.

adverb is a word which limits, describes, or qualifies a verb, an adjective, or another adverb. In English, "quickly," "soon," "primarily," "very," etc., are adverbs.

adversative describes something opposed to or in contrast with something already stated. "But" and "however" are adversative conjunctions.

aspect is a grammatical category which specifies the nature of an action; for example, whether the action is completed, uncompleted, repeated, begun, continuing, increasing in intensity, decreasing in intensity, etc. "Was built" indicates completed aspect, while "was running" indicates continuing aspect.

clause is a grammatical construction, normally consisting of a subject and a predicate.

comparative refers to the form of an adjective or adverb that indicates that the object or event described possesses a certain quality to a greater degree than does another object or event. See also superlative.

complex sentence contains at least one modifying clause in addition to the main clause.

components are the parts or elements which go together to form the whole of an object. For example, the components of bread are flour, salt, shortening, yeast, and water. In a similar way, the phrases, words, and other elements in a sentence may be considered its components.

Glossary

conditional refers to a clause or phrase which expresses or implies a condition, in English usually introduced by "if."

construction. See structure.

context is that which precedes and/or follows any part of a discourse. For example, the context of a word or phrase in Scripture would be the other words and phrases associated with it in the sentence, paragraph, section, and even the entire book in which it occurs. The context of a term often affects its meaning, so that a word does not mean exactly the same thing in one context that it does in another.

copyists were men who made handwritten copies of books, before the invention of printing. See manuscripts.

cultural equivalent is a kind of translation in which certain details from the culture of the source language are changed because they have no meaning or may even carry a wrong meaning for speakers of the receptor language. Cultural equivalent translation should be used only when absolutely necessary for conveying the intended meaning, and it may be important to add an explanatory note. See culture.

culture is the sum total of the ways of living built up by the people living in a certain geographic area. A culture is passed on from one generation to another, but undergoes development or gradual change. See cultural equivalent.

declarative refers to forms of a verb or verb phrase which indicate statements assumed to be certain; for example, "prepared" in "She prepared a meal." Such a statement is, for example, declarative rather than imperative or interrogative.

direct address, direct discourse. See discourse.

direct object is the goal of an event or action specified by a verb. In "John hit the ball," the direct object of "hit" is "ball."

discourse is the connected and continuous communication of thought by means of language, whether spoken or written. The way in which the elements of a discourse are arranged is called discourse structure. Direct discourse is the reproduction of the actual words of one person quoted and included in the discourse of another person; for example, "He declared, 'I will have nothing to do with this man.'" Indirect discourse is the reporting of the words of one person within the discourse of another person, but in an altered grammatical form rather than as an exact quotation; for example, "He said he would have nothing to do with that man."

double negative is a grammatical construction in which two negative words are used in the same clause. Usually two negatives produce a positive meaning ("He did not say nothing" means "He did say something"). In some languages, however, a double negative is an emphatic negative (as in Greek, where "not no" means "definitely not").

emphasis (emphatic) is the special importance given to an element in a discourse, sometimes indicated by the choice of words or by position in the sentence. For example, in "Never will I eat pork again," "Never" is given emphasis by placing it at the beginning of the sentence.

exclusive first person plural excludes the person(s) addressed. That is, a speaker may use "we" to refer to himself and his companions, while specifically excluding the person(s) to whom he is speaking. See inclusive.

explicit refers to information which is expressed in the words of a discourse. This is in contrast to implicit information. See implicit.

figure, figure of speech, or figurative expression involves the use of words in other than their literal or ordinary sense, in order to bring out some aspect of meaning by means of comparison or association. For example, "raindrops dancing on the street," or "his speech was like thunder." Metaphors and similes are figures of speech.

future. See tense.

general. See generic.

generic has reference to a general class or kind of objects, events, or abstracts; it is the opposite of specific. For example, the term "animal" is generic in relation to "dog," which is a specific kind of animal. However, "dog" is generic in relation to the more specific term "poodle."

idiom or idiomatic expression is a combination of terms whose meanings cannot be understood by adding up the meanings of the parts. "To hang one's head," "to have a green thumb," and "behind the eightball" are English idioms. Idioms almost always lose their meaning or convey a wrong meaning when translated from one language to another.

imperative refers to forms of a verb which indicate commands or requests. In "Go and do likewise," the verbs "Go" and "do" are imperatives. In most languages, imperatives are confined to the grammatical second person; but some languages have corresponding forms for the first and third persons. These are usually expressed in English by the use of "may" or "let"; for example, "May we not have to beg!" "Let them work harder!"

implicit (implied, implication) refers to information that is not formally represented in a discourse, since it is assumed that it is already known to the receptor, or evident from the meaning of the words in

[399]

question. For example, the phrase "the other son" carries with it the implicit information that there is a son in addition to the one mentioned. This is in contrast to explicit information, which is expressly stated in a discourse. See explicit.

inclusive first person plural includes both the speaker and the one(s) to whom that person is speaking. See exclusive.

indirect address, indirect discourse, indirect form. See discourse.

ironical is having the quality of irony, which is a sarcastic or humorous manner of discourse in which what is said is intended to express its opposite; for example, "That was a wise thing to do!" when intended to convey the meaning, "That was a stupid thing to do!"

literal means the ordinary or primary meaning of a term or expression, in contrast with a figurative meaning. A literal translation is one which represents the exact words and word order of the source language; such a translation frequently is unnatural or awkward in the receptor language.

manuscripts are books, documents, letters, etc., written by hand. Thousands of manuscript copies of various Old and New Testament books still exist, but none of the original manuscripts.

markers (marking) are features of words or of a discourse which signal some special meaning or some particular structure. For example, words for speaking may mark the onset of direct discourse, a phrase such as "once upon a time" may mark the beginning of a fairy story, and certain features of parallelism are the dominant markers of poetry. The word "body" may require a marker to clarify whether a person, a group, or a corpse is meant.

metaphor is likening one object, event, or state to another by speaking of it as if it were the other; for example, "flowers dancing in the breeze." Metaphors are the most commonly used figures of speech and are often so subtle that a speaker or writer is not conscious of the fact that he is using figurative language. See simile.

middle voice. See voice.

mood (or mode) defines the psychological background of the action, and involves such categories as possibility, necessity, and desire. Some languages (for example, the Greek) use specific verb forms to express mood.

neuter is one of the Greek genders. A "gender" is any of the three subclasses of Greek nouns and pronouns (called "masculine," "feminine," and "neuter"), which determine agreement with and selection of other words or grammatical forms.

noun is a word that names a person, place, thing, idea, etc., and often
     serves to specify a subject or topic of a discourse.

object. See direct object.

parallel, parallelism generally refers to some similarity in the content
     and/or form of a construction; for example, "The man was blind, and
     he could not see." The structures that correspond to each other in
     the two statements are said to be parallel.

participle is a verbal adjective, that is, a word which retains some of
     the characteristics of a verb while functioning as an adjective. In
     "singing waters" and "painted desert," "singing" and "painted" are
     participles.

particular is the opposite of general. See generic.

passive. See voice.

past tense. See tense.

person, as a grammatical term, refers to the speaker, the person spoken
     to, or the person or thing spoken about. First person is the person(s)
     speaking ("I," "me," "my," "mine," "we," "us," "our," "ours"). Second
     person is the person(s) or thing(s) spoken to ("thou," "thee," "thy,"
     "thine," "ye," "you," "your," "yours"). Third person is the person(s)
     or thing(s) spoken about ("he," "she," "it," "his," "her," "them,"
     "their," etc.). The examples here given are all pronouns, but in many
     languages the verb forms have affixes which indicate first, second,
     or third person and also indicate whether they are singular or plural.

phrase is a grammatical construction of two or more words, but less than
     a complete clause or a sentence. A phrase is usually given a name
     according to its function in a sentence, such as "noun phrase,"
     "verb phrase," "prepositional phrase," etc.

plural refers to the form of a word which indicates more than one. See
     singular.

pronouns are words which are used in place of nouns, such as "he," "him,"
     "his," "she," "we," "them," "who," "which," "this," "these," etc.

proper name or proper noun is the name of a unique object, as "Jerusalem,"
     "Joshua," "Jordan." However, the same name may be applied to more
     than one object; for example, "John" (the Baptist or the Apostle)
     and "Antioch" (of Syria or of Pisidia).

redundant refers to anything which is entirely predictable from the
     context. For example, in "John, he did it," the pronoun "he" is
     redundant. A feature may be redundant and yet may be important to
     retain in certain languages, perhaps for stylistic or for grammatical
     reasons.

[401]

Glossary

relative clause is a dependent clause which qualifies the object to which it refers. In "the man whom you saw," the clause "whom you saw" is relative because it relates to and qualifies "man."

restructure is to reconstruct or rearrange. See structure.

rhetorical question is an expression which is put in the form of a question but which is not intended to ask for information. Rhetorical questions are usually employed for the sake of emphasis.

sentence is a grammatical construction composed of one or more clauses and capable of standing alone.

Septuagint is a translation of the Old Testament into Greek, made some two hundred years before Christ. It is often abbreviated as LXX.

simile (pronounced SIM-i-lee) is a figure of speech which describes one event or object by comparing it to another, using "like," "as," or some other word to mark or signal the comparison. For example, "She runs like a deer," "He is as straight as an arrow." Similes are less subtle than metaphors in that metaphors do not mark the comparison with words such as "like" or "as." See metaphor.

singular refers to the form of a word which indicates one thing or person, in contrast to plural, which indicates more than one. See plural.

specific refers to the opposite of general, generic. See generic.

structure is the systematic arrangement of the elements of language, including the ways in which words combine into phrases, phrases into clauses, and clauses into sentences. Because this process may be compared to the building of a house or a bridge, such words as structure and construction are used in reference to it. To separate and rearrange the various components of a sentence or other unit of discourse in the translation process is to restructure it.

subject is one of the major divisions of a clause, the other being the predicate. Typically the subject is a noun phrase. It should not be confused with semantic "agent."

superlative refers to the form of an adjective or adverb that indicates that the object or event described possesses a certain quality to a greater degree than does any other object or event. See also comparative.

synonyms are words which are different in form but similar in meaning, as "boy" and "lad." Expressions which have essentially the same meaning are said to be synonymous. No two words are completely synonymous.

tense is usually a form of a verb which indicates time relative to a
discourse or some event in a discourse. The most common forms of
tense are past, present, and future.

text, textual refers to the various Greek and Hebrew manuscripts of the
Scriptures. Textual variants are forms of the same passage that differ
in one or more details in some manuscripts. Textual evidence is the
cumulative evidence for a particular form of the text. See manuscripts.

transitive is a predicate construction in which the verb has a direct
object; for example, "hit the man." By contrast, in an intransitive
construction the verb does not have or need a direct object to
complete its meaning; for example, "he lives."

translation is the reproduction in a receptor language of the closest
natural equivalent of a message in the source language, first, in
terms of meaning, and second, in terms of style.

verbs are a grammatical class of words which express existence, action,
or occurence, as "be," "become," "run," "think," etc.

versions are translations. The ancient, or early, versions are translations of the Bible, or of portions of the Bible, made in early times;
for example, the Greek Septuagint, the ancient Syriac, or the
Ethiopic versions.

voice in grammar is the relation of the action expressed by a verb to
the participants in the action. In English and many other languages,
the active voice indicates that the subject performs the action
("John hit the man"), while the passive voice indicates that the
subject is being acted upon ("the man was hit"). The Greek language
has a middle voice, in which the subject may be regarded as doing
something to or for himself (or itself); for example, "He washed,"
meaning "He washed himself."

Vulgate is the Latin version of the Bible translated and/or edited
originally by Saint Jerome. It has been traditionally the official
version of the Roman Catholic Church.

wordplay (play on words) in a discourse is the use of the similarity in
the sounds of two words to produce a special effect.

Index

This index includes concepts, key words, and terms for which the Guide contains a discussion useful for translators.

Index

[406]

Printed in the United States of America